TWO OLD FOOLS DOWN UNDER

NEW YORK TIMES BESTSELLING AUTHOR

VICTORIA TWEAD

Ant
Press

Copyright © 2019 by Victoria Twead

Published by AntPress.org

Paperback ISBN: 978-1-922476-12-8

For Thea, who wears many hats: baker, guide, medic, ranger, weather forecaster, dog-sitter, etc.

And for Debbie Reynolds, my confidante, my guide to all things Australian, one of Lola's favourite aunties and a brave lady.

And to the memory of Linda, a very special friend, much missed by her family and all who knew her. Readers may remember Linda. She was proclaimed the Pudding Queen in El Hoyo after winning the village fiesta Pudding Contest with her bread-and-butter pudding.

CONTENTS

THE OLD FOOLS SERIES

AVAILABLE IN PAPERBACK, LARGE PRINT AND
EBOOK EDITIONS

Two Old Fools Down Under is the sixth book in the *Old Fools* series by New York Times and Wall Street Journal bestselling author, Victoria Twead.

Chickens, Mules and Two Old Fools
Two Old Fools ~ Olé!
Two Old Fools on a Camel
Two Old Fools in Spain Again
Two Old Fools in Turmoil
Two Old Fools Down Under

Prequels
One Young Fool in Dorset
One Young Fool in South Africa

FREE PHOTO BOOK
TO BROWSE OR DOWNLOAD

For photographs and additional unpublished material to accompany
this book, browse or download the

FREE PHOTO BOOK
from
www.victoriatwead.com / free-stuff

1

DOWN UNDER

I've always wanted a dog. I've had cats, all big personalities and all much missed. I remember Fortnum and her brother, Mason, who grew up with the children. Fortnum was a beautiful, delicate tabby with the heart of a lion, unlike her brother, Mason. He was huge, but cowered behind his little sister as she fought all the battles with the neighbouring feline community.

And there was Chox, the Siamese mix who enchanted us in Spain and ended up living in Germany.

There were always excellent reasons for us *not* to have a dog: we were working and out of the house all day. Or travelling too much and unable to give a dog the time or stability it deserved.

So I made myself a promise. One day, when the time was *exactly* right, we'd have a dog.

It was September 2015, and I had just landed in Australia clutching my precious, newly-granted Permanent Residence visa.

We no longer needed to travel. Our year working in Bahrain had cured my itchy feet and Joe was probably not well enough to explore the far-flung corners of the earth.

We'd stopped looking for greener pastures because we'd found them. Home is where the family is. Australia was where the family was and Australia was where we would put down our roots.

The possibility of owning a dog was suddenly within my reach for the first time in my life.

"You won't rush out and get a dog the moment you land in Australia, will you?" Joe had asked, watching me carefully.

"No! Of course not! I'm going to be far too busy catching up with little Indy, and house-hunting, to think about getting a dog."

But I lied.

"Good. When I've finished my treatment in the UK, and we've got a place of our own to live, then there'll be plenty of time to discuss whether we want a dog or not."

※ ※ ※

Back in Spain, Joe and I had discussed what type of home might suit us best in Australia. At one point in the past, Karly and Cam had considered building a granny flat for us, but it hadn't been feasible.

"I'll leave it totally up to you," said Joe. "Something not too big, something easy to look after, low maintenance. A place that doesn't need any work done at all."

I had agreed, but I was in for a shock. House prices in Sydney were amongst the highest in the world. Our budget would barely buy a flat, or unit as they are called in Australia, let alone a house.

"I had no idea they were so expensive!" I said to my daughter. "I think I'm going to have to think again. Perhaps a retirement village might be the answer? Some of them look really nice. They have nice grounds, swimming pools, gyms, medical facilities. You can even have pets in some of them."

"A wrinkly-ville? Are you quite sure?" A 'wrinkly-ville' was Karly's rather disparaging description of a retirement village. She was dubious. "I don't think you're old enough to be happy in one of those. Not yet."

"Well, I think it's worth considering. I'd enjoy having big gardens."

"Shared with all the other residents."

"And some of these places are close to a beach. And there are some not too far from you. If it's comfortable and affordable, I should at least look. I think it might suit Joe very well, and there'd always be doctors available."

"Okay, we'll look."

There was so much to think about.

Indy was delightful. Three years old and full of mischief and imagination. Her favourite game was Princesses and she chose to wear tiaras on most days. Not only did *she* wear bejewelled crowns, but Princess Nanny was expected to wear them, too. In addition, Indy had sheets of multicoloured plastic sticky-back jewels.

"Di' monds," she said as she pressed huge sparkling 'jewels' onto my earlobes. "I make you a little bit quite pretty."

Sometimes I would completely forget about my tiara and generously-sized earrings when I answered the door.

"Sign here, please," said the delivery man, looking at me strangely.

Only much later, when I caught sight of myself in a mirror, did I remember my finery.

Often we'd play 'mermaids' and swim together across the dining room floorboards. Or 'shops' in the side garden where my son-in-law, Cam, had set up a Wendy house, called a cubby house in Australia. That little side garden was full of interest with its chicken coop, Balinese hut, cubby house and trampoline.

Adjoining the chicken garden was my den. If I needed peace, I could retreat to this, my writers' lair, which had been created especially for me. I had a desk, Internet access, a TV, a kettle for coffee, a sofa, and a cupboard where I kept a few toys for visits from Indy.

It was here, sometimes accompanied by Indy's tabby cat, Bandsaw, that I conducted all my research into retirement villages and houses for sale. In the evenings, I would Skype with Joe, or write, while bugs the size of small family cars threw themselves at my window.

During the day my lair was cool and I could gaze out of the window at the blue sky. It was springtime and the air was full of birdsong. Not the polite, tuneful tweeting we expect from British wild birds, but the raucous shrieks of cockatoos and the repeated snaps of whiplash birds.

The Happy Birthday bird sometimes sang his song, although

nobody ever believed me when I mentioned it. Now that I know a little more about Australia and its wildlife, I'm guessing it might have been a magpie. Magpies sing beautifully and can be excellent mimics. They also live for many years, which would explain why I heard this particular bird repeatedly over several years. I'd first heard it on previous visits from Spain, and it was still performing the same birthday song.

Not so melodic was the sound of next door's dog. He was an enormous basset hound, usually silent, but given to occasional bouts of miserable howling. I wondered what was making him so unhappy.

"So how is the house-hunting going?" asked Joe during one of our online sessions. "Any possibilities yet?"

"Well, actually, I'm quite excited. We've got an appointment in the morning at a wrinkly-ville that's only about ten minutes away from here. It looks fabulous. Very leafy, lots of trees, and it's built round a lake."

"Hmmm. I'm still not convinced that we'd be happy in a retirement home. Mini-bus outings and weaving baskets in craft clubs are not exactly my scene."

I tried to imagine Joe basket-weaving and failed.

"Oh, I'm sure they're not really like that. I'll bring back a full report after the visit tomorrow. Has the hospital given you a start date for your radiotherapy?"

Joe already had the tiny gold beads (called fiducial markers) inserted in preparation for his radiation therapy. They are inserted painlessly and provide greater accuracy for targeting the cancer whilst sparing healthy tissue. We hoped that this course would successfully eliminate his prostate cancer.

"Ah, yes. I have to endure twenty sessions spread over four weeks. It's all going to happen in December."

"So it'll all be finished by Christmas?"

"Yes, that's the plan."

"That's good news! How's your breathing?"

"Not great. I get very out of breath at the slightest thing. I have an appointment at the medical centre this week."

We'd been given the dreadful news that Joe had COPD, or Chronic

Obstructive Pulmonary Disease, and we knew there was no cure. However, it could be managed.

"Perhaps they'll give you stronger inhalers."

"Maybe. It's just so cold here. I'm not used to it after Spain."

"Well, you'll soon be out here in the sunshine and moaning about the heat. Right, I must go. Speak again tomorrow."

Finding somewhere to live was a matter of urgency. Of course, we could both stay with Karly and Cam as long as we needed, but I wanted to have found somewhere to live before Joe arrived. He needed a tranquil environment. Sharing a house with a young family, which included an active toddler, a large dog, a cat and a baby on the way was not ideal. Neither did I want us to outstay our welcome.

I had three months to find us a home.

And the clock was ticking.

As I hadn't bought a car yet, Karly was chauffeuring me around. Indy was at her paternal grandmother's house, so Karly and I set off alone. I was excited. Maybe finding somewhere to live would be easy.

I'd read the particulars of the retirement village we were visiting from cover to cover, and it seemed ideal. There was usually a waiting list for new residents but they had a vacancy pending. Whenever a home became empty, the policy was to strip it out entirely, paint it throughout, and refit it with new flooring and appliances.

This village wasn't near any beach, which was a pity, but as we turned in, we admired the homes shaded by pine trees. A pretty fountain played in the centre of a small lake. At Reception, we were met by Margo, who shook our hands enthusiastically.

"Welcome!" she said. "I'll give you a tour, and I can show you the unit. It's got workmen in it at the moment, but it'll give you an idea of what it's like."

"Perfect!"

"This way! I'll show you the clubhouse and dining hall first. If you do join us, you may like to eat in the dining hall occasionally."

She clicked off in her high heels with Karly by her side. I trailed behind a little, absorbing the ambience, trying to imagine living there. Would we fit in? Would Joe like it?

"And here's the gym! Hello, Stan!"

The gym was well-equipped but deserted, apart from an ancient chap wearing shorts and T-shirt perched on an exercise bike. He stared straight ahead with glazed eyes, veins standing out on his forehead. His lips were drawn back revealing clenched teeth, and his knuckles were white as he gripped the handlebars. Sweat poured from him as his skinny white legs pumped relentlessly.

"How's it going, Stan?" cried our guide, but Stan didn't even glance our way.

"I'll show you our pool," said Margo gaily, not at all troubled by Stan's lack of response. "It's hugely popular with our residents. Bye, Stan! Catch up with you later!"

But Stan ignored her cheery wave. Whether he was hard of hearing or deep in some kind of sporting coma, I couldn't say.

The pool was nice. Two ladies stood at one end, chattering. They didn't look very wet.

"Muriel, Evie!" hailed Margo. "How are you?"

They waved back then continued their discussion.

"We have weekly aqua-aerobics classes," said Margo.

I tried to imagine Joe jogging and bouncing alongside a bunch of others but doubted that would ever happen.

"And we have loads of other activities! We have trips to places of interest and clubs. Do you like crafts? We have a thriving scrapbooking club and a make-your-own Christmas decorations club!"

Oh dear.

I might enjoy marching to music in the swimming pool, and even fashioning a festive Christmas bauble or two, but Joe would regard it all with horror. I consoled myself with the knowledge that none of these activities was compulsory. If Joe didn't want to join in, he wouldn't have to. He could simply pop out to the clubhouse and take part in the occasional Happy Hour if he felt like it.

"And here's the library," crowed Margo, pushing open some swing doors. "We have thousands of books and the library is always buzzing."

I could see the books but there wasn't a soul in the library. Definitely no buzzing. Just a rattling snore rising from one of the armchairs in the far corner.

"Oh, I think that may be Lily," said our guide in hushed tones. "We won't disturb her. I'll take you to see the houses and the vacant property instead."

Many of Sydney's suburbs are hilly and this retirement village was no exception. The little streets were nicely laid out, but steep. Joe would struggle. Karly and Margo chatted and I did my best to keep up.

"Do you have much of a problem with big spiders?" asked Karly. "I imagine these big trees would attract them." Karly and I shared a spider phobia.

"No, never heard anybody complain about spiders," said Margo, shaking her head. "I probably shouldn't tell you this, but we do see quite a few pythons."

Karly and I stared at her. Pythons were not part of our lives in England. Or in Spain for that matter.

"Ah, here we are," said Margo. "Number 75. Just as I thought, the tradies are busy working on it." In Australia, tradesmen are often referred to as 'tradies'.

She knocked on the door but the power tools within drowned out the sound and nobody answered.

"Never mind! I don't have the key but we can go around the back and through the garden gate. This house is particularly nice because the back faces onto the lake. Follow me!"

The lake looked cool and peaceful. Tall trees and the sky above were reflected on the surface which was undisturbed except by the fountain in the middle, and two black coots paddling furiously away from us. Dragonflies flitted and doves cooed in pine trees. A pretty walking track encircled the lake and inviting wooden benches stood at intervals.

"This is lovely!" I said to Karly.

A movement caught my attention and I stared, enchanted. Basking on the bank in the sunshine was a beautiful water dragon. It was a large one, perhaps about a metre (three feet) nose to tail, so probably a male. He regarded us haughtily, his proud nose in the air. Then there was a plop, and the dragon vanished, leaving just a ripple as the only clue to where he had dived.

Although Australian water dragons are shy in the wild, they can become used to constant human presence in their habitat. It's common to see water dragons in city parks where they have become accustomed to sharing the grounds with people. However, if necessary, they are fast runners and strong climbers, able to clamber up tree trunks in seconds. If alarmed, they will usually hide in thick vegetation, or they may scale a tree and drop from an overhanging branch into water. There they can sit on the bed of shallow creeks or lakes for well over an hour, hiding from enemies.

Joe would love this! I thought. We share a passion for wildlife and Joe has always been fascinated by reptiles.

And I could walk our future dog around the lake, I thought. I hoped the house itself wouldn't disappoint.

"Coo-ee!" called Margo. "Over here! We can get into the house via the patio doors."

She was beckoning to us, walking backwards up the narrow garden path towards the big sliding glass doors, which stood open.

"This way!"

We turned and headed towards her. Karly was ahead of me and had almost reached Margo when something caught my attention. Something wasn't right.

"Stop!" I shouted. "Don't move!"

AUSSIE BREAKFAST BOWLS

A fabulous, nutritious way to start the day. Garnish with avocado slices and cherry tomatoes for extra colour and flavour.

Ingredients (serves 4)

4 large bread rolls

4 tablespoons melted butter

4 rashers cooked bacon, each rasher cut in half

4 small handfuls baby spinach leaves

4 cherry tomatoes, finely sliced

1 cup grated tasty cheese

4 eggs

Salt and pepper

Avocado slices and cherry tomatoes for garnish

Method

Cut about 2-3 cm (1 inch) off the top off each of the bread rolls and remove and discard bread filling.

Place one tablespoon of melted butter into each of the bread rolls.

Place two bacon pieces into each bread roll.

Place a small handful of baby spinach leaves into each bread roll.

Share the cherry tomato slices between each of the bread rolls.

Share the cup of grated cheese between each of the bread rolls.

Break an egg into each of the bread rolls.

Carefully place loaves/rolls onto a baking tray lined with aluminium foil and place in a 180°C (350°F) oven for 15-20 minutes, until the egg is cooked to your liking.

Serve each roll on a plate and top with salt and pepper.

Garnish with avocado slices and cherry tomatoes.

From newideafood.com.au

2

HOUSE HUNTING

Margo stumbled back in surprise. I pointed at the ground by her feet and her hand flew to her mouth. Her eyes grew huge.

A huge diamond python, as thick as a man's arm, was draped across the path.

"Ohmigosh, ohmigosh," squeaked Karly, sidestepping neatly.

"I can't believe it! I stepped over it," whispered Margo, her eyes still the size of two full moons. "I nearly trod on it!"

The python wasn't bothered. Perfectly camouflaged, he was warming himself on the pavers and not in the mood to move.

"Hey!" called a workman, appearing at the patio door. He must have seen us approaching. "Is there a problem?"

He was a large man, wearing the obligatory Aussie tradie uniform comprising work boots, shorts and neon T-shirt. A tool belt was slung around his hips. His burly mate appeared beside him, ear defenders still in place, a power tool in his hand. The pair of them began to walk down the path towards us, unaware of the reptilian obstacle.

Margo's voice had returned.

"Watch out, there's a snake there!" she warned, pointing to the python. "Could you please remove…"

But she never finished the sentence. Like magic, the pair turned on their heels and vanished back into the house. The glass doors closed behind them with a decisive click.

"Well!" exclaimed Margo, exasperated.

"That wasn't very gallant," said Karly.

"It's just a diamond python," shouted Margo at the blank glass doors. "It's harmless!"

No reply from within.

Diamond pythons are common in Sydney. They are no threat to humans and exist by hunting lizards, rats, mice, and the occasional possum if they can catch it. They usually live in the bush but also take up residence in the roof spaces of private houses.

Understandably, many people are not keen to have snakes in their roofs, but perhaps they should welcome their lodgers. The pythons will happily eliminate any unwanted rodent pests, and once the food supply is exhausted, the snakes will move on. They provide an excellent free service.

The sunlight caught our snake's beautiful yellow and black scales, making them shimmer. He rippled ever so slightly, stirring from his slumber.

Margo clacked up the path to the patio doors and peered in through cupped hands.

"Honestly!" she said to us over her shoulder. "They've locked themselves in!"

She rapped sharply on the glass with her knuckles.

Nothing. She tried again.

"Hey! Guys! Give me one of your brooms or something so I can chase it away!"

There was a pause, and then the doors slid apart just wide enough to allow a broom to be passed out. I saw the workman's tattooed fist, but not its owner, and the doors snapped together again the instant Margo accepted the broom.

Margo was made of sterner stuff.

"Off you go, Mr Python," she said, preparing to sweep him away.

The python reared his head slightly to assess the situation. Then, in one sinuous, fluid movement, melted away into the undergrowth. He was gone.

"Wow!" I said.

"Gosh!" said Karly.

"Oh dear, I expect all this wildlife has put you off considering Fernview Village," said Margo.

"On the contrary!" I exclaimed. "I think it's wonderful to be so close to nature and watch water dragons and waterfowl on the lake. And the odd python is very welcome, too. Joe would love it."

"Oh good. Let's go inside and I'll show you around the house."

The tradies must have seen Margot deal with our uninvited reptilian visitor because the patio doors were now miraculously unlocked and the pair were working extra busily. I noticed they looked a little sheepish and made no eye contact with any of us.

Stepping inside, I was disappointed.

Obviously it was being refurbished and not looking its best, but I was struck by the size. The place was tiny. Although it had two bedrooms, the entire home was smaller than our roof terrace in Spain. Not big enough to swing a koala.

"No good, then?" asked Karly as we drove home.

"No. It was just too small. We would be really cramped."

"Well, that's the trouble with property in Sydney. Land is so expensive."

"Yes, I'm beginning to understand that now."

We collected Princess Indy and headed home. Indy was at that age when she loved to sing. As we drove, we all belted out her current favourite:

> Five cheeky monkeys a-sitting in the tree
> Teasing the crocodile,
> "You can't catch me!"
> Along came the crocodile, quiet as can be
> And snapped one monkey out of that tree.

Back home, Cam had finished his working day. We retreated to the chicken garden with cool drinks to discuss the day's events and watch Princess Indy playing in the sandpit.

"Never mind," I said, "there are plenty more places to see. I like the look of that one near the beach. We have an appointment..."

But my voice was drowned out by the mournful howling of next door's basset hound. Further conversation was impossible.

We looked at each other and rolled our eyes.

Suddenly, a head popped up over the fence, immediately above us. A man with huge, sweeping moustaches was peering down at us. The fence was extremely high at that point and I assumed he was standing on a ladder. I'm not sure who was the most surprised.

"Oh!" squeaked Karly, nearly spilling her drink.

"Oh!" said Moustache Man. "Sorry! I wasn't spying on you, honestly. I was just wondering what was making my dog howl like that."

"We were wondering the same thing," said Cam.

"Well, I think it's a cat," said our neighbour.

"Really?"

"Yes, I've seen one a few times. It seems to enjoy teasing my dog."

"Oh dear. How?"

"It sits on that branch up there," he said, pointing, "then it walks along the fence just out of reach. It drives my dog crazy."

"Oh dear. What sort of cat?"

"A tabby one."

"Oh."

"Anyway, the cat seems to enjoy it more than the dog. Sorry to have bothered you."

And the head vanished as suddenly as it had appeared.

We looked at each other guiltily, trying not to laugh. Next time we sang Indy's song, the words had changed:

> One cheeky Bandsaw a-sitting in the tree
> Teasing the basset hound,
> "You can't catch me!"
> Along came Moustaches, quiet as can be
> And snapped naughty Bandsaw out of that tree.

Those neighbours sold their house and moved away soon after. We can only hope that the cats in their new neighbourhood are a little more charitable than Bandsaw.

We visited many more retirement villages during the weeks that followed. Looking back on them now, they kind of merge into each other in a blur. Most were pleasant, but I couldn't really imagine us living in any of them.

I remember one in particular, not because of the village itself, but because of Karly's latest health craze. She'd just discovered smart water bottles. I had no idea what these were until she explained that they automatically tracked one's water intake and reminded one when a drink was recommended. I believe sensors monitor the water level, and the weight of the bottle, and the information is relayed to a phone app that activates an alarm.

My daughter is a fitness freak and quick to embrace new health discoveries. Somehow I was also persuaded that life could not possibly be complete without my very own smart water bottle. So that day we set off, each armed with our smart bottles, Indy in tow.

Beep, beep.

"Drink, Mummy. Drink, Princess Nanny."

Obediently swigging water whenever our apps (and Indy) ordered us to, we headed for the retirement village. Unfortunately, we took a wrong turning somewhere and the water was beginning to have an effect.

"Where's the guest parking?" asked Karly.

"I don't know. Hope it's close. I really need the loo."

"Me too."

"Me too! I a little bit quite need a wee," announced Indy who was fascinated by anything to do with lavatories, particularly public ones.

We parked quickly and hurried into Reception. A well-dressed lady stepped forward to greet us.

"Good afternoon and welcome to Forest Glen! Allow me to introduce myself. I'm Sandra, and I imagine you are Mrs Twead." She shook my hand. "And you must be her daughter?" she said, turning to Karly.

"Yes!" said Karly, looking flushed and hopping up and down.

I'm sure I was wearing the same anxious expression and twitching just as much.

"Ah," said Sandra. "You look flushed. Is it hot outside? Can I get you a glass of water before the tour?"

"No, thank you!" we said in unison.

"Could we possibly use your bathroom?" asked Karly.

Beep, beep.

"Drink, Mummy. Drink, Princess Nanny," ordered Indy.

Poor Sandra was looking uncomfortable. These twitchy viewers were clearly not behaving like her usual potential buyers. However, she directed us to the bathroom and we emerged much relieved and ready for the tour.

We boarded a golf buggy with Sandra chauffeuring.

"We are just passing Forest Glen's own nine-hole golf course," she said, warming to her task. "And over there is the clubhouse where..."

Beep, beep.

"Drink, Mummy. Drink, Princess Nanny," Indy commanded.

"I'm so sorry. We should explain," I said, seeing the poor lady's baffled expression. "We have new smart water bottles that tell us when we should hydrate."

"Actually, we're not used to drinking quite so much water," Karly added apologetically.

"Ah!" said Sandra, now understanding the situation and becoming the perfect guide. "Shall we pop into the clubhouse? There's a nice bathroom in there."

Beep, beep.

"Drink, Mummy! Drink, Princess Nanny!"

The remainder of the tour was punctuated by beeps and bathroom stops.

Forest Glen Village was nice, I think. Although it boasted plenty of toilets, and Sandra was exceptionally attentive, the villas were tiny and I didn't feel it was for us.

On another occasion, we'd just completed a guided tour around a village that had also seemed promising. Our guide had stopped to show us their program of events, talking us through the activities on offer. The knitting clubs and craft sessions were becoming familiar now.

"And on the first Tuesday of every month, we have a get-together. We barbecue beef burgers, or serve a curry, or Thai food, and drinks are half price at the bar."

"Gosh, that sounds fun," exclaimed an elderly lady who had joined our little group and was listening avidly. She was rather eccentrically dressed in a floaty dress and lace cardigan. Her feet were clad in white ankle socks and sandals. She had a friendly smile. I assumed she was also considering moving into this retirement village.

Our guide returned her smile and continued.

"On those Tuesdays, we sometimes organise a ten-pin bowling event or a quiz night."

"Oh, how super!" enthused our new companion. "I love ten-pin bowling!"

Our guide didn't comment but carried on listing future events.

"Next week we're going to order in fish and chips and have a darts night," she said, pointing at dates on the calendar.

"Darts? How lovely!" thrilled the lady. "I've *always* wanted to play darts. Can I come?"

Our guide sighed and patted her arm.

"Edna, dear, you've been coming to our Tuesday get-togethers since 2004."

"Have I?"

"Yes, dear. Now, would you like to sit in the shade and I'll organise a nice cuppa for you?"

With a cheery wave, Edna allowed herself to be led away. Our guided tour was over.

"The thing is," said Karly, as we drove home. "I don't think you're ready for a retirement home. The average age of the residents seems to be in the eighties, and you're only sixty."

This wasn't a new refrain from my daughter, and I was beginning to agree. The age factor was definitely a worry, not eased by the knowledge that Sydney accommodation was expensive and would be much smaller than Joe and I were used to.

"Cam suggested that we drive up the coast this weekend. Out of Sydney, but not too far away. We could look around, maybe visit some open houses. That way, you could see what you *could* get for your money."

"Not retirement villages?"

"No. Not retirement villages."

When I discussed it with Joe, he agreed that it was a good plan.

"I know some of the villages are really nice places," he said, "but I'm not sure we're ready for a wrinkly-ville yet. I think we like our privacy and independence too much."

I agreed and in the quiet of my den, I researched possibilities using Google maps. Luckily, my family lived in the northern suburbs of Sydney. It would be a simple matter to join the motorway and head north to the area known as the Central Coast.

Could this be the answer? Could I find a property here that gave us what we wanted? House prices looked attractive, much lower than those in Sydney and its suburbs. I began to feel quite excited.

No, we wouldn't be very close to the family, and city attractions would be less accessible. But there were huge compensations. Heaps of pristine beaches stretching for kilometres, including dog beaches, I noted. Forests, open grassland, lakes, dense bushland, national parks. The Central Coast seemed to have it all.

Then I saw a couple of sentences that made my heart race.

The Central Coast offers dozens of lookout points where watchers can view the humpback whale migration twice a year. Humpbacks swim north to breed in the winter, then return with their newborn calves later in the year.

Yes, for wildlife enthusiasts like Joe and me, the Central Coast had a lot to offer.

"That sounds amazing," said Joe. "But look carefully. We definitely don't want to take on a renovation job. I think we've had quite enough of those! I don't think I could cope with another."

"I agree! I'm going to look for a house which doesn't need *anything* doing to it."

"And we don't want a swimming pool. They require far too much maintenance."

"Absolutely."

"And take your time. Don't make up your mind too quickly. The right place will come along."

"I know. Don't worry. We're only going to look, anyway."

SUMMER VEGETABLE LASAGNE

Australia has every climate and it's possible to source most ingredients, from tropical fruit to Brussels sprouts without importing from abroad. Even cheeses like ricotta and parmesan, or baby zucchini with flowers attached, are produced in Australia. Recipe from Delicious.com.au

Ingredients

500g (17oz) ricotta

2 cups (160g) finely grated parmesan

200g (7oz) frozen peas

½ bunch basil, leaves torn

Finely grated zest and juice of 1 lemon

1 tsp dried chilli flakes

¾ cup (120g) roasted almonds, chopped

½ cup (750g) butternut pumpkin (butternut squash), seeds removed, halved, peeled

2 tbs extra virgin olive oil

2 tbs honey

4 yellow squash

4 baby zucchinis (courgettes) with flowers attached

1 tbs apple cider vinegar

Method

Preheat oven to 200°C (390°F)

Place ricotta, parmesan, peas, basil, lemon zest and chilli flakes in a food processor and whiz until roughly combined.

Transfer to a bowl and stir through ½ cup (80g) almonds.

Season. Cover and chill until ready to use.

Thinly slice pumpkin into 5mm-thick slices. Combine 1 tbs each oil and honey in a bowl.

Microwave the pumpkin in a heatproof bowl on high for 3 minutes. (Alternatively, steam pumpkin for 1 minute.)

Brush with honey mixture, then place one-quarter of pumpkin in a single layer in a 22cm (8 inches) baking dish and spread with one-third of the ricotta mixture.

Repeat process two more times, finishing with a layer of pumpkin.

Bake for 35 minutes or until pumpkin top is golden and caramelised. Cool slightly.

Meanwhile, thinly slice squash.

Cut zucchini into thin rounds and gently remove petals.

Combine vinegar, lemon juice and remaining 1 tbs each oil and honey in a small bowl. Set aside.

Top lasagne with squash, zucchini rounds and flowers, and remaining ¼ cup (40g) almonds.

Drizzle with the honey dressing to serve.

3

PURCHASES

The weekend couldn't come quickly enough. Cam drove, Karly was in charge of navigation, using estate agents' apps to guide us to houses for sale, and Indy and I sat in the back. We played a game that I hoped she had grown out of but it remained a firm favourite. She had a toy CD player and every time she pressed the Start button, a nursery rhyme played.

"Dance, Princess Nanny!" she cried.

I would jig and pretend to dance until she pressed the Stop button, whereupon I froze. It was like a solitary game of musical statues and it amused Indy endlessly. Me, after the first five minutes, not so much.

When she finally dozed off to the hum of the car's engine, I could concentrate on the passing scenery. The motorway passed over the giant Hawkesbury River and cut through towering rock for many miles. After an hour, we turned off and began our property quest.

I liked what I saw. We'd left the Sydney traffic behind and the roads were wide. There were plenty of trees and untouched bushland. Many districts had inviting-looking beaches. People looked relaxed, tanned and unhurried. Many didn't even bother with footwear as they strolled along ample sidewalks.

"Sea-girls!" cried Indy as gulls wheeled overhead.

As with any region, there were salubrious areas and others less so. Some houses were in smart streets, while other, cheaper houses, appeared scruffy and neglected.

It was helpful that my son-in-law was a builder. He could offer advice, and we rejected some properties for reasons I may not have noticed had I been alone.

The business of house-buying is very different in Australia, compared with England and Spain, where the buyer arranges a private viewing through an estate agent. Cam explained to me how it worked.

"In Australia, we hold 'open homes'," he said. "The sellers will arrange times with the real estate agent for property-hunters to have a look around. It's usually for just an hour, or even half an hour."

"So there are lots of viewers all walking around at the same time?"

"Yes. Sometimes people will make an offer after the viewing, and if one is accepted, the sellers take it off the market."

"I can see it's a good, informal method of viewing," I said, "but if houses are only open for half an hour, could potential buyers miss seeing properties if the times coincide?"

"Yes, but houses often have a couple of open days or more. And you could request a private viewing if you really wanted."

"Oh, I see."

"Often a house goes to auction if a seller thinks it'll reach a higher price if potential buyers bid against each other. Homeowners usually set a reserve price, and if bidding doesn't reach this price, they aren't forced to sell the house."

"How about this one?" interrupted Karly, passing me her phone.

"Looks nice!"

It was a wooden, chalet-type, but we dismissed it after a quick viewing. Apart from being tiny, it could only be reached by a shared drive, and many of its timbers were rotten.

"No, thank you," I said, staring into dark corners where half-dead cockroaches lay on their backs waving their legs.

"This one?"

"No, it's on a main road."

"How about this one?"

"No, too close to the railway."

One was very nice, but I felt the vast, manicured garden would need too much work. Another was too crowded in by its neighbours.

The last house on our list was in a cul-de-sac. It was a typically Aussie, unpretentious, brick-built, single-level house and I liked the look of it immediately.

"The photos look amazing," said Karly, looking at her phone.

The estate agent was waiting to welcome us on the doorstep, and we could see other viewing parties milling around inside.

I don't know what it was about that house, but I felt right at home as soon as we walked in. Perhaps if I'd looked more closely, or if I hadn't left my glasses at home, I might have thought differently. But there was a smile on my face because I could actually visualise Joe and I living in this house. It had three bedrooms (perfect) and wasn't too big or too small.

"You really like this one, don't you?" asked Karly, watching me.

"I do!"

The kitchen was very cramped, and the bathroom badly in need of a makeover, but Cam swept those problems aside.

"Easy to refurbish those," he said, "and you'd still have money left over in your budget."

And when I saw the pool I was in love.

It wasn't the regular rectangular blue-painted pool, the type that is often formed by a prefabricated fibre-glass liner or tiles. No, this was a sparkling oasis pool edged with giant boulders and palm trees. It was extravagantly exotic and unusual, and I wanted to jump straight in.

"Well?" asked Karly as we got back into the car. "You haven't said anything for ages."

We clipped on our seat-belts and set off.

"Dance, Princess Nanny," said Indy, but my head was too full of thoughts and ideas.

"I'm going to put in an offer," I said.

That evening, I talked with Joe.

"You did what?" he asked.

"I put in an offer."

"Vicky, have you gone crazy? Whatever made you do such a thing? Is the house perfect?"

"No, not really, but you should see the pool."

"Pool? Pool? We agreed we didn't want a swimming pool!"

"I know, but this one is different. It's fringed with palm trees and..."

"How many bedrooms?"

"Three."

"Okay. Bathrooms?"

"Only one, but Cam explained that's the brilliant thing about Aussie houses! They're not built like British houses. All the interior walls are just plasterboard. Nothing structural or load-bearing. They can all be demolished, and the whole house can be reconfigured to suit ourselves."

"Wait a minute," said Joe from the other side of the world. "Are you saying we are taking on another huge renovation job?"

"Well..."

"We agreed! No pool! No renovations!"

"Anyway, my offer was rejected."

"Well, hallelujah! Thank goodness for that!"

"So I put in a higher offer."

By the end of September, I had bought a car. It was terrific to be mobile and I felt much more independent. It had a reversing camera, it switched on its own lights at dusk, and the windscreen wipers automatically leapt into life when it rained. I was delighted with these and all manner of mod cons I didn't know even existed when we lived in Spain. I named our car Bruce and was grateful to his satnav voice for nagging me if I exceeded the speed limit.

Bruce was roomy, which I secretly thought might be useful for our future dog.

Karly's pregnancy was progressing well, and I felt I could be useful by watching Indy while Karly and Cam made preparations for the new baby. Indy still had no idea about the new addition to the family.

After hospital scans assured them that things were proceeding exactly as they should, Cam and Karly decided the time had come.

"Indy, we've got something very important to tell you."

Indy's blue eyes couldn't have been wider.

"Some very exciting news."

Indy put her head on one side, listening intently.

"Indy, you are going to be a… BIG SISTER!"

Indy's mouth dropped open as her three-year-old brain tried to process this information.

"Mummy has a baby in her tummy and when it comes out, you'll be a big sister!"

"A baby?"

"Yes, a really tiny one."

"A little bit quite tiny one?"

"Yes! You can help look after it."

"I can help!"

"Yes, you can help, and when the baby grows, you can play with it."

"Tomorrow?"

"No, not tomorrow. Not for a long time because it has to do some more growing. When it's ready, Mummy will go to the hospital, and they'll help it come out of Mummy's tummy."

"Yes! And when I was a baby I used to go waaaah!"

"That's right, and our new baby will go waaaah, too."

"And I can play with it."

"Yes, you can. Would you like a little sister or a little brother?"

"Sister. We can play Princesses."

"And what name shall we choose for our new baby?"

"Um, Dragon."

My second offer for the house was also refused. With Cam and Karly's help, I made my last offer. I instructed the estate agent to tell the sellers that I would not be attending an auction, if they chose to hold one and that this was my final offer. If they accepted, I wanted the big mirror in the dining area included in the sale.

Twenty-four hours later I had a response. The sellers accepted my offer and called off the upcoming auction.

The house was ours.

"You're going to love it, honestly!"

"Are you sure?"

"Absolutely sure. It's got great potential."

"Great potential?" echoed Joe. "Great potential? But we weren't looking for a house with great potential!"

"Oh, and did I tell you about Splinterbone Crag? Seriously, it's a cliff literally less than a five-minute drive away. Apparently, it's a fabulous place to watch the whale migration! I can't wait!"

"Yes, but…"

"And there are so many gorgeous beaches!" I didn't add that many of them welcomed dogs. "We could go to a different one every day of the week, all within a fifteen minutes drive away."

"Vicky, I…"

"And three good shopping centres within easy reach. Oh, and a chemist, veg shop, butcher, and supermarket all within walking distance."

I heard Joe exhale and sensed he had given up, but I hurried on, just in case he hadn't.

"Have you been to the medical centre? Any news? Did they give you a new puffer?"

"Yes, the nurse gave me a new inhaler. It seems to help a little bit."

"That's good. Oh, and I forgot to tell you. I got an email today, and you'll never guess in a million years who it was from!"

There was a long pause, then, "So are you going to tell me?"

"I'll give you a clue. Somebody in Spain. Somebody from the village."

"Gosh! I can't think of anybody who would sit down and write us an email. I give up. Who?"

"One of the Ufarte twins!"

"Really? Which one?"

"Catalina."

"Which one's that?"

"I'm not sure, I never could tell them apart."

"Why did she write?"

"Listen, I must go, Karly's calling me. I'll forward the email."

After dinner, it was time for Indy's bath, and then her bedtime. She was no trouble at all to put to bed. After her story, she'd want to play Princesses, so we told her she could be Sleeping Beauty. She must pretend to be asleep under a spell, waiting for a handsome prince to arrive. She closed her eyes and we kissed her goodnight.

She was fast asleep within minutes. It worked every time.

Later, I read the email through again.

Hola tía Vicky y tío Joe,

I hop you are well. I am well and my sister and family is completely wells. My teacher at school she say all the class will take english penpalls. please can you be my english penpall. The grades of my sister is good and I like to be good too.

How are you like Australia? Are there much kangaroos near your house? My mother she say *tío* Joe is sick. I am sorry *tío* Joe is sick.

If you can be my english penpall i am very happy,

Felicitations, Catalina xx

I could picture the Ufarte twins labouring over their homework at the kitchen table while Mama Ufarte stirred a saucepan behind them. It was late September so the weather would still be mild in the village of El Hoyo. Perhaps, later, the family would sit outside. There would be the smell of over-ripe grapes in the air from nearby vines, as unpicked fruit began to ferment. When the sky darkened, the hum of wasps would subside, and Papa Ufarte would sit on the doorstep, picking out chords on his guitar.

I sighed. Was it only a month since we had left Spain?

So much had happened already. I now had a car that talked to me and knew when it was getting dark. I'd bought a house with a swimming pool in a district I'd never even heard of before. In a couple of months, I'd be moving up the coast. And we were expecting another grandchild.

Hopefully, Joe would be joining me soon.

Catalina's email had reminded me of what we'd left behind, but I didn't feel homesick. I had too much to look forward to.

I wrote back to Catalina telling her that I'd be absolutely delighted to be her penpal and sent my best regards to her parents and family. I couldn't resist also asking her a few questions about the village. Joe would probably say I was being a nosy parker, but I prefer to think that I was just exercising the linguistic skills of Ufarte Twin #1 (or was it #2?).

When we left Spain, we'd brought very little with us, deciding that we didn't know where we'd be living or whether our old furniture would fit. The cost, too, of shipping from Spain to Australia would have been enormous.

It was a little bit like getting married in the old days. I began collecting stuff for our future home and soon the goods began to pile up in my lair. Karly and Cam had a bed they could lend me, but I had no sheets, pillows or bed linen of any kind.

During these shopping trips, I learned unexpected language differences, particularly in the field of bed linen.

"Can you tell me where your linen department is, please?" I asked once.

"Um, linen? What are you looking for, exactly?" asked the shop assistant, tilting her head to one side and raising one painted eyebrow.

"Well, a duvet, actually."

"Duvet?" Blank look.

"Yes, for the bed… Like a quilt, you know?"

"Oh! You mean a doona!"

"Do I?"

"Yes, I'm sure you do."

"And where would I find one?"

"In Manchester."

Now it was my turn to look completely baffled. Manchester, England seemed an unreasonably long journey to make in order to buy a duvet.

"Manchester?"

"At the back of the store, on your right."

The lady was right, of course. Under a big MANCHESTER sign were plenty of pillows, sheets, quilts and bedcovers to choose from.

And doonas.

I am told that during the 18th and 19th centuries, Australian settlers had little success growing cotton crops. This meant that linen had to be imported. Much of it came from the northern cities of England, and wooden boxes and crates packed with cotton goods were stamped *Manchester*. The word stuck and came to mean table linen and bedding. Nowhere else in the world is that word used to describe cotton merchandise.

Soon I became the proud owner of a new set of saucepans, some wine glasses, a knife set, and all manner of kitchen utensils. Imagine starting from scratch at the age of sixty. It was great fun and thanks to stores like Kmart, it wasn't expensive.

I soon had an intimate knowledge of all the local shops. But there was one shop that I frequently walked past, but never entered. My head would turn, and my footsteps slowed to a stop as I stared in.

And what was displayed in the window of this particular shop which drew me like a magnet?

Puppies.

It was a pet shop.

STRAWBERRY SWIRL PAVLOVAS

Australians adore pavlovas, and family celebrations are rarely without one. This is a wonderfully easy variation from www.taste.com.au

Ingredients (makes 8)

250g (9oz) fresh strawberries, hulled, quartered

2 tablespoons caster sugar

150ml (5 floz) thickened cream

150g (5oz) mascarpone

1 teaspoon vanilla bean paste

8 meringue nests

Strawberries, extra, to decorate

Mint leaves, extra, to decorate

Method

Place quartered strawberries in a bowl. Sprinkle with 1 tablespoon caster sugar. Set aside for 30 mins or until they begin to release their juices.

Place strawberries in a food processor and process until coarsely chopped.

Place cream, mascarpone, vanilla bean paste and remaining sugar in a bowl. Use an electric beater to whip until soft peaks form.

Gently fold in the strawberries, being careful not to over-mix.

Arrange meringue nests on a serving platter.

Divide strawberry cream among the meringues and top with fresh strawberries and mint leaves.

4

A FRENZY AND PHONE CALLS

I was on the verge of moving into our forever home, and I felt that dog ownership was almost within my grasp.

I'd reluctantly dismissed the idea of adopting a rescue dog. This would be my first dog and I didn't feel confident enough to take on a dog with unknown traits or background.

Australian dog rescue centres are crammed with large breeds, most being staffie or pitbull crosses. I'd heard they can be excellent with small children but are not always good with other dogs. I didn't feel experienced enough to offer one a home.

I carried out a lot of research and already had an idea of the dog I wanted someday. I narrowed the type and traits down and created a wish list:

- A dog that didn't moult would be excellent because of Joe's breathing problems and Indy's asthma.
- A reasonably small dog would be ideal because our new home wasn't very big.
- A breed that is known to be good with children, adults and other dogs would be perfect.
- A dog that enjoys walks and is easy to train would be nice.

It was a lot to ask.

The pet shop was scrupulously clean and always busy. Sometimes there were baby rabbits or guinea pigs in the window. Occasionally there were kittens or puppies, delightful little bundles that soon found homes.

Well, it wouldn't do any harm just to go in and wander around, would it?

I walked in, admiring the tanks of exotic fish and bright green stick insects.

A notice caught my eye.

We prefer not to display puppies for long because they can become distressed. However, if you are looking for a puppy, we may be able to help. We obtain our puppies from a handful of trusted breeders and never deal with puppy farms. If you would like more information, please ask.

"Can I help at all?" asked a voice beside me. "Were you interested in getting a puppy?"

"Oh! Um, not really, I was just looking… I mean, I would like a puppy, but I'm not ready to have one yet."

"What breed were you thinking of?"

"Well, we have asthma and breathing problems in the family so…"

"Ah, a poodle might suit you. They don't shed at all."

I couldn't quite picture Joe sharing a home with a poodle. I'm not sure why.

"I'd like a breed that is known to be good with children. I have a three-year-old granddaughter and another grandchild on the way."

The assistant nodded wisely.

"It would be my first dog, so a breed that is easy to train? And not too big and loves walks." I was thinking of how owning a dog might also benefit our health. Going out for daily walks would be good for both Joe and me.

"I think I know the perfect puppy breed for you," said the assistant brightly. "I think either a cavoodle or a spoodle would suit you perfectly."

"A what?"

"A cavoodle is a poodle crossed with a cavalier spaniel. Cavalier spaniels are very loving dogs. They were bred to be lap dogs for royalty."

I adore cavalier King Charles spaniels, but I think they get a rough deal. The way they have been bred to make their eyes bulge means they are prone to eye problems and even epilepsy in later life. I feel the same about dogs who have been bred with short snouts. It might make them look super-cute, but it doesn't seem fair to breed dogs with deformities that can make them struggle to breathe.

"What's a spoodle?" I asked.

"You're English, aren't you? I believe they're called cockerpoos in England. Half poodle and half cocker spaniel. A very intelligent breed. They don't shed and are always ready for a walk."

She pulled out a picture from a drawer, and I was smitten.

"Funnily enough," she said, "we are expecting a litter of spoodles in about a month. Shall I take your phone number and contact you when they're ready?"

"So how's it going?"

"Fine. All the house paperwork is going through smoothly. It looks like the final exchange and moving date is going to be November 6th. I'm going up to see it again, a week before moving day, to walk around and check that everything is okay. That's the way they do it here. I can't wait, it's all so exciting!"

"And you've been collecting stuff for the house?"

"Yup. Cam is going to lend us a bed, and I've been gathering bits and pieces. I'm taking the sofa that's in my lair, and the desk. As soon as I move in, I'm going to look for tradies to get stuff done as quickly as possible. It would be terrific if work can begin before you arrive."

"Do you think there's much work to be done?"

"A little bit. Not too much, though."

As I type these words, I can't believe how naïve I was. Perhaps it was just as well that I didn't know what the future held.

"Gosh, I wish I was there to help you, Vicky."

"Concentrate on your health, Joe. That's the most important thing. Don't worry. I'll manage perfectly."

"Well, at least you didn't rush out and get a dog. I was afraid you were going to. If you had it would have made things even harder."

"Er, yes."

Moving day drew closer. I now had the plans of the house and spent hours poring over them, considering the best way to use the space available. I felt the two most significant drawbacks were the single bathroom and the tiny kitchen which was almost a kitchenette. Maybe we could build an extension, or knock a few walls down and reconfigure the layout.

"Have you seen the widescreen smart TVs they're offering at Aldi on Saturday?" asked Karly, interrupting my thoughts.

There was no doubt about it. The TVs were a bargain. We would need a TV, so perhaps I should buy one. But Aldi isn't an ordinary store. Their special deals change every week and bargains quickly sell out.

"We'll have to be there, ready and waiting, queueing before the shop opens," said Karly. "Deals like this get snapped up immediately. In fact, I suggest you and I go to our Aldi store, and Cam can go to one in a different district."

That Saturday, Karly, Indy and I sped towards the local mall, while Cam went to another.

We parked and joined the queue that was already forming at the store's entrance. We were third in line, so I felt we were safe. As the minutes ticked by, more people gathered, and by the time the manager approached to unlock the glass doors, quite a crowd had assembled.

As he jiggled his key into the lock, I felt the atmosphere change. The doors slid apart and the manager hastily stepped back as a horde of shoppers surged into the store, polite queue forgotten.

"Quick!" yelled Karly. "Make for the centre aisle!"

But the stampede was too much for me, and I was tossed aside as it raged through the store. Everybody wanted a widescreen smart TV.

"Excuse me!" my valiant daughter cried, knuckles white on the trolley, elbows at right angles as she forged ahead.

"Skooze meee!" echoed Indy, standing in the prow of the shopping trolley, like Rose in the film *Titanic*, her hair flowing behind.

I arrived at the flatscreen TV display just after my daughter and granddaughter did. Where a mountain of TV boxes had once existed, now only one remained, and a man was already reaching for it. I shouted the first thing that came into my head.

"Look out! Pregnant lady!"

It was just enough to make the man hesitate for a second, allowing Karly to grab the heavy box.

"My mummy has a baby in her tummy and it's called Dragon," Indy informed the man, as we attempted to manhandle it onto the trolley.

He rolled his eyes and walked away, defeated.

The box was enormous and wouldn't fit in the trolley, so progress was slow to the checkout.

"My mummy has a baby in her tummy," Indy told everybody in the queue.

The fellow customers who could see over their widescreen TV boxes smiled at her.

"My mummy's baby is called Dragon," Indy told the checkout girl.

Somehow we managed to wrestle the TV out without crippling too many people, and reached the car. Our next problem was getting it into the vehicle. It soon became apparent that it was never going to fit.

As we took a breath to plan our next move, our phones rang simultaneously.

I didn't recognise the number that flicked up on mine, so ignored it. Meanwhile, Cam was ringing Karly.

"Sorry," he said, "I got there before they opened, but I couldn't reach the TVs in time. Seriously, it was crazy! As soon as the doors opened, it was like a feeding frenzy."

"I know, it was the same here! I managed to grab the last one but we can't get it into the car. We've tried all sorts of ways and it just won't fit."

"Okay, on my way."

As we waited for Cam to arrive in his ute, I checked who had phoned me. Whoever it was had left me a message. I held the phone up to my ear and listened.

"Hello, this is June from the pet shop. Our spoodle breeder has just informed us that the litter will be ready next week. Can you please ring back and confirm that you still want a golden female? If it's too early for you, we can put you down for one from the next litter, early in the new year."

My heart raced. Next week?

I wasn't moving into our house for another two weeks. It would make no sense to get a puppy yet. Besides, it would be very unfair to ask Karly and Cam if I could bring a new puppy into their home. And what would LJ, their huge husky/staffie mix, think of a puppy in his domain? Would he harm it? And what would Bandsaw, the cat, make of a pup?

And Joe?

I knew exactly what his advice would be...

I struggled with these thoughts but, for the moment, kept them to myself.

Cam arrived and lifted the TV onto his ute as though it was a feather. He strapped it securely and we followed him home.

"You're quiet," observed Karly.

"Um, yes. I just listened to a message from the pet shop. The spoodle puppy is ready to collect next week. I just wondered if you'd mind me bringing her back to your house for the two weeks before I move."

Karly hardly hesitated.

"I can't see a problem with that. We'll have to check with Cam, of course."

"Okay with me," said Cam later, smiling.

I could have hugged them. Instead, I rushed away and called the pet shop.

I'd already spent a lot of time researching how to look after and train a puppy. Now that the big day was just a week away, my research intensified. I have a lot of respect for the RSPCA and appreciated any advice they gave. Crate training soon came to my notice.

Although many Australians have never heard of it, crate training is popular in the UK and the US. I decided it was the way to go and it was probably the best decision I could have made.

I made lots of doggy purchases but the most important item was a crate. I made sure it was large enough to allow for my puppy to grow. The RSPCA site clearly explained how a crate is intended to provide a haven for a dog. By nature, dogs feel secure in small, enclosed spaces. A mother dog will hide her pups in a hole or den while she goes hunting. The pups will feel safe in the den and sleep until she returns.

Apparently, if carried out properly, crate training would help my new pup to become toilet trained. It would also give it security if I had to go out and provide a retreat where it could escape for peace and quiet.

It all made sense to me and sounded quite easy. I couldn't wait to get started.

Joe and I had chatted for a while about the move, but I didn't broach the other subject occupying my mind.

"So, how's it all going?" he asked. "All set for the move?"

"I think so. The TV we got was a bargain. And I bought a big crate today, too."

"Crate?"

"Um, a crate for packing."

"What, a wooden one?"

I'm hopeless at telling lies. I tie myself up in knots and always get caught out in the end. So I took a deep breath.

"Well, no. It's a big, plastic one. And it's not for packing."

"What's it for, then?"

So I told him about the puppy.

There was a long pause. I waited, holding my breath.

"A what? A cockerpoo? What on earth is that? A cross between a cockatoo and a...poo?"

But at least Joe was only questioning the breed. He wasn't putting his foot down and demanding that I cancel the collection of the pup.

"You're not furious?"

"No, what would be the point? I absolutely knew you were going to get a puppy. I'm just surprised it took you so long."

It seems Joe knows me better than I know myself.

I had a crate. I had food and water bowls. I had a frisbee, balls and dog toys, including a plush platypus with soft eggs in its pouch. I had dog treats and dog chews. I had puppy training pads. I had puppy shampoo and special ear-cleaning liquid.

I had everything except a dog.

And that was about to change.

On Monday morning my phone rang again and this time I recognised the number.

"Hi, June here again. Just to let you know your puppy has arrived and you can pick her up as soon as you're ready."

EASY SALMON MOUSSE

Serve on crackers, little toasts, or even cucumber slices. Super-easy to make in advance and can be stored in an airtight container in the fridge.

Ingredients

1 large pack of Philadelphia cream cheese

250g or 8oz sour cream

1 stick celery

2 spring onions, finely chopped

Ground pepper

2 x 220g tins or 8oz tinned red salmon

Juice of 1 lemon

¾ tablespoon gelatine, softened

Method

Beat cheese and cream together until fluffy. Add finely chopped vegetables.

Fold in salmon and lemon juice.

Blend in gelatine.

Pour into mould and refrigerate overnight.

5

LOLA AND COLD FEET

June, the manager of the pet shop, recognised me as soon as I arrived and showed me into the office.

"I expect you'd like to see her before we embark on the paperwork," she said.

On the floor, lined with newspaper, was a wooden playpen. Even before I saw the tiny puppies, I heard squeaks.

"There are three in the litter," she said, "all girls. The two brown and white ones, fast asleep in the far corner, are already sold, too. Yours is the gold one trying to escape."

My puppy was the one that was squeaking, standing on her stubby little hind legs, trying to scrabble up the bars of the playpen.

"Oh my, she's just *gorgeous...*" I said and felt my eyes misting over.

"Any idea what you're going to call her?" asked June.

I had thought of all manner of names over the past month. I'd made long lists of possibilities, then shortlists, staring at them for ages but not really liking any.

Never mind, I had thought, *I'll wait until I actually meet the puppy. Maybe a name will occur to me then.*

"No, I haven't decided yet."

And then, as I gazed at this beautiful young creature, it came to me like a bolt of lightning. The perfect name.

This puppy was breathtakingly beautiful, and golden, and naughty. I knew somebody else with those identical qualities. Lola Ufarte. Our wayward young neighbour in the Spanish mountain village we had left behind. Now this little pup would always remind me of Spain and the wonderful years we spent in El Hoyo.

"Actually, I think I will name her Lola," I said.

"Good name," said June, and we began the lengthy paperwork.

After I'd signed numerous papers and was given others to take with me, including records of her microchip number and an appointment for a puppy check with the local vet, I left, cradling Lola against my chest. She was soaking wet, having just waded through the puppies' water bowl.

"She's tiny!" said Karly when we got home.

Of course Indy wanted to play with her but we explained that Lola needed a few days to settle in first. LJ sniffed her all over and appeared to decide she wasn't worth wasting his time. Bandsaw growled, her tabby fur standing on end, but she seemed to know that Lola was too young and silly to be any threat.

I'd been warned that taking on a puppy was similar to caring for a newborn baby. I hadn't really believed that but soon discovered it was true. Puppies are extremely hard work.

For the first two days Lola cried a lot, which broke my heart. She only stopped when I cuddled her. I got nothing done and worried that I might be spoiling her. But slowly she began to adjust and settle.

The vet pronounced her bouncing with health, and I started her crate training, another challenge.

I began by making the crate an attractive place by putting in soft bedding, a cuddly toy, and an occasional treat. I didn't close the door and she entered the crate by herself when she was tired. After a few days, I could play with her, feed her, take her outside to relieve herself, then pop her in the crate to sleep. As her crate time increased, I was able to get some writing done and was even able to shoot off to the shops.

Now, as I look at her first collar, I find it hard to believe she was ever so small. She had hardly any neck, just rolls of fat. Her tail and legs were mere stubs and her coat was short and dark gold. But every day she grew.

We spent nearly all our time together. At night, Lola slept in her crate in my lair. I knew that allowing her to sleep on my bed, or even in my bedroom, would be a mistake because Joe would never approve. But I set my alarm to take her to the toilet twice during the night. She stumbled out of the crate, went outside, then snuggled back down without a murmur. Her training was going pretty well.

A week before the day of the move, I left Lola behind and drove up the coast to take a final look at the house and make sure all was in order. I met the estate agent outside, and he unlocked the front door.

"The present owners are out at the moment," he said, but his eyes didn't quite meet mine.

I knew they were young men and was prepared to make allowances. Even so, I was shocked at the scene that met my eyes.

Junk was piled in the living room, waist-high. Black garbage bags spewed clothes over a jumble of fishing rods and tackle. Cardboard boxes barely contained the audio equipment and vinyl records stuffed into them.

It was clear that the house had been cleverly, probably professionally, styled the day of the sale. Now that the tasteful furniture and extravagant vases of flowers had disappeared, things looked very different.

Chipped floor tiles were no longer hidden. Window blinds, tied up and out of sight for the viewing, now hung broken. Loose cables spilled out from untidy holes in the walls. There was an underlying smell of cigarette smoke and animal urine, and I noticed that most of the interior doors were gouged, as though by claws. And how had I missed the disgusting stained and threadbare bedroom carpets?

Outside there were piles of dog faeces, buzzing with flies. And it seemed I had overlooked the window frames that had been crudely spray-painted without first masking the surrounding brickwork. The pool water was green, with leaves and debris floating in dirty islands. In the few short weeks since I'd seen the house, masses of weeds had sprung through the cracks of the brick paths.

There were even shocks in store for me in the garage. Somebody had fed hose pipes, to supply water through the hatch into the loft, and had set up lights in the cramped roof space. Even I could see that something very odd had been going on here.

"Everything okay?" asked the estate agent after I'd finished my inspection. "Seen enough?"

No, everything *wasn't* okay, and yes, I *had* seen enough. But I was too shocked to voice my emotions. I'd been an idiot. I shouldn't have rushed into it. I knew it was too late, so I nodded dumbly and crept back into the sanctuary of my car.

I cried all the way back to Sydney.

I couldn't bring myself to tell Joe just how ghastly the house was. After all, he had enough on his plate with his health. He'd trusted me to find us the right home, and I'd let him down.

At first, I said nothing to Karly and Cam. Then I finally admitted that I was convinced I had made a terrible mistake.

"The house is awful. I've been an idiot. I can't believe I was so stupid to rush into such a ridiculous purchase."

"Now just a minute," said Cam, always able to think clearly in a crisis. "You had a budget, didn't you?"

"Yes."

"Well, according to my calculations, you got the house pretty cheap. If you spend the rest of the budget fixing it up, you'll end up with a beautiful house."

"Exactly the way you want it," agreed Karly.

"But you should have seen it! It was disgusting! I can't expect Joe to move into that!"

"We'll bring loads of cleaning stuff on the day of the move. We'll make it habitable, and you can start bringing in tradies to sort it out as quickly as possible. You can get a lot done before he gets here."

"Do you really think so?"

"Definitely!" they chorused.

"There is nothing about that house that can't be easily fixed," said Cam. "Honestly, as we discussed before, Aussie homes are shells. You can knock down walls or change things as much as you want. When the house is finished, it'll be worth a lot of money. It'll be like brand new and built to your personal specifications."

"You like the area, don't you?" asked Karly.

"Yes! I love it."

"Well, there you are then. No problems."

The more I thought about it, the more I realised they were right.

My spirits lifted.

Lola's crate training progressed quite well, although the toilet training was a bit more miss than hit. After she had napped, or finished playing, I took her outside and praised her when she performed. However, there were still plenty of times when I'd find puddles on the wood floor. But she never soiled her crate. I tried as much as possible to keep to my lair in case she disgraced herself on a carpet in the house.

Indy often joined us while her mum was busy or preparing dinner. I had a special cupboard for Indy's toys, but Lola was her favourite playmate. Many a time I would laugh because Indy was inside the crate and Lola was on the outside, wagging her tail so fast it was just a blur.

"Would you mind looking after Indy for an hour or so? I want to bake the reveal cake for tonight," said Karly one day.

"Of course!"

Reveal cake? I'd never heard of a reveal cake and I'm pretty sure they didn't exist when I was giving birth to babies. When it was explained, I understood why we didn't have reveal cakes in our day.

I knew Karly and Cam had gone to the hospital for a scan and they had returned, hand in hand, bursting with excitement. They had immediately phoned to invite Cam's parents and grandmother to dinner that evening.

"Everything go okay at the hospital?" I asked, although I could tell by their expressions that all was well.

"Yup! Cam and I know whether Indy is going to have a baby brother or sister. The hospital told us today!"

"Really? Wow!" I squeaked. "What are you having?"

"Not telling! When we cut into the cake tonight, it'll be either blue or pink inside. That's a reveal cake!"

"I'm going to be a big sister," Indy told Lola. "My mummy's got a baby in her tummy and it's called Dragon."

Lola licked her and they played their favourite game together. Indy pretended to be a puppy and the pair of them romped. Then Indy crawled into the crate, closely followed by Lola. There they flopped down together, resting, before springing back into life and more games.

Dinner that night was a happy affair. Indy wore one of her favourite princess costumes and both grandmothers, and great grandmother were ordered to wear tiaras.

Karly is a fabulous cook but I don't remember what she served that evening. However, I do remember that most of us couldn't resist glancing furtively at the splendid cake on the sideboard.

GENDER REVEAL CAKE

Three layers of moist, delicious vanilla cake dyed with food colouring, and frosted with easy, creamy vanilla buttercream. From prettysweetsimple.com

Ingredients

Cake

3 cups (15oz) plain (all-purpose) flour

1 tablespoon baking powder

½ teaspoon salt

1 cup (8oz) unsalted butter, softened

¼ cup (2floz) canola or vegetable oil

2 cups (14oz) granulated sugar

4 large eggs

1 tablespoon pure vanilla extract

1¾ cups (14floz) whole milk

Vanilla Buttercream Frosting

1½ cups (12oz) unsalted butter, softened

⅛ teaspoon salt

5 cups (22oz) powdered (icing) sugar, sifted, plus more as needed

5 tablespoons (2½floz) heavy (thickened) cream

1 tablespoon pure vanilla extract

Method

Preheat oven to 350°F/180°C. Butter three 9-inch (22 cm) cake pans, and line the bottoms with parchment paper.

Cake: In a medium bowl, sift together flour, baking powder, and salt. Set aside.

In the bowl of an electric mixer fitted with the paddle attachment, beat butter, oil, and sugar on medium speed until light and fluffy, 3-4 minutes. Scrape down the sides and bottom of the bowl as needed.

Add eggs, one at a time, beating well after each addition.

Beat in vanilla extract. With the mixer on low speed, add the flour mixture in three additions alternating with the milk in two additions, beginning and ending with the flour mixture. Do not over-mix the batter. The less you mix, the lighter the cake will be.

Divide the batter as evenly as possible into three bowls. Add food colouring to each bowl until desired colour is reached. Add just a tiny drop at first because food colourings can be very concentrated.

Pour each bowl of batter into prepared pans.

Bake for 25-30 minutes until a toothpick inserted into the centre of the cakes comes out clean.

Allow cakes to cool for 15 minutes, then gently remove from pans and allow them to cool completely on a wire rack.

Frosting: In the bowl of an electric mixer fitted with the paddle or whisk attachment, beat butter and salt on medium speed until smooth and creamy, about 2 minutes.

Add 5 cups icing sugar, heavy cream, and vanilla. Beat on low speed for 30 seconds, then increase speed to high and beat for 2 minutes. Beat in more powdered sugar if frosting is too thin.

Assembly: If the cakes have risen too much, cut their rounded tops off with a knife to make them flat. Set one cake layer on a plate or cake stand. Evenly spread a thick layer of the frosting over the cake to the edge. Top with the second cake layer and spread a thick layer of the frosting. Finish with the third cake layer. Spread frosting over the top and sides of the cake.

Store cake in the fridge, but bring it to room temperature before serving.

The cake can be made a day in advance.

6

MOVING

At last it was time for dessert — time to cut the cake.

"I think Princess Indy should do the honours," said Karly, and we all agreed.

Cam carried the cake from the sideboard and placed it on the table in front of an empty chair. All eyes were on Indy as she climbed up and knelt on the chair. Her hands were too small to manage the cake slice but, with help from her mum, the cake was cut. We all held our breaths.

A few crumbs fell out and we gasped. The inside of the cake was pink.

"A girl!"

"A little sister!"

"Indy, you're going to have a baby sister!"

Indy, caught up in the excitement, stood on her chair.

"My mummy's got a baby in her tummy and she's called Dragon!" she shouted to the world. "And she's my sister!"

Days passed, and Lola and I continued to enjoy each other. I took her to play in the chicken garden where the hens towered over her. Nervous of them at first, she learned to ignore them.

One day she found her bark and life was never quite so peaceful again. She also discovered the joys of fetching a ball, a passion she has never lost.

I needed to buy a set of essential tools and Cam had suggested I should also buy bug bombs which would kill any insects in the empty house. Bunnings, a vast Australian chain of DIY stores, stocked everything I needed. Bunnings allowed dogs in their stores provided they are carried or ride in a trolley. So I took Lola with us.

"Where's the rest of it?" asked a burly assistant, peering down at her. "Is that all there is?"

Lola wagged her stubby little tail and earned herself a smile and a pat.

"My mummy's got a baby in her tummy and she's called Dragon," Indy told him.

"Not me," I said hurriedly, "her mum is over there."

It was a good thing that her parents weren't trying to keep the baby news a secret because Indy told everybody. She informed the postman, the girl at the bakery, the cleaner in the mall, the waitress, complete strangers on the street, and all the staff of Bunnings. She told the street cleaner and the man who read the meter. She even told the wallabies in the park.

"Hey, wobblies! Guys! My mummy has a baby in her tummy and her name's Dragon."

The wallabies stared at her for a moment, then hopped away.

At the beach, anybody who would listen was told, and even the seagulls were informed.

"Hey, sea-girls! Guys! My mummy has a baby in her tummy and her name's Dragon."

At that age, Indy had a particularly clear voice that rang out, and her announcements and questions often embarrassed her mother.

On one occasion, the pair were standing in a queue at a cafe counter, waiting to be served. A man passed by, wearing the typical neon tradie shirt that all tradies, including her builder daddy, wear.

"Is that my daddy?" she asked, her voice clear and shrill.

"No, Indy, that's not your daddy," said Karly smiling.

Another man appeared some distance away, also wearing a lime green tradie shirt, but otherwise looking nothing like Cam.

"Is that my daddy?" she asked loudly, pointing.

"No, Indy, of course not!"

A third man entered the cafe, and Indy sang out again.

"Is *that* one my daddy?"

Karly knew Indy was being silly and she was beginning to tire of being stared at by everybody in the cafe.

"Indy, you know perfectly well who your daddy is," she hissed.

A man in the queue in front of them half-turned.

"As long as *you* do, love," he said, grinning.

"Good luck for tomorrow," Joe had said. "How does it all work?"

"Well, my solicitor will phone me to say that the money has arrived with the vendor's solicitor, then I go to the house and collect the keys from the estate agent."

"Wish I was there to help."

"Don't worry. I'll be fine. I'm only driving up and collecting the keys and letting off the bug bombs I told you about. Then, on Saturday, I'll have Karly and Cam with me. I'll load up the car with as much as I can carry, and Lola of course, and they'll bring the ute with the bed, mattress and other stuff."

"It seems strange to think that just as I'm going to bed, you're doing all this stuff on the other side of the world."

"Relax. Sleep well, I'm sure it'll go smoothly."

Hola tía Vicky y tío Joe,

Thank you to be my english penpall. My teacher she say she will surprise if my english will become better. I am well and my sister and family is completely wells but Pollito my little brother he say he does not like school and learning english is stupid.

Here the weather is very cold but we do not have snow. I want have snow because it is fun to have snow.

My *tía* Lola has a big diamond ring from father Samuel and they will marrys next year. Mama says it will be a very little weeding civil down in the city not like the weeding of Sofía and Antonio in the village. I will buy a new dress and my sister will buy a new dress but my brothers they say they don't want to go to the weeding but my Mama she say they are not permitted to not go. I am sorry we are not dance flamenco in the weeding civil but my Mama she say we can dance flamenco in the village later.

My teacher she say there are very much kangaroos in Australia so why they not coming to your house?

Please sending me picture of koala near your house.

We do not very much see the lady and man they are living in your house. At Christmas we will come to the village and perhaps we will see them. I will say you.

We remember when *tío* Joe say that there are sabre-toth tiger in the woods by the village. Please tell *tío* Joe we know there are not sabre-toth tiger in the woods by the village but we tell my little brother Pollito there are sabre-toth tiger in the woods by the village.

Felicitations, Catalina xx

Moving day dawned with clear summer skies. Just as I'd been instructed, the solicitor phoned to say everything was in place and the estate agent would meet me at the house to hand over the keys.

Lola and I arrived and the scene that greeted me filled me with dismay.

All manner of vehicles were parked in front of the house and on the grass. People milled around and piles of boxes, furniture, and black garbage bags were heaped on the drive. Two giant mastiffs were tethered to a ute. One napped while the other lifted his giant head and barked at anyone who came too close. He was so big, he could have inhaled Lola and not even noticed.

The vendors were nowhere near ready.

The estate agent sprung out of a parked car and stuck his head through my car window.

"I'm very sorry but my clients aren't quite ready to leave."

"I can see that."

"Perhaps you could come back in a couple of hours?"

It was very inconvenient because I couldn't use the time to take Lola for a walk or explore the beaches. She hadn't finished her course of puppy injections and wasn't allowed in public places yet. I would have to sit in the car and wait.

We discussed the problem and he offered to detonate my bug bombs when the vendors left. As we talked, I watched the vendors over his shoulder and made a mental note to buy gallons of disinfectant and bleach before Saturday. He gave me a set of keys and I was free to drive back to Sydney. Even though I was the owner of the house, I still couldn't enter.

On Saturday, I returned in convoy with Cam and Karly and a bizarre thing happened.

The street was quiet when we arrived but, as soon as I put the key in the lock of our door, numerous *other* front doors opened. Faces peeped out, heads appeared and then people strolled towards us with big grins on their faces. It was like a massive welcoming committee.

"We live opposite," said one couple. "Welcome! We are *so delighted* the old owners have gone, they were *dreadful*."

"We couldn't walk past the house because their terrible big dogs were always loose," said an older lady wearing a white hat. I detected a German accent. "You are very welcome to the street. My name is Thea, and this is Nixi."

I looked down and smiled. Nixi was a small, tubby Jack Russell, with a permanently smiling face. She wagged her tail then rolled over for tummy rubs.

"Perhaps we can walk together when my puppy, Lola, has had her injections," I said to Thea, smiling.

"We used to call it the duff-duff house," said another neighbour.

"Duff-duff?"

"Yes, on account of the music. The double-bass, *duff-duff*. Used to go on all through the night."

"The lads were quite nice when they weren't high," said my next-door neighbour. "But that wasn't very often."

"He had his girlfriend there, and her baby. They used to have terrible rows. Once he came running out in the middle of the night, shouting at the top of his voice. He got into his car, then rammed her car over and over again in the drive."

"There were people coming and going all hours of the day and night."

"We reckon they were dealers."

"Why else would they have cameras set up everywhere?"

"And lights in the roof space."

"And the dogs! They kept having litters of puppies and selling them. I heard dead puppies were found in the pool."

"Oh no!" I was aghast.

And so it went on. Yes, it was a kind of welcoming committee, but only because the neighbourhood was so heartily relieved that the troublesome former residents had finally moved away.

But it was nice to introduce ourselves and meet some of the neighbours, whatever the reason for them turning out *en masse*.

The house, as I expected, was filthy, but the bug bombs had done their business and dead cockroaches, spiders and insects littered the floor. We set to work with brooms and bleach. I disinfected every light switch and door handle and discovered that many were loose or didn't work.

Karly tackled the bathroom. She did her best, but the bath had cigarette burns along its edge, and the grime on the tiles was so ingrained that they wouldn't scrub clean.

Meanwhile, I set to work in the 'kitchen', which was yet another disaster area. The oven and hob did not work at all, but there was a microwave. Several drawers wouldn't open. Cupboard doors hung from a single hinge or had no handles. There was no fridge, or even space for one, and the tap in the sink dripped constantly.

Nevertheless, by the time Karly and Cam left that evening, the house was habitable. Just about.

Cam had kindly concentrated on one bedroom, the one with the least disgusting carpet. He'd put up the bed, ensuring I had somewhere to sleep. Lola was already fast asleep in her crate. Worn out, I prepared for bed.

It was my first night in our new house.

I pulled the cord to shut the wooden window blinds and, to my horror, they came crashing down. The room was filled with clouds of dust that settled on everything. Dead insects covered the windowsill, my clean bed, and the floor.

Coughing and sneezing, I cleaned up the mess and finally climbed into bed. When I switched off the bedside lamp, I discovered that my next-door neighbours had a fondness for multi-coloured flashing garden lights. Having no window shades, these illuminated my bedroom all night long. Even with my eyes closed, the flickering lights seemed to pierce my eyelids and nearly drove me crazy. That night I slept with my head under the pillow.

In the morning, I started making a list of jobs labelling them either VU, QU or just U. (Very Urgent, Quite Urgent or just Urgent.) The length of the list was terrifying. Then I sat down with my phone, and a copy of the Yellow Pages, and began work.

First, I called the local vet to make an appointment for Lola's next injections and enrol her in Puppy School. Not a moment too soon as she was getting naughtier by the day. Paper, cardboard, and even plastic were not safe from her shredding puppy teeth.

I was just beginning on a list of builders to call when I heard a car draw up outside, footsteps approached and my front door flew open.

I don't know who was the more surprised, me, Lola or the enormous bald man covered in tattoos who had just crashed into my house.

"Oh! Has the house changed hands?" my uninvited visitor shouted over Lola's welcoming yaps, as she tried to scrabble up his tattooed leg.

"Yes!"

The visitor looked shocked, and I could hardly blame him. The previous, nocturnal, drug-dealing occupants, with their colossal dogs couldn't be more different to me, an elderly lady with a cute, fluffy puppy.

"Sorry!" he said, eyes wide, and he backed away out of the house.

Unfortunately, Lola ran out with him. Thus began an embarrassing sequence of events: me calling Lola, she ignoring me, and all three of us running up and down the street like idiots. I finally grabbed her in an unladylike rugby tackle while Tattooed Man's mates in the rusty parked car watched in amusement.

Returning to the house, I edited my list. 'Locksmith - change locks' was moved from Urgent to Very Urgent. Who knew how many people had keys? I wanted no more unexpected visitors.

Now it was November and temperatures soared. Christmas decorations appeared in all the shopping malls and I was struggling to find builders. I had the same conversation with many.

"Sorry, since that hail storm in September, we're completely booked up for months. We couldn't even *look* at your job until maybe July next year."

July? I wanted the work started before Joe arrived in January.

But it was not to be.

In September, monstrous hailstones had hammered down, leaving 1,200 homes without power and hundreds of homes without roofs, including the local shopping centre. The ceiling had partially collapsed and everyone had to be evacuated. The event made national news and aerial views showed the area cloaked in white, as though by snow.

My house was one of only a couple in our street that wasn't damaged. I had to face it; finding a builder was going to be almost impossible.

Or was it?

Being new to the area, I knew nobody, so I was forced to rely on my instincts. An advert in the local paper caught my eye.

All building work and renovations undertaken.

I phoned the number supplied and spoke to Fred for the first time.

TERIYAKI STEAKS

Asian food of all kinds is extremely popular in Australia. Teriyaki is a Japanese marinade, quite similar to Chinese sweet and sour sauce.

Ingredients (serves 6)

6 pieces rib eye steak

⅓ cup soy sauce

¼ cup red wine

2 cloves garlic, crushed

2 teaspoons grated ginger

2 tablespoons brown sugar

1 tablespoon barbecue sauce

Method

Marinate steaks in soy sauce, wine, garlic, ginger, brown sugar and barbecue sauce for several hours or refrigerate, covered, overnight.

Drain steaks and barbecue or grill on both sides until cooked to your liking.

7

TRADIES

Fred sounded like a decent chap on the phone and very Australian. He explained that he had been a builder in Sydney, but had just moved to the Central Coast and was in the process of setting up his business again. He agreed to inspect the job and give me a quote.

I'd already invited three other builders, but two hadn't turned up, and the third was so young I feared he might need help with his school homework.

Fred promised to come round the following week, but Friday passed without a sign of him. However, he did call and apologise, which was a point in his favour.

"I had a bit of an emergency," he explained.

"Oh, I'm sorry to hear that."

"My house was flooded."

"Oh, right. Plumbing problems."

"Not really, the seal broke on one of my breeding aquariums. Water everywhere and I had to mop it up and sort out a new home for my fish."

"Is everything okay now?"

"I think so, thank you. Dwarf cichlids are fussy blighters so it wasn't easy. They like their water soft and slightly acidic. Sometimes you have to try mimicking the coming of the rainy season with a cool and soft water change."

He'd lost me. I didn't even know what a dwarf cichlid was.

Listening to him on the phone, I imagined Fred to be a large man, perhaps in his mid-thirties, possibly with tattoos, and probably a rugby player. Eventually I would discover I was wrong on all counts.

Around that time, I had an army of tradesmen coming to the door to give me quotes for various jobs. Lola welcomed them all like long-lost friends. They generally tolerated her enthusiasm, but sometimes her unruly behaviour made life difficult for me. I distinctly remember a lady, smartly dressed in a pencil skirt and high heels who arrived to give me a quote for window blinds.

"Would you mind keeping your dog under control?" she asked politely. She was smiling pleasantly but the smile never quite reached her eyes. "This is a very exacting job and I need to be as accurate as possible."

With that, she produced a pink retractable tape-measure as a signal that she was ready to begin.

"Of course! I'm so sorry, she's just a few months old and hasn't learned any manners yet. I'll shut her in the laundry."

Lola did not accept her banishment lightly. She yapped and scratched the door so loudly that the lady had to shout to make herself heard.

"This is ridiculous!" I said, and reluctantly let Lola back in.

Lola struggled against my grip on her collar, eager to reach the lady and cover her with a thousand unwanted wet licks. The lady continued to talk and take measurements but unfortunately, just for the merest millisecond, I was distracted and loosened my hold on the straining puppy. Lola bounded joyfully over to our visitor, firmly believing she was desperate for another exuberant puppy welcome.

"Ouch!" said the lady as Lola's sharp little claws raked her bare legs.

"I'm so sorry!" I cried and grabbed Lola, but not before she had completely disgraced herself.

In her excitement, Lola lost control. The lady's white high heels were now standing in a yellow puddle.

"That bloody thing has peed all over my shoes!" she shrieked, all attempts at politeness abandoned.

"I'm so sorry," I gasped, grabbing Lola.

But it was too late. Not only had Lola soaked the lady's shoes, but the puddle had seeped to the samples book laid out on the floor. Even the pink tape-measure hadn't escaped.

"I'm so sorry..." I started to say again, but the lady was taking herself, her wet shoes, her dripping samples book, and pink tape-measure, out of the door.

I didn't blame her.

I told Lola her behaviour had been absolutely appalling and hoped that the lady's pink tape-measure would dry sufficiently to run smoothly again soon.

I didn't invite the lady back and neither did she contact me.

I had learned a lesson: whoever I employed had to accept Lola as part of the deal.

Most tradesmen passed with flying colours, as far as Lola was concerned.

I remember one chap who came to give me a quote for an innovative method of capturing solar energy. His name was Sam and he had an engaging manner. Lola gave him her usual frantic welcome which he accepted, smiling. I offered him a cup of tea, and we sat at the table as he showed me leaflets and talked me through various facts and figures.

After a short while, he shook his head and packed up his paperwork.

"Nope," he said, "I don't think our company can help you. We're geared up for more industrial-type premises. But I'll enjoy this cup of tea with you and Lola, anyway."

A tiny spider walked across the table and he squashed it with one finger.

"Oh, poor thing," I said, "it was just a small one."

"You haven't been in Australia long, have you?" he asked, looking at me sideways.

"Well, no. Just a couple of months, really..."

"Let me tell you, you need to be careful. Take my mum, for

instance. She was pegging out her washing, and a white-tailed spider dropped down on her from above and got inside her shirt. She felt something and patted it, and it bit her in the small of her back."

"You are kidding!"

"No, white-tailed spider bites can be really nasty. Anyway, the wound swelled up and festered, and she had to go to the hospital to get it gouged out and cleaned."

"Oh no!"

"Three years later she's still suffering. The wound won't heal, and numerous hospital visits haven't helped. Have you been to the beach yet?"

"Yes, but not to swim. I haven't been here long."

"Take my word for it, swim *only* between the red and yellow flags."

"Right."

"Australian currents are crazy. Have you heard of rips?"

"Yes, but I'm not sure what they are."

"Rip currents can form when waves break near the shoreline. The water piles up between the breaking waves and a narrow stream of water, like a river, can move swiftly away from the shore. It can whip your legs away from under you and drag you out, even if you are only standing knee-high in the water."

My mouth dropped open.

"Seriously. The ocean is a very dangerous place. A couple of years ago, I was out in a boat with some of my mates. We were fishing for lobster. As we were pulling up the pots, a school of humpback whales swam past."

"How wonderful!"

"Yes, they're a common sight around here, but I never get bored with them. Well, I happened to have my underwater camera with me, so I dived into the water to try and get some pictures. Never again."

"Sharks?"

"Nope. Although it could have been. I didn't know then that Great Whites follow the humpbacks, picking off calves, or old, or sick humpbacks."

"So what happened?"

"I had no idea just how fierce the currents were. I did some underwater filming, then looked up and saw I'd drifted quite a long way from the boat. And I was still travelling. I shouted to my mates, telling them I was in trouble. They didn't notice at first. When they did, they sprang into action straight away, but it takes a good five minutes to pull up the anchor with that kind of boat."

"And you were still drifting?"

"Yup! One of my mates just stood in the boat, never taking his eyes off me as I drifted further and further away. I don't mind telling you, I was crying with fright. I thought I was going to die. By the time they weighed anchor and turned the boat round to pick me up, I was probably a kilometre away, and I was more scared than I'd ever been. I was exhausted by the time they reached me. It was a close thing."

Lola gave a little snore under the table and Sam checked his watch.

"Is that the time? I must go! It's been a pleasure chatting and thank you for the tea. I hope you settle in quickly and sorry if I've been rabbiting on."

"No, you haven't! It's been fascinating, thank you, and you've taught me a lot!"

I vowed never to swim anywhere except between the flags. In fact, the talk of sharks and currents made me doubt I'd ever swim in the ocean fearlessly again. I reminded myself that we had our own swimming pool now.

The problem was, the pool was becoming a darker green by the day and definitely wasn't the place to enjoy a swim. It was beginning to resemble spinach soup.

Australian law stipulates that pools must be enclosed by a fence. Mine was, although the metal railings were horribly rusty. However, on my first day at the house, I discovered something very worrying.

Lola was small enough to slip between the railings.

And she did.

The first time it happened, I didn't notice what she had done. What alerted me was hearing a small wet *plop* coming from the pool.

To my absolute horror, I saw Lola had fallen in. A split second later I was at the pool's edge, grabbing her by her fur and rolls of fat. She was underwater, but I had her out in a trice.

"You could have drowned!" I scolded her, and set her down.

Not bothered in the slightest, she launched herself back into the pool.

That day I learned that Lola was a water dog. She added swimming to her list of passions along with tennis balls, visitors, shredding things, and digging.

So we made another trip to Bunnings to buy plastic mesh. I tied it to the pool fence to stop Lola slipping through and swimming without supervision.

By the beginning of December, the weather was hot, but I couldn't cool down in the pool, it was just too dirty.

I knew nothing about swimming pools or their upkeep. The pool had looked wonderful on the day of the house sale, and I was sure I could restore it to its former glory.

I called a pool company for help. Two men promptly turned up and didn't seem too shocked by the murky, green water that looked fit for nothing but hippos. After Lola had finished welcoming them, and stopped trying to scrabble up their legs, they delivered their verdict.

"We can fix the pool and you'll be swimming in it in a week," said one.

"But I'm afraid your pump has seen better days and needs replacing," said the other.

"And your chlorinator doesn't work. You'll have to buy a new one or keep adding chlorine manually every day."

"Honestly," I said to Joe that evening, "I don't believe *anything* works in this house."

Then I reminded myself that my problems were tiny compared with his. I may not have had a working kitchen, or bathroom, and the pool may look as inviting as minestrone soup, but at least I didn't have breathing problems. And I wasn't facing a course of radiotherapy to destroy the prostate cancer that was threatening my life.

I wouldn't have wanted to swap places with Joe.

"How did your first radiotherapy session go?"

"Not too bad. It's just the journey to the hospital and back every day that's going to be such a pain. The bridge is closed so I have to make a detour. It should be a forty minute drive but now it takes me four hours."

"Oh, that's not good."

"The radiotherapy itself was easy. The nurse told me to strip down to my underpants and socks…"

"Socks? Why socks?"

"I don't know. Then she told me to lie on a very narrow table which I did. I was a bit nervous."

"Why?"

"Because the nurse was huge, with great rippling biceps and a bosom to match. And the table was like an ironing board. 'Don't move,' she said. No fear of that. I wasn't going to argue with her and anyway, I reckoned I'd fall off if I moved."

"Then what?"

"Well, she lumbered out of the door into some sort of outside control room, and her voice suddenly boomed from loudspeakers. 'Don't move and don't be concerned,' she said and then a huge doughnut-shaped machine moved and I felt myself being manoeuvred into the doughnut's hole."

"How odd."

"Yes, it was. Anyway, I lay very still and I guess the zapping started. The beam would have been aimed at those gold seeds they inserted in me before. I didn't feel anything and it only took a few minutes. Then the doughnut backed away. I guessed it was all over so I sat up, which was definitely the wrong thing to do."

"Why?"

"The door flew open and the big nurse came charging in. 'I told you not to move!' she shouted. That's when I realised that the table had been raised and I was close to the ceiling."

"Oops."

"She wasn't happy. I got a real scolding. She said if I fell off the table and broke my legs I only had myself to blame."

"She was right. She told you not to move."

"I know, I know."

"Oh well, I'm sure you'll be better behaved next time." *Pigs might fly.*

"So you have to attend twenty sessions of radiotherapy and it'll all be over?"

"Hopefully. Monday to Friday, weekends off."

"Only nineteen sessions left, then."

"Yes. And it'll be done by Christmas."

"Good! You'll be here in the new year."

"I can't wait!"

I had a lot to do in one month. Fred, the builder, was due to give me a quote for a new kitchen and bathroom, and Lola was booked to have her final puppy injections. Then she'd start puppy school, not a moment too soon.

Perhaps school would teach her some manners.

LOBSTER AND SUMMER FRUITS SALAD

A delightful, refreshing, colourful lobster dish from www.taste.com.au Enjoy with a glass of chilled chardonnay.

Ingredients

3 baby cos lettuce, leaves separated, torn

1 bunch rocket, trimmed

1 large avocado

½ medium red onion, thinly sliced

½ cup small fresh mint leaves

½ cup small fresh coriander leaves

1 large mango, thinly sliced

150g (4-5oz) fresh raspberries

2 cooked lobster tails, meat removed, sliced

¼ cup lemon juice

2 tablespoons olive oil

2 teaspoons Dijon mustard

Pinch caster sugar

Method

Arrange lettuce and rocket on a platter.

Cut avocado in half and remove the stone. Peel and slice. Arrange over salad with onion, mint, coriander, mango slices and raspberries.

Top with lobster meat.

Whisk juice, oil, mustard and sugar together in a small bowl until combined.

Drizzle over salad.

Serve.

8

NEW FRIENDS

I'd just about given up on Fred, the builder I had booked to give me a quote. He was two hours late and I assumed he wasn't going to show. But then a white tradie ute pulled up and parked outside the house.

The driver's door opened, and out stepped Fred, allowing me to take a good look at him for the first time.

Fred wasn't what I expected at all. He wasn't the athletic rugby type in his mid-thirties that I'd imagined. No. Fred was short for a man, perhaps five feet four inches, not even as tall as me. He was thickset and in his late fifties. Thick-lensed horn-rimmed glasses sat on his nose. He wore heavy boots, the usual tradie neon shirt, and shorts. Later I discovered that he always wore shorts, whatever the weather. Lola hurled herself at him declaring her undying love as I tried to greet him.

"I'm Vicky, thanks for coming out. I'm sorry about the puppy."

"I'm Fred," he said, giving my hand a firm shake. "Pleased to meet you, and I'm sorry I'm late."

Then he crouched down on the doorstep and fussed Lola.

So far, so good. He had passed the first test.

"I'm sorry I was so late today. I was driving along the motorway, and a truck in front of me shed its load. It was carrying cartons of milk.

You've never seen such a mess! There was milk everywhere, all over the road — rivers of it. I stopped and helped out because I had brooms on board. All the traffic had to be redirected and we were sweeping milk and trying to clear the cartons."

"Oh my goodness!"

"Eventually the fire brigade arrived. They'd been held up because they'd been attending a bush fire. Bush fires always come before spilt milk here in Aus!"

We both laughed and I was just inviting him in when something appeared at his feet.

"Dinks, how on earth did you get out of the car?" he said, addressing the strange-looking little dog looking up at him.

"Dinks?" I asked.

"Her name's Fair Dinkum. I rescued her when she was a puppy, but she's getting on a bit now."

Another point in Fred's favour.

Dinkum had a sprinkling of Jack Russell genes somewhere, in addition to a multitude of other breeds which I couldn't even begin to identify. I doubted that she would ever win a dog beauty contest but kept that thought to myself.

In Australia, many tradies own large breeds of dogs, most often of the pitbull variety. These dogs ride in the back of their owners' open-topped utes. I'm not sure why these big, ferocious-looking dogs are so popular with tradies. Maybe the dogs guard the tools, but I think it's more likely that their owners are making a statement.

Fred definitely wasn't making any statement with Dinks. She wagged her tail, then marched into the house ignoring Lola and me and heading straight for Lola's bed. She flopped down and dozed, one eye cracked open and fixed on her master.

"Dinks!" said Fred, catching sight of her relaxing on Lola's bed. "Come here!"

"She's okay," I said, "don't worry."

Fred insisted on removing his boots before entering the house. He set them neatly side by side at the front door. Lola immediately ran off with one of them but he didn't seem to mind.

I took Fred on a guided tour of the house, explaining what needed doing. He snapped heaps of photographs and didn't seem shocked by any of my rather dramatic suggestions.

"Two things really bother me," I explained. "The kitchen, apart from needing to be ripped out and re-done, is much too small."

Fred nodded.

"And we only have one bathroom and that's in a terrible state. I wondered whether we could sacrifice the garage and convert it to a new master bedroom and en suite."

We discussed possible new configurations over a cup of tea. Lola, exhausted by her visitor-welcoming duties, fell asleep under my chair. Dinkum snored on Lola's bed.

"I'll prepare a quote for you," said Fred. "I'll include my licence number so you can check me out."

Business over, we discussed other things. Fred told me about himself. He'd raised two children alone, as his wife had abandoned them all a long time ago when the kids were toddlers. After the children left home, he decided to move from Sydney to the Central Coast, to be near his ageing mother.

I couldn't help but like this man who wore his heart on his sleeve. I forgave him the broken appointments and decided that, if his quotes were reasonable, I'd give him the job. I was keen to get started. It didn't matter, I reasoned to myself, that Fred didn't actually look like a builder.

"I liked him," I told Joe later that evening. "He looks more like a nerdy accountant than a builder, and his dog won't win any dog shows either. But I think he's a nice bloke. I felt a bit sorry for him, actually."

"Why?"

"Well, I kind of got the impression that he's very lonely. He's not been in the area long and spends most of his spare time looking after his mum. Anyway, he seemed to know his stuff. He made lots of good suggestions."

"Did you believe his milk lorry story?"

"Yes, I did. And when he left, there were two milky stains on the ground where his boots had been standing."

When the quote arrived, I felt it was fair. I contacted Fred and told him he'd got the job. It turned out that my decision was a good one and Fred was a good, competent worker.

However, he was often late and sometimes didn't turn up at all. When this happened, he was most apologetic and his excuses were often unusual. We were to discover that Fred was a man who attracted rather outlandish occurrences.

Bizarre things just seemed to happen to him.

I'd already visited the vet's surgery a couple of times, when I'd registered Lola and booked her into puppy school, so I was familiar with the young lady receptionist. Apart from her, the waiting room was empty when we arrived.

"Hello," I said, "I've brought Lola for her injections."

"Ah yes," she replied, "do take a seat. The vet won't keep you waiting long."

But there was something different about the receptionist today and I couldn't quite put my finger on it. I kept snatching furtive glances at her, trying to work out what it was. I didn't think she'd changed her hairstyle, and her clothes seemed ordinary enough.

And then it clicked. It was her bosom! Surely she hadn't been quite so, um, well-endowed before?

To my embarrassment, she caught me staring at her upper body.

"Ah, you noticed my boobs," she said, grinning.

"Well, I…"

"It's okay. I'm not normally this shape. Come and see."

I really didn't know how to react. I guessed she'd had surgery, some kind of breast augmentation, and I had absolutely no wish to inspect the results up close. However, it was kind of her to extend the offer. Hiding my reluctance, I trotted up to the desk and obediently peered down the front of her top.

What I saw took my breath away.

"What are they?"

"Two possums. Somebody brought in an adult possum that had

been hit by a car. Unfortunately, she died but the vet found these newborn joeys in her pouch."

"Oh my goodness!" I breathed, staring at the baby animals, wrapped in towelling, squirming in her cleavage. "Will they survive?"

"Yes, they should do. It's not the first time we've had to be mum to newborn possums or wallabies."

"Oh, my," I said, gently touching a warm, fuzzy little body with the tip of my finger. It's dark eyes gazed up at me. "I've never seen baby possums before."

"We've got the proper formula to give them, and they should thrive. I'm going to be a double D-cup size for a while though," she said, smiling.

The street door opened behind me. An Asian man entered and I looked over my shoulder, just in time to catch the look of shock on his face. He was clearly surprised to see me leaning over the counter, peering down the receptionist's front, with my hand down her top.

"It's okay, I'm just admiring her little possums," I said, then flushed scarlet.

That didn't sound right at all.

The telephone rang and the receptionist turned to answer it, leaving me to explain. The new arrival was still looking at me strangely. He had an elderly labrador on a leash, and Lola strained to give both dog and master one of her exuberant welcomes.

"I'm sorry, she's very young," I said, trying to restrain her. "We've enrolled her in puppy school, and I'm hoping that will calm her down." I cleared my throat. "Oh, and if you were wondering what I was doing just now…"

The man stared at me, blank-faced. I persevered, keen to clear up the situation.

"The receptionist was just showing me her two little orphans…" Again, I flushed scarlet.

Just then, the vet popped her head out from the surgery.

"Lola?" she asked. "This way."

My moment was lost forever.

"Oh! Must go," I said, and left him, his eyes bulging.

Lola greeted the vet like a long-lost favourite relative and was given her injection. By the time we returned to the waiting-room the man and his labrador had gone and the receptionist was taking another call, her bosom undulating slightly as she talked.

I can only hope that she had explained what was going on to the poor man with the labrador.

I'd never owned a puppy before and, although I was finding it to be utterly delightful, it was extremely hard work. As far as I was concerned, the day of Lola's first puppy class couldn't come soon enough.

Thanks to the crate-training, she was brilliant at night and settled quickly. The crate-training allowed me to go shopping without her, knowing she would snooze until I returned. When I returned, she welcomed me as though I'd been away for weeks, often, in her excitement, leaving a puddle on the floor.

I couldn't leave any paper or cardboard in her reach or she would shred it, scattering numerous tiny pieces all over the floor. Neither was any footwear safe from her needle-sharp puppy teeth. Nor any item of clothing, particularly underwear. Hanging up laundry was a fight because Lola leapt for each item as I pulled it out of the washing basket. And woe betide if I allowed anything to hang within her reach as a glorious game of tug-of-war would ensue. Any dropped pegs were immediately chewed to oblivion.

She drove me to distraction when I showered, scratching at the bathroom door, yapping and crying until I'd finished. Then, before I had a chance to dry myself, she'd burst in and lick all the drops off my legs, making me dance like a possum on a hot tin roof.

Sometimes, when I was trying to write, she was quiet. A little *too* quiet. Like children when they are up to no good. On one occasion, I jumped up to look for her.

"Lola, where are you?"

I searched for her, then glanced out of the window.

I had planned to pave an area in the garden which was muddy and unplanted, but Lola loved it just the way it was.

She adored mud, the wetter the better.

To my horror, her bottom was in the air and her front paws were digging so fast they were almost a blur. Clods of sticky mud were flying into the air.

"LOLA!"

She stopped for a second, just long enough for me to see her black, muddy face.

She's never lost her passion for mud and I have to remember that fact. I choose walking routes that avoid puddles. Even now, when I walk her on our local oval, an Aussie term for a sports field, I avoid a particular area which becomes a quagmire after rain. I call it the Ten Dollar Puddle because, if I forget, Lola jumps straight in and executes a kind of commando crawl through the mud. Only a stripe of clean golden coat remains, along her back and the top of her head. The rest of her body is caked with gloop.

Why Ten Dollar Puddle? Because we have to march straight back to Bruce and drive to the nearest dog-wash, which costs ten dollars.

Incredible inventions, those auto dog washes. They've rescued me many a time. I've taken Lola, covered in mud from head to foot after her latest puddle wallow, and fifteen minutes later, after shampoos, conditioner and warm air dryers, I've transformed her into a scented, golden ball of fluffy fur.

But never for long. Only until she finds the next muddy hole to dig, or something disgusting to roll in.

Now that her course of puppy injections was complete, we had much more freedom. I started to walk her up and down the street to accustom her to walking on a lead.

I often walked with my German neighbour, Thea, and her little dog, Nixi. We became good friends.

Nixi and Lola were about the same size, but that's where the similarity ended. Lola was a whirling dervish of energy and naughtiness. One glimpse of Thea and Lola became a frenzy of excitement, jumping and pulling me along to reach her German friend and Nixi. She knew that Thea's pockets were stuffed full of dog treats.

Nixi, the Jack Russell, was not so lively. She was older, more polite and calm, a sweet-natured dog and a huge favourite with local children. She'd trot over to them, wagging her tail happily as she waited for pats, then roll over for tummy rubs.

If one researches the personality traits of the Jack Russell terrier, one discovers they are considered high-energy dogs that need a lot of exercise. They are vocal, feisty and, because of their hunting instinct, have an innate urge to explore.

Nobody told Nixi that. She'd never read the Jack Russell manual.

Unlike any Jack Russell I've ever met, Nixi was neither energetic, nor keen to explore, or even inclined to walk. On the contrary, she'd rather not bother with walks at all. I've often seen Thea throw little treats ahead to encourage Nixi to walk on. The ruse worked, but no doubt contributed to Nixi's expanding waistline.

When Thea pulled out a dog treat from her pocket, Nixi would sit and wait patiently. Not Lola. She leapt and wriggled, unable to contain her excitement.

"*Donnerwetter!*" Thea would exclaim. "Keep your snoot away! No snatching!"

Treats gobbled up, Lola would dive onto Nixi, trying to initiate a game of rough-and-tumble. But Nixi wanted none of it. Tired of Lola's puppy exuberance, she would roll on her back, wave her stubby paws in the air and expose her very round tummy. It was her signal that she didn't want to play.

But Lola didn't heed signals or requests. She had no manners at all, just an enormous zest for life and everything in it.

The time had come for her to go to school and learn some manners. And as soon as possible. Time was running out because Joe would be joining us in less than a month.

WHITE CHOCOLATE AND MACADAMIA BISCUITS

These cookies from www.kidspot.com.au are very decadent. Rich, crunchy and easy to make, they also make perfect wrapped gifts.

Ingredients

125g (4oz) butter

½ cup white sugar

½ cup brown sugar

1 egg, lightly beaten

1 tsp vanilla extract

¼ tsp salt

¼ cup self-raising flour, sifted

100g (3½oz) white chocolate chips

100g (3½oz) macadamia nuts, chopped roughly

Method

Preheat oven to 180°C (350°F).

Line 3 trays with baking paper.

In a mixing bowl, cream the butter and both sugars with the vanilla extract until fluffy.

Add the egg and mix well.

Add the flour, salt and beat for a minute or two.

Stir in the nuts and chocolate chips.

Roll into tablespoon-size balls and gently press on the baking tray.

Bake for 8-12 minutes.

Leave to cool on a wire rack.

9

PUPPY SCHOOL

Even simple tasks like putting a harness or lead on Lola were a challenge. She thought everything was just one huge game. She bounced about like a fluffy yo-yo and, when I finally succeeded, I then had to wrestle her vaccination papers out of her jaws. Lola and I were the last to arrive at the first session of puppy school.

The teacher took our details and we were asked to sit on chairs in a circle.

"Just tell us your name and a little bit about your puppy," said the teacher, addressing the group. "Perhaps you could share what you'd like your puppy to learn."

I looked around. There was a labrador, a boxer, a staffie, a white terrier like the one from the movie, *Oliver*, and a German shepherd. All were perfectly calm, well-behaved, and sitting nicely at their owners' feet.

And then there was Lola.

Although Lola had grown a lot in the short time I'd had her, she was still the smallest, fluffiest dog there, and by far the most unruly. She wasn't going to sit still for even a second. She was like a hyperactive child, unable to settle, impervious to commands.

We introduced ourselves, while Lola strained this way and that, desperate to reach everyone. I spent all the time apologising and untangling her leash from my neighbours' chair legs.

"And who is this?" the teacher asked the boxer's owner.

"This is Wesley," said the owner. "I'd like Wesley to join me on my jogs and help me get fit. I'm hoping he'll learn to run beside me without tripping me up."

The teacher turned to the anxious-looking lady with the German shepherd.

"Hello, I'm Barb, and this is Jet. His mother is a police dog, so he should be clever. I want to do agility training with him one day."

It was my turn, and Lola was still excited, jumping around like popcorn in the microwave. My wishes seemed trivial compared with those of my classmates.

"I'm Vicky," I said, "and this is Lola. I'd like Lola to learn not to chew every shoe and piece of paper she encounters. I wish she wouldn't bark at everything and jump up at visitors and complete strangers. I wish she wouldn't steal my underwear or snatch the washing from the clothesline. I'd love it if she didn't jump in muddy puddles. It would also be fantastic if she didn't roll in dead things, or eat beetles. Oh, and I'd be grateful if she'd just be still for a minute."

Lola knew we were talking about her. She panted, tongue lolling and her tail wagged so fast it was a blur. Everybody smiled.

"I take it you've never had a puppy before?" asked the teacher.

I shook my head.

"Honestly," I said to Thea as we walked together one hot day in December. "Lola is easily the naughtiest puppy at puppy school. I was hoping she'd be better behaved by now. Joe will be here after Christmas and I don't think he'll be too thrilled with her bad behaviour."

"After Christmas?"

"Yes, his radiation treatment will be finished by then."

"Good!" she said, adjusting her white hat. "I will bake him a cake."

I was to learn that Thea's cakes were legendary. Apart from tasting delicious, they were produced for a variety of reasons. I was given a cake to welcome me to the neighbourhood, for my birthday, because my family was visiting, and when I wasn't feeling well. Cakes were baked to solve every problem and mark every occasion.

Thea recommended the man who came to mow my lawn, and he blamed his rotund shape on Thea.

"I've been mowing her lawn for years," he told me, patting his stomach, "and whenever I turn up, there's a huge slice of German cake waiting for me. Delicious!"

Thea had other skills beside cake-baking. For instance, she knew exactly what the weather was going to do.

"Take an umbrella, this afternoon it will rain," she would say.

I would look up at the cloudless sky and ignore her warning. Sure enough, it rained, and because I hadn't heeded her advice and armed myself with an umbrella, I was soaked.

Thea was also an excellent visual weather warning. She never went outside without wearing a hat over her silver hair. She owned two, a white one for hot days and a brown, fleecy one for cold days. As she walked, (or dragged) the reluctant Nixi past our house, I knew whether it was a hot or cold day by her headgear. A few consecutive days of brown hats meant that winter was on the way. A week of white hats indicated that spring was in the air.

I rarely missed Thea and Nixi's walk-past: Lola made sure of that. One glimpse of Thea's hat would send her off into a frenzy of barking. One would have thought we were being invaded by a horde of burglars. She hurled herself at the window, scrabbling at the glass until I was afraid it would break.

Lola and I often joined Thea and Nixi on their neighbourhood strolls and I devised a scheme to inform them that Lola and I wished to accompany them. I drew a simple outline of a walking dog on a big piece of cardboard and placed it in the window (out of Lola's reach). This was my signal to Thea to say we'd love to join her and Nixi and prompted her to knock on our door.

I soon discovered that Lola might have been naughty, but she was also extremely bright. She was eager to learn, and I easily taught her the basics, like sit, stay, and lie down. She gave me her paw if I asked for it and rolled over on command. She quickly learned how to pick up her toys and put them away in a bucket, if asked, and ring a bell to go out. I began to run out of things to teach her and googled new tricks.

With such an impressive repertoire of skills, one would think she was the star pupil at puppy school.

Not so.

Would she sit, stay and lie down on command at school? She would not. Would she come when called, or walk nicely on the lead? No.

All the other puppies showed off their skills, while Lola dashed about, tangling herself in other dogs' leads and making a general nuisance of herself.

"Don't worry," the teacher said, trying to reassure me. "Some pups take longer to learn than others."

"But she does *loads* of clever stuff at home," I protested, perfectly aware that the teacher probably didn't believe me.

"Today, I'm going to give you and your pups extra homework," our teacher announced, handing out sheets of paper. "This is a checklist. I want you to make sure that your puppies are introduced to all the things on this list. I know it may take weeks to get through, but do your best. The more things your puppies encounter early on, the more confident they will be throughout their lives."

There's nothing I like more than a good meaty list. I stared at it with interest, mentally ticking off as many as I could.

Physical Contact
• Being picked up ~ No problem
• Brushed ~ No problem
• Patted ~ No problem
• Nails clipped (or pretend touch) ~ Practice needed
• Teeth examined ~ Practice needed
• Ears examined ~Practice needed

People
• Babies ~ Not tested yet. Must work on that, Indy's new baby sister is due in April
• Children ~ No problem, loves them. Indy and Lola are best friends

- Men ~ Loves them
- Women ~ Loves them
- Groups of people ~ Loves them, the more people to give her attention, the better
- People with hats ~ No problem, she adores Thea whether she is wearing her white or brown hat
- People with glasses ~ No problem
- People with disabilities ~ This one made me stop and recall a recent event.

The family had visited and we'd driven to The Entrance, a favourite place of ours because of the beach, the big children's play area and the daily pelican feeding sessions. I'd stood at the back of the crowd, concerned that Lola's unruliness might unsettle the pelicans. She loved to chase seagulls and I was sure she'd do the same with these birds, in spite of their size.

As usual, Lola bounced and tugged this way and that, making friends, licking hands and thrashing her tail. I was watching the show and listening intently to the commentary from the lady feeding the pelicans when I suddenly realised that Lola was no longer panting or straining.

I hadn't noticed the group of severely disabled adults and children arriving and surrounding us. Some were in wheelchairs, others walked with difficulty, aided by sticks. But it was Lola's behaviour that astonished me. Instead of her usual rowdy boisterousness, she was utterly calm, allowing herself to be patted and stroked by their many faltering hands. All the time, her tail wagged slowly and steadily, so unlike its customary frenzied lashing.

Did she know these people had disabilities and couldn't cope with her usual excessive energy? I'm positive she did because, when the carers wheeled their charges away, Lola returned to her usual unruly self.

One day, I thought, *I'll look into training Lola to be a therapy dog. I think she would take to it like a pelican to water.*

But now, back to the list…

- Elderly people ~ Loves them
- Police officers ~ I don't know

• Men with facial hair ~ No problem

• Postmen ~ No problem

We'd actually had a stroke of luck with these last two. Our postman was a lovely man who weaved his way from mailbox to mailbox, riding a bright green moped. He had a full beard and the first time Lola saw him, she barked with fright. The postman saw this and slowed right down, then stopped. He held his hand out and allowed her to sniff him.

Of course Lola could never resist making a new friend and was soon licking his hand, oblivious of his bushy beard or the revving of his moped. Thanks to the postman's kindness, we could knock three items off our list: men with facial hair, postmen and motorcycles.

Animals

• Dogs (all shapes & sizes) ~ No problem, maybe *too* friendly? Not all dogs like their faces licked at the first meeting

• Cats ~ Oh dear. She seemed to have forgotten those early days, living in Sydney and sharing a house with Bandsaw

• Chickens ~ She used to be okay with them, but now? I wasn't sure.

• Birds ~ Oh dear again. In Lola's opinion, seagulls, magpies, cockatoos, kookaburras, in fact anything feathered, was put on earth for her to chase. Big fail.

• Horses/cattle/sheep/pigs ~ I don't know.

The list went on for another page and included items such as umbrellas, wheelie bins, vacuum cleaners and fireworks. I was lucky, Lola didn't have a problem with any of them.

The final lesson of the course fell on the week before Christmas, and our teacher suggested we dress our pups to look festive. I had a little reindeer costume for Lola, but she shredded it in minutes so I made do with a strand of glittery tinsel around her neck. Wesley, the boxer, won the prize with a Santa outfit.

"Any news?" the teacher asked us, as she always did.

"Wesley has finally got the idea of jogging beside me," said my classmate happily.

Barb, the lady who owned the German shepherd, was also looking pleased, if somewhat tired.

"I've had a bit of a breakthrough with Jet, too," she said. "You know I bought that really nice, expensive outdoor kennel for him?"

We all nodded.

"And he flatly refused to sleep in it? Well, I wasn't going to give up. I decided the only way to force him to try it out was to sleep in the kennel *with* him. I've had three of the most uncomfortable nights of my life, and my husband said I was completely crazy. But it worked! Jet now sleeps outside in the kennel!"

We all clapped and the teacher turned to me.

"Any news?" she asked.

I shook my head. I wasn't going to brag about Lola's accomplishments because I knew she'd never perform in public. I certainly wasn't going to risk asking her to salute or roll over because we'd both look silly when she ignored me.

To be honest, I doubted she had even earned a puppy school graduation certificate, which I knew were being handed out that day. I eyed the stack of papers in the teacher's hand.

"Never mind," she said. "Lola will get there in the end."

THEA'S GERMAN CHEESECAKE
QUARKTORTE

Thea's cheesecake is legendary. She is asked for the recipe so frequently, she has typed it out and printed a stack so that she can hand it out to anyone who asks. The recipe below is copied straight from Thea's sheet.

Ingredients

1kg (35oz) plain yogurt (European style)

6 eggs

250g butter or margarine

375g (14oz) sugar

6 tsp semolina

Lemon peel (chopped to very small pieces)

Lemon juice from 1-2 lemons

Vanilla sugar or a few drops of vanilla extract

A few drops of rum / bitter almond

Some raisins

Some crushed almonds

1½ tsp baking powder

How to do

Put the melted butter in a bowl, add the eggs and sugar and mix with an electric mixer thoroughly.

Add the yogurt and mix.

Add all the other ingredients and mix again.

Prepare your baking form. (I wipe the baking form with a little butter.)

Pour the rather liquid mass into the form and bake for 60 minutes at 180°C or 350°F in a preheated oven or microwave, if you have a microwave with convection.

Enjoy!

Yours,

Thea

10

GRASS

"Right," said the teacher at the end of the lesson. "Let's see which puppies deserve one of these!"

I held my breath as the certificates were handed out. To my relief, Lola was given one. She jumped up on her hind legs and tried to snatch it from my grasp. Another game.

"Oh no you don't, young lady," I said, and held on firmly. After all, she may never be awarded another.

Hola tía Vicky y tío Joe,

I hop you are well. I am well and my sister and family is completely wells but Pollito my little brother he is in big troubles.

My class is studied prehistoric times and we rided on a bus to Los Millares to see the settlement where the very old people lived. We maked notes and we drawed pictures. Pollito he like very much crazy about dinosaurs and saber-toth tiger and he want to go with me and my sister.

One day Pollito is not at home and we are very much worry because he is very bad and sometimes he goes into mountains like that other time he falled in the old mine. This day Mama cried a lot and want to call the Guardia Civil but then Geronimo and my neighbour Paco and his son Paco they find Pollito again. Bad Pollito was in a old sheepherd place my teacher say shelter. It is a place made by stones for when the weather is very terrible.

My mother cry and ask Pollito why for you go to that old sheepherd place. Pollito say he is search for bones from a dinosaur and maybe a saber-toth tiger. My mother she cry more when they find Pollito and she say that Geronimo is the angel guardian of Pollito. My father he say that he will put a big chain on the leg of Pollito so he not go in the mountains alone no more again. My big brothers are not happy because they hop to go in a Guardia Civil helicopter to seek for Pollito.

My *tía* Lola has a new friend from the new apartments his name is called Esteban. Mama say we not talk about it to father Samuel and it is not the business of children.

I am very sorry you do not have a koala near your house. My teacher say you has redback spider. My big brothers say redback spider kill you.

Felicitations, Catalina xx

I was living on a different continent, in a new country, in a totally strange neighbourhood where I knew nobody. But even though I missed Joe's company, I was never lonely. Thanks to Lola, I made friends wherever I went.

Thea and I often walked together. She showed me places I may not have discovered had I been alone, and introduced me to more people. I also met dog owners at the oval, where I took Lola for her daily run, and so I always had somebody to chat with.

Lola's very best doggy friend at that time was Tilly, another spoodle, the same age but black. When the pair saw each other, they would race around in big circles, tumbling joyously over each other. Exhausted, they'd lie panting side by side in the long grass, gathering up enough energy to do it all over again. It was an absolute delight to watch the puppies having such fun.

I often chatted with Tilly's owner, Sophie. Mostly, we talked about the puppies, comparing notes, but I also learned some surprising facts about Australian fauna and flora from Sophie.

"Does Lola eat mole crickets?" she asked once. "Tilly does."

"Mole crickets? What on earth are they? I've never heard of them."

"Oh, mole crickets are insects, very common and a real pest around here," Sophie explained. "They look a bit strange because the front is like a mole with black beady eyes and forelegs like shovels. But the back end looks like a cricket. And it has wings."

"No way! Where do they live?"

"Underground. They burrow and live on grass roots. They are nocturnal, and you can actually go out into the garden at night and hear them munching. They drive me crazy. Every year my lawn dies because of them."

"Really? Is there any cure?"

"Detergent. I had a really clever idea last week. I redirected my washing machine hose out onto the lawn so that it soaked the grass in soapy water. All the mole crickets came up. It worked a treat. The trouble was, it never occurred to me that Tilly would find mole crickets delicious. She must have eaten dozens of them before I realised what she was doing."

"Did they do her any harm?"

"No. I rang the vet and he said they were harmless to eat. She was fine but her poo looked very peculiar for a couple of days."

Our front lawn was looking very bald and patchy, and I was keen to get it looking a bit better before Joe arrived. There wasn't much I could do about the interior of the house until Fred came and started work, but I could try and improve the look of the front.

Had I been in England, I'd have known what to do. But Australian grass is very different. Instead of just spreading fairly politely, as my lawn in England used to do, this grass threw out great runners. The runners rooted on the drive and across the path, instead of populating the bald areas of the lawn. Not only that, but clover and dandelions made up a large proportion of the green. Another visit to Bunnings was required.

There was plenty of choice, in fact a dazzling display of treatments.

I finally settled on a large box of a 'weed 'n' feed' mixture which boasted that it would speedily destroy all weeds and feed and nourish the grass simultaneously.

Perfect!

I applied it exactly as the instructions set out, sprinkling the granular mixture evenly over the area just before wet weather was forecast. Australian weather forecasters are very accurate, and Thea agreed we should expect rain. On cue, we had a good, heavy shower.

Then I waited.

I checked daily, but nothing happened for a week or so. Then I noticed that the weeds were turning brown and dying.

Good!

Unfortunately, it seemed that the grass was also dying. I knew I had followed the instructions to the letter, so I was horrified to see the grass browning and withering in front of my eyes. I was mystified.

"It's as though the whole lawn has been poisoned," I told Sophie. "All the grass is brown. It looks awful!"

Sophie looked puzzled, then put her head on one side.

"Your lawn isn't buffalo grass, is it?" she asked.

"I don't know. What's buffalo grass?"

"It's fast-growing grass, with wide leaf blades, very closely related to weeds. It spreads by shooting out runners."

"Yes! That's what I have, I think."

"Oh dear."

"Why?"

"Well, like I said, buffalo grass is very closely related to weeds, so it looks as though your weedkiller killed it as well as the weeds."

"Oh no!"

"I think if you read the box carefully, you'll see it says 'not suitable for buffalo grass lawns'. You need a weedkiller that is safe for buffalo grass."

It was too late. Actually, it didn't matter. It turned out that when Fred started work, our front lawn would have died anyway. The numerous garbage skips, piles of rubble, and other building materials heaped on it for months made sure of that.

"I can't believe you'll be here in a couple of weeks," I said to Joe. "Please don't be disappointed by the state of the house. I wish I'd managed to get it more ready for you."

"Don't be silly, Vicky! I'm just delighted that the radiation treatment is over and that I'm free to fly to Australia. I couldn't care less if the place is a complete hovel."

"It is."

"I'm sure you're exaggerating."

"I'm not."

"Never mind, we'll sort it together. I'm not worried about the house at all. But I have to admit I'm quite worried about the journey."

"Why?"

"I'm just not as strong as I used to be. I get out of breath so quickly, and I hope I can cope with my heavy luggage."

"You don't need to bring much! You'll only need to wear shorts and T-shirts and we can easily buy those here."

"I know. I plan to travel light, but I can't help worrying about everything."

I felt sad, remembering how strong Joe used to be and how he never let anything bother him. This illness was taking its toll.

"Well, once you're here, I'll be able to look after you properly."

"Thank you, I know you will. It's so cold here in Britain, but at least I'll be arriving in time to catch the Australian summer. Maybe I'll feel better in the warmth. Maybe I'll find it easier to breathe."

COPD is a terrible, terrible disease. We both knew there is no cure and that it would gradually get worse over time. However, we also knew that we could manage it by maintaining a healthy lifestyle, with good food and plenty of exercise. I was determined to help Joe do all the right things to keep the disease at bay.

"It's a shame you can't be here for Christmas," I commented.

"There were no flights, but actually I think it's a good thing. I don't think I could cope with a rowdy family Christmas straight after that journey."

It made me sad, but I understood what he meant.

In the days that followed, I tried to look at the house with fresh eyes, to see it as Joe would see it. I secured the services of a floor layer who ripped up the disgusting carpets in two of the three bedrooms. The many litters of puppies, raised by the previous owners, had left the carpets threadbare and stinking of dog urine. It was a massive relief to have them replaced with fresh, clean wood floors.

One of these rooms would soon serve as the main bedroom. I painted the inside of the fitted wardrobe and polished the mirrors on the wardrobe doors. I also painted the walls, bought two bedside tables and bedside lamps, and a new bed. Assembling the bed by myself was a challenge because Lola insisted on washing my face liberally every time I sat on the floor. But I eventually succeeded. I was satisfied that this room was now as clean and fresh as it could be.

It was a start.

The other bedroom, with its new wood floor, I converted into an office. I painted the walls white and Karly and Cam gave me an old desk they no longer needed.

I couldn't, as yet, extend the new flooring into the living areas because I planned to have walls knocked down, and change the layout of the kitchen and bathroom.

One of the walls I planned to remove belonged to the third bedroom, which I had slept in while I worked on the main bedroom. The third bedroom door was a problem because the previous owners had fixed the door handle so that it could only be opened from the outside. During the day, when I wasn't in the room, I kept the door closed to prevent Lola from getting in. At night, when she was in her crate, I slept with the door wide open.

This room still had its original vile brown carpet and the blanket still hung over the window to block out next door's flashing fairy lights. Now that the main bedroom was finished, I could move out of this nasty room. I wouldn't be sorry not to be sleeping in there any more.

I carried a small tool box into the room, hoping to repair the door handle. Joe would have enjoyed tinkering with it but he was in the UK.

Lola ran in and bounded onto the bed as I pulled the linen off. Another game. I tried to grab her but she jumped off and sped towards the half-open door.

"Lola! No!" I shouted, but it was too late. She leapt at the door. It slammed shut.

We were trapped.

I climbed onto the bed and removed the blanket covering the window. I tried to open it but it was painted shut. It probably hadn't been opened in years. I reached for my phone, hoping to call Thea, who lived just a few houses away in the same street. Then I remembered it was on the table on the other side of the door.

I rapped on the window glass with my knuckles.

"Help!" I called.

Nobody heard me.

What to do? Smash the window? That would be a last resort.

Then I remembered the toolbox and fetched a screwdriver. I couldn't use it to fix the door handle because the door needed to be ajar in order to reach the screws. However, I could use it to work away at the window clasp and was rewarded when the window slid open. I say 'slid', but it was more of a jolt than a slide because the channel was filthy, filled with the debris of years.

I leaned out of the window and looked down. I didn't relish setting foot in the dense undergrowth I saw below. It probably hid snakes and giant spiders.

Although the house was single-level, the land below the window sloped away. It was a considerable drop. If I jumped I might twist my ankle on some unseen rock when I landed. And what if I broke a leg? I would be of no use to Joe then.

"Help!" I called again. "Help! I'm locked in!"

SILVERBEET, BROCCOLINI AND MOZZARELLA PIZZA

This recipe is from Phoebe Wood who says, "Sunday night is pizza night. Enjoy this better-than-takeaway version, filled with healthy gourmet toppings."

Ingredients

1 bunch broccolini

½ bunch silverbeet, finely shredded

1 garlic clove, crushed

Finely grated zest of 1 lemon

1 tablespoon extra virgin olive oil

¼ cup pesto

2 round pizza bases

2 tablespoons finely grated parmesan

250g (9oz) fresh mozzarella or bocconcini, roughly torn

2 bacon rashers, cut into large pieces

Method

Preheat the oven to 200°C (390°F). Line 2 baking trays with baking paper.

Thinly slice the stalks of the broccolini and set aside.

Blanch the broccolini tops in boiling, salted water for 1-2 minutes until just tender, adding the silverbeet for the final 10 seconds. Drain and refresh under cold water.

Combine garlic, lemon zest and oil in a bowl, then toss with drained broccolini tops and silverbeet. Season and set aside.

Spread the pesto over the pizza bases and scatter with the parmesan and sliced broccolini stalks.

Divide the mozzarella, bacon and greens between the pizza bases.

Bake for 12-14 minutes until the crust is golden and crisp, and the cheese has melted.

Cut into slices and serve immediately.

11

NEIGHBOURS

I kneeled on the bed, leaned out of the window and yelled as loudly as I could.

"Help!"

Beside me, Lola stood on the bed on her hind legs, front paws planted on the windowsill. Every time I shouted, she joined in.

It was a weekday, and nobody heard our duet. It seemed none of my neighbours were at home.

Through the gap between the houses, I saw the occasional car flash past. Our house was in a *cul de sac* and there wasn't much traffic.

An hour went by, and my voice was becoming hoarse. As nobody heeded our calls, I considered taking risks. Perhaps I could use the bed linen to lower myself into the undergrowth?

Then I thought of snakes and broken legs. I tried shouting again.

"Help!" I rasped. "Please! I'm locked in..."

No response. A flock of cockatoos flew overhead, screeching. My cries and Lola's yaps were in vain. In despair, I rested my chin in my hands, trying to decide what to do next.

Suddenly, I heard a murmur of voices. Peeping through my fingers, I saw two pale-faced, saucer-eyed ladies peering around the house wall up at me. For a second, I lost all power of speech. Lola, still standing beside me on the bed, front paws on the windowsill, head stuck out next to mine, didn't hesitate. She barked her head off in excitement, her tail thrashing me.

The ladies gaped at us.

"Thank goodness," I croaked. "We're locked in the bedroom."

The ladies looked shocked and didn't move. I tried again, raising my voice over Lola's yaps.

"We're locked in! Please could you go round the house? The front door is locked but you can use the side gate. The glass sliding doors at the back should be open."

The two heads hung for a moment longer, then withdrew. I waited, then heard the side gate rattle and the glass doors slide open. Footsteps entered the house.

It occurred to me that I had just allowed two complete strangers to enter the house. They could have made off with all my possessions and I couldn't have done a thing about it.

Of course, nothing like that happened.

"We're in here!" I called.

They hurried over to the room we were trapped in and opened the door easily. I could have hugged them, but I didn't need to. Lola treated them to one of her bumper welcomes, regaling them with liberal licks and excited yelps.

The ladies introduced themselves as neighbours from further down the street. I hadn't met them when I first arrived. They had heard my cries for help but couldn't make out where they were coming from. They were about to abandon their search when they saw me. I would have preferred being introduced in less fraught circumstances, but never mind.

I sheepishly explained what had happened, and they were very sympathetic. Like so many others in our street, they had nothing positive to say about the previous owners, and the poor state of the house was of no surprise to them.

"You have got a lot of work to do here," said one, looking around.

I had to agree.

"Have you met many of the neighbours?" asked the other.

"Yes, briefly. There's the lady next door, and Emma down the road, with her cocker spaniel, Baxter. Lola and I meet Emma and Baxter at the oval sometimes, dog-walking. And there's Thea, who is always bringing me cake. We walk together sometimes, too."

"Have you picked up your invitation to the Christmas street party yet?"

"No! When's that?"

"I don't know the exact date but it's the first Saturday in December. Your next-door neighbours, the couple with all the gnomes and garden ornaments, organise one every year along with the Tongan family. Their house is opposite yours, over the road."

"Sounds good! I'll look forward to that!"

Sure enough, the next time I visited our ancient and dented mailbox that leaned at a dangerous angle and badly needed replacing, I found an invitation to the Christmas street party in it.

"Just bring a bottle, nibbles and a chair," it stated.

Karly, Cam and Indy drove up from Sydney to join me for the street party. We carried out garden chairs and introduced ourselves. Indy instantly made friends with the youngest of the Tongan family's five children. They, and a bunch of other kids, were soon bouncing on the trampoline that was a permanent fixture on the front lawn of the Tongans' house. The crowd kept growing, and the children ran excitedly from house to house. I smiled. It reminded me of the street parties in our Spanish village.

Lola was supposed to be shut away in our house, but she soon escaped with Indy and the other children, and joined the party.

Tables had been set out and were being laden with all manner of food and nibbles. Thea had baked a cake. I brought out a tray of sausage rolls, intending to put it alongside the other food platters already there.

"Stop!" hissed Karly. "You can't serve them like that!"

"Why not? What's wrong with them?"

"They're nude!"

"Pardon?"

"We're in Australia! You can't just serve them plain. You have to serve them with some type of sauce." said Karly. "Hold on. I'll find something."

She disappeared back inside the house, into my shambles of a kitchen, and came out with a small bowl filled with tomato sauce, for dipping.

"Oh, they look good," said someone, and the sausage rolls and tomato sauce vanished in minutes.

Flocks of cockatoos shrieked overhead, intent on reaching their roosts before dark. The huge, hot Australian sun dipped behind the distant ridge, leaving the sky stained tangerine, peach and orange.

As the sky grew darker, and the cockatoos' shrieks faded, the night shift arrived. The cicadas stopped their grating buzz and were replaced by the more melodic trilling of crickets. Monstrous black silhouettes flapped across the apricot sky on silent wings.

"Look at those huge crows," I commented.

"They're not crows, they're fruit bats," somebody corrected. "They always fly over at about this time. They're leaving their colonies in the bush to head out and search for food."

The moon hung above us and the sky became black velvet studded with stars. It was December. In Spain, we would have been sitting huddled in front of a roaring fire. Here, in Australia, I was wearing short sleeves and rubbing insect repellent on my bare skin to ward off the mosquitoes.

Somebody switched on music. The children played, barefoot, while the adults' voices grew in volume. We met people we hadn't met before and chatted with ones I already knew: Emma, Thea, and her husband, Reinhard.

Then Indy and the younger children were put to bed, protesting, and the party carried on into the night. When I awoke the next morning there was still a jumble of abandoned chairs in the street, and empty bottles stood on tables. I suspect the party continued well after we'd gone to bed.

Before I could blink, Christmas was upon us. Our local shopping village was already blasting out Christmas carols, and the shops were decorated with Christmas bling. When I visited the mall one day, a pen had been set up in the central aisle, housing live reindeer for children to pet.

All the Christmas traditions seemed to match those I remembered in England. There were mince pies for sale, and people decorated their houses inside and out with flashing Christmas lights.

Groups of carol singers came to the door. But, unlike England, where pale-faced, red-nosed carol singers would be wrapped in scarves and woolly hats, these carol singers wore shorts and their hair was bleached and skin bronzed by the Australian sun.

Lola and I spent a wonderful Christmas in Sydney with the family. It was so good to be there and watch Indy open her gifts. As usual, the strict *No Presents for Adults* rule was completely ignored. I reminded myself that Indy's baby sister would be part of the festivities next year. I smiled, knowing that I'd be here, God willing, in Australia for that. Never again would I need to miss precious family events because I lived in a distant land.

We ate, drank and laughed a lot. Karly, fantastic cook that she is, produced a banquet that was both typically Aussie and totally English. Oysters and seafood began the feast, followed by roast turkey with all the trimmings.

The sun beat down, and I thought of Joe in chilly Britain. It was such a shame he couldn't be here, but it was only a matter of days before he arrived. I joined in the laughter and chatter, but my mind often wandered because Joe was due to land in Australia on New Year's Eve.

"Is everybody coming back here for New Year's Eve?" Karly wanted to know. "You're all invited, of course. Shall we all wear red underwear again and eat a grape for every chime of the clock?"

Everybody laughed. Was it really a whole year since I'd brought that Spanish custom to Australia on my last visit?

"I'll have to miss it this year," I said. "Joe's timing is awful."

Hola tía Vicky y tío Joe,
   I hop you are well. My family is completely wells and I am writing

you a letter. Now we have no school because it is christmas and we are helping my mother with cookings for christmas. My mother she say if I don't want do cookings i must study because my school statement from my teacher is not so good. I do not like to do study and i do not like to write letters. Mama is not happy i don't like cookings. I like only dancing flamenco and talking with my friends but my mother she say I must study and do cookings like my sister.

Tía Lola and father Samuel they have big loud words in the street. My mother she say to my father that Lola is not knowing when she has the honey on her bread. My sister say it is the fault of Lola and Esteban because Lola she always go to the house of Esteban. My mother say we not talk about it and it is not business for children.

I am very happy that you have redback spider in your house. Pollito say how many peoples your friends they are kill by redback spider.

Felicitations, Catalina xx

The roads were deserted as I drove in Bruce to the railway station. This was hardly surprising because it was New Year's Eve, approaching midnight. I had the radio on, and as the clock struck twelve, the sky was illuminated by fireworks. As rockets exploded in all directions, I thought about the family who would be raising a glass and watching the fabulous Sydney Harbour firework display on TV. Then I thought of Joe, nearing the end of his long journey from the UK.

I glanced at Lola in the back seat, fast asleep, looking like a fluffy mop. What would he think of her? Would her unstoppable energy irritate him? Would he approve of the house I had rushed into buying?

The railway station car park was almost empty. I parked under a lamp post that barely illuminated the parking lot.

"Come on, Lola," I said, opening the back door and unclipping her seat-belt harness. "I want you to be on your very best behaviour. That means no pulling on the lead and no jumping up. I want Joe to be impressed by you."

Of course, I wasted my breath. She sprang out of the car, a ball of hairy excitement, bouncing and tugging this way and that as the train rumbled in and stopped at the platform.

A few doors opened, and suddenly, there he was.

Joe.

I remember he looked tired and pale, and somewhat frail, but mostly I remember his smile as he saw me and the unruly ball of golden, bouncing fur.

And then I was in his arms.

"So this is Lola!" he laughed, as she stood on her hind legs, trying to get in on the act, licking us both frantically. "Hello, Lollipop!"

Lola's tail wagged so hard I thought it would fly off, and from that day, the silly name stuck. Lola answered to the name of Lollipop as readily as she did to her proper name.

The fireworks were dying in the sky as we walked hand in hand back to Bruce, Lola trotting beside us.

"I'm so tired, but it's wonderful to be here at last," said Joe. "So this is Bruce! And I can't wait to see the house."

"Please don't expect too much… It's going to take a lot of work to get right."

"I know. It doesn't matter. We'll sort it out like we always sort everything out. We're a team."

We smiled at each other. He was right.

A brand new year had just begun. Joe was home, and I stopped worrying.

BAKED PUMPKIN RISOTTO

If you like, add in some chopped, cooked chicken about 10 minutes from the end. Also stir in some baby spinach leaves or peas for extra colour.

Ingredients

1 cup arborio rice (or any short grain rice)

2½ cups chicken or vegetable stock

60g (2oz) butter

350g (12oz) jap or butternut pumpkin, peeled and diced into bite-sized pieces

½ cup finely grated parmesan cheese

Cracked black pepper and sea salt

1 tablespoon chopped flat leaf parsley

Method

Preheat oven to 190°C (375°F)

Place arborio rice, stock, butter and pumpkin into an ovenproof dish and cover tightly with a lid or aluminium foil.

Bake for 30 minutes (although may need up to 50 minutes) until rice is soft.

Stir through parmesan, pepper, salt and parsley and serve garnished with extra parmesan and parsley.

12

BATS

Joe tried to absorb everything as we drove home, but it was dark, and he was exhausted. He didn't even notice the dead, brown area that used to be our front lawn. There would be plenty of time to show him everything in the morning.

When he awoke, rested, I took him on a tour of the house. I showed him the plans I had sketched and described how I hoped the house would look. He'd seen my sketches before, but now that he could actually see the layout, he understood.

"You're very good at this sort of stuff," he said. "I'm sure the house will be brilliant when it's finished. I'm so pleased that you've already organised a builder. Very well done!"

I nodded, privately hoping that, one day, Fred might actually materialise and begin work.

As the days passed, I showed Joe all the local places I had told him about. Like me, he was in awe of the lake, the white sandy beaches, the wide-open spaces, the bush, and the abundant birdlife. Fabulous colourful parrots often landed in our trees.

Gradually, we fell into a routine. Temperatures were hot, and we would either walk Lola on the beach or at the local oval. We swam in our pool and did odd jobs around the house. Often we just sat drinking coffee in our garden, eating slices of Thea's delicious 'Welcome' cake and chatting. Even though we had managed to keep in touch every day we had been apart, there was still so much catching up to do, so much to discuss.

"Have you had any more news from El Hoyo?" he asked. "You know, from your cute little penpal, the Ufarte twin?"

"Catalina? Yes, didn't I tell you? Hold on. This is the latest." I reached for the iPad and passed it over to him.

Hola tía Vicky y tío Joe,

It is I Catalina your penpall again. I hop you are well again. My family is completely wells again. I am writing you a letter today because my mother she say i must write again a letter.

Pollito my brother he say he is sorry no peoples your friends have kill from a redback. Pollito he say he now not want to be a scientist for dinosaurs he want to be a detective famous because today he find a diamond ring in the street. My mother say it belong to *tía* Lola and we must carry the ring to her because it is lost. i think the diamond ring not lost because I see *tía* throw when they have loud words and talk about Esteban. My mother say we not talk about it and say it is not business for children.

Pollito say please to tell me if you are seeing a great white shark.

Felicitations, Catalina xx

Joe smiled before commenting. "If I read between the lines, I'd say that Catalina's little brother, Pollito, is still a handful. More importantly, I'd absolutely lay money on the fact that Lola Ufarte hasn't changed her ways one little bit."

"Huh! And you are the one who always accuses *me* of being a gossip!"

"Remind me who Esteban is."

"I don't think we ever met him. He bought one of the apartments in the Monstrosity."

I remembered our horror when the foundations of the new apartment block were laid. As it grew, we named it the Monstrosity, convinced it would ruin the look of our beloved white-washed village.

We needn't have worried because in time, it blended quite well with the other buildings.

"Ah, right. Poor Father Samuel. I don't think anybody could ever stop Lola Ufarte from misbehaving. Certainly not an ex-priest who's probably had absolutely no experience handling women."

"Poor man. He was so besotted with her, and he dotes on her little daughter. I wonder if he regrets leaving the church for her?"

"It's a wonder nobody warned him."

"They probably did, but we all thought Lola had changed. Perhaps this will pass."

"Well, if they are having 'loud words' in the street and if she's throwing her diamond ring at him, I don't hold out much hope for their future relationship," said Joe drily.

I had to agree.

We were new to Australia, and the mini-beasts we encountered astounded us. Our garden heaved with extraordinary insects. At night, colossal winged creatures battered our window panes, attracted by the light. Something made peculiar chattering, bickering noises outside, causing Lola to growl into the darkness.

By day, huge black, shiny centipedes, with red legs, marched through the leaf litter. I saw massive ants with jaws that made me flinch, and others as tiny as pinpoints. We rescued delicate insects with lacy wings from the pool, and gawked at giant praying mantises that landed on our windows, inviting scrutiny.

We had never seen stranger creatures. It was as though some joker had been given permission to design the craziest animals imaginable from a mountain of spare parts, and then placed them all in Australia.

Cockroaches were plentiful, but they were three times the size of the cockroaches we had in Spain. Mosquitoes, too, were different from the ones we used to have in England and Spain. Some were tiny, and others were huge. They didn't play fair, either, because they were perfectly happy to suck one's blood in the full glare of daylight, without waiting for the cover of night. Strangely, I discovered that the itching caused by Aussie mosquito bites stopped quite quickly. I recalled that their European cousins' punctures swelled into angry lumps and itched for a full two weeks.

"I guess there's no such thing as paradise," said Joe, as an unusually large cockroach scuttled past his foot.

But I didn't agree. I thought, and still do, that Australia is as close to paradise as one can get. But I felt that about Spain, too.

When I was handed the keys of the house, I discovered a fantastic surprise. I already loved the view from the back of the house and enjoyed seeing flocks of cockatoos rise from it. But the surprise came at dusk.

The back of the house faced west and when the sun set behind the distant and thickly-forested bush, I was treated nightly to the most awesome, breathtaking sunsets imaginable.

About an hour before the sun sank from view, bird activity increased. Great flocks of white cockatoos, their wings tinted pink by the sunset, squawked overhead as they headed for their roosts in the bush. Groups of rainbow lorikeets flashed by at high speed. Loud and hyperactive as always, they darted past, as though dangerously late for some seriously important appointment, shrieking instructions at each other over their shoulders.

"Quick! Quick! We're late! Follow me, hurry up!"

Indian Mynah birds, considered pests and not native to Australia, landed in our palm trees and settled to roost. By day they were regular visitors to our pool and garden. We often saw them teasing visiting magpies and kookaburras by perching alongside them. Their bold behaviour and cheekiness earned them our nickname of The Hooligans.

Then the kookaburras began their twilight laugh-in. Perched on telegraph wires and silhouetted against the orange sky, they exchanged their raucous calls. They are extremely territorial, and that loud laugh is a warning to other kookaburras to stay away. I know now that kookaburras are almost exclusively carnivorous, feeding on mice, snakes, insects, small reptiles, and even the young of other birds.

"Do you remember the first time we saw kookaburras?" I asked Joe.

"Oh yes, when we were camping in Queensland."

"Yes!"

We both smiled at the memory. In 2008, we travelled in a campervan up the east coast of Australia, stopping anywhere we liked. We had a whole month to please ourselves. It was a trip full of adventures, discoveries, and a great sense of freedom.

At one particular campsite, Joe was serving up barbecued sausages. The smell was making me hungry, but I wasn't the only one watching him intently. I happened to look up and caught sight of a kookaburra perched nearby on a low branch, its head on one side, studying Joe.

"I think we've made a new friend," said Joe. "Perhaps he'd like a sausage? I'll put one on that post over there."

He picked up one of the cooling sausages and walked towards the post. But he never reached it. Without warning, the kookaburra left his perch and with a soft whoosh of feathers, swooped past, snatching the sausage from Joe's fingers.

"Wow!" we chorused.

The kookaburra swerved, the sausage still dangling from his beak, and landed on the back of one of our camp chairs. But he didn't immediately gobble down his dinner. He first thrashed the sausage violently and repeatedly against the back of the chair.

"He thinks it's a snake!" I said.

"And now he's dispatching it!" said Joe.

At last the kookaburra was satisfied that he'd knocked the sausage senseless, and that it would give him no further trouble. He gulped it down. Then, having preened himself with an air of self-importance, he flew away. We never forgot the incident.

When the kookaburras had ceased their cackling, twilight cries, the sun vanished. As the orange backdrop darkened to burnt umber, the stage was set for the next show.

At first, just one or two appeared, then more and more, until the sky seemed to be filled with them. Black, silent shapes flapped overhead and only when they flew very low could one hear the whisper of their giant wings. Unless we looked up, we'd be unaware of the fruit bats above.

My first visit to Australia was way back in the early 90s when my son, Shealan, and his little sister, Karly, were still kids. We visited northern Queensland and were experiencing a nature walk through a conservation area within a rain forest. We followed our guide along a twisting specially constructed boardwalk. The area was vast and had been netted to protect the enclosed rescued wildlife. We saw a wombat asleep in his den, and kangaroos in trees. I was surprised to learn that there is a species of kangaroo that climbs and lives in trees.

"Look out for Charles and Diana," said our guide, ducking to avoid a huge fruit bat dangling upside down from a branch above our path. "I see Charles has chosen a rather silly place to snooze today. Don't worry. He won't harm you."

The whole party filed past Charles, who regarded us with big dark eyes. I couldn't see Diana.

We were the last to pass, Shealan bringing up the rear and perhaps stopping to stare at Charles a little too long. Without warning, Charles dropped and wrapped himself around our son.

We gaped for a second and then attempted to gently detach Charles from Shealan. But Charles was thoroughly enjoying his new perch, and it was proving impossible to remove him. In addition to wrapping his enormous wings around my son, Charles also clung with the hooks on his wings. As fast as we unhooked him, he found a new hookhold, wrapping Shealan in a cosy embrace. Shealan wasn't in the least bit concerned.

"I think we need help," I said. "Karly, run on ahead and tell the guide."

Off she ran, her feet pattering on the wooden boardwalk. The guide was busy explaining how the eco-system of the rainforest worked and how it was affected by the seasons. Karly came to a halt in front of him and looked up. He didn't pause with his explanation, so she tapped him lightly on his leg with her knuckles. He looked down in surprise.

"Excuse me," she said, flushed but polite. "A fruit bat's got my bruvver."

Everyone stared, then swung around and smiled. Now the guide understood and trotted back to rescue Shealan from Charles's enveloping embrace. He succeeded and hung Charles on a nearby branch, well away from the boardwalk.

"Now behave," he told Charles. "No more dropping down on unsuspecting visitors."

Unfortunately, many Australians dislike fruit bats. They believe the bats will raid fruit harvests, unaware that they prefer pollen, nectar and bush fruit, in that order. As usual, it is a problem of diminishing habitat. The bush has been cleared to make room for the ever-growing human population. Existing bat colonies have been lost to new housing schemes and farms. Farm-grown fruit is bound to attract hungry flying foxes, even though they prefer bush fruit to the cultivated hybrid varieties.

The problem is severe, and flying fox numbers are in sharp decline. These native 'gardeners of the sky' have a crucial part to play. They help regenerate by spreading seeds which develop into new forests.

There are other reasons why fruit bats get a bad press. Their colonies are noisy and give off a terrible smell of ammonia. Fruit bats don't smell at all, they are fastidious creatures, but the stench of their guano and urine, which collects on the ground below their colonies, is overpowering.

I didn't appreciate this until Joe and I encountered our first fruit bat colony in Queensland. We'd parked the campervan on a grass verge and got out to stretch our legs. Cars sped past us on the road and beyond the verge was typical Australian bushland, edged with tall trees.

That's when the stench hit us.

"Boy, that's a *horrendous* smell," said Joe, clapping his hand over his nose. "It's enough to make my nose-hair shrivel and die."

"Every cloud has a silver lining," I said.

"Where's the smell coming from?"

We looked around, and then we saw the source.

"Over there! Bats! Quick, grab the binoculars, let's go and look!"

FIG AND WALNUT BREAKFAST LOAF

A change from banana bread and delicious topped with cream cheese and sliced strawberries. From newideafood.com.au

Ingredients

125g (4oz) unsalted butter, chopped

1½ cups water

250g (8½oz) dried figs, chopped

½ cup buttermilk

2 eggs, beaten

1¼ cups brown sugar

2 cups white spelt flour, sifted

2 teaspoons baking powder

1 teaspoon mixed spice

1 cup walnuts, chopped

½ cup desiccated coconut

Method

Grease and line a non-stick loaf tin and set aside.

Place butter and water in a large saucepan and heat over medium heat.

When butter is melted, add figs.

Bring to the boil and remove from heat.

Transfer figs and butter mixture to a large bowl and allow to cool.

Add buttermilk, eggs, brown sugar, flour, baking powder and mixed spice to bowl and stir to combine.

Add walnuts and coconut and stir one last time.

Pour into prepared tin.

Bake in 160°C (320°F) oven for 90 minutes.

Slice and serve.

13

A BANANA AND BEETLES

"Look out for snakes," said Joe as we stumbled through the long grass and headed towards the trees.

"Make lots of noise and they'll slither away."

"I think the bats are making enough noise for both of us!"

We could see the colony ahead of us, each individual hanging upside-down from a branch, encased in its leathery wings. Sometimes they stretched out a wing or changed branches. They chattered, jabbered, and bickered with their neighbours.

"There must be hundreds of them!"

"Thousands!"

And there were. Some branches had as many as ten bats hanging from it, others only one. But there were dozens and dozens of them. We didn't want to scare them away by getting too close, but an all-pervading smell and a deep ditch kept us at a distance.

We raised our binoculars and stared. I focused on a particularly large, restless specimen.

"I didn't realise they had such bulgy black eyes and long dangly noses," I commented.

Joe said nothing for a moment and appeared to be thinking.

"Long dangly noses? I don't think so. They're called flying foxes because they have faces like foxes. And foxes don't have long dangly noses."

"Well, the one I'm looking at has. Focus on that big one, on the high branch on its own, with the family of about six under him."

"Ah yes, I see it…"

"Well?"

"Honestly, Vicky!"

"What?"

"I can see what you're looking at, and it isn't his face."

"It isn't?"

"No, it's a particularly well-endowed specimen of a male fruit bat. You're not looking at his face at all."

"Oh."

As though aware of our scrutiny, the bat scratched himself.

"Oh, he's scratching himself. Now, who does that remind me of, I wonder…" I commented.

"Humph!"

Scratching his nethers is a horrible habit I have never managed to cure Joe from doing.

For a long time we watched the bats bicker, gibber, scratch and snooze.

"Let's come back at dusk and watch them fly out," I suggested.

"Great idea!" said Joe.

That evening we managed to park a little closer to the colony, but far enough away not to be overpowered by the stench. As the sun dipped, we barbecued our dinner, keeping an eye on the colony. It may have appeared a strange spot to choose to cook one's dinner, but the roadside gave us a perfect vantage point, and we were rewarded.

As the sky darkened, the bats grew more restless and twitchy. They stretched and flapped their wings, and the noise level rose. One sensed a mounting excitement.

First one bat dropped from its perch and rose into the sky, followed by a few more. Then more lifted into the air, flying in ones and twos, then groups, then dozens. Eventually the evening sky was almost black with bats.

"They're all heading in the same direction," Joe remarked.

"Yes, I read somewhere that they can smell ripe fruit from three miles away."

We finished our meal and watched until the last bat launched into the sky. Then we drove back to our campsite, delighted with our evening's entertainment.

The next day, we were discussing fruit bats when a nugget of previously forgotten information jumped into my head.

"Did you know that fruit bats don't actually bite, chew and swallow as we do?"

"Don't they? What do they do then?"

"They crush the fruit against the roof of their mouths, suck out the juice, then spit out all the fibrous remains."

"Really?"

"Yes, really."

"We could test that theory," said Joe. "I'm sure they eat bananas. Why don't we leave a banana out and watch it tonight?"

"How would the fruit bats find it?"

"You said they could smell ripe fruit from three miles away. I bet they'd easily find our banana."

"Where would we put it?"

"Hmm... Up one of these trees, I reckon," said Joe, looking up at the tall pine trees surrounding our campervan. "Nice and high."

"Don't be ridiculous! Are you suggesting we climb one of these trees and put a banana up there?"

Joe was deep in thought, absent-mindedly scratching himself down below.

"No, of course not. We've got a big ball of string, haven't we?"

"Yes..."

"Well, we could attach a stone to the string and throw it up over a high branch. Then we lower the stone, and exchange the stone for a banana. Then we pull the banana up."

"Are you serious?"

"Yes, of course."

"Right..."

The first throw proved nowhere near high enough. The second one hit the trunk of the tree, ricocheted and nearly took Joe's eye out. The third throw sailed over the branch, precisely as planned.

"There you go, easy!" said Joe, rubbing his eye.

He lowered the stone, exchanged it for our banana, and pulled on the string until the banana swung high in the air above us. It looked very odd.

"Perfect!" said Joe, securing the string to another branch.

"Now what?"

"Well, we sit outside tonight and watch the banana. A fruit bat is bound to come along and find it."

That evening, we set up our camp chairs, opened a bottle of wine, and waited. We watched bush turkeys flap into the trees to roost for the night. We heard owls and a dozen strange noises, including the chitter of bats, but saw nothing else. The yellow banana swung high over our heads in the moonlight.

Eventually we gave up and went to bed, confident that some fortunate bat would devour the banana during the night.

But none did.

We left that campsite two days later and the banana was still hanging there, untouched. I wondered whether any future campers might notice it and scratch their heads, asking themselves why anybody would want to dangle a banana high in a tree.

We'd driven about a hundred kilometres towards our next destination when another thought occurred to me. What if the banana rotted and fell on somebody's head? I doubt they would ever solve the mystery of the banana that fell from a pine tree.

Joe had been in Australia a few weeks and still hadn't met our builder, Fred. We had no working kitchen but we were coping, cooking on a camp stove and using a microwave. It wasn't worth investing in a proper cooker yet, not before the kitchen was remodelled.

The bathroom was dire, but everything worked, and one could enjoy a proper shower if one averted one's eyes from the deeply ingrained mould, the cracked tiles and dripping taps.

At last, Fred got in touch and arranged to come over. I introduced him (and Dinkum) to Joe, and as they shook hands, I noticed cuts and scratches on Fred's forearms.

"Sorry I'm late," he said, "I've just rescued a puppy, and he's a bit of a handful."

"Oh, really? What kind of puppy?"

"He's a Great Dane. He doesn't take no for an answer when he wants to play. Actually, he grabs my arm with his teeth and drags me into the garden."

He rolled up his sleeves to reveal more cuts and grazes.

"Oh my goodness," I said, shocked. "What does Dinkum make of him?"

"Dinks is fine; she's the boss. She can control Hulk better than I can."

Dinkum had already marched in and plonked herself on Lola's bed. I tried to picture this small dog and the Great Dane together and failed.

"Lola's grown a lot since I last saw her," he said, patting her as she gave him her usual exuberant welcome.

It was true. Lola was growing very fast. She was a lot bigger than Thea's dog, Nixi, and was even taller than Emma's cocker spaniel, Baxter, down the road. I had thought Lola would be a small dog, but she was still growing. Later, I checked her papers and was surprised to discover that one of her parents was a standard poodle. That would explain a great deal because standard poodles are big dogs.

"Have you any idea when you'll start work, Fred?" Joe asked.

I held my breath.

"Well, that's one of the reasons why I've come around today. It seems to me that we'll have to go about it all in a certain order."

"How do you mean?"

Dinkum snored, opened her eyes a crack to check her master was still there, then went back to her slumbers.

"I'm desperate for a decent kitchen and bathroom," I said, trying not to whine.

"Yes, but we can't start with the kitchen because of the kitchen wall that needs knocking down. And we can't start with the bathroom, or you'll have no toilet or shower for quite a long time. So it makes sense to start with the new bedroom and en suite. That'll give you a bathroom to use when we knock the other one down."

Joe and I looked at each other, then back at Fred.

"I suppose that makes sense," I said.

"Yes, I see," said Joe. "So when can you start?"

"First we'll need to get planning permission. I'll leave you with the name of an architect. You can make an appointment with him."

"An architect?" spluttered Joe. "Planning permission? We only want to convert the garage into a bedroom with en suite."

"I'm afraid it's necessary," explained Fred. "And we'll need to set up things like termite protection."

We were a bit depressed when Fred and Dinkum left. Things were going to take a lot longer than we'd planned.

It's hard to stay depressed in Australia when the sky is bluer than a roll of washed denim, the sun shines nearly every day, and your puppy wants to romp on the beach with you.

We began to explore further afield and fell in love with the area more and more. Thea showed us a beautiful lakeside path which soon became a favourite walk. There were clifftop lookouts from which we planned to watch the whale migration, and more beaches than one can count on two hands.

And, as if that wasn't enough, we had our pool, although that wasn't without its problems. Thank goodness for our friend Emma, Baxter's owner, because she worked in a pool shop and could answer our numerous questions.

One summer day we were taking a dip. It was an excellent place to be because of the heat. Pelicans flew in formation overhead, and a gentle breeze fanned the palm fronds above us.

"Ouch! That hurt!" I said.

"What's the matter?"

"Something nipped me!"

"What sort of something?"

"I don't know!" I said, peering into the water.

Actually, it crossed my mind that it could be a funnel-web spider, because I knew they sometimes lurked in swimming pools, having fallen in when searching for a mate.

Thankfully, it wasn't a funnel-web; it was something entirely unexpected.

"I see it! It's a water beetle!"

"A water beetle? Don't be ridiculous. The pool has chlorine in it, how could a water beetle survive in it?"

"I don't know! Look, there's another! And another…"

"Ow!"

Joe had just discovered that, not only were there indeed water beetles in our pool, but that they were armed with surprisingly powerful jaws. We jumped out of the water.

"Look, there are *hundreds* of them," I said, pointing at the pool filter where dozens of little black beetles were merrily swimming in and out.

"Oh, you've got them, too?" asked Emma when I told her about it. "We've had loads of calls from customers who've found beetles in their pools recently. Seems there's some kind of water beetle epidemic going on."

"How can they survive in chlorinated pool water?"

"I don't know. Chlorine will kill them, but you'd have to put so much in that you won't be able to swim."

"Oh no! I don't want to do that. Is there anything else we can do?"

"Well, there is a chemical you can add, but lots of our customers have complained that it doesn't work."

I reported the conversation back to Joe, who wasn't pleased.

"Don't worry," I said. "I've got an idea."

Without telling him where I was going, I shot off to the nearest dollar store and purchased two children's shrimping nets, the type with very fine mesh.

"Correct me if I'm wrong, Vicky, but are you suggesting we catch all those beetles with these nets?"

"Yes."

"Don't be ridiculous."

"Have you got a better idea?"

"No, but do you realise how many there are? I think they've been holding some kind of beetle love-in because I'm sure there are hundreds more since I last looked."

"Never mind, it'll be fun. And then we can release them into the wild."

"Excuse me? Do what?"

"Well, as we catch them, we can put them into this Tupperware box. Then we can take them to the lake and set them free."

"Now I know you are crazy."

We added a new activity to our list of hobbies: beetle catching. It might not have been as good as swimming, but it was surprisingly entertaining. We set ourselves small targets, like how many could we catch in one scoop of the net. On the eighth day, we caught the last one and swam in the pool to celebrate.

Lola had no idea why we didn't use our pool for a week, but she enjoyed the lake visits. We emptied our daily catch into the water, and the beetles scooted off to hide in the reeds. Perhaps the lake water wasn't their natural habitat, but we'd given them a chance, and I'm sure the local frogs, fish and egrets enjoyed snacking on them.

Slowly, as summer slipped away, the water in our pool became too cool to swim in. It was essential that Joe continued to exercise and keep his lungs as active as possible. He joined a local gym that also offered a decent, very warm, indoor swimming pool. He began a daily regime of a workout in the gym followed by a swim in the pool.

How could we know that this place was to change our lives? We can't be sure, but we suspect that this innocent gym subscription was the cause of a catastrophe waiting to happen in the not too distant future.

CREAMY CAMEMBERT POTATOES

A delicious vegetarian side dish for any meal or barbecue. This recipe came from a 20-year-old Australian Women's Weekly magazine.

Ingredients

750g (1½lb) potatoes

2 tbs sour cream

15g (½oz) butter

1 clove garlic

125g (5oz) camembert

salt, pepper

2 tbs chopped chives

Method

Boil or steam potatoes in the usual way until tender. Drain.

Mash with sour cream until smooth.

Remove rind from cheese, chop cheese roughly.

Melt butter in pan.

Add crushed garlic and cheese, stir over a low heat until the cheese melts, then add to potato.

Season with salt and pepper then stir through the chives and serve hot.

14

CLONES AND A RUSSIAN

The architect came and took measurements. He drew plans to convert our garage into a bedroom with an en suite bathroom. We submitted the proposals to the council and waited for permission to be granted.

Lola continued to grow, and so did her hair. She didn't shed at all, which was a blessing, but every three months her curly coat needed clipping or it would begin to mat. It surprised me that she was such an enthusiastic swimmer and puddle-splasher, yet she wasn't very fond of being bathed. And she was even less keen on having her fur dried with a hairdryer.

But Lola had no choice, and a very nice lady regularly visited our house with her mobile dog-wash salon. She parked the trailer in our drive and set to work on Lola. She lathered her, dried her, trimmed her coat, cut her nails, until Lola looked and smelled delicious. That was until her next muddy puddle paddle or roadkill encounter. She loved to roll in anything that stank, and the stinkier the better. A rotting fish on the beach, a dead bird riddled with maggots, whatever. Sometimes she stayed clean and perfumed for no more than an hour.

I couldn't really blame Lola for not enjoying her salon experience. I don't enjoy visiting a hair salon either. When I first arrived in Australia, I was quite excited, knowing that I'd be able to chat with a hairdresser in my own language. In Spain, I always took my English-Spanish pocket dictionary with me, in case I forgot essential words like 'fringe' or 'layers' or phrases like 'low maintenance'.

I was still living in Sydney when I made my first hair appointment. The receptionist led me to a chair and introduced me to my stylist.

"This is Li Na," she said, and a delicate Chinese girl smiled at me and bowed her head respectfully.

I hadn't expected that, although I shouldn't have been surprised. Australia is exceptionally multi-cultural and Asians are the largest ethnic group to settle and start new lives here, followed by the British.

We didn't talk much, although Li Na smiled a lot and told me her name meant 'elegant'. I didn't know the word for 'fringe' or indeed anything at all in Mandarin, so I gave her free rein. She did an excellent job and seemed to understand the sign language I had perfected in Spain. Although we couldn't chat, I was very satisfied with the result.

The next salon I visited was near my new home and only employed Australian staff. Communication wouldn't be a problem. When I arrived and gave my name, the receptionist looked at me strangely. She stared intently at the appointment book. Her eyes narrowed. Adjusting her spectacles, she checked the book again.

"Is there a problem?" I asked.

"Well, no, not really," she said. "It's just I think we've got some client names mixed up."

"Well, my name is Vicky. Vicky Twead."

"Yes, that's what I have written down here." She lowered her voice to a whisper. "The strange thing is, the lady in the chair over there is also named Twead."

"Twead with an EA instead of double E?"

"Yes."

"You're kidding! It's a really unusual name. Apart from family, I don't believe I've ever met any other Tweads."

"Oh, I expect we've made a mistake in the appointment book," she said, leading me to the empty chair beside the other Ms Twead.

But they hadn't made a mistake. As soon as I was settled, and my stylist had begun her work, I couldn't resist starting a conversation with the lady next to me. She was roughly my age and seemed friendly.

"Hello," I said. "Excuse me for asking, but I wondered whether your surname really is Twead, like mine? With an A? That would be such a coincidence if it was!"

"Good heavens! Really? Yes, I'm Val Twead. Twead with an A. My husband is an only child, and I've never met any other Tweads."

"Me neither! How extraordinary! I'm Vicky so both our names begin with V. Do you get called V often? I do."

"All the time!"

As the stylists mixed colour and snipped, we chatted on, making discovery after discovery. I was beginning to think I had entered some kind of twilight zone or alternative universe.

"I can hear from your accent that you're English," said Val. "So am I! I've been here for over forty years, but I originally came from Dorset."

"Dorset? No way! So did I! When's your birthday?"

"February."

"So's mine!"

We gaped at each other, then carried on firing questions to and fro. A few details were different, but the vast majority were staggeringly similar.

"Do you have any grandchildren?"

"Yes, a granddaughter, and another one due in April."

"I have two granddaughters! The eldest is called India and the one-year-old is called Summer."

I didn't yet know the name of Indy's new baby sister who would be born that coming April. But India and Indy were undoubtedly very similar names.

By this time, the staff members were equally fascinated and joined in the conversation, firing more questions and comparing answers. Val and I drove similar cars, liked similar foods, we both had a dog, although she also had a cat.

And so it went on. It was one of the most surreal hair appointments I have ever attended. Readers may remember I had another, more unnerving experience, in Spain before emigrating to Australia. I documented that one in *Two Old Fools in Turmoil*, and it still causes shivers to run down my spine when I recall it.

Val left before me, and I never saw her again because the salon changed hands soon after and closed. In fact, the incident slipped my mind until Indy's baby sister was born. When her parents finally decided on a name, I was profoundly shocked. The name they announced was so similar to that of Val's youngest granddaughter, Summer, that I wondered whether I had imagined the whole episode.

"It just isn't possible," said Joe, always the cynic. "I don't believe in *doppelgängers*, and I think you dreamed the whole thing."

I didn't dream it. And it *did* happen. I did meet a lady called Val Twead, and we definitely shared numerous personal details.

But I can't prove it.

So if you know somebody called Val Twead, do tell me. And if Val ever reads this book, please do get in touch so that I can prove to Joe that the salon incident was not a figment of my imagination.

Oh, and Val, I wonder if you can guess what name my daughter and son-in-law chose for my youngest granddaughter that April?

Meanwhile, another problem was distracting us. Australia's National Broadcast Network (NBN) was being rolled out across the country, designed to provide fast broadband Internet for all businesses and households. It was a government sponsored scheme and I had to apply for it through an Internet provider. I chose a popular one from a list of many and, when I moved into our house, I visited their outlet in the shopping village.

"The NBN is coming to this district," an assistant informed me, checking my address.

"That's good to hear," I said happily. "When is it coming?"

"We're not exactly sure. It will probably be several months."

That was disappointing, but I was pleased that it was definitely on its way. Fast Internet access was vital to me.

"Can I arrange for ordinary cable Internet to be set up? To tide me over until the NBN arrives?"

The assistant checked his computer, and his voice was solemn.

"I'm sorry, we're not allowed to install that service to your address."

"Why ever not?"

"Because the NBN is coming to your district. There's no point setting you up for cable Internet because you will soon be getting NBN."

"Yes, but it's not coming quite yet?"

"That's right. Not yet."

"So how do I get Internet access until then?"

"You'll need to use your phone as a hotspot and pay as you go."

That was double-Dutch to me but I had no choice. I knew I'd have to master it and rely on that until the NBN arrived.

"I've checked the system. I can now see the NBN should be available for you in December."

"Good, thank you. I guess that's not too long to wait."

"Would you like to put your name down for it?"

"Yes please."

In December, I phoned to see if there was any NBN news, and they admitted to having lost my order. The next date I was given was February. This was a blow because the pay-as-you-go system was proving to be expensive.

It also meant that my beautiful new flat-screen TV that Karly had so valiantly fought for, was useless. It could only pick up two local channels, one of which was dedicated to horse-racing. Not my personal viewing choice. It was probably just as well that I didn't want to watch horse-racing because the horses were blurry and disappeared at the slightest breeze.

When Joe arrived in Australia, he was horrified.

"What? Only two channels? Well, only one really as I have no intention of spending my evenings watching a pack of ghost horses galloping around a track. And that's only if the weather is good."

He called out a TV aerial expert who marched outside and looked up.

"Is that your TV aerial?" asked Mr Aussie Aerials, his eyes wide.

"Er, yes. That's what the previous owners left behind."

"Well, no wonder you've been having trouble. That's a caravan aerial, and I'm surprised you receive any TV channels at all. I doubt whether that thing could catch a cold, let alone a signal. It's about as useful as a glass door on a dunny."

Ah, another new Aussie word to add to my growing collection. Dunny: Australian/New Zealand slang for toilet or WC.

The flimsy TV aerial shook and wobbled, as though seriously affronted.

Mr Aussie Aerials erected a much more robust model, and hey presto, we had a dozen new TV channels.

Nothing happened in February, but in March, we received fantastic news. The NBN had arrived in our suburb. A team of workers attached a box to the outside of our house, and we were told somebody would soon appear to connect it to a smaller box inside.

We were given a date and at seven-thirty in the morning, a burly technician arrived carrying a toolbox and an assortment of levels, drills and square plastic tubing. Everything looked suspiciously shiny and new.

"I am Vladimir," he said, bowing slightly. "I am from Russia."

"Come in, Vladimir," said Joe cheerily. "We'd like to have the box put up in the office, please. It's very close to the outside box so there shouldn't be any problem connecting them through the wall. I suggest that if you run the tube along the wall just under the edge of the desktop, it'll be hidden."

Vladimir's lips stretched into a smile, but the smile never quite reached his eyes. I wondered whether he had actually understood us and if he'd ever done this job before.

"Would you like a cup of coffee or tea?" I asked.

"I am Vladimir," he said, bowing slightly.

"Oh dear. Let's leave Vladimir to get on with it, shall we?" said Joe, backing out of the office. "I'm sure he knows what he's doing."

Before long, we heard the clatter of tools and the encouraging sounds of industrious drilling.

"How wonderful!" I yelled above the noise. "We'll soon have fast Internet access! Would you mind holding the fort while I take Lola for a quick walk around the block?"

"No, you go ahead. I'll keep an eye on things here," shouted Joe over the deafening sound of brickwork and masonry under duress.

The closed office door was vibrating as I walked past, and in the bedroom the noise, if possible, was even louder. I wanted my favourite cardigan and opened the sliding doors of the wardrobe.

What I saw inside made me gasp.

SPEEDY BEEF STROGANOFF

This stroganoff recipe is fast and flavoursome. Using evaporated milk, it minimises the fat. Delicious poured over pasta or creamy mashed potatoes. From Taste.com.au

Ingredients (serves 4)

300g (10½oz) dried spiral pasta

600g (1¼lb) beef rump steak, trimmed, thinly sliced

2 tablespoons plain (all-purpose) flour

2 tablespoons olive oil

1 large brown onion, thinly sliced

200g (7oz) button mushrooms, thinly sliced

2 garlic cloves, crushed

2 teaspoons sweet paprika

1 tablespoon tomato paste

2 teaspoons dijon mustard

2 teaspoons Worcestershire sauce

½ cup beef stock

185ml (7fl oz) can light and creamy evaporated milk

Chopped fresh flat-leaf parsley leaves, to serve

Method

Cook pasta in a saucepan of boiling, salted water following packet directions, until tender. Drain.

Meanwhile, place steak in a large bowl. Add flour. Season with salt and pepper. Toss to coat.

Heat oil in a large, deep frying pan over medium-high heat. Cook beef, in batches, for 2 to 3 minutes or until browned. Transfer to a bowl.

Add onion to pan. Cook, stirring, for 5 minutes or until softened.

Add mushrooms and garlic. Cook for 5 minutes or until mushrooms are tender.

Return beef to pan.

Add paprika. Cook for 1 minute or until fragrant.

Add tomato paste, mustard, Worcestershire sauce and stock. Bring to the boil.

Reduce heat to low. Simmer for 5 minutes or until slightly thickened.

Remove from heat.

Stir in milk.

Divide pasta between plates.

Spoon over stroganoff mixture.

Sprinkle with parsley. Serve.

15

TERRY

I clapped my hands over my ears to muffle the roar of the drill, but I STILL couldn't believe my eyes. Surely this wasn't my neat, orderly wardrobe?

Vladimir had missed the outside wall entirely. The NBN technician had drilled through the office wall straight into our bedroom wardrobe.

Worse still, brick dust coated my hanging clothes and chunks of brick filled my shoes. I could see something soft and ragged wrapped around the drill bit, spinning crazily.

My favourite cardigan had suffered a terrible fate.

"Stop!" I yelled.

In the office, Vladimir didn't hear me, but Joe came running.

"What the…"

He turned back and burst into the office where our Russian friend was still drilling purposefully. Joe tapped him on the shoulder and the Russian stopped abruptly, but looked puzzled when he found he couldn't withdraw the drill from the wall.

"Are you aware that you're drilling into our wardrobe?" asked Joe, his voice calm but icy, a mirthless smile on his lips. "You can't pull your drill out of the wall because my wife's cardigan is wrapped around it."

Vladimir looked nervous.

"I am Vladimir," he said, bowing his head slightly.

"I know you are…" said Joe, but then caught sight of the box fixed to the wall.

"What the…"

Even an inebriated wombat would never have declared that box to be level. And as if that wasn't bad enough, the cable that led to the box was fixed to the wall in full view. It ran merrily along for at least a metre, halfway up the wall. And it wasn't level either.

I sensed Joe might implode and quickly intervened.

"Vladimir, come with me," I said, grabbing his sleeve and pulling him into the bedroom. It briefly crossed my mind that this was the first time I had *ever* dragged a man into a bedroom, let alone a burly young Russian.

Vladimir was goggle-eyed and even more shocked when I pointed at the debris and ugly hole in the wardrobe. His eyes nearly popped out when he saw my shredded cardigan wrapped in a ball around the end of his drill.

Back we marched to the office to find Joe busy herding our technician's tools into a heap.

"What are you doing?" I asked.

Joe knows two words of Russian, 'Hello' and 'Goodbye', and he was about to employ one of them for the first time in his life.

"I don't believe I have ever, EVER, seen a worse job," he said grimly. "I'm just gathering up these shiny new tools which have *clearly* never been used before. Then we're going to say Прощай (pronounced *proshchay*) to Vlad the Impaler, because he is leaving now."

Vladimir jumped. He may not have understood much English, but Joe's tone and expression, and the word Прощай, left him in no doubt. Grabbing his tools, he made a hasty exit. He might have left even faster had he not been delayed by needing to cut away my balled-up cardigan from his drill before he could extract it from the wall.

Poor man. I could see his hands shaking as he ripped away the last shreds.

Probably wisely, he didn't stop to say *Прощай*.

Next, we made numerous phone calls. These were fielded by helpful, polite representatives called Rashid or Sanjay, who were based in a call centre in Mumbai. Each listened sympathetically. Finally, we were invited to submit emails with attached photographic evidence of the disaster in the wardrobe, and the crooked NBN box.

Countless phone calls and emails later, a proper, skilled technician arrived and put everything right. Of course, he couldn't re-knit my favourite cardigan. Our Internet Provider gave us a router that we connected to the internal NBN box. Then, one happy day, a remote switch was flicked, and the little red and green lights on the router lit up and blinked cheerily. We finally had fast Internet access.

I danced with joy.

It seemed everybody had their own NBN horror story to tell. Our tale wasn't unique. We heard of telegraph poles falling without warning, and holes left in walls that allowed armies of insects to march into people's houses. We heard of installed NBN suddenly dropping out, and streets where houses on only one side had access to the Internet.

It was enough to make us quite twitchy.

One day, while driving down our street, we saw a parked NBN truck. A bunch of workmen were poring over an NBN switchboard located in a roadside electrical box. Joe stopped Bruce.

"Don't you dare mess with our NBN," he called out of the window.

The workmen stared at him.

"There, that's told them!" said Joe, satisfied, and drove off.

I've mentioned before that I don't enjoy visiting a hair salon, but that changed when I met Terry. The closure of the salon where I had met my clone, Val Twead, meant I needed to find another hairdresser, and one of my new dog-walking pals suggested Terry's place.

"I've been going there for years," she said. "You'll love Terry."

She gave me directions to the salon, and I drove slowly past. It wasn't in the smartest district of town, and empty shops flanked the building, but I parked Bruce and entered the salon.

Inside, it looked as though time had stood still and nothing had changed very much in the last twenty years or more. It didn't boast the flashy decor one often sees in modern salons. There were no vivid colours or posters of lithe young models sporting edgy hairstyles.

Nevertheless, this salon had a unique attraction of its own. It was clean and homely, and there were little displays of lovingly-knitted toys and homemade cot quilts. Greetings cards were being sold for charity. It reminded me of a bygone England, when Women's Institutes thrived, before we began importing everything from China.

But what I caught sight of, in a corner, convinced me to make an appointment. It was an overflowing bookcase with shelves bowed into crescents by the weight of stacked books.

A tiny, blonde lady detached herself from her customer and smiled at me. I judged her to be in her sixties, like me, and couldn't help noticing she had a gap between her front teeth, exactly like my own.

"Hello, can I help you?"

"Are you, Terry?"

"I am."

"Oh good! A friend recommended you. I wonder whether I could make an appointment, please?"

"Of course," she said, pulling out a big, dog-eared appointment book and thumbing through the pages. No fancy computer system here. "When would suit you?"

My first session with Terry was a delight. She was perfectly satisfied with my request of 'just a tidy-up, please' and didn't attempt to convince me I needed 'foils' or other baffling hair treatments. Instead, we had a good old-fashioned gossip, and I left feeling I'd made a new friend, not just acquired a new hairdresser.

As we nattered, ladies would come in, and Terry would look up.

"Hi, Beryl, how are you?"

"Good, thanks, Terry. I'm just bringing in a few new books and returning that one you recommended. I really enjoyed it."

"Oh good, I thought you would. There's another one by that author on the second shelf somewhere. Unless somebody else borrowed it."

A steady stream of readers arrived to swap and donate books. I feared for the shelves that groaned beneath the weight of each new book.

Terry knew everybody, and I began to understand why her appointment book bulged.

"I don't think I'll ever retire," she said, shaking her blonde tresses. "It's not like going to work. It's like meeting friends. I've known some of my clients for more than twenty-five years."

I felt relaxed and was actually enjoying my appointment. We had plenty in common, like our love of wildlife.

"I have two Indian mynah birds in my garden," she said, "I call them Heckle and Jeckle."

Most Australians dislike the Indian mynah bird, perhaps not without reason. This cheeky chap should not be confused with the Noisy Mynah, which is an Australian native, grey in colour and much better behaved.

Deliberately introduced in the 1860s to keep insects down in Melbourne's market gardens, Indian mynahs thrived and multiplied, reaching almost epidemic proportions and making life difficult for native species. Apart from competing for food, the mynahs take over the native birds' traditional nesting hollows, and their ability to multiply is breathtaking. One bird can lay six eggs in one clutch, and they often breed three times a year. It has been estimated that one breeding pair could potentially be responsible for 13,000 birds within five years.

Scary.

Often called 'flying rats' or even 'cane toads of the sky' they have earned a place on the list of the world's 100 most invasive species.

I guess it's understandable that some councils have taken steps to keep the numbers down. I read that Bundaberg Regional Council, in Queensland, offers a bounty of two dollars per head for Indian mynahs, delivered alive and unharmed. It kills them humanely, and some are sent to the *Snakes Down Under Reptile Park* in Childers, where crocodiles regularly snack on them.

Of course, we can't blame the mynah birds for being so successful. It was man's fault for meddling and introducing them to Australia in the first place. Like the disastrous introduction of rabbits and cane toads. And, like Terry, I couldn't help liking these bold, mischievous birds. The gang we had christened The Hooligans entertained us greatly.

"Oh my stars!" exclaimed Terry. "You wouldn't believe how cheeky Heckle and Jeckle are! If the door is open, the pair of them march straight into our laundry and help themselves to the dog's kibble out of her bowl. And Bridie just watches them!"

I laughed.

"And you know what? My husband got a different brand of kibble and Heckle and Jeckle just turned their beaks up at it. So when he went shopping again, I asked him to get the usual stuff. 'Why?' he asks, 'doesn't Bridie like the new brand?' 'Nah,' I said, 'Heckle and Jeckle don't like it.' Well, he just rolled his eyes at me."

We chatted on, and I discovered other things about Terry. For instance, although Australian through and through, she was a staunch royalist and her knowledge of the British royal family put me to shame. The year 2016 was quite a busy one for the Royals, and Terry followed their every move. She celebrated the Queen's 90th birthday and was delighted when Prince Harry made headlines by confirming he was dating Meghan Markle. She knew what outfits were worn at what official occasions, and the names of all the little princes and princesses. The very mention of Princess Diana made Terry's eyes mist over.

"I remember it like it was yesterday," she said. "I couldn't stop crying. Then, when the day came to lay Diana to rest, I said to my family, 'Listen, I'm going into the lounge room with a scotch to attend a funeral. Do not disturb on any account.'"

Not only was Terry an avid reader and Royal Family watcher, but she could tell stories that held me spellbound. We were discussing Australian wildlife once when Terry recalled an incident.

"Oh my stars! I remember when my daughter was a baby, and I was making our bed. She was crawling around the floor by my feet when she lost her toy. I think it went under the bed and we couldn't reach it. So I moved the bed back from the wall and peered down. Oh my stars! Something was moving!"

"What was it?"

"Well, it was dark down there so I couldn't make it out at first. I know it's crazy, but I thought it might be a turtle or a lizard. When it moved again, it suddenly dawned on me. Oh my stars, it was a snake! So I grabbed the baby and flew out of the room. Then I rolled up some towels to block the gap under the door. I don't think it could have come out, but I wanted to be sure. I thought it was probably harmless, but I didn't know what sort of snake it was and I certainly wasn't going to risk it."

"Wow! What did you do then?"

"I ran over to a neighbour and left the baby with her, and then I didn't know what to do. It was the days before mobile phones, and my husband was away and couldn't be reached. I thought of ringing my dad, but he was an hour away. Anyway, my neighbour's husband said he'd go and have a look and when he came back, he'd gone pale. 'Did you see it?' I asked him. 'Yes,' he says, 'it's a five and a half foot red-bellied black snake.' Well, I nearly died!"

Red-bellied black snakes are beautiful creatures, but highly venomous. They have forward-facing fangs and although their bite is rarely fatal, anyone bitten must seek immediate hospital attention. They are very common along the eastern coast of Australia and usually hide in moist vegetation. They can climb trees and are excellent swimmers, being able to stay underwater for twenty minutes or more.

"What on earth was it doing in your bedroom?"

"I have no idea."

"How do you think it got in?"

"I don't know!"

"I wonder how long it had been there?"

"Who knows? In the end, I called out the council, and a ranger came. He said they hibernate in cold weather. We might have been sleeping in that bed, with a red-bellied black snake underneath us, for weeks!"

"Did he take it away?"

"No, he killed it."

I was sorry to hear that. I think we are a little wiser nowadays. Had it happened today, the snake would probably be relocated to a place where it wouldn't be a nuisance.

When Terry's husband came home, he thought the whole tale was just a huge prank. He refused to believe they had been slumbering blissfully between the sheets, unaware of the red-bellied black snake that lay under their bed.

FAST FOOD MINESTRONE

With stock in the freezer and a few veggies in the fridge, you can make this steaming bowl of minestrone in just under half an hour.

Ingredients

2 cups prepared chicken stock

2 cups water

1 tin tomatoes

1-1½ cups small macaroni

2 zucchini (courgette) sliced

2 carrots, peeled and sliced

Handful of frozen peas

1 can red kidney beans, drained

2 tablespoons tomato paste

½ bunch spinach or 1 small packet frozen spinach

Parmesan cheese

Salt and ground black pepper to taste

Method

Bring the stock and water to the boil.

Chop the tinned tomatoes a little and add to the stock with macaroni and tomato paste.

Simmer for about 10 minutes.

While that is simmering, chop the spinach, then add carrots, zucchini and kidney beans.

Simmer for a further 10 minutes or so until carrots are tender.

Add salt and pepper to taste.

Stir in the spinach and peas, cook for a minute or two, then serve.

16

HOSTIBALS

Hola tía Vicky y tío Joe,

It is I Catalina your penpall again. I hop you are well again. My family is completely wells. I do not know what things I can write but my mother say to tell you here are many almond flowers on the trees today and everybody say we will have good lots of almonds. Valentina say if she marry Geronimo she will make a dress the same colour of almond flowers and she want Geronimo wear a necktie of blue colour same of sky above mountains.

I ask Valentina if she marrys Geronimo soon because I want to dance flamenco at the weeding. But Valentina she say no because first she must hit Geronimo into a shape. I do not understand hit Geronimo into a shape. I like the shape of Geronimo. I say Valentina that my mother she say Geronimo is a guardian angel because he always save my little brother Pollito from dead. Valentina she laughs much but she not very happy. She say me if Geronimo is a angel why he not fly out of the valley more??? She say if Geronimo has wings he can see some more of the world.

I say the words of Valentina to my mother and she say we not talk about it and say it is not business for children. But she say me that

Valentina has visit many places in the world. Perhaps she wish Geronimo come with her for some travellings.

I say Geronimo I care for his donkey with straw then he can make travels with Valentina. Then he be the right shape for Valentina. Then they can marrys and I can dance flamenco at the weeding. Geronimo make an noise like PAH then say he like Andalucía much and why for he want see more???

Pollito say you not remember write if you have great white shark near your house.

Felicitations, Catalina xx

Before we knew it, summer tiptoed out, and autumn crept in. The water in our pool cooled but Lola, the water-dog that she was, didn't care. I'm sure she'd be willing to break through ice to have a swim, although I've yet to see frost in our part of Australia.

It was April, the month when, in Spain, the almond blossom petals would litter the ground like confetti, to be replaced by new leaves in the branches overhead. Our grapevine in Spain was, no doubt, bursting into life. But here, in Australia, the forests turned red and gold.

We still had no kitchen or a decent bathroom. Neither did we have a date when the promised work would begin.

But that April a very exciting thing happened which took our minds off such trivia.

At dawn on the 25th of April, 1915, armed forces from France, Great Britain, and the British Empire, including Australia and New Zealand, landed on the Gallipoli peninsula. Battles raged, and many lives were lost on both sides. More than 8,000 Australian soldiers were killed.

A year later, in 1916, the 25th of April was officially named Anzac Day. ANZAC is an abbreviation for Australian and New Zealand Army Corps. Declared a public holiday, it became the day on which Australians remember the sacrifice of those who died in the Great War.

Every year, on the 25th of April, memorial services are held at dawn, the time of the original landing in Gallipoli.

One hundred and one years later, in 2016, Anzac Day fell on a Monday and saw me driving to Sydney. I'd left Joe at home to look after Lola. I would be looking after Indy in Sydney. But this wasn't an ordinary babysitting engagement.

"Are you ready to go?" I asked when I arrived at Karly and Cam's house and had finished hugging Indy.

"I think so!" said Karly. "My case is all packed. I've left a list on the table of what Indy can have for meals, and Cam will be back late tonight. Help yourself to anything."

"Gosh, so exciting! This time tomorrow, I'll have another granddaughter."

Karly and Cam left, and I had Indy all to myself.

"Do you know where your mummy and daddy have gone?" I asked her.

She looked back at me with those wise, wide three-and-a-half-year-old blue eyes fringed with thick lashes.

"Yes."

"Where are they?"

"Hostibal."

"That's right! And why have they gone to hostibal?"

"To get my new sister!" she squealed, clapping her hands.

And that's precisely what the plan was. Karly was booked to go into hospital to be induced, and we all expected the baby to be born the next day.

It was exciting going to sleep that night knowing that the new day would bring another little person into our lives.

In the morning there was no news, and I tried to concentrate on playing Princesses with Indy, but my heart wasn't in it. The morning wore on, and I drove us over to Cam's parents' house so that we could all wait for news together. A gathering of the clan was always fun, but this time we were all breathless with expectancy.

"Have they decided on a name yet?" somebody asked.

"No, they have a shortlist, but they haven't picked one yet."

How slowly the time crawled by. Had the baby been born? Was everything okay?

At last, the telephone call came through. The baby had arrived, and mother and daughter were both doing well.

"Indy, your new baby sister is here! She's in the hospital!"

"Can we go and get her?"

"Not yet, Mummy and Daddy will bring her home soon, but we can go and see her."

We bundled into our cars and drove to the hospital. We shared a lift to the third floor with an elderly couple.

"Oh," they said to Indy, noting her costume and tiara, "are you a princess?"

"Yes, and I've got a baby and its name is called Dragon."

"Oh, that's nice…"

Cam was in the waiting area, grinning.

"Everything's great," he said, "it all went really well. Karly's tired but doing fine and the baby's perfect."

"Still no name yet?"

"My baby's name is called Dragon," announced Indy.

"Hmm, maybe…" said her daddy, smiling down at her. Then he turned to all of us. "Now, I hope you don't mind, but I'd like to take Indy in first, on her own, to meet her baby sister."

We all nodded.

"Of course!"

We understood this was a very special family moment and watched, moist-eyed, as the pair walked away, hand in hand, up the corridor. Cam, tall, strong and capable, holding the princess's little hand in his big one. Her long blonde hair streamed out behind her as she ran alongside him, three of her steps matching his single stride. In her other hand, she clutched a soft little teddy, a gift for her new sister.

"Well, we'll never forget this baby's birthday," I said, while we waited. "The day after Anzac Day."

Then, at last, they appeared, coming back towards us down the corridor, Cam marching while his eldest daughter skipped beside him. We all stood.

"Did you see your new sister?" I asked Indy.

"Yes!"

"Oooh! Have you got a new baby sister?" asked a passing nurse, overhearing the conversation. "What's her name?"

"Her name is called Dragon."

The nurse smiled and walked on.

A weary but radiant Karly, with her new daughter, were in a little side room. We all flooded in. Of course, the baby was perfect and slept through the whole experience of being examined, and cooed over, and passed from family member to family member.

"She's got heaps of hair," said Karly, "and she's quite a lot darker than Indy was. We still haven't decided on a name."

Meanwhile, Indy and her little cousin, who had just arrived, discovered that if they pressed individual buttons on a remote control, the bed would rise or lower, or tip this way and that. They almost folded poor Karly in half. Probably wisely, she escaped the levitating mattress by vacating the bed. I heard later that the bed eventually broke, but the hospital was very nice about it. They claimed it must have been faulty, and quickly replaced it with a new one.

It wasn't until a couple of days later that Cam and Karly finally settled on a name for their baby daughter. We were all delighted that it wasn't Dragon.

"We're going to call her Winter," Karly said. "She'll always remind us of when Cam and I met in the snow."

Having lived so many years in Spain, I was aware that I had neglected routine medical procedures that I might have been encouraged to pursue had I been living in the UK. I received no reminders for bowel cancer tests or mammograms; neither did I ever have my blood routinely tested. Now, as an Australian permanent resident, all that would change.

I registered Joe and myself at the local Medical Centre and was delighted with my new doctor. Dr Sarah happened to be English, and she was one of those special people who listen to you as though you are the only person in the world. I immediately felt at ease, and I trusted all the advice she gave me. If she didn't know the answer, she said so, and never made me feel I was wasting her time.

Joe's doctor was South African, a man who didn't make small talk and called a spade a spade. Joe liked him very much, so we were both happy.

Dr Sarah conducted a smear test, which pronounced me clear of cervical cancer. Dr Botha kept an eye on Joe's high blood pressure and prescribed medication for that, and his COPD and prostate cancer.

I received a parcel in the mail. I ripped it open to find that it was a 'self-administer' bowel cancer test kit. I'd never heard of such a thing in Spain. I followed the instructions and found it a straightforward process, in spite of my horror at the thought of it. I labelled my specimen and sent it off in the envelope provided. In due course, I was thrilled to be told that no evidence of bowel cancer had been detected.

One day, I noticed a huge pink van parked in our local shopping centre car park, with the legend *BreastScreen NSW* painted in enormous letters on the side. *Book your free mammogram*, it invited.

I nervously climbed the steps, entered the little waiting room and made an appointment.

It was the first time I had ever had a mammogram, and I now understand why women don't like it very much. I had no idea that breasts can be squeezed and compressed so dramatically. Bread dough being flattened under a rolling-pin springs to mind. The actual compression only lasts a few seconds and is utterly necessary, but I was heartily glad when it was all over.

"We'll be in touch," said the receptionist as I left.

I put it out of my mind until I received an ominous letter.

Thank you for attending your appointment at Breast Screening, New South Wales. We would like you to return to have further tests to complete your screening. This appointment usually takes from two to four hours, however, occasionally an appointment can take longer. It is therefore recommended that you commit the day to your visit just in case.

I checked in and was directed to a waiting room. I remember

thinking it must be tea-break time because there was a bunch of ladies in blue overalls already seated there, some with white cups and saucers, sipping tea.

A nurse bobbed up from nowhere.

"Victoria? If you'd like to go into one of those cubicles over there, you'll find a pile of gowns on the bench. Just pick one that's your size and change into it. Pop all your clothes and personal items into one of those lockers."

Ah. So the other ladies weren't cleaners or hospital staff. Like me, they were patients.

"Thank you," I said and made my way to a cubicle.

A pile of neatly folded gowns awaited me on the bench, and I selected one marked *Medium to Large* because I didn't want anything too skimpy. Then I struggled with the crossover ties, trying to work out how they were supposed to hold the gown together. By the time I'd just about fathomed it, I realised that the gown was far too big for me and threatened to reveal large portions of my naked self unless I kept it clamped together with a firm grip. It was too late to exchange it for a smaller one because I heard my name being called. I bundled my clothes and handbag into a locker and hurried back out into the waiting room to join the seven other ladies.

ANZAC BISCUITS

ANZAC biscuits were originally made by the wives and mothers of soldiers fighting in World War 1 and were sent to them in packages. From bakeplaysmile.com

Ingredients (serves 2)

110g (4½oz) rolled oats

150g (5oz) plain flour

125g (4½oz) brown sugar

70g (2½oz) desiccated coconut

125g (4½oz) butter

2 tbs golden syrup

½ tsp bicarbonate of soda

Method

Preheat oven to 160°C (fan-forced) or 320°F. Grease and line three flat baking trays with baking paper.

Combine the rolled oats, flour, brown sugar and coconut in a bowl.

Place butter, golden syrup and 2 tablespoons cold water into a microwave-safe bowl and heat for 3 minutes, 50% power or until melted.

Stir through the bicarbonate of soda.

Pour the butter mixture over the oat mixture and stir to combine.

Roll level tablespoons of mixture into balls.

Place on trays, 5cm (2 inches) apart and flatten slightly.

For chewy biscuits, bake for 10 to 12 minutes or until light golden. For crunchy biscuits, increase cooking time to 12-15 minutes.

Leave on the baking trays for 5 minutes before transferring to a wire rack to cool completely.

17

CATS AND DOGS

I was taken to a little side room where the doctor asked me lots of questions. She ticked boxes on her forms.

"We called you back because we noticed a shadow on one x-ray," she explained. "It's probably nothing, but we need to check it out and investigate further."

She pointed to an area on the screen. I peered at it, but it wasn't obvious to my untrained eye.

"We'll run a few different types of tests to check your breasts in more detail," she continued. "A specialist will give you a thorough examination, both visually and by manipulation. She'll be feeling for abnormalities. We'll give you a second mammogram, and we'll also conduct an ultrasound scan. This uses harmless sound waves. The test is done by moving a probe over the surface of your skin, and it's completely painless."

"That's a lot of tests," I remarked.

"Yes, I'm afraid it's going to be a long day for you. Now, if you'd like to return to the waiting room, we'll call you when we're ready for the first test."

I joined the gown-clad ladies and waited, probably wearing the same anxious expression as all the others. Gradually, the ice began to break and some ladies chatted. A few flicked the pages of magazines or concentrated on finding pieces of a giant jigsaw puzzle that lay partially finished on a table.

At regular intervals, a nurse popped her head around the door and called out a name. That person would stand and follow the nurse to carry out the next test.

I grabbed some multi-coloured knitting out of a basket. I hadn't knitted for years, but it would keep my hands busy. I looked at the rows knitted so far. It was evident that this square had been taken up by a variety of knitters. Some rows were tighter than others, some of the stitches smaller or looser. There were plenty of dropped stitches. I wondered how many anxious women had added rows to this misshapen woollen piece. I hoped that none of them had to hear those words all women dread.

It was a strange day. Gradually, the eight of us were whittled down as individuals were given a clean bill of health and sent home. They dressed and waved a cheery goodbye, wishing the remaining few the best of luck.

By late in the afternoon, there were only two of us left. Barbara was in her forties and had discovered a lump when taking a shower. And there was me.

Why hadn't I been sent home already? What had they found? My fingers knitted furiously, row after row.

"Victoria? Sorry to keep you waiting, but would you mind coming through for another mammogram?"

"Another one?"

"Yes, we just want to repeat the sideways section on the right side. The doctor felt it wasn't clear enough."

My heart lurched. Had they found something?

"Good luck!" called Barbara as I trotted after the nurse.

I was already feeling somewhat bruised and tender after all the other tests, but I followed her. The top plate descended and squashed me, holding me firmly in place for the x-ray.

Another interval in the waiting room. Another four rows of knitting.

Then the nurse returned.

"Victoria? The doctor is happy with your x-rays now. We can't see any problems. You can get dressed and go home. Expect a letter from us in due course confirming that all is well."

"Oh, thank you!" I was beaming from ear to ear.

"I'm very pleased for you!" said a voice at my elbow.

I'd forgotten Barbara, the only remaining patient, and my smile vanished.

"Oh, I'm sure that any minute now they'll come in and say the same thing to you," I said quickly.

I retrieved my clothes and dressed. When I came out, the waiting room was empty. Barbara wasn't there.

Perhaps she'd been called in for another test, or maybe she been given good news, like me, and was getting dressed.

I sometimes think about Barbara. Had she been declared clear, or did she have to listen to those words that none of us ever want to hear?

I'll never know.

The month of June brought the shock news that Britain was leaving the European Union. In a referendum, held on 23 June 2016 in the UK, 51.9 per cent of voters supported leaving the EU. Brexit, a combination of the words 'Britain' and 'exit', was dominating the news headlines.

Everybody we knew seemed to have a passionate opinion on the matter, and I was surprised that my friends and family in the UK were also split on the issue.

Me? I have no head for politics and couldn't substantiate any argument, for or against. I hadn't lived in England since 2004, and didn't feel qualified to vote. However, although I'm aware of being hopelessly naïve and over-simplifying the matter horribly, I dream of a world with no borders, no wars, and mankind living at peace with each other. Somehow, leaving the EU feels like we are taking a step backwards.

"Hear! Hear!" said Joe when he read these words over my shoulder.

July in Australia is midwinter, and we were delighted that the temperature didn't drop very low. In fact, when there was no southerly wind, and the sun shone, it was as warm as a British summer's day. The only complaint we had was that our house seemed to be much colder inside than out.

Most Australian houses are not built to combat cold temperatures. I have yet to see double-glazed windows, and cavity-wall insulation is not automatically installed.

"We'll make sure we get insulation put in the roof when the reno starts," I said.

"Reno?"

"That's Aussie for 'renovation'."

"Oh. You mean *if* the reno ever starts. We've got the planning permission in place, what's holding Fred up?"

Fred did contact me that week, although not in quite the way we had expected.

Out of the blue, a text appeared on my phone. I read it, and my eyes popped.

U sound lovely. Would u like to meet up some time? I've not been well but I'm ready for some fun now.

"Who's texting you?" asked Joe.

"Fred," I answered, and passed him the phone. We both started laughing.

"I think he sent that message to the wrong person," I said. "What shall I do?"

"Nothing. Don't embarrass him. At least we know why he hasn't been in touch, anyway."

I followed Joe's advice, and sure enough, Fred phoned the following day.

"Sorry I've been a bit delayed. I've actually been in hospital. They're not sure what was wrong with me, except for being diagnosed as diabetic, but I'm okay again now."

"Oh, that's good."

"Right, expect a bin to arrive on Monday morning. They'll put it on your front grass. Then I'll be coming later with building materials and my plumber. He'll be mapping out how your new en suite bathroom plumbing will be laid."

"So, what fantastic excuse did he come up with this time?" asked Joe, ever the cynic. "Did aliens whisk him away and experiment on him?"

"No. As we suspected, he was crook."

"What? He was what?"

"Crook. It's Aussie for 'unwell'."

"Oh."

"Anyway, work begins on Monday."

"Hmm… I'll believe that when I see it."

Very early on Monday morning, before I'd even finished my first cup of coffee, the rubbish skip arrived. Lola barked so hard I feared she would give herself a sore throat. And she didn't stop, even after the skip had been lowered onto our front lawn and the lorry had driven off. She carried on barking at the skip until I took her outside and introduced her to it. When she understood that it wasn't a huge yellow intruder, she calmed down.

"That dog never stops barking," said Joe. "She barks at everything. Can't you do something about it?"

"Like what?"

"I don't know. She barks at people walking past the house, birds, cats, everything."

Actually, he was right. She spent much of her time peering through the living room window studying the goings-on in our street. Anybody passing got a good barking at. If The Hooligans, or any other birds, invaded the front lawn, they were barked at. And cats infuriated her.

The rascally cats knew how to wind her up. They would deliberately preen themselves just a few feet beyond the window, in full view of Lola, sending her into a frenzy. Memories of the days when she was a tiny puppy and friends with Bandsaw in Sydney, had apparently faded away.

"She's only a puppy…"

"Well, you need to get it sorted now before she gets any older."

Joe was right, of course. We had three cats living next door, and several more in the street. At night a tomcat roamed, howling at the moon. The thought of Lola forevermore going berserk every time she saw or heard a cat was not pleasant.

What to do? Consult the Internet, of course.

Apparently, desensitisation is the answer. Get one's dog so accustomed to whatever sets them off that they eventually cease to notice it.

I couldn't physically introduce Lola to a hoard of cats, but I could do the next best thing. I could expose her to cats meowing. I found a soundtrack on Youtube called *12 hours of cats meowing*, or something like that, and warned Joe.

"Now, before I start this therapy, I want your promise that you won't interfere, and you won't tell me to stop."

"What are you going to do?"

"I'm going to play a soundtrack I found, and it's twelve hours long."

"Twelve hours? What is it, music?"

"Um, no, not really. Not unless you're a cat, I suppose."

"Go on, then, if it cures Lola's barking, it'll be worth it. I promise not to interfere."

I slipped my phone out of my pocket and pressed Play. The unearthly sound of a cat yowling filled the room and Lola went ballistic. She barked and rushed around searching every room and nook and cranny for cats.

Joe and I looked at each other.

"Are you sure?" shouted Joe, scratching.

To be honest, I'd had enough after one minute. The never-ending howling of the cats combined with Lola's hysterical barking was almost unbearable. But we had to give this therapy a chance to work.

"Let's just carry on as normal, and she should start to ignore it soon."

Actually, it did work. After five minutes of searching for the noisy feline invaders, Lola gave up and went to sleep. I wondered what she dreamed of as the soundtrack continued with litters of kittens mewling and tomcats singing. Joe had shut himself away and clamped earphones over his ears, enjoying Beatles' songs, and successfully drowning out the caterwauling. I tried to write, but I couldn't string any coherent thoughts together.

Hour after hour, the cats howled, nearly driving me insane. Occasionally, when they changed note, Lola would begin to bark, then lost interest. I felt the treatment was working.

There was a knock on the door, and I opened it to Fred who had brought the plumber. Joe heard nothing because he was still shut away with the Beatles. I held Lola back as she tried to give both men her usual enthusiastic welcome. Dinkum marched in and stole her bed while Lola was otherwise occupied. The sound of meows didn't bother Dinks in the slightest.

"Have you got some new kittens?" asked the plumber.

"I was going to ask the same thing," said Fred.

"No," I replied and explained. "Lola barks every time she hears a cat. I'm playing a soundtrack of cats meowing so that she learns to ignore it."

"She isn't barking now so perhaps it's working." the plumber commented.

"Yes, I hope so."

We discussed pipes and water pressure for a while, then Fred and the plumber left. I looked at my watch. It was time to take Lola for her run on the oval so I gathered her up, shouted goodbye to Joe and drove away. I put my phone in my pocket, the cat soundtrack still running.

As I got out of the car, a mum passed with a toddler.

"Mummy, where are the pussy cats?"

"What pussy cats? There are no pussy cats here, silly!"

In the distance, I could see some of my dog-walking pals and Lola raced over to greet them. Frankie was an elderly lady who had never lost her Scottish accent despite having moved to Australia more than fifty years ago. She had two little white fluffy rescue dogs.

I met so many people through Lola, and many of them had stories to tell about their dogs.

For instance, there was Monty, or Mounty as I called him privately. Monty was an ancient, black, miniature poodle, greying around the face. He was quiet and relaxed until he saw another dog. Then his demeanour would change. Suddenly he became an ardent lover with just one thing on his mind.

His owner admitted that it didn't matter to Monty whether the other dog was male or female.

"In fact, it doesn't even have to be a dog; he humps everything. He humps cushions, legs, anything. We had him de-sexed, but it made no difference."

"Oh dear!"

"He has a favourite soft toy at home which he won't leave alone. Even the kids accept it. We call it Tigger-time."

I couldn't help laughing.

"I know! He's a pedigree, and he was supposed to be a stud dog at a breeder's place. But he didn't do the business so they gave him away. We reckon he's spending the rest of his life making up for it. He's got something to prove."

Monty always tried his luck with Lola but she just shrugged him off. No doubt she was baffled by his advances.

Another owner, Chris, had a pug named Riley, and he had a very different story to tell. He paid $1000 for Riley but when he got him home, he discovered his dog was riddled with worms. However, medication sorted the problem, and all was well.

Until the day Riley disappeared.

HOME-MADE DOG BISCUITS

I had to wait until I actually had a kitchen with a working oven before I could try this recipe. It's good to know what goes into your dog's treats, and they didn't taste too bad to me, either.

Ingredients

Dog Biscuits

1 cup cooked pumpkin

½ cup peanut butter

2 eggs

¼ cup cooking oil

2½ cups of wholewheat flour

1 tsp baking powder

Glaze

2 tablespoons of bacon grease or similar

¼ cup of smooth peanut butter

Method

Preheat oven to 350°C (650°F)

Combine pumpkin, peanut butter, eggs and oil in a bowl. Add baking powder and flour and stir until a stiff dough forms.

Knead or mix dough until all the flour is incorporated.

Roll out the dough with a rolling pin and use a cookie cutter to cut out dog bone shapes, or just bake in little circles like cookies.

Bake for 15 minutes.

Whisk the bacon grease and peanut butter until very smooth. Drizzle over the treats and cool in the fridge until the glaze sets.

18

MORE CATS AND DOGS

"Riley disappeared? Was he stolen?"

"No," said Chris. "He was just a puppy at the time, and he was always into mischief. I don't know how he managed to get out through a tiny hole under the fence, but he did. I was beside myself! I looked for him everywhere and went to three local vets in case he'd been handed in. They asked if Riley was microchipped and I told them he was."

"So what happened?"

"Then I got a call from one of the vets saying somebody had found a pug and that it seemed to fit Riley's description. The vet said that the people who found him were bringing him in to get the microchip checked. The vet would phone me back as soon as that was done."

"Oh, thank goodness for that!"

"I was overjoyed! But that wasn't the end of the story."

"Why? Wasn't the puppy they found Riley?"

"Well, that's the thing! The vet called me back, as he promised, but he said there was a problem. They'd scanned the microchip and looked it up, and it belonged to a seven-year-old black German shepherd. That dog was registered at a breeder's address in a town several miles away. The vet phoned the breeder and was told that there must have been a mix-up with the microchip. But they said Riley belonged to them."

"Belonged to who? The breeder?"

"Yes."

"That's very odd!"

"I know, and the story nearly had a horrible ending!"

"Why?"

"The vet gave the finder's address to the breeder, and they said they were setting off straight away to collect Riley. I jumped in my car and drove around to the finder's address, too, praying that I'd get there before the breeder did. As it happened, we arrived at exactly the same time. The breeder was just walking up the path to the finder's front door. I saw the finder looking out of the window, and then the front door opened. Riley burst out and charged down the path. He swerved straight past the breeder and his wife and jumped up at me, giving me a massive welcome."

"Wow!"

"Yup, there wasn't any doubt that it was Riley! Or that I was the genuine owner. The breeder couldn't leave fast enough. Thank goodness I arrived in time because they would have taken him and resold him, I'm sure of it."

I heaved a sigh of relief, hearing the end of the story. That had been a close call.

At the oval I joined my dog-walking pals, Frankie, with her two fluffy rescue dogs, and Jean, who owned another pug named Bella.

"Can you hear cats in the distance?" asked Jean. "Kind of muffled?"

"No," said Frankie, "but I am rather deaf."

"I'm sorry, but the cats are my fault," I said, sighing. I explained, pulling out my phone from my pocket.

Frankie and Jean laughed. We chatted and watched the dogs play, ignoring the sounds of the cats which kept up their infernal meowing.

Eventually, it was time to go home, and I was pleased that Lola was no longer showing any interest in the cats' chorus. I parked Bruce and was about to enter the house when I saw a large white card tucked into the screen door. It said:

Council Ranger Section

We visited this property at 15.30 on urgent business. Please contact us as soon as possible using the above telephone number. Fines may apply if you disregard this notice.

"Joe? What's this card on the door? What do they mean?"

Joe was making himself a coffee and examined the card.

"I have no idea! I didn't hear anybody come to the door. I've been listening to music with my earphones on. Ranger? Urgent business? Whatever do they mean?" He scratched below, deep in thought. "What are Australian rangers responsible for, anyway?"

"Um, litter, bush fire matters, animal control..."

"That's it!"

"What? Lola hardly needs controlling!"

"Not Lollipop. It's the cats! Somebody has complained about the incessant cat noises coming from this address! And I don't blame them either! Hours and hours of continuous yowling? I bet you've been driving our poor neighbours insane!"

"You don't think..."

"You mark my words, our neighbours have had enough. They probably think we're cat hoarders and have cats in every room. Not to mention the litters and litters of kittens and marauding tomcats!"

"Oh, don't be ridiculous..."

But his words struck home, and I hastily switched off the cats' chorus. I called the number on the card.

"Ah yes, we called today, thank you for getting in touch."

"What exactly is the problem?" I asked nervously.

"Our records show you have a number of dogs on the premises."

"A number? We have just one."

"Our records indicate that you have three mastiffs. Two females and a male..."

"Excuse me, can I just stop you there?"

"…and that none of these dogs has been properly registered."

"No! We just…"

"In New South Wales, all cats and dogs, other than exempt cats and dogs, must be microchipped by twelve weeks of age, or before being sold or given away, whichever happens first."

"Yes, I know, but…"

"Are they exempt? Perhaps they are guide dogs? Although that would be most unusual as mastiffs are very large and don't make good guide dogs."

"No! We have just *one* dog, and she's not a guide dog. Or a mastiff, for that matter. She's a cross between a cocker spaniel and a poodle. And she's microchipped and registered. I think your records need updating because I believe the previous owners of this house had mastiffs. And they had heaps of puppies, too."

I went back to Joe with a smile on my face, delighted that my cats' chorus recording wasn't to blame. However, I had no wish to hear the cats any longer and never pressed 'Play' again.

I'm sorry to report that Lola still reacts when she hears a cat, but I refuse to resume the caterwauling therapy. And Joe's next suggestion hardly deserved a reply.

"Here's an idea! Why don't we make a load of cardboard cut-outs of cats? We could attach them to a string and keep pulling them past the window for Lola to see. Then maybe she'll lose interest and won't bark when she sees a real cat."

"Don't be ridiculous."

I guess we'll just have to accept that she'll always bark at cats.

As for the previous owners of our house, I have no idea where they went, or whether they still have heaps of unregistered mastiffs. I do know that, even now, we get a constant stream of mail for them from Foxtel, Mastercard, utility companies, and various debt-collecting agencies, all demanding money.

That August we celebrated Indy's fourth birthday.

"You can choose any theme you like," said her mother. "What sort of party would you like? A princess party?"

"A cat party, please," said Indy, carrying a long-suffering Bandsaw.

"Are you sure?"

"Yes, I love cats."

A cat party? Easy!

Karly had lots of ideas. I reverted to infant-teacher mode and thoroughly enjoyed myself making preparations.

Everything was cat-themed. The cake was a cat, there were blue jellies with little fish set in them, cat-shaped cookies and sandwiches, and I made some strawberry mice with long liquorice tails.

The toilets had signs saying, 'Litter Tray'. Karly set up games including 'Pin the Tail on the Cat' and 'Find the Prize' in a (new) litter tray using a poop scoop. There were stick-on cat tattoos and a host of other feline activities.

While her four-month-old baby sister slept, Indy's little friends arrived, and the party began. I'd made a cat collar, using wide ribbon and velcro, for each child to wear. Attached to the collar, like a pet tag, was a disc with the child's name on it. Karly also presented each child with a set of cat ears and a tail.

The birthday party was a huge success.

By August, work had begun in earnest on our house, although, as Joe pointed out at regular intervals, *ad nauseum*, they weren't exactly racing along.

We couldn't argue with the quality of Fred's work; it was consistently good. But everything moved at a snail's pace. Fred and Dinkum never arrived early, which we understood because we knew he had his elderly mother to look after. However, he was often extremely late, and although his excuses were probably genuine, they were colourful.

"I'd have been here earlier, but Hulk chewed the sole off one of my work boots. I had to stop and get some more."

"Hulk?" asked Joe, eyebrows high.

"You remember, the Great Dane Fred rescued," I reminded him.

"Ah. Yes."

Another time it was:

"I'm sorry I'm late, but Hulk ate Mum's medication, and I had to take him to the vet for a stomach pump."

"I suppose we should be grateful he doesn't bring Hulk here," said Joe. "At least Dinkum just walks in and makes herself at home on Lola's bed."

Dinkum was never any trouble, but Lola was dreadful. She dug holes in sand piles, destined for making cement, scattering it all over the place. She dived into the sacks of plaster, sending up great white clouds that made us all cough, poor Joe in particular.

Once, when the rubbish skip was too full to take any more, Lola discovered the best toy ever. A huge roll of disgusting old carpet was left unattended. She found that if she pulled and worried a ragged end, the ancient, smelly carpet, amidst loud ripping noises, fell apart. She would have happily unravelled that carpet all day had I let her.

It was no wonder that Joe escaped to the gym every day. Apart from needing to maintain his exercise regime, there was too much dust, noise and activity at home.

The doctors had always impressed on us how vital exercise is to patients suffering from Chronic Obstructive Pulmonary Disease. COPD is a condition in which the air sacs of the lungs are damaged and enlarged, causing breathlessness. Therefore, any exercise that strengthens the heart and lungs may improve the body's ability to use oxygen. We knew there was no cure, but exercise would definitely slow down the inevitable and cruel progress of the disease.

I didn't stay at home much, either. My lovely German neighbour, Thea, and her dog, Nixi, often accompanied Lola and me on walks beside the lake.

Thea was great company and always made me smile.

"No! You can't park there," she would say as I searched for a car parking space. "That's for the limping ones."

She was warning me not to park in a slot reserved for the disabled.

Or, when telling me about a detective show she had watched on the TV the night before. "It is about a policeman wearing clean clothes."

That had me thinking for a moment until I realised she was referring to a plain-clothes policeman.

It was impossible to wear Lola out, but poor Nixi was older and stouter with much shorter legs. She often sat down and refused to walk any further.

"Are you sure she's a dog?" I would ask Thea. "I think she might be a guinea pig."

Thea would throw treats in front of her to encourage her to keep moving. But only when we turned around and headed for home did she show any spring in her step.

The lake path is many kilometres in length. It is flat and meanders as it hugs the shore. At intervals there are children's play areas and shelters with barbecues and benches. In typical Aussie style, families hold their children's parties there, decorating the shelters with bunting and balloons, and bringing party food.

The lake was also a favourite place for cyclists, joggers and dog walkers. You never knew who you were going to meet, or what strange sight you might see. I once met a young couple walking their pet dingo. They told me its mother had been killed in Queensland. The litter of puppies she'd left behind had been rescued and given to suitable homes. Lola was very interested in saying hello to the young dingo, but it was extremely shy.

It is believed that primitive man brought the dingo to Australia around 15,000 years ago. Dingoes hunt alone or in packs, and prey on small animals such as rabbits, birds, lizards, and rodents. They are usually shy creatures, avoiding humans, and they choose a mate for life. When a dingo's partner dies, it is not uncommon for the living mate to pine away.

Dingoes are also known to be great tree climbers, which astonishes me. Imagine going for a stroll and seeing a dingo up a tree.

One day, Thea and I met a tall, thin man with long black hair, his face hidden behind sunglasses. Accompanying him were three giant white standard poodles, each wearing little booties.

Both Thea and I avoid big dogs whenever possible because both Nixi and Lola are very submissive. If a large dog approaches Lola, she throws herself on her back, cringing and frantically wagging her tail, showing the other dog she is no threat. Nixi does the same.

Therefore, when both Lola, and the usually placid Nixi, began to strain on their leashes, pulling us towards the three giants, we were rather taken aback.

The three poodles were male and rather haughty, quite disdainful of Lola and Nixi who were both displaying embarrassingly skittish behaviour.

Dogs are instant ice-breakers, and we were soon chatting to the poodles' owner. The poodles were beautifully trained and perfectly behaved, unlike Lola, who was wild with excitement. They sniffed her politely, then looked down their long noses at her, maintaining their dignity, even while wearing the little booties.

The booties, their owner told us, were to protect the dogs' pads from pine needles. The whole incident was a little surreal.

But it was the birdlife at the lake that really took my breath away. Pelicans flew overhead or sailed like galleons on the water. White and grey egrets stood motionless in the water, apart from one particularly magnificent specimen that frequently flapped up to perch on a parked car's roof. Sulphur-crested cockatoos screeched overhead. Pink and grey galahs sat in rows on telegraph wires. Rainbow lorikeets swooped and shrieked through the trees.

On the several jetties that stretched out into the lake, cormorants stood with outspread wings, drying off, allowing one to approach quite close before launching themselves and flapping away. In the water, fish jumped, breaking the surface. I saw fish of all sizes, huge stingrays and little needlefish. I saw jellyfish the size of dinner plates feeding on the weed. There was so much life, both in the water and out.

"Huh," said Joe when he joined me for a walk one day. "I wish there was this much activity going on at our house."

STRAWBERRY MICE

These mice are simple to make and were a big hit at Indy's cat-themed birthday party. Each strawberry makes one mouse.

Ingredients

Strawberries

Black writing-icing

Silver or coloured cake decoration balls

Mini chocolate chips

Almond flakes

A few straps of black or raspberry liquorice

Swiss cheese for garnish, optional

Method

Remove the green stems from each strawberry. Slice a small slice from one side of each strawberry so it will sit flat on the plate.

Use the black writing-icing to stick a choc chip on the pointy end as a nose.

Use the writing-icing to create eyes and push in a silver ball while still wet.

Poke 2 slots with a sharp knife and slide in 2 almond flakes as ears per mouse.

Use a skewer to poke a hole into the berry and slide in the liquorice as a tail.

Cut the cheese into little wedges and serve with the strawberry mice.

19

WATER BALLET

I had to agree with Joe. Things were not moving very fast at all, and each tradie that arrived seemed to be odder than the last. The only thing they seemed to have in common was that they were all aged 55 or older. That didn't matter to us, but we wondered whether Fred deliberately employed older tradies, or if it was just coincidence.

Fred's attendance was erratic, but his work was of a high standard, and he remained polite and respectful. For instance, he insisted on removing his boots before entering the house. This was probably a waste of time because our old, chipped white floor tiles were destined to be replaced soon.

Fred would place his boots, side by side, at the front door. The moment he turned his back, Lola would charge in and drag one of them away. Then there would be a mighty tug of war between Fred and Lola, which was one of Lola's favourite games. Fred would pretend to be cross with her, but he was laughing at the same time, and it was hard to decide who enjoyed the game more.

Every day, Fred revealed more details about Hulk, his Great Dane puppy. Apparently, even though he already weighed 80kg (176 pounds, well over 12 stone), he was an absolute coward. He was frightened of everything, even his own reflection in a puddle. A manhole cover in the pavement sent him bolting in the opposite direction. Poor Fred, who weighed less than his dog, had to hang on for dear life. Bicycles and motorbikes terrified Hulk. The sight of a helmet strapped to a parked motorcycle by the side of the road spooked him so violently, he knocked Fred and a passerby over in his attempt to flee.

Apart from recapturing his work boots from Lola, Fred had his work cut out overseeing all the other trades. Work was being carried out on both inside and outside the house and I wanted the drive to be widened to allow two cars to park, side by side.

"Why would we want to park two cars?" asked Joe. "We only have Bruce. Surely a narrow drive is enough for us?"

"What about when the family visit? They will need a place to park."

"Yes, I suppose so."

"And if we ever bought a boat or a caravan, there'd easily be enough space to keep it."

"I can't see us ever buying a boat! Hmm. A caravan could be a possibility, though. I'd love to see more of Australia and that might be a rather fun way of doing it."

Aha! I'd succeeded in sowing a little seed in Joe's mind. I'd always loved the idea of travelling around Australia in a caravan.

"And the wide drive would be a good selling point if we ever sell. Also, it's all cracked and breaking up! While they are digging it up and re-laying it, they may as well widen it."

"Okay, okay, you've made your point. Let's go with the double drive."

At the back of the house, the area outside the sliding patio doors was a mixture of poorly-laid paving and grass. Lola easily identified where the grass was thinnest and loved to excavate, leaving a moonscape of holes. Stepping out, we had to wade through mud, particularly when it rained. This area, and that around the pool, needed to be concreted in preparation for laying pavers.

I couldn't wait for the concrete to be laid.

There are not many people I dislike on sight, but I confess that Seth, the concreter, was one of them. I guess he was in his mid-sixties, but his skin was so shrivelled and sun-dried, it was hard to tell what age he was. He was covered in tattoos. Huge likenesses of his children's faces decorated his chest. But the giant features had puckered and dropped over time, making them look like evil, deformed monsters. Every square inch of his remaining flesh was covered with vast swathes of roses and rolls of barbed-wire, phoenixes and mermaids. He never wore a shirt and constant exposure to the Australian sun had turned his skin to dirty brown parchment.

"Don't you ever protect your skin at all?" I asked him, one particularly hot day.

"Nope! And if I find any new lumps and bumps, I just cut 'em out meself, or burn 'em with me cigarette. That's all a doctor would do, anyways."

It wasn't the tattoos or how he looked that made me dislike him so much; it was his attitude. He was small and sly, and had the habit of creeping up on me unnoticed. Then he'd peer at whatever I was doing and pass an opinion on a better way to do it, whether it was painting, planting, or whatever.

"Oh, you don't want to use *that* paintbrush for corners. Get yourself one of those cut-away ones. You're wasting your time using *that*."

Another time, I was gardening.

"You're not thinking of planting *that* there, are you? You might as well throw your money in the bin. It won't like *that* spot at all," he said. Then he turned the label over and read the price on it. "What? Did you pay $25 for *that*? You were robbed. You should have asked me, I've got a mate who sells those for half that."

A mate? Personally, I found him so objectionable that I was surprised he had any mates at all.

When we discussed the job, I told him what I'd like done. His response was predictable.

"Oh, you don't want to do it like *that*."

I'm rarely rude to people, but Seth brought out the worst in me. I took a deep breath.

"I do, actually. That's exactly how I'd like it done."

"Well, don't say I haven't warned you. It's your money. If you ask me, *that* just won't work."

When I told Joe about it, he was circumspect.

"I know he's rather an irritating little man, but just ignore him. The sooner he gets on with the job, the sooner he leaves. Perhaps you should pass on any instructions through Fred. That way you won't have to deal with him directly."

Easier said than done, because often Fred wasn't around. But it was good advice, and I promised to behave myself.

Seth often worked alone, and despite his age and size, he was very strong. Even in the baking sun, he dug up yards of soil and ripped up old paving slabs as though they were made of polystyrene. Shouldering two at once, he dropped them into the waiting skip.

Sometimes he'd bring an assistant labourer, who he called Simp, which I assumed was short for Simpson. Simp was in his twenties and twice the size of his boss, Seth. He was also shockingly lazy, and I often caught him hiding down the side of the house, puffing away on a cigarette or busy on his mobile phone.

"I just twisted my ankle," he said quickly, when I caught him one day. "Giving myself a bit of a break."

Or his excuse was the heat.

"The sun's so hot, it was making me dizzy. Just cooling off for a moment."

I couldn't decide whether Simp was a delicate little blossom, or just lazy and fabricated stories to get out of doing any work. Whichever it was, I don't believe I've ever met a grown man, let alone a labourer, who was more of a whining hypochondriac.

One day somebody knocked on the back door. I opened it to see Simp the Wimp holding up a finger.

"I think the shovel is giving me a blister," he said. "Have you got any band-aids?"

I invited him in, of course, and found a plaster, which I offered him.

"Thank you," he said, "could you put it on for me, please?"

What could I say? I was forced to put the plaster on his finger while he screwed his face up in pain. Joe sniggered in the background.

"Vicky is really good at getting splinters out, too," Joe volunteered.

I could have kicked him.

But there was one time when Seth and his labourer, Simp the

Wimp, had me laughing until I cried. It could have developed into something more serious, definitely no laughing matter, but the memory makes me laugh even now, just thinking about it.

Seth had arranged for a man to dig out our driveway, using a JCB digger and loader, in preparation for the laying of concrete. I watched from inside the house as the digger gouged the ground before the shovel swung in and removed the excess soil.

All was going well. The JCB toiled away. Seth yelled instructions to the driver while Simp the Wimp leaned on his shovel, no doubt resting his exhausted body.

"More to the right," yelled Seth, waving his arms. "Yeah, that's it! Deeper than *that*, for —sake, we're goin' to be here all week otherwise!"

I was just thinking how rude Seth was, and how there was no need to curse, when something unexpected happened. A spout of water shot up into the air.

"You — idiot! Not like *that*!" Seth roared. "You've bloody dug up the mains water pipe!"

The Wimp gaped. From inside, I gaped. The driver gaped and shut off his engine.

Thinking quickly, Seth put his foot on the pipe, temporarily blocking the hole. But the water pressure was too powerful and was lifting his foot off the pipe.

"Simp, come here! I'm going to have to stand on it with both feet. I need you to steady me."

Reluctantly, Simp stepped forward, offering Seth his shoulders so the older man could balance himself while standing with both feet on the pipe.

"Dan, call the bloody council!" Seth roared at the digger driver who was still watching events with his mouth hanging open. "This is an emergency! If I take me bloody feet off, the road will flood!"

Dan jumped to it, jabbing the keys on his mobile phone.

Seth was heroically stemming the flow. However, the occasional spout of cold water still managed to escape, drenching him, and his leaning post, Simp.

"Get a b-bloody m-move on!" shouted Seth, his teeth beginning to chatter. "This water is freezing!"

"The council is asking whether the break in the pipe is within the nature strip," Dan announced.

I didn't know this before, but in Australia, a 'nature strip' is the name given to the council-owned land located between a constructed road and private property. In England, I believe the property holder owns and maintains the verge, all the way from the property down to the street. In Australia, this area is council-owned, although most residents maintain the strip themselves. I knew this because I had to get planning permission for our drive as it would pass through council property.

"Nah, the leak's on p-p-private p-p-property," said Seth. "C-c-call an emergency p-plumber."

Seth was shivering, and I took pity on him.

"I'll take him some towels," I said to Joe. I grabbed a pile and hurried outside.

"Me b-b-bloody feet have gone numb," Seth was saying. "S-S-Simp, you're going to have to t-take over."

"What?"

"Listen," said his boss, "p-put your hands on me shoulders and I'll keep m-m-mine on yours. When I say 'now', I'm going to s-s-step back. And you're going to take a step f-f-forward and take me place on the p-p-pipe."

Simp had gone pale and looked horrified.

"S-s-o on 'one', I take me f-f-foot off the hole, and 'two', you put your f-f-foot *over* the hole. Then 'one' I s-s-step off the pipe and 'two' you s-s-step on. Only after I s-s-say 'now'. G-g-geddit?" "

His bottom lip trembled. But Seth had no pity.

"G-Geddit?"

"Yes, I think so."

"It has to be quick and smooth, or we'll b-b-both get satched."

I'd never heard that word before, but I looked it up later. Apparently it's one of those new words creeping into our language.

Satched: To be soaked through or drenched to the skin.

"S-S-Simp, you r-r-eady?"

"Yep."

The two men tensed and took deep breaths, tightening their grip on each other's shoulders and concentrating on their feet.

"NOW! Back one-two, forward one-two!"

Any competition ballroom dancer would have been proud of the fancy footwork those two men executed. My face ached from trying not to laugh. I didn't dare look at Dan, the digger driver. If he was laughing, I would have lost control.

Just one small burst of water escaped, squirting Simp in the face, but the operation was mostly successful. Now Simp was balanced, feet glued to the pipe, while Seth supported him.

"Plumber will be here in twenty minutes," said Dan gruffly, his face deadpan. I was sure he found it as funny as I did.

"Towels for you," I said, handing them to Seth who slung one round his naked shoulders, mercifully covering his hideous tattoos. "I'll bring out some more."

It was an excuse to get away, really. I couldn't keep a straight face.

Every few minutes, the pair repeated their dancing duet. Back one-two, forward one-two. We watched, hidden, from inside the house and I laughed so hard my ribs became painful. Joe became breathless with laughter and had to turn away.

I was almost sorry when the emergency plumber arrived.

It wasn't our last broken pipe; we had two more. One was caused again by Seth, this time in the back garden when he severed a swimming pool pipe, and the other was in the bathroom when a tradie drilled through a cold water pipe.

But neither incident came close to being as entertaining or memorable as Simp and Seth performing the spellbinding Dance of the Shattered Water Pipe.

By the end of August, we were seeing signs of spring.

Welcome as spring always is, there is one significant downside in Australia. Magpies, a perfectly well-behaved, intelligent species during all other seasons, turn into monsters in spring. Once their eggs hatch, magpies will swoop and attack any child, adult or animal that gets too close to their nests.

I haven't been attacked yet, but I guess it's just a question of time. I've seen other people being swooped, especially when I take Lola for a run. Magpies on the ground or sitting on fences are not a threat. It's the hidden ones high in the trees who attack if anyone, however unknowingly, dares to approach their nests. I've often seen small boys innocently playing football being chased off the pitch by angry magpies.

In September, Karly was due to take her Australian Citizenship exam.

"I'm so nervous," she said. "I've been studying loads, but what if I fail?"

"You won't fail. You were always the same when you were at school. You used to work really hard and worry yourself sick that you'd fail. But you never did!"

"Yes, but this time it's different."

"You always used to say that, too! But you still got straight A's for most subjects and ended up with a degree in Law."

"I know, but…"

DEAD-EASY DAMPER

Damper is a traditional Australian soda bread, historically prepared by swagmen, drovers, stockmen and other travellers.

Ingredients

250g (9oz) self-raising flour

½ tsp salt

25g (1oz) unsalted butter, chilled and cubed

175ml (6floz) milk

Method

Mix the flour with the salt in a large bowl. Add the butter and rub it into the flour with the tips of your fingers, until it resembles fine crumbs.

Stir in the milk with a round blade knife (butter knife) to make a soft, but not sticky dough.

Turn out onto a lightly-floured work surface and shape into a soft, smooth ball.

Set the ball of dough onto a tray or baking sheet and flatten gently to make a round about 17cm (7in) across. Cut a deep cross in the dough and brush lightly with milk.

Bake at 190°C (375°F) for 30 minutes until golden.

Serve warm or at room temperature.

20

DEBBIE REYNOLDS

When the results of the Australian Citizenship exam were announced, nobody was surprised except Karly.

"What did you get?" I asked.

"Um, 100%."

"There! Didn't I tell you? I knew you had nothing to worry about!"

I was very proud of my daughter. There would be a ceremony in Sydney where Karly, and many others who had passed the exam, would be officially awarded citizenship.

A few days before the ceremony, Karly rang me.

"I'm not sure I want to be an Australian citizen, after all," she said.

"What? Why ever not?"

"Well, I was out walking LJ, and I got dive-bombed by a magpie. That wouldn't happen in England!"

We both laughed. She was right.

With the renovations going on, there were a million things to do every day. In Spain, when we renovated our cottage, Joe and I did most of the work. Joe did all the plumbing and electrical stuff, and I did the tiling and carpentry. We both painted and attempted to plaster. The results were rustic which suited the ambience, luckily.

In Australia, we were handing most of the jobs over to skilled workmen instead of tackling them ourselves. However, there were decisions to be made, items to order, and I undertook all the exterior and interior painting. Joe couldn't be exposed to dust or paint fumes and, frankly, he didn't know a travertine paver from a slab of toffee. So I made most of the design decisions.

He helped out, assuming the shopping and cooking duties, which was an enormous help. We still had no kitchen, but we had a microwave and portable gas stove, and as the weather improved, we cooked our food outside.

In addition to all these tasks, Joe forced himself to visit the gym as the doctors insisted he should. And Lola needed a good walk every day, which was my responsibility.

Lola and I visited the oval regularly and always enjoyed a chat with the other dog owners. It was rare not to see somebody we knew.

Sometimes it was Jean, with her pug, Bella. Bella and Lola liked each other, but Bella had a mischievous streak. She wasn't as fast as Lola, but she was patient. When I threw Lola's ball, Bella would rarely join Lola in running for it. Instead, she'd watch and wait for Lola's attention to wander. Sure enough, an opportunity arose, and Bella would snatch the ball and race off with it. Then she hunched over it and shredded it to pieces.

Lola would watch, heartbroken, but wasn't the type of dog to stand up for herself and fight for her possessions.

"Bella!" Jean would shout. "Drop it! Leave it! Give it back! That's Lola's ball!"

But it was usually too late. Bella, the ball thief, had struck again and another tennis ball was reduced to green strips.

It didn't matter one bit because I kept a supply of balls for Lola in the car. Lola soon learnt never to leave her ball unattended near Bella. Even when she drank water from a bowl, she would first drop the ball in the bowl and drink round it, never leaving her precious toy unguarded or open to theft.

Sometimes Frankie was there, with her two white fluffy dogs,

Sandy and Suzy. Both were rescue dogs, both lucky to end up with Frankie. Suzy was tiny and terribly timid. Not really surprising as Suzy had been rescued from a breeder who kept her permanently confined in a cage producing litter after litter of puppies.

The result of this horrific treatment was that Suzy's hips were deformed and she had no idea how to be a dog or how to interact with humans.

Frankie's heart went out to her, and she adopted her. It was a long haul, but, after expensive surgery on her hips, Suzy gradually healed, mentally and physically. She adored Frankie, who was the only person she allowed to touch her. She learned how to walk, then run and even became confident enough to yap at visitors. In future years, Suzy's health failed prematurely, but that didn't stop Frankie from taking her out. She bought a dog stroller and took her out in that instead.

We often saw an older man with two terriers whose routine was utterly cast in stone. Privately, I called him Mr Grunt. He parked in the same space, at the same time, every day. Then he opened his car door, and the terriers tumbled out. Pulling on a wide-brimmed hat, he'd walk around the three ovals, always anti-clockwise, never taking his eyes off the ground in front of him, or deviating from his daily route.

If their paths crossed, Lola and the dogs always greeted each other briefly, which was more than I ever got from their owner.

"Beautiful day!" I would sing out when we passed.

But, other than a grunt, I never received a response.

Sometimes I saw Scottish Irene, who didn't actually own a dog herself. Irene, like Frankie, still retained her strong Scottish accent, despite moving to Australia decades ago. She was excellent company, and I always enjoyed our chats as we walked.

Sometimes I wouldn't see Irene for ages, but then she would reappear. This was because Irene looked after Bella, an elderly golden retriever owned by locum doctors, who were often called away to work in other parts of Australia.

Big Bella, as we called her to differentiate her from Bella, the pug, was gentle and in her nineties, if one calculated her age in dog years. However, she and Lola liked each other and Bella became quite frisky when they met up, which was lovely to see.

Although older than me, Irene kept fit by swimming across the bay at some unearthly hour every morning. The fact that she could be sharing the water with sharks bothered her not at all. Her idea of an annual holiday was to cycle across Eastern Europe, and I sometimes met her when she was in training, cycling by the lake. She was easy to spot because her cycling helmet was adorned with a bunch of cable ties that pointed skyward.

"What are they for?" I asked, not having been in Australia very long.

"They are supposed to discourage the magpies from swooping me," she explained.

Apart from her obvious love of dogs, and the fuss she made of Lola every time we met, there was another aspect of her personality that endeared Irene to me. I love gadgets, apps, computers and labour-saving devices. Irene was the exact opposite.

"I'm a Luddite," she confessed. "I don't own a microwave. I don't have a mobile phone or a computer. Personally, I don't like technology, and it isn't something I want to learn. I won't even use the self-checkout at the supermarket; I'd rather queue and be served by a human."

As Irene and I walked around the oval, chatting, I clipped Lola's lead on her when we approached the Ten Dollar Puddle.

"I don't want her jumping in that," I said, "or we'll have to go straight to the dog wash."

"The what?" asked Irene, "you mean take her home for a bath?"

"No, the automatic dog wash. It's fantastic! Have you never used one?"

"No. How does it work?"

"Well, it's a coin-operated kiosk with a dog bath in it. The dog hops in. When it starts, there's a dial with options like 'Shampoo', 'Conditioner', 'Rinse', and then 'Dryer'. The water is warm and controlled by a soft-touch gun. Lola quite likes it. If she's rolled in something disgusting, I can get her clean and dry in ten minutes. Worth every cent."

"You're joking!" said technophobe Irene in disbelief. "I'd like to see that in action!"

So, one day, I took her with me to the dog wash. I even put her in charge of the dial.

"Oh my!" she said, thoroughly impressed.

"Conditioner, please!" I said, then, "Rinse!"

Irene dutifully turned the dial and may have been more in touch with her techy self that day than she'd ever been in her life.

On one particular day, I was in such deep conversation with Irene that I forgot about the Ten Dollar Puddle. Too late to stop her, Lola threw herself into it and happily splashed and commando-crawled through the mud.

"Lola!" I cried in horror, and she bounded over to me.

I had Lola's ball in my hand and she spotted it. She jumped up and, moments later, I, too, was plastered with mud.

Irene managed to get a photo of the subsequent disaster which you'll see if you browse the Down Under photo book on my website.

One day, I met Debbie Reynolds.

Lola and I were walking around the oval when I noticed a lady on the far side. She appeared to have a dog that was very similar to Lola.

I always keep to the outer edge of the oval, throwing the ball for Lola to fetch as I walk along. By the time I reached the lady, she had seated herself on one of the wooden benches. Her dog was panting in the shade beneath it. Lola, as she always did when she saw another dog, rushed up to say hello. The two dogs wagged tails, touched noses and decided they liked each other.

"Hello!" I said, to both the cute Lola look-alike and her owner.

"Hello," she answered, smiling.

It's strange how one can meet dozens of random people and like them all. Then, for no reason you can explain, you meet someone and connect on a different, special level. Somehow you know that you have much in common and that you will become close friends. That's how it was with Deb.

Of course, it helped that Lola and Molly were the same breed and of a similar age, so we had plenty of doggy details to discuss. Both were spoodles, both had boundless energy, and both loved running after a ball. They also both had a passion for beach walks.

"Do you go to the beach much?" asked Molly's owner.

"Not very much," I said, resisting the urge to explain about Joe and how he struggled to walk far. "I don't know the area very well yet."

"Molly and I'll show you," offered the lady, "if you'd like."

"Lola and I would love that!" I said, delighted to be asked.

We chatted on until it was time to leave.

"Let's exchange numbers then we can sort out a beach date," she said. "I'm Deb, by the way."

"And I'm Vicky," I said, fiddling with the Add Contacts app on my phone. "What's your surname?"

"Reynolds."

"Debbie Reynolds?"

"Yup. My mum had a sense of humour."

Our first doggie date was perfect, as I knew it would be. Deb and I had already risen above the polite 'just met' level, and we were now confiding in each other, sharing our hopes, fears, and future plans.

We strolled along the beach, enjoying miles of deserted white sand lapped by frothy waves. The dogs galloped together, running so closely across the sand that their footprints were entwined.

Meanwhile, Deb and I chatted. I told her that I was a writer, a fact I rarely mention to people I meet. I also told her about my family and Joe's illness.

In return, Deb told me about her family and the fact that she'd recently overcome breast cancer. She explained she was looking for a job, and how difficult life was at that time because her sister had been diagnosed with cancer.

"I drive up north at least once a week to see her and help out," she said. "I spend a fortune at Doggy Day Care centres. Molly can't handle being left alone."

It seemed both dogs shared the same traits, like separation anxiety, although poor Molly appeared to have more than her share of it.

"It's a real problem," Deb said, sighing. "I installed one of those pet minder apps on my phone to see what happened when I went out. It's like a baby alarm, but for dogs."

"Did she bark?"

"Worse than that. I tested it by driving around the corner. I knew she'd be anxious, but I expected her just to wait and watch out of the window until I came home."

"What did she do?"

"She lifted her nose to the sky, and she howled. She didn't stop until I came home. And that's what she does every time I go out."

"Oh no! Poor thing."

"I know. I can't bear to think she's so distressed, and the noise probably drives the neighbours crazy. That's why I'd rather drop her off at a Doggy Day Care centre. She's fine as long as she's with a human. She just can't bear to be alone."

"That's so sad."

"I know. But what am I going to do when I go back to work?"

I shook my head. I didn't know what to suggest. I would love to have offered to look after Molly, but I knew that was impractical. Our house was a shambles, and Joe could never have coped with another dog in the house, especially one with issues. He'd only just accepted Lola, and he had done that reluctantly.

DEBBIE REYNOLD'S MUM'S PAVLOVA

"Hellooooo! Here is Mum's pavlova recipe.

It's been our family's celebration dessert for as long as I can remember and I think of my wonderful Mum every time I make it." — Deb

Ingredients

4 egg whites, room temperature

1½ cups caster sugar

1 dessertspoon cornflour

1 teaspoon vanilla essence

1 teaspoon white vinegar

Whipped cream and fruit for decoration (any combination of strawberries, blueberries, raspberries, mango slices, pineapple pieces or for a Christmassy theme, strawberries and kiwi fruit are lovely).

Method

Preheat oven to 150°C (300°F).

Line a large oven tray (such as a biscuit/cookie tray) with baking paper.

Beat egg whites until just stiff, then add sugar a dessertspoon at a time, beating well after each addition. Beat until the sugar is dissolved so there is no "grit" in the mixture.

Add cornflour, vanilla essence, white vinegar and mix in lightly but thoroughly.

Spoon mixture onto the oven tray in a round. Turn oven down to 110°C (230°F).

Bake 1½ hours then leave to cool in oven with door open. (If you close the oven door the pavlova will be flat and sticky!)

Decorate with whipped cream and your chosen fruit, maybe with either passionfruit pulp or chocolate grated over the top.

21

A FRIGHT

Meeting up with Deb and Molly became a regular event. She showed me beaches in our area that I had never heard of, so stunning they almost hurt my eyes. Molly and Lola ran together on endless pristine stretches of sand, before stopping to dig a hole, or roll, or chase each other down to the sea's edge.

Meanwhile, Deb and I chatted non-stop. For me, it was a wonderful break from house renovations, and I'm guessing it took Deb's mind off her own problems. Her sister's health wasn't improving. Deb was dividing her time between driving up to see her and hunting for a part-time job. She needed to find work that would allow her enough free time to visit her sister. Meanwhile, Molly was a regular Doggy Day Care attendee.

"I don't know what you two find to talk about," Joe often said when Lola and I returned from a walk. I suspect he was a little jealous of our friendship, but Deb and I never ran dry.

Nor did Molly and Lola ever tire of running on the sand together.

Our tiler arrived and measured up the jobs in hand, namely the en suite bathroom and the outside patio and pool areas. We needed to choose tiles.

Reg, the tiler, was in his sixties with a rather red, flushed complexion. He had a lot of hair of which he was clearly very proud, and dyed it strawberry blond. He always sported a sharp haircut. He informed us that his son, Kurt, would sometimes be joining him on the job.

At first, I quite liked Reg, although that sentiment would gradually change to a hearty dislike for a number of reasons, later on.

"There's a tile shop up the road on the industrial estate," said Reg. "I know the owner. His name's Jonas, tell him I sent you. He'll look after you."

We headed off happily to the tile shop, intent on finding precisely the right tile for our new en suite bathroom. We found the store easily and entered.

When shopping, I prefer to browse in peace, considering each item carefully. I dislike feeling rushed into purchase decisions. Joe is the opposite; he'll grab the first thing he sees, hoping to curtail the painful shopping experience.

Unfortunately for me, we seemed to be the only customers in the shop. This meant that we had the undivided attention of the man behind the counter and it would have been rude not to speak to him.

"Hello, how are you?" I asked. "Our tiler, Reg, sent us. Are you Jonas?"

"I certainly am! What can I help you with today?"

"Oh, we're just browsing really…"

"We need to order some tiles," interrupted Joe.

Oh dear. No preamble. Joe didn't want to discuss the merits of matte versus glossy tiles, or colour schemes.

Jonas leaned forward, getting so close I could see the pores on his nose.

"And what are the tiles for exactly?" he asked.

"Oh, just the en suite bathroom," I said, stepping back pretending to examine a display of coloured grouts and trying to hide the fact I was backing away from him.

Jonas darted out from behind the counter.

"I have just the thing! Follow me," he ordered.

We trailed behind. Well, I trailed, but Joe trotted along like an enthusiastic little pony, no doubt imagining that our tile quest would be over in a trice, if we stuck close to our new friend, Jonas.

"Here we are!" said Jonas, triumphantly. "Wall tiles and matching non-slip floor tiles."

"I like these," said Joe hopefully, pointing at the nearest tile which happened to be a garish pink colour.

"Very fashionable," Jonas chimed in. "I have those in my downstairs bathroom at home."

"Gosh! What do you think, Vicky?"

"Our bathroom is a very small space," I said. "I don't think a bright pink tile would do at all."

Joe looked disappointed.

"I think I'd prefer to go for something more classic. Like a white marble, perhaps?" I said, thinking aloud.

"Good choice," said Jonas, leaning in and seriously invading my personal space. "I have those in my guest en suite at home."

"Gosh!" said Joe, perking up.

"Can you show us the different sizes, please?" I asked, and Joe sighed.

Jonas pulled out some samples, and I deliberated over the bewildering array of choices. At last, when I sensed that Joe was losing the will to live, I made my choice.

"Excellent," said Jonas, rubbing his hands together. "Exactly the sizes I have in my home."

Really?

"Is that it, then?" asked Joe, smiling again.

"Niches," said Jonas.

"Pardon?"

"I was suggesting you might consider shower niches. Everybody has them now. I have them in my home."

But of course.

"A niche is a storage space in the wall of your shower to put your soap and shampoo bottles. You can use the same tile to line it or choose something ornamental like these little mosaic tiles."

Joe groaned and I gave him one of my Looks.

"I think that's a very nice idea," I said and began to browse the ornamental tile section, eventually picking a grey and white mosaic that tied in well with the marble.

"Excellent choice," said Jonas, copying down the reference number. "I have those in my bathroom niches at home."

What a surprise...

"Good," said Joe. "That's it, then, isn't it? All done."

"Except for the grout colour. I think I'd like white for the wall tiles and black for the floor."

"Oh yes," said Jonas, adding those to the order. "Very stylish. That's what we did in our laundry at home."

Naturally.

Mission complete. The order was successfully placed, and Joe and I exited with a spring in our steps.

"Careful!" I squeaked, pointing. "Don't step in that!"

"Yuk! I nearly did! Why don't people clean up after their dogs?"

"Do you think I should go back in and tell Jonas there's a massive pile of dog poo on his path?"

"No, I wouldn't. He'll just say he's got one of those at home."

We were still laughing when we drove off.

On Monday, the 26th September, Joe complained that he wasn't feeling great and he skipped his gym session, which was unusual for him.

"We'll make an appointment at the medical centre in the morning if you don't feel any better," I suggested.

The next day, he looked a strange colour and said he had no energy. He said he felt nauseous and was more breathless than usual. In fact, he kept closing his eyes and drifting off. I know nothing about medical matters, but I thought it was a good thing he was having a snooze. Perhaps he needed the rest. Nevertheless, I made an appointment for him.

"They can see you later this morning," I told him. "Do you want me to drive you there?"

"No, I'll be fine. I'll see what Dr Botha says then I'll come straight home."

He later told me that he hardly remembered the drive to the medical centre. He parked and made his way into the building and headed for the receptionists' desk. The staff took one look at him and summoned a doctor, who shot out of his consulting room, leaving behind an astonished patient who was in mid-sentence.

Joe was helped through the waiting room and into the treatment room where the doctor immediately gave him oxygen. Slowly, Joe's breathing began to ease, and his colour improved.

"I'm sorry," said the doctor, a young visiting locum, "but I'm not happy with the state of you. You need to go to the hospital."

"Hospital?"

"Definitely. I don't mind telling you, it's a very good thing you came into the surgery when you did, because you may have died if we hadn't given you oxygen. You say you've been drifting off recently?"

"Yes. I just seem to doze off…"

"You were losing consciousness. When you get to the hospital, they'll give you proper tests."

"Can I call my wife?"

"Of course. Now, how did you get here?"

"I drove."

"You are kidding! I'm amazed you got here in one piece."

While Joe was away, I had decided to take the opportunity to do some small painting jobs. I had barely prepared an area and picked up a brush when the phone rang.

"Joe? Are you okay?"

"Well, no. I don't think I am."

"What?"

"I'm in the medical centre. The doctor here seems to think I'm not at all well, and I need to go straight to the hospital."

"What?" My paintbrush dropped to the ground.

"They're giving me oxygen. I'm not allowed to drive, of course, and we're waiting for an ambulance. Do you think you could grab a few wash-things for me? Toothbrush, a change of underwear, that sort of thing?"

"Right! Of course! I'm on my way!" I said, utterly horrified by the news, but glad to be given an important job to do.

I rushed around collecting bits and pieces and throwing them into his holdall. Lola watched me with interest, but I was too busy to give her any attention. I couldn't pack any pyjamas because Joe didn't possess any. Until I could buy him some, I hoped the hospital might provide something temporary.

There were no workmen at our house that day, but, by now, Lola was accustomed to being left alone for a few hours.

I was ready. I reached for the car keys, but they weren't on their usual hook. And then I remembered. Joe had driven Bruce to the medical centre.

What to do?

"I'll be home soon," I said to Lola, and flew out of the door.

Luckily, my friend and neighbour, Thea, was at home. I knew she didn't drive, but her husband, Reinhard, did.

I gabbled my story and Reinhard didn't hesitate.

"Jump in," he said, and very kindly drove me to the medical centre.

"I'll bake a cake for Joe when he comes home," promised Thea as we left.

It was a shock to see Joe wearing a nasal cannula (a word I'd never heard before) attached to an oxygen tank. He smiled when he saw me, and I sat down beside him. He reached for my hand.

"It's okay," he said, "I'm in the best place here in the medical centre. And when I get to the hospital, they'll be able to work out what's going wrong."

A smiling nurse clipped an oximeter onto one of his fingertips and studied it.

"That's a better number, Mr Twead," she said. "You had us all worried earlier."

We sat quietly for a little while until the ambulance arrived. The nurses brought the two female paramedics up to speed.

"May I go with him in the ambulance?" I asked.

"You can if you like," said the paramedic. "Your husband may have to wait in Emergency for a while, and then I imagine they might want to keep him in, which means he'll need to be allocated a bed. It's quite often a lengthy process."

"No, I think you should go home," said Joe. "I'll be fine now. There's so much to do at home, so it's silly wasting time sitting around in waiting rooms. Anyway, if you come with me in the ambulance, you'll be stranded without a car. And you can't leave Lola alone for too long."

"Okay. I'll see to Lola and buy you some pyjamas," I said. "I don't want you making a spectacle of yourself in front of all those nurses. Keep in touch, and I'll be right over as soon as you phone me. I think the hospital is only forty minutes away."

Hola tía Vicky y tío Joe,

It is I Catalina your penpall again. I hop you are well again. My family is entirely wells but i am much unhappy. My grandmother is wells.

Every person in El Hoyo is occupied because we must take the grapes for the wine. My neighbour Paco he say it is best year for his wine but he always say it is best year for his wine.

Next month I am dancing flamenco with my sister at the *fiesta*.

Valentina say she will holidays in London after the *fiesta* and if Geronimo not accompany then she not have an weeding. I am much unhappy. i want dance flamenco at the weeding.

Felicitations, Catalina xx

I bought a couple of pairs of pyjamas and a bathrobe and slippers and waited for Joe's phone call. The day wore on but I heard nothing from him.

At last, my phone rang.

TROUT WITH LEMON PARSLEY BUTTER

There is no need to bother to de-scale fish when cooked this way because the skin will peel away easily with the aluminium foil.

Serves 2

Ingredients

2 trout

60g (2oz) butter

1 teaspoon grated lemon rind

1 small clove garlic

1 tablespoon chopped parsley

1 tablespoon lemon juice

Salt and pepper

Method

Wash and dry the trout.

Fold a large piece of aluminium foil in half for extra strength. Lay the fish on the foil so it is completely enclosed, wrapping tightly.

Bake on a tray in a moderately hot oven for 20 minutes. The fish can also be cooked on a barbecue, turning the parcel regularly.

Blend softened butter with lemon rind, crushed garlic, parsley and lemon juice. season with salt and pepper and mix well.

Serve fish topped with the lemon butter.

22

BREATHLESS

"Joe? How are you?"

"Hello sweetheart, I'm not bad at all, but they want to keep me in for a day or so for observation."

"Are you in a general ward now?"

"Yes, they've put me in the respiratory ward."

"Are you okay? Are you still on oxygen?"

"No, I seem to be coping by myself at the moment. I'm a bit breathless, but not too bad."

"I bought some pyjamas. Shall I come over now?"

"No, Vicky, don't worry about it tonight. I've been lent some pyjamas for the time being, so I can manage. I'm exhausted, so I think I'll just go to sleep now. Anyway, I know you can't see a thing when you drive at night. It's getting dark, so you'd better not drive."

Joe was right. I suffer from night blindness, and it would have been foolish to drive in the dark to an address I'd never been to before.

"Well, if you're sure. I'll come tomorrow morning."

"Yes, that'll be best. The doctors will come on their rounds tomorrow, and perhaps they can shed some light on what happened to me. Have you got a busy day planned tomorrow?"

"Oh, nothing to worry about. I'll let you sleep and we can talk properly tomorrow. Goodnight."

It was a bit of a white lie. I was expecting the wardrobe fitter, the pool man, and the plumber. I asked Fred to handle it, and, thankfully, he agreed. He also kindly agreed to make sure Lola was okay, which was a relief. I didn't want her 'helping' the wardrobe fitter, pool man or plumber. Fred was accustomed to her foibles.

I phoned the family to keep them up to date. Then I sorted myself and Lola out and dropped into bed.

The weather was beautiful the next day as I drove to the hospital. I'd already given Lola a run on the oval, and I knew Fred could cope with the day's agenda. I hoped Joe was feeling better this morning.

I found him sitting up in bed, looking quite cheery. He was definitely a better colour than he had been the day before.

We chatted, and he told me a little about the other patients in his ward. Some were extremely ill and lay still; I never even saw their faces. Others were more lively, like the flatulent old gentleman called Brian, in the opposite bed, who kept letting off a stream of muffled explosions under his bedclothes.

"So what did the doctor say?" I asked. "Has he shed any light on what happened?"

"No, not at all. Not yet. They want me to stay a little longer, but I think I may be allowed home soon."

"Oh, that's good news. At least the pyjamas I brought you won't be wasted."

Joe grinned. He knew I was joking.

Just then, a little girl ran into the ward, blonde hair and toy stethoscope swinging as she turned her head looking for someone.

"Grumps!" she called. "Where are you?"

"She looks just like Indy!" said Joe, astonished.

"It is Indy!"

Indy caught sight of us and cantered over.

"Grumps! I got my stethes-poke and my doctor bag. I'll make you all better!"

Karly and Cam, carrying baby Winter, were hot on her heels and hugs were exchanged all round.

"I can't believe you're all here," said Joe. "You shouldn't have taken the trouble to drive all the way from Sydney! I'm much better; I think I'll be going home soon."

"Oh, we had to come. Indy needed to try out her new doctor's kit."

It was a lovely visit. Indy climbed up on the bed and subjected Joe to a series of extensive medical tests, including having his ears examined and giving him several injections. We laughed and joked and generally shattered the peace in the ward.

At one point, Brian, in the bed opposite, let off a particularly violent explosion of wind. It sounded like a gunshot. We all politely ignored it, looking away avoiding any eye contact with each other.

"Pop goes the weasel," Joe said quietly, his face deadpan, and we all lost it.

Karly and I laughed so much our sides ached. It was probably just a reaction to the potentially serious situation, but it did us all a lot of good.

I stayed for another hour or so after the family left. When I finally left, Joe was cheerful and waved me goodbye.

The next day was packed with events, and I scarcely had time to catch my breath. Fred had texted me to say that he couldn't come to work because he needed to take his elderly mother to a hospital appointment. The bathroom tiles were scheduled to be delivered, and the man was arriving to measure up for the shower screen and a glass fence for the pool. Thea had kindly offered to take Lola for a while, but I didn't want Lola to outstay her welcome. Consequently, I couldn't stay long during my visit to the hospital.

"It's okay," said Joe, "I'm absolutely sure they'll discharge me tomorrow. I'm feeling so much better, and they all seem pleased with my progress. Off you go, and pat Lola for me. And do thank Thea."

I shot off and arrived home just in time to receive and sign for the tiles. It was going to be a frantic day.

I had no idea that the next day would turn into an utter nightmare.

I arrived at the hospital early the next morning looking forward to bringing Joe home.

As I passed the nurses' station, the sister in charge looked up, then dropped the papers she was holding on the desk.

"Mrs Twead?" she asked, darting out.

"Yes," I smiled. "Is my husband being discharged today? I've brought some more clothes and shoes."

"Er, I was just about to call you, Mrs Twead. Would you mind coming into the Relatives' Room for a moment, then I can explain everything."

"Shall I drop this off with him first?" I asked, holding up the bag containing Joe's clothes.

"No, bring it with you."

I stared at her dumbly.

Relatives' Room?

I've watched enough TV medical dramas to know that if a doctor or nurse calls you into the Relatives' Room, things were serious. They were not about to hand out good news.

My legs began to shake. My mouth went dry. She was already heading off, so I followed like a lamb to slaughter. A thousand questions jumped into my head, but I couldn't form any words.

The little room had some comfy chairs, a low coffee table and a couch. The window looked down onto a car park. I felt detached, as though I was floating above.

I saw somebody helping a young man into a wheelchair. Some distance away, a little family hurried towards the hospital entrance. The father held the little girl's hand, and she clutched the string of a pink helium balloon which bobbed as she walked.

Little dramas were taking place wherever I looked. It dawned on me that Joe, the sister, and I, were about to star in one of them.

"I'm afraid your husband has literally just been moved, no more than half an hour ago. He isn't in this ward anymore," she said.

"Where is he? Why has he been moved?"

"The doctor is on his way, he'll be able to explain everything. Would you like a cup of tea or coffee?"

"No, thank you. Can you tell me…"

"Doctor will be along in a minute," she said with a smile, as though talking to a child. But I could see pity in her eyes.

"But…"

Then she uttered that ghastly phrase guaranteed to make one frantic with worry.

"Try not to worry."

The doctor was a tall, pleasant-faced, white-haired man, although I imagine he was no more than fifty. He wore his shirt sleeves rolled up and his handshake was firm.

"I'm Gordon," he said, "the doctor in charge of the ICU."

Did I mishear? Did he say ICU? Doesn't that mean Intensive Care Unit?

I opened my mouth to speak, but absolutely nothing came out. The sister excused herself and backed out of the door.

It's strange how trivial, irrelevant, unbidden thoughts crowd into one's mind at the most stressful moments in our lives. Perhaps it's a kind of safety valve. I remember thinking, *That's a nice necktie. Goes well with the shirt. I wonder if his wife chose it for him?*

"Mrs Twead."

"Vicky, call me Vicky."

"Vicky, let me try to explain what's happened," said Gordon, gently.

Gordon? Whoever addresses one of the most prominent doctors in the hospital by his first name? We wouldn't dream of doing that in England…

I tried to concentrate on Gordon's words.

"Your husband ate well last evening then had a good night. However, something happened this morning. He couldn't breathe, and he lost consciousness."

I gasped.

"Normally, we use a type of non-invasive ventilator in cases like this. We call them BiPAPs. This BiPAP machine is designed to increase the pressure when you inhale. To prevent the airways in the nose and throat from closing. Have you heard of sleep apnea and a CPAP machine?"

"Yes."

"Well, it's similar to that except it provides help with both inhalation and exhalation. The patient wears a mask, and the machine pushes air into his airways. It helps open the lungs with air pressure."

I nodded.

"So we set up a BiPAP which usually helps immediately. However, in Joe's case, he didn't respond. We had to act quickly."

I could hear the muffled noises of a hospital day beyond the closed door in the corridor. Somebody was laughing. Outside, a flock of white cockatoos screeched as they swooped over the hospital car park.

"So he's been taken to the Intensive Care Unit?"

"Yes. We thought it best to put your husband into an induced coma. We are getting him settled now. We have set him up on a ventilator that will breathe for him until we know what's happening."

"A ventilator? A life-support machine?"

"Yes..."

"He can't breathe for himself at all?"

"No, not at the moment, but we're hoping this is a temporary situation."

"Does he know what's happening? Is he in any pain?"

"No, he's asleep. He won't have any pain, and he wouldn't have been aware of the intubation."

"Intubation?"

"That's what we call the insertion of a tube into a patient's body, especially that of an artificial ventilation tube into the trachea. He would have known nothing about it."

"I don't understand. What would have caused all this so suddenly? He seemed so much better. We thought he was coming home today."

"We'll be running tests. People with COPD are very susceptible to viruses. It could be a virus. We'll know more later."

A hundred other questions that I could have asked, popped into my mind later, but for now, I was numb.

"Can I see him?" I managed to say.

"I suggest you go home," Gordon said gently. "There's nothing more you can do here today. He's in the best hands. You can phone the ICU later on, and the staff will be able to let you know how he's doing."

I drove home in a daze, my hands gripping the steering-wheel far too tightly. Somehow, I greeted Fred and the other tradies and served them a tray of tea and biscuits. I felt like a zombie. I didn't tell them what was happening in the hospital. Then I went into our bedroom with Lola and locked the door.

I couldn't function properly. All I could think of was Joe on a life support machine. Joe with a tube down his throat.

I leaned my back against the wall. Lola, sensing something wasn't right, watched me with her head on one side. Her tail waved slowly, uncertainly. I slid down the wall, put my arms around her, buried my face in her soft coat, and wept.

For once, Lola didn't bounce or wriggle. She didn't tug my clothes or roll on her back. Instead, she sat quite still, occasionally licking my hand, allowing me to soak her with my tears.

I phoned the hospital later and was put through to the ICU. The nurse in charge informed me that there was no discernible change.

"We do have the results of the tests, though," she said. "Your husband definitely contracted a virus, and that's what caused this to happen. At least we have that information now, and can treat the virus accordingly."

"If I come over, will I be allowed to see him? Will he know I'm there?"

"Yes, of course you can come if you like, but I'm afraid he won't know you are there. He's still in an induced coma to give his body a rest. He's settled now. He'll have a nurse at his bedside the whole time, day and night. You may decide to wait and visit him tomorrow."

"I see."

"Do phone us in the morning. If you come in then, you'll be able to have a chat with the doctor."

I had an early night, but sleep eluded me for a long time. Finally, I drifted off, but the scenes my mind created were far from restful.

I entered a world where the Spanish village *fiesta* was in full swing. The stage was set up in the square, just as it always was every year when we lived there. Coloured lights hung in the trees, but they were swinging dangerously low, forcing villagers to duck out of their reach or be struck on the head. The twins danced flamenco, but the music was all wrong. The band was playing, and the dancing villagers gyrated around something in the middle of the stage. I saw Paco and Carmen, then caught a glimpse of Geronimo and Valentina. I think I saw Lola Ufarte but Father Samuel was not among the throng of dancers. Everybody looked solemn. And then, as the dancers parted momentarily, I saw what everybody was ignoring, but dancing around.

It was Joe, laid out on a hospital bed.

SPINACH AND FETA QUICHE

A lovely vegetarian quiche, hot or cold. If you prefer, use half a pack of frozen spinach, defrosted and drained of water.

Ingredients

3 eggs

100g (3½oz) feta cheese, crumbled

125g (4½oz) spinach

½ cup self-raising flour

1½ cups skim milk

½ cup cheese, grated

1 onion thinly sliced

200g (7oz) mushrooms

Method

Sauté onion and mushrooms until just cooked.

Mix flour, eggs, cheese and milk together in a bowl.

Add the feta to the spinach and combine with the onion and egg mixtures.

Spray a quiche dish with non-stick spray.

Pour mixture into dish and bake at 180°C (350°F) for 30-35 minutes.

23

BED NUMBER FIVE

As soon as I had shaken off the disturbing dream, I phoned the hospital and was put through to the ICU.

"Your husband has had a reasonable night," said the nurse. "There hasn't been much change. We're trying to give him the lowest dose of sedation possible, and he's doing okay. If you are planning to come in today, I know the doctor would like to ask you a few questions."

"Yes, of course, I'll be in as soon as I can."

I was so lucky to have such fantastic neighbours. Thea had already helped me out, and that morning, when I gave Lola a quick run on the oval, I met up with Emma and her cocker spaniel, Baxter. I told her what was going on.

"Leave Lola with me," she said, "I'm not going into work today so she can hang out with Baxter. I'll have her any time. And if you're stuck when I'm at work, I'll just pick her up from your house when I get back."

I could have hugged her. I'd been worried because I couldn't always expect Fred to look after Lola when I was away. Neither could I trust the workmen to remember to keep the garden gate and front door closed all the time. If either one was left open, Lola would be out faster than a rat up a drainpipe, searching for me. Thea had already been so kind. I couldn't keep asking her to look after a boisterous puppy. Emma's offer was heaven sent.

I headed for the hospital. Now that Lola was sorted, and I'd left keys and instructions for Fred, I could focus on the day ahead.

And I was absolutely terrified.

I'd never entered an intensive care unit before. Apart from scenes in television dramas, I'd never seen a patient on a life support machine. And now I had to steel myself to see Joe hooked up on one.

Could I cope? Could I bear to see Joe like that? What if I broke down?

Parking in the multi-storey car park wasn't easy, and I wasted twenty minutes slowly driving from floor to floor, waiting for somebody to leave. All the time, my heart was hammering in my chest.

I was directed to the ICU, and my feet felt like lumps of lead as I made my way along the corridor until it forked.

No Entry - Staff Only, ordered one sign. *Visitors - This Way*, pointed the other.

I pushed the door open and found myself in a gloomy, windowless waiting room, with a wall-hung television screen flickering away to nobody. A middle-aged lady seemed to be demonstrating some kind of cooking device, but the volume was off, so she was wasting her time here.

I caught sight of a telephone with a notice beside it, inviting visitors to call the ward, after which someone would arrive to escort me in. I dialled the number.

"I've come to see Joe Twead," I said. I was struggling to keep the tremble out of my voice.

"And you are?"

"Vicky. His wife."

"Ah, yes. Bed number five. I have a note in Joe's file to say that the doctor would like a word with you. Could you please wait, and I'll let her know you're here."

I didn't have to wait long. A door I hadn't noticed before swung open to admit a young lady doctor into the waiting room.

"Mrs Twead? May I call you Vicky? I'm Cherry, the doctor in charge today. Thank you for coming in."

The door behind me opened, and an elderly couple entered, pain etched on their faces. Above their heads, the silent chef lady was still demonstrating her cookware.

Cherry put her hand on my arm.

"Would you mind following me to the Relatives' Room?" she asked. "We won't be disturbed there."

My heart lurched. Not again! *Please, not the Relatives' Room!* There must be more bad news because that's the place where distressing news is delivered.

She kept her hand on my arm, and I allowed myself to be led away. The Relatives' Room was very similar to the one off the respiratory ward. The walls were painted a soothing soft green and comfy chairs were placed around a low coffee table. There was no window.

"I know how hard this is for you," said Cherry, looking into my face. "Your husband is quite stable. Now that we know what we're dealing with, we can make headway. It's best that Joe remains sedated for the moment. The machine will breathe for him, which will put much less strain on his heart. Before we go on, do you have any questions?"

I nodded. "Can you tell me more about the virus?"

"Well, actually, we discovered that he contracted *two* viruses. Neither is very serious; in fact, one is similar to babies' croup. That particular virus leads to the swelling of the larynx and windpipe. Although they are fairly minor viruses, it's very serious for him as his lung disease is quite advanced."

"I wonder where he could have caught them?"

"Oh, it could be anywhere. Any public places, like supermarkets. Quite often these sort of viruses are picked up in gyms or swimming pools. Coughs and sneezes spread them."

Perhaps I am being unfair, but I've always blamed Joe's gym. It never seemed very clean to me, and the indoor pool water was always exceptionally warm.

"How will you know when he's able to breathe by himself again?"

"We'll be monitoring him very closely. We'll be checking his heart, and we'll be waiting for these viruses to abate. Which brings me to a couple of questions."

"Yes?"

"Do we have your permission to include Joe in a clinical trial? There are two sedation drugs we'd like to use. There's no risk involved, but the data would be very useful for our research."

I didn't have to think very hard about that one. Joe has donated gallons of blood in his time, earning himself all sorts of awards. He's always declared that, after death, he'd like to gift his entire body to medical research, if it was useful, and medical science were welcome to any organs they fancied. I was positive he'd be delighted to be part of a clinical trial.

"Yes, that's fine."

"Thank you so much. I'll get the relevant papers prepared for you to sign. There's just one more thing I need to discuss with you before I take you to him."

I could feel my hands still shaking, but the chat with the doctor had calmed me. She hadn't delivered any additional terrible news. Was she going to do that now?

And then it came. Cherry's brown eyes watched me as she spoke.

"Vicky, in the course of our examinations, we discovered a mass in Joe's pituitary gland. Was he aware of it before?"

"What? A mass? Do you mean a tumour?"

"Yes, but it's not necessarily anything sinister or aggressive."

"No! We knew nothing about any tumour! Are you saying he has cancer?"

"No, in over 99% of patients, this is not a cancer; it is benign. Actually, it's surprisingly common."

Poor Joe. He already had high blood pressure, COPD, and prostate cancer to deal with, and now life had thrown him another curveball. A tumour, for goodness sake.

"Where and what is the pituitary gland, exactly?"

"The pituitary gland is a tiny organ," explained Cherry, "no bigger than a pea. It's found at the base of the brain. It makes or stores many different hormones."

"So, what happens now?"

"I'm going to request an MRI for him. Although the tumour is more than likely harmless, we need an image of it now, so we can compare it with future images and check that it's not growing."

"And if it *is* growing?"

"Well, although a tumour may be benign, it can cause problems if it grows. It can cause loss of vision, for instance, or headaches."

"What sort of treatmen…" I began, but I never finished the sentence because I was interrupted by an urgent-sounding rap on the door.

A nurse stuck her head around the door.

"Cherry, could you please attend to bed number five as soon as you can? We have a little problem."

Cherry jumped up. "Vicky, would you mind waiting? I'll just go and see what's needed and then I'll be right back."

I leant back in the armchair and replayed our conversation in my head. All in all, it didn't sound *too* negative, I told myself. If all went according to plan, the viruses would be dealt with; Joe would emerge from the coma and get his strength back. The tumour was a shock, but Cherry didn't seem unduly worried. Or was she just pacifying me?

I'm ashamed to admit that my next worry was utterly selfish. I was terrified of being taken to Joe's bedside and not being able to handle what I would see. I never watch medical procedures on television, and I turn away when receiving routine injections. How would I cope with seeing Joe on a life-support machine? I closed my eyes and took a deep breath. In a minute, I would be tested.

Suddenly, a shocking thought occurred to me. Had the nurse just said *bed number five*? Wasn't that the bed number the other nurse on the phone had said that Joe was occupying?

If I was right, something was happening to Joe in the ICU.

Right now. This minute.

With that realisation, my fears flew away. Now I was desperate to see Joe, life-support machine or not. I sprang up and began pacing back and forth, back and forth, waiting for Cherry to return.

At last, the door opened, and Cherry walked in.

"Everything's fine," she said, reading my expression. "We've been keeping Joe on the lowest possible dose of sedatives, and perhaps it was too low. He suddenly became very agitated and was attempting to pull out the ventilation tube from his trachea."

I stared at her, shocked.

"So we had to increase the dose, I'm afraid. Don't worry, this often happens. Would you like to see him now?"

I nodded.

I stared straight ahead, refusing to glance at the other beds we passed. Each bed was occupied, I knew, and a nurse was attending every patient.

Cherry pulled back the cubicle curtain surrounding bed number five, to reveal Joe. A nurse stepped forward.

"I'm Katrina," she said. "Are you okay?"

I knew all the colour had drained from my face, but I *was* okay. Just.

I had never seen so much medical equipment in all my life. Monitors flashed coloured numbers and graphs. Tubes, drips, cables, plugs, machines on wheels, lights on stands, shelves laden with more equipment. Strange beeps and hums kept up a constant background noise.

And in the middle of it all was Joe.

Lifeless, laid out like a shop display dummy, he was mostly covered by a white sheet. Both his arms were lying outside the sheet, but I couldn't see much of them because they were wrapped in bandages from which lines and tubes led to machines and drips.

I forced myself to look at his head. Electrodes were taped to his skull and forehead. Worst of all, his mouth was open and his dry lips were parted to allow entry for a fat plastic tube.

"Here," said Katrina, "use this gel to sterilise your hands. He's doing fine, don't worry."

Cherry smiled reassuringly. "Will you be alright now?" she asked. "Stay as long as you like, and you can touch him. I must go now, but remember, you can phone any time of day or night."

I thanked her, and she left.

Katrina had pulled up a chair for me. I sat down and slowly reached out for Joe's hand. It was reassuringly warm in mine. I wasn't frightened any more.

"Hello, Joe," I said quietly. "I'm here."

Katrina smiled approvingly.

"Does he know anything of what's going on?" I asked.

"No, I doubt it. He was having a temper tantrum earlier. He was determined to pull out that tube so he's quite heavily sedated for now."

Temper tantrum? Yup, that would be Joe.

I sat there for a long time, holding his hand. Katrina busied herself with charts and dials, frequently checking her watch and recording readouts. The ward was calm. Every cubicle held a human in crisis, but there was very little noise apart from footsteps and machines.

There was nothing I could do except sit with him. As time ticked away, I sat there, watching him, stroking his fingers.

GERMAN BUTTER CAKE (BUTTERKUCHEN)

Instead of making a batch of cinnamon rolls, try this German sheet cake with crunchy sugar, cinnamon, and butter topping. It freezes well and is perfect with a cup of coffee.

From thespruceeats.com

Ingredients

The Sponge

4½ cups plain (all-purpose) flour, divided

2½ teaspoons dry yeast

1 cup lukewarm milk

Pinch of sugar

The Yeast Cake

½ teaspoon salt

1 large room-temperature egg

225g (8oz) room-temperature butter, divided

1 ¼ cups sugar, divided

2 teaspoons cinnamon

Method

The Sponge

Place 4 cups of flour in a large mixing bowl or stand mixer and make a hollow in it with the back of a spoon.

Sprinkle dry yeast in the hollow and fill with the lukewarm milk. Add a pinch of sugar and mix a little to incorporate some of the flour.

Let the sponge sit in a warm place for 15 minutes.

The Cake Batter

After the yeast is activated and showing strong growth, add the salt, egg, 7 tablespoons of the softened butter and ¾cup of the sugar to the yeast mixture.

Mix until the dough is smooth and forms a ball. Add up to ½ cup additional flour if necessary. Form dough into a ball, place in a greased bowl, turning the dough once and cover. Let rise 15 to 30 minutes.

Roll the dough out to 1cm (½ inch) thickness on a lightly floured board and transfer to a baking sheet with edges, like a jellyroll pan. (Approx. 30 x 25cm or 10 x 15 inches.) Let it rest again for 15 minutes while heating oven to 190°C (375°F).

Dimple the top of the dough all over, using your fingers or the back of a wooden spoon.

Mix remaining ½ cup of sugar and 2 teaspoons of cinnamon together and sprinkle evenly over dough. Cut remaining 9 tablespoons of butter into small pieces and spread it evenly over the dough.

Bake the Cake

Bake for 25 minutes, or until cake is done and the sugar/cinnamon mixture has melted together and caramelised a little.

Optional: Mix ¼ cup of sugar with enough water (¼ to ½ cup) to dissolve the sugar and brush this sugar water on the hot cake right after you take it out of the oven.

This cake freezes well. After defrosting, crisp it up for a few minutes in a 175°C (350°F) oven. Top this *butterkuchen* with sliced, blanched (or toasted) almonds.

24

ROLLERCOASTER

During those early days of October, I felt as though I needed to split myself into two, with separate heads. I had a 'House' head and a 'Hospital' head. Both required my undivided attention, and every night I went to bed drained and exhausted.

Only when I walked Lola could I relax to some degree. If we could arrange it, Deb and I would walk the full length of the beach, stopping for coffee at a cafe before walking back. Lola and Molly sniffed at seaweed and ran together along the wet sand, frothy waves erasing their paw prints.

We were in the middle of spring, and the weather was already balmy. Thea wore her white hat, and the magpies' babies had grown into awkward teenagers. They were easy to spot, hopping after their parents, because their plumage was grey and black. As they grew older, the grey feathers would turn white.

Australian magpie youngsters are hilarious to watch. The ones I observed that spring followed their parents in flight, their flying skills already impressive. However, they still had a lot to learn when it came to landing.

Instead of slowing down before reaching their target, they would come in much too fast, consequently crashing into the tree. With a loud shriek and a flurry of feathers, they scrabbled to grab a branch with their claws. Often they spun upside down, hanging like a circus acrobat, before righting themselves with the help of their beaks. There they would stand, swaying and hanging on for dear life. Mum or Dad could be seen on a branch nearby, rolling their eyes in exasperation as their offspring steadied themselves. Then Mum and Dad would swoop away, and the kids were forced to relaunch or be left behind. With an indignant squawk, they would take off only to repeat the performance and crash-land into yet another tree.

As strange as it sounds, magpie parents actually play with their youngsters. Joe and I have seen teenage magpies lying on their backs while their parents appear to be tickling their tummies. We've seen siblings on their backs, side by side, play-fighting like puppies. They are remarkable birds, extremely intelligent with long memories.

"Pooh! Magpies never bother me," Thea told me. "When I walk with Nixi, I throw some dog treats to them. When spring comes, magpies never swoop me. I think they know my hat."

Then there are the plovers. These large, common and conspicuous creatures are arguably some of the most bad-tempered birds in Australia. Magpies only lose their patience during their breeding season, but plovers seem to spend their whole life in a rage. Most streets and ovals in our area have pairs of patrolling plovers, and if anybody gets too close, they scream abuse before flying away in a shrieking fury.

In my opinion, the plover, or masked lapwing, isn't a pretty bird. It has a white stomach and brown back, a dangly yellow wattle, black scalp and long skinny legs. It never tolerates interference, but during the breeding season, it becomes a menace. Plovers lay their eggs on almost any stretch of open ground, including front gardens, school ovals, and even supermarket carparks. Woe betide any unsuspecting human or creature that dares approach. Hurling abuse, the plover parents will swoop and attack.

One spring, poor Jean, one of my dog-walking pals, was unable to leave her house to walk Bella. Plovers had made a nest and laid eggs in her front garden. Every time Jean and Bella attempted to leave the house, they were attacked.

However over-zealous the plover parents might be, it is impossible not to love plover chicks. The babies can leave the nest and feed themselves a few hours after hatching and are extremely cute. Like round, fluffy pom-poms on knitting-needle legs, they scuttle after their parents who zealously guard them.

Such scenes warmed my heart during those dark, dark days when Joe fought for his life in hospital, and our home was a demolition site.

The first thing I did when I awoke every morning was phone the hospital, which, by now, was on speed-dial. I was usually put through to the nurse currently in charge of Joe's care. It was never the same person.

On 2nd October, I phoned the hospital and was told Joe had enjoyed a restful night. I arrived, expecting to sit quietly at his bedside, watching the machines breathe for him, as I always did.

"Hello, I'm Nita," said his nurse. She glanced at her notes. "You must be Vicky?"

"Yes, that's right."

"Good, I'm sure he'll be pleased you are here."

"Really? Is he awake?"

I looked at Joe, and he seemed the same. He lay motionless, eyes closed, the tube still inserted into his mouth, breathing for him. The machines hummed and beeped. Numbers flickered.

"Well, he's still sedated, but he definitely knows what's going on around him. You'll see."

I sat down quickly and reached for his hand, taking care not to dislodge the confusion of plastic lines taped to it.

"Speak to him," said Nita.

"Joe. Joe, can you hear me?"

Nothing.

"Joe? It's me."

Slowly, slowly, Joe's heavy eyelids lifted. His eyes looked straight ahead.

"I'm here," I said, leaning over and putting my face into his line of vision.

There was immediate and utter recognition.

A little moan came from somewhere, and a single tear ran out of the corner of his eye.

"There! You see!" said Nita triumphantly.

I could hardly believe it. My heart leapt in my chest, and I grinned from ear to ear. I could tell he was trying to smile, but the tube and his poor, dry, cracked lips wouldn't allow him. But the look in his eyes spoke volumes.

"You're back!" I said, and felt a little pressure on my hand as Joe tried to communicate.

He slowly withdrew his hand from mine and lifted it to stroke my face with his fingertips. He didn't need words.

I sat with him for most of the day. He was weak, and couldn't talk because of the ventilator. I didn't mind, I would talk for both of us.

"I expect you want to know how Lollipop is?"

Tiny nod of the head.

"Well, she's in Germany again today."

Small questioning frown.

"Thea is looking after her, bless her. Thea talks to her in German all the time, so I think we're going to have a bilingual dog by the time you come out of the hospital."

Tiny twitch of the lips.

"Thea is going to make you one of those delicious German lemon and almond cakes when you come home. Oh, and Reinhard has a book he thinks you'll like. It's all about the First Fleet, you know, the eleven ships carrying convicts from Portsmouth to settle in Australia in 1787."

I prattled on and on. I told him about Emma's kindness and how her dog, Baxter, treated Lola like an annoying little sister. I told him about the antics of the magpies and about the baby plovers on the oval.

I described how things were progressing at home.

"Reg, the tiler, is coming along nicely with the en suite tiling. Should be finished soon and then the plumber can come in and fit the sink and toilet. And then Reg can start laying the travertine pavers outside. I've met his son, Kurt, by the way."

A minuscule questioning flick of the eyebrows.

"Kurt? He's really just a younger version of his dad. Red-faced, a bit belligerent. He doesn't make eye contact when you speak to him."

I didn't tell Joe that Fred had voiced his misgivings about the father and son duo. That was an issue Fred and I needed to tackle and wasn't Joe's worry.

I drove home in high spirits and sat down to write an email to our friends and family in the UK, who were justifiably anxious for news.

At ten o'clock, I phoned the hospital to be reassured that Joe was still doing well.

"It won't be long before we remove the tube and let him try to breathe by himself," the nurse informed me.

That was very good news.

The next day, Monday 3rd October, was a public holiday and I had no tradesmen in the house to worry about. Looking at my phone, I saw I'd received a text from Fred that I hadn't noticed before.

I'm thinking about you tonite babe

I snorted. It didn't bother me because I was one hundred per cent certain that Fred had sent it to me in error, but I wondered who his 'babe' was. It reminded me I needed to discuss the tilers with him, but that could wait.

I phoned the hospital and was told that Joe had enjoyed a good night. A plan was in place to reduce his sedation still further, then take him off the ventilator later in the morning. Consequently, I waited until later before driving over to see him. I remember singing happily along with Sia as the radio played *Cheap Thrills*.

In the ICU, I was surprised to be met by the senior doctor.

"Hello, Vicky, I hoped I'd see you," said Gordon. "Not great news, I'm afraid."

"Oh no!"

"We reduced the sedation level in order to remove the tube, but Joe suffered a panic attack. His blood pressure sky-rocketed and was putting a dangerous strain on his heart. I'm afraid we had to abandon the attempt and increase the sedation again. So he's still on the ventilator."

"On no!"

"I'm so sorry."

"Is he back in an induced coma?"

"Yes, I'm afraid so."

"Will he know me?"

"No. He's heavily sedated. We'll see how it goes and maybe try again tomorrow."

I didn't stay long. On the return journey, when Sia came back on the car radio, I switched her off. I wasn't in the mood for singing.

That night, wild weather arrived. The wind howled around our house like an angry monster, throwing branches into our pool, which was already green from neglect. The storm raged all night.

The next day was calm, and I can tell from my journal entries that Joe had turned a bit of a corner. Things were looking more positive.

4th October, 2016.

He's now been in the hospital for one week! High winds brought down power cables last night. The radio says the road to hospital is blocked so won't attempt to go in. Phoned. Sedation reduced again, removal of tube successful (HOORAY) although he still can't breathe by himself. Oxygen and BiPAP machine but at least he's no longer on a ventilator. Sedation increased again but coping on BiPAP. Good sign?

In the morning, the staff in the ICU told me that Joe was conscious but still being fed intravenously and unable to communicate because of the oxygen mask.

As usual, I waited to be escorted into the ward and entered in some trepidation. I peeped around the curtain to see Joe propped up almost into a sitting position. A mask was clamped over his nose and mouth, and I saw the many dials and numbers flickering on monitors behind him. His eyes were closed.

"How is he?" I asked his nurse quietly.

"Why don't you ask him yourself?" she said, smiling.

I tiptoed to his bedside.

"Joe?" His eyes sprang open, and his arms reached for me. "How are you?" I whispered.

He tried to speak, but the mask transformed his words into comical grunts.

"Here," said the nurse, passing us a stack of paper and a thick marker pen.

Joe nodded his thanks and accepted them. He clutched the pen and began scribbling. Joe's writing is usually meticulous, but all spelling and punctuation flew out of the window in his need to communicate.

its so god to see you

"Hah! It's so good seeing you sitting up and awake! How are you feeling?"

sor throat

"I'm not surprised. You've had that tube down your throat, and every time they tried to take it out, you panicked, and they had to push it back in again."

i know nurse rebeca said

I looked up at Rebecca, and she smiled.

"He's doing really well, isn't he?" she said, then went back to her paperwork.

how long i ben here

"Well, you've been in hospital for more than a week, but not in the ICU all the time. Can you remember anything?"

resp ward then no more

I explained to him how we'd all expected him to come home after the family had visited, which he remembered. Beyond that, he could recall nothing.

i nearly died yes?

"Yes, I think you did," I said, nodding my head. "I reckon you were only good for landfill a couple of days ago."

I stayed for three hours. I told him almost everything that was happening at home, keeping it all very light. I still didn't tell him about Fred having a problem with the tilers.

"Guess what? I got another message from Fred. Hang on, I'll find it for you. Ah, here it is: *I'm thinking about you tonight babe.*"

I couldn't help giggling.

babe?

"Haha! I know! Don't worry. I'll never be Fred's babe!"

Now Joe was laughing too, but the mask turned his chuckles into monstrous snorts. This only made us both laugh more, and even Nurse Rebecca was laughing until Joe managed to scribble:

stop hurts to larf

Joe was worn out, and it was my cue to leave. I kissed him goodbye and left, confident that things were finally looking up.

Sometimes it's a good thing we can't see into the future. Our rollercoaster of a journey hadn't come to a halt quite yet.

HONEY-GLAZED SPARE RIBS

Here's a really simple special crowd-pleaser for summer get-togethers. Prepare the night before, then sling them on the barbecue. They also cook beautifully in a slow cooker.

Ingredients

2kg beef spare ribs

2 tablespoons tomato paste

½ cup diced tomatoes

⅓ cup honey

1 tablespoon Worcestershire sauce

2 teaspoons soy sauce

1 tablespoon white vinegar

Method

Trim spare ribs. Make the marinade by combining tomato paste, diced tomatoes, honey, Worcestershire sauce, soy sauce and vinegar.

Mix well and stand for several hours or refrigerate overnight.

Barbecue until tender and golden-brown.

25

MONSTERS BENEATH

Unaware of what was in store for us in the future, I drove home, singing along with Ed Sheeran. I laughed again, remembering Joe's snorts behind his mask.

Sometimes in life, the faintest whiff or scent, or a glimpse of a view will remind us of some past event. Often it's difficult to place the exact time and location of the memory, even though it might be intensely familiar. I *knew* I'd heard those snorts before, behind a mask, and I suddenly remembered the occasion.

It was at our beach in Spain, when Joe walked into the sea, already wearing his mask, snorkel and flippers. As the cool water lapped his sun-warmed skin, he bellowed. Of course, he sounded and looked ridiculous. I imagine a cornered wildebeest might make the same sound. Small wonder that I used to pretend he wasn't with me.

There was another time, many years ago, when Joe heard that same sound, and we often used to chuckle about it. Way back in 2008, before we even dreamed of living in Australia, we had a fantastic holiday driving up the Australian east coast. At Airlie Beach, in Queensland, we took a boat trip and headed for a section of the Great Barrier Reef. Arriving at our destination, the boat was moored, and we were provided with wetsuits, masks, snorkels and flippers, and encouraged to explore the reef.

"You'll have two hours here," said our guide. "There is a lot to see, and you'll be able to identify many species of fish and coral from this chart. This section is not deep but beware of swimming beyond the markers. The ocean suddenly becomes very deep past them."

It is unwise to tell Joe what he must *not* do; it's like a red rag to a bull. I never break laws or disobey rules without making myself extremely uncomfortable, but Joe thrives on risk-taking.

We had a fabulous time watching the fish and admiring the exotic creatures that call the coral home. But that wasn't enough for Joe. He's a much better, stronger swimmer than I am and we soon parted company. I didn't follow him. I stayed quite close to the boat where the water was shallow, and the reef was quite near the surface.

Joe swam much further afield, to the edge of the reef shelf where it suddenly dropped away and became immeasurably deep. He wasn't the only one: there was a little group of Chinese tourists also intent on pushing the boundaries.

I knew nothing of what happened next until he returned to the boat, beetroot with excitement.

"What happened?" I asked.

"Well, I swam to the edge of the shallow part, then past the marker. The reef edge drops like a cliff, and you can actually feel the temperature of the water change. I was watching all these little fish disappear into crevices in the cliff face; it was fascinating. Then I heard this weird noise!"

"Noise?"

"Yes! I bobbed straight up to the surface and looked around. The noise was coming from three Chinese swimmers. They were all hanging onto the buoy for dear life, making these extraordinary noises as they yelled through their snorkels. I could see their faces behind their masks. They were terrified!"

"Why? What was the matter? Had they just discovered they were out of their depth?"

"No! They were all climbing over each other, trying to get out of the water onto this buoy that kept bobbing about, and they were pointing down. I couldn't see anything so I went underwater to take a look."

"Weren't you scared?"

"Yes! Terrified! But I had to see what they were pointing at. I saw it straight away..."

Joe paused and took a deep breath, reliving the moment.

"Well?"

"It was the biggest fish I have ever seen! A *monster* fish!"

"Wow! How big? Not a shark?"

"No, it wasn't a shark; it was the wrong shape. I don't know what it was, but it was *enormous*! Well, my eyes nearly popped out of my head. And all I could hear were these noises coming from our snorkels as we all shouted! Kind of 'Hoo!' 'Hoo!' 'Hoo!' noises! No wonder they were clinging onto the buoy, and I wasn't hanging around either. I swam back onto the shelf as fast as I could."

"And the Asians?"

"They let go of the buoy, one by one, and swam like the clappers back onto the shallow area. They were only small, and I reckon that the monster could have swallowed one in a single bite."

Still breathless with excitement, Joe described the fish to our guide, hoping she could identify it.

"It was *huge*, with a massive mouth!"

"Was it kind of mottled and spotted?"

"Yes!"

"Oh, you must have met George!" she said, smiling. "He's a giant Queensland groper, or grouper. He's harmless, but he would be dead scary if you met him face to face. You'll probably see him again soon because he often comes up to be hand-fed when we leave."

She was right, and I was lucky enough to see George at close quarters, too, later. And what a magnificent fellow he was! However, I think I would have died of fright if I had come across him while snorkelling.

When I got the chance, I researched the giant Queensland groper species.[1] Apparently, they are the biggest reef-dwelling fish in the world and are renowned for their curiosity. They are usually solitary in nature and live to a ripe old age. Giant Queensland gropers are commonly seen in caves on coral reefs and around wrecks. They feed on small sharks, juvenile sea turtles, crustaceans and molluscs, all of which are sucked into that colossal mouth and swallowed whole.

Perhaps those Asian swimmers, being so slight, had a lucky escape.

Reluctantly shaking off thoughts of those happy bygone days, when Joe's breathing was strong and taken for granted, I arrived home. All the tradies had finished for the day and already left. All, that is, except Reg. To my huge surprise, Reg, the tiler, was mowing our front lawn. Or as much as he could reach between the stacks of tiles, bricks, and the rubbish skip.

Had Fred misjudged him? Was there a heart of gold lurking somewhere within that we hadn't seen any sign of yet? I thanked Reg sincerely for his kindness.

"That's okay," he said. "While I've got you, we need some more cash to go to the suppliers tomorrow. We're running short of tile cement and suchlike."

"No problem," I said, and paid him the sum he requested.

It was time to find out from Fred exactly what was concerning him about Reg. I resolved to tackle him about it as soon as possible.

Thursday, 6th October was a good day. Joe was still in the ICU, attached to oxygen via a lightweight tube, the cannula placed in his nostrils, delivering a mixture of air and oxygen. The BiPAP mask was almost dispensed with, and he was inhaling and exhaling without help. Better still, he was encouraged to get up for the first time and spent three-quarters of an hour out of bed. He told me he managed a hearty breakfast, and his spirits were high.

That afternoon, I sat down with Fred, and we quietly discussed the progress of the renovations.

The tiling in the en suite bathroom had been completed in spite of Reg's haphazard attendance. He and his son, Kurt, were now beginning to lay the beautiful travertine pavers outside.

"The tiling looks fantastic," I said, patting Dinkum, who had commandeered Lola's bed again. "So what's the problem with Reg?"

"The tiling in the en suite should have been finished ages ago," said Fred. "It's only a tiny area. And I think I know part of the problem. Booze. I've caught him and his son, Kurt, drinking on the job many a time. Have you noticed they always have a tinny nearby?"

"Yes, but I thought that was just a can of cold drink, I didn't realise it was alcoholic. No wonder they always refuse my offers of tea and biscuits. But their work is good, isn't it?"

"It is now. I've had to tell him to re-do those niches twice, and I'm not sure that he's sloped the floor tiles enough for the shower water to drain away. And there's something else bothering me."

"Oh dear, what?"

"He comes straight to you for more money for materials, doesn't he?"

"Yes…"

"Well, I think he's using some of your materials, like the tile cement, for other jobs. He can't possibly get through the amount he says he uses. I've also noticed that whenever you pay him, the pair of them disappear for a few days. I reckon they're doing another job, or they're going on a bender, and when they run out of money, they come back."

"Oh no!"

"I'm afraid so. Did you pay Reg last night?"

"I did."

"Well, I've not seen them at all today, and I'll wager they won't rock up for a couple of days. I've had my suspicions for a while. I had a quiet word with Seth, the concreter."

"Oh, I wouldn't take *his* word for anything…"

"I know, but he's worked with those two on another job, and it seems they got the sack from that job for the same thing."

"Are you sure?"

"Pretty sure. I'm going to watch them closely from now on. It's your call, but I recommend you terminate them."

"So we'll have to find another tiler?"

"'Fraid so. If I'm right."

I nodded. It couldn't be helped. I desperately wanted the new bedroom and en suite finished before Joe came out of the hospital, so that he could have a clean, comfortable retreat.

"The good news," said Fred, as though reading my mind, "is that the plumber is all set up to come in and put in the vanity, toilet and shower."

"Oh, that's good! I'll carry on painting the bedroom and organise the fitted wardrobe, carpet, bed and bedside tables."

I was making lists as we talked.

By the end of the meeting, I felt pretty overwhelmed by all that needed to be done. But there wasn't time to complain. I had a bedroom to paint. And I had to control an enthusiastic puppy determined to be my assistant.

I finished painting late that night. I washed my brushes and cleared up, then made myself something to eat. As usual, I phoned the ICU and was told that Joe was doing well, and was asleep. It was already past ten o'clock, but I thought I'd eat with a tray on my lap and watch half an hour of TV before going to bed.

I was just finishing up when I heard an unusual noise. Although I'd never heard her do it before, I knew exactly what it was. Lola was growling.

Perfectly aware that her hearing was one hundred times better than mine, I paid attention. Had she heard something unusual outside? I stood up to investigate.

To my surprise, she was growling at something under the dining table.

"What's the matter, Lola? Why are you growling?"

She didn't even look up. More deep, throaty growls.

I bent down to take a look, and then I saw it.

A spider. A spider (almost) the size of an upturned soup bowl. A *monstrous* spider.

I froze. I'm terrified of spiders even though I have great respect for them. Knowing that some can be aggressive and dangerous, I grabbed Lola's collar. I certainly didn't want her bitten by this crouching monster.

Australians reading this will be scoffing and rolling their eyes by now, but they have always lived alongside snakes and spiders. Me? I was terrified, and my knees were trembling. Was it a harmless huntsman? Or one of those jumping ones?

What to do? It was far too late to call Thea; I knew she and Nixi would be tucked up in bed by now. Emma? She went to bed early, too. I had to deal with the situation myself.

The spider sat there, all eight eyes staring at me.

I had to do something, but what?

Everything is much worse at night. Shadows are deeper, and every tiny sound is augmented. Lola was still growling, setting my nerves on edge.

I needed a plan. I didn't want to kill it, but it certainly wasn't going to leave by itself, however politely I asked.

Then I remembered. There was a can of One-Shot on the windowsill on the other side of the room. This insect killer works like a dream on flies which instantly drop and soon die. I had to trust that it had the same effect on giant arachnids.

"Listen, my friend," I whispered, "I don't want to do this, but you leave me no choice. You weren't invited, and you don't pay rent."

Reluctantly, I prepared myself for the ordeal ahead. Anybody who shares my fear of spiders will understand what I am going to say next.

I had to keep my eye on this intruder at all times.

I had to know where it was. To lose sight of it would mean it was still somewhere in the house and could reappear at any time.

Slowly, smoothly, I backed away, never for one second losing sight of the monster…

I felt behind me, groping blindly until my fingers found the can of insecticide spray. Success. Lola's leash was also within reach. I quickly clipped that on her collar. I couldn't allow her to run free. My eye never lost sight of the spider.

Slowly, smoothly, I approached my quarry again, getting as close as I dared.

---

1. This Youtube clip shows just how big the giant Queensland gropers are: https://www.youtube.com/watch?v=5FaDq_k1ZQM

SLOW COOKER CHOCOLATE FUDGE

Slow and constant heat is all you need to make this delicious chocolate fudge. A great recipe to make with the kids. From kidspot.com.au

Ingredients

2 blocks cooking chocolate (broken into pieces)

1 tin sweetened condensed milk

1 tbs butter

1 packet mini M&Ms for final decoration

Method

Place chocolate, condensed milk and butter into slow cooker on High with the lid off.

Stir with a metal or silicone spoon every 15 minutes until melted.

Turn setting down to Low and continue to stir every 15 mins for up to 2 hours.

Pour into a lined 20cm x 20cm (7″ or 8″) square cake tin and smooth over the top.

Sprinkle with mini M&M's and place into the fridge to cool for 1 hour.

Cut into squares and serve.

26

BAD STUFF

Lola and I stared at the spider while the digital clock on the wall ticked the seconds away. The spider stared back at us. I clutched Lola's lead tightly.

A car drove past and, just for a moment, I toyed with the idea of running out and flagging it down. Our house was in a cul-de-sac so it must have been a neighbour. But what might a neighbour think, seeing a crazed elderly woman in Disney pyjamas, with a dog on a lead, running from her house in the middle of the night?

And anyway, I couldn't leave the spider. What if it scuttled somewhere and hid, only to come out later at night and join me in bed?

No, I had to fight this battle on my own.

And then something horrible happened.

The spider's eyes and mine were locked into a stare when, without warning, the spider lifted one leg and beckoned me.

"Aaagh!" I gasped and jerked back.

My unexpected reaction made Lola jump, and she barked in excitement, first at me, then at nothing in particular, bouncing around as much as the lead would allow.

It took a while for her to calm down but I never took my eyes off the spider. Thank goodness, the commotion didn't seem to disturb it, and it put its leg down again. It remained still, silent. I hoped it wasn't limbering up for a sprint.

"Right, Lola," I said quietly, "I'm going to spray it now."

Perhaps I believed that if I voiced my intent, it would give me the courage to do it.

I did spray it, long and hard, but it just sat there in a cloud of insecticide. It didn't even cough. I tried again, hating myself for punishing a spider for being a spider. It wasn't its fault that it terrified me.

Then it gathered itself up, seemingly unaffected by the spray, and ran out from under the table, across the floor and up the back of the sofa. At the top, it rested, waving two defiant legs at me.

For more than half an hour, it sat there. I was at the other side of the room by now, all lights switched on, the spider always in sight. Lola was asleep at my feet, but I was transfixed. I couldn't allow myself to lose sight of the enemy.

Which way would it run next? Reluctantly, and cautiously, I moved in and sprayed it again. It ran down the other side of the sofa and across the cushions. I sensed it had slowed down, as though the spray was finally affecting it.

It came to a halt on a cream-coloured cushion. The pale background provided a perfect backdrop for it, the contrast showing every hair on every leg in sharp relief.

I watched that spider until it crawled behind a cushion, out of sight. A sensible person would have called it a day and gone to bed, but I couldn't do that. I had to watch the cushion in case the spider emerged.

I waited nearly all night, eyes glued to the cushion, but the spider didn't reappear. I wasn't brave enough to move the cushion and try to find it, but neither did I want to leave it and go to bed.

Eventually, absolutely exhausted, I convinced myself the spray had probably done its job by now, and the spider had died somewhere in the depths of the sofa. I went to bed, taking Lola with me.

But before I could sleep, I stuffed rolled-up towels along the bottom of the door to fill any gap, in case the spider revived and came looking for me.

I didn't sleep well, and the next day dawned much too soon. I phoned the hospital to check on Joe's progress.

"Oh, he's doing really well," said the nurse. "We're going to take the IV line out of his groin today, and the one in his hand. If there's a bed free, he may go back to the general ward later today or tomorrow."

That was *fabulous* news. Joe was on the mend, and he no longer needed to be in the Intensive Care Unit! I looked forward to visiting him, but first I had to deal with the eight-legged midnight intruder.

I emerged from the bedroom. Sunlight flooded through the windows, and I was beginning to feel rather foolish. However, I couldn't pluck up enough courage to move the cushion aside and look for the spider.

When I'd given Lola her breakfast, I checked it wasn't too early, then phoned Thea.

"Thea, can I ask you a favour?" I asked, attempting to sound casual. "Would you mind popping round as soon as you have a moment?"

"I come now."

I loved her Teutonic abruptness. She must have sensed that this was an emergency and was on my doorstep within minutes, not even bothering to don either her white or brown hat. Lola treated her to an over-enthusiastic welcome. She couldn't believe she was seeing one of her best friends so early in the morning.

"*Donnerwetter!*" Thea exclaimed as Lola jumped up, nearly knocking her over.

I grabbed Lola.

"You look tired," remarked Thea. "Are you sick?"

"No, there's a gigantic spider in the depths of my sofa. I sprayed it last night then I saw it crawl behind a cushion and I had to stay up all night to make sure it didn't come out."

"Pardon? You stayed up all night watching your sofa?"

I nodded. "Yes. I think the spider must be dead, but I'm too scared to look. Could you please check?"

"Where did you last see this creature?"

I pointed at the cushion and held Lola back as Thea approached it. She moved it aside.

"Ah, here it is!" she said.

"Is it dead?"

"Oh yes, very dead."

"Can you get rid of it, please?"

"Yes. Perhaps I don't touch it. Do you have a bag and a tweezer?"

I scuttled off to find the items and handed them to her.

"*Donnerwetter*, it's a big one," she said and held the corpse up for me to see, dangling off the tweezers.

Of course, Lola also wanted to see and nearly broke away from my grasp.

"*Donnerwetter*, Lola! No, take your snoot away; this is not for you."

I shuddered. The spider *was* big, but it had looked ten times bigger last night. Now it was scrunched up and stiff, poor thing. I wasn't proud of myself at all.

Thea dropped it into the plastic bag I'd given her and threw it away in the bin. Had she not removed it, I would never have sat on that sofa again. In fact, I may have considered selling the house.

Thea, the Ranger, had saved the day.

It was still quite early in the morning, and there was a lot to do.

In Australia, some days are so perfect that I wish I could preserve them and take them out again to enjoy later. A photograph isn't good enough because it doesn't capture the sounds and scents.

The 7th of October was a day such as this.

I took Lola for a run at the oval, hoping to tire her out before I went to the hospital. The sky was unblemished by even the smallest, puffiest of clouds, and stretched, bluer than an ocean of forget-me-nots. A warm, gentle breeze tickled the leaves on the trees, and a line of pink and grey galahs sat on the high fence glowering down at us.

Galahs weren't the only parrots present that day. A huge flock of screeching white cockatoos flapped overhead, clearly disturbed by something. Shielding my eyes from the sun, I saw the reason for their indignation. High in the sky, an eagle wheeled, wings motionless as it harnessed a column of rising warm air.

The eagle wasn't the only one making use of the thermals. A dozen multi-coloured paragliders soared silently above the distant bush. Conditions would have been perfect at Splinterbone Crag, a favourite spot for paragliding enthusiasts.

Lola romped, and my heart sang. The day couldn't have been more beautiful, and Joe was out of danger and on the mend.

It was just as well that I didn't know what was in store for me just hours later. I still have the email I sent that evening to family members in Britain, outlining the events of the day.

7th October

Dear All,

Today has been a very mixed, somewhat surreal day, which I will try to describe...

As you know, Joe was doing great when I phoned this morning, and the plans were to send him back to the general ward. I went in about two hours later, and (after circling the carpark for 20 mins waiting for a space) I finally got to the ICU. You have to phone from a large waiting room to be let in. They said I couldn't come in for a while, because the doctors were having a meeting at his bedside, so I waited.

And waited.

After three-quarters of an hour, I was allowed in. Joe was asleep and had the BiPap mask back on, and the arterial and other line were back in place. He wasn't sedated, but in a very deep sleep, and the mask was breathing for him. This was pretty disappointing as he seemed to have gone backwards again. The consultant said they were puzzled because Joe had appeared so much better, but then he kept falling asleep again. They were going to run more tests, and do a CT scan of his chest.

Joe didn't know I was there. He was totally out of it. I finally left.

The journey from the hospital to our house is about 35/40 minutes. I had reached about halfway when my phone rang. (Here's the surreal bit.) It was Joe, asking why I hadn't come in, and could I go in now? So I turned the car around immediately.

At the ICU, they wouldn't allow me in again. I was shown into the

Relatives' Room that I was taken into once before, when Joe was first admitted into the ICU, and asked to wait for the consultant.

He arrived and explained that they'd had no choice but to put him back on the ventilator. Square One. He explained that they were baffled by the test results. He has got over his chest infection, and his chest is relatively clear. But something is making him slip into unconsciousness with no warning. He said it was a good thing that he hadn't made it down to the general ward, or they may not have noticed it happening.

So the next thing is to find out what this "something else" is. He will have an MRI, fully sedated, which is a good thing, and maybe that will throw some light on the matter.

So that is where we are now. I will phone the hospital later tonight and again in the morning, as I always do. One step forward and two back. I am exhausted.

Really hoping I have better news soon,

Vicky x

CREAMY CURRIED SNAGS

These curried snags (sausages) have a mild creamy sauce and a good variety of vegetables. Another great recipe from kidspot.com.au

Ingredients (serves 3)

5 beef sausages (thick)

1 onion (sliced)

1 carrot (diced)

1 tsp sweet paprika

1 tsp turmeric

1 tsp curry powder

freshly cracked pepper

2 zucchini (courgettes), sliced

100g (3½oz) green beans

375 ml (12½floz) light evaporated milk

1 cup water

1 tsp cornflour

1 tbs brown sugar

Method

In a frying pan, cook the sausages until just done, slice and set aside. Discard residual oil from the pan.

In the same pan, add the onion, carrot and cook until the onion is transparent.

Add the paprika, turmeric, pepper, brown sugar and curry powder. Fry this for 2 minutes.

Add the sliced sausages to the pan with the evaporated milk and stir.

Mix the cornflour into the glass of water and add to the pan. Stir continuously until the sauce thickens.

Add the zucchini (courgette) and beans and cook for 3 minutes.

Serve with rice or mashed potatoes.

27

DIFFICULT DAYS

By now I was sure I could have driven to and from the hospital blindfolded. Every day I wasted precious time trying to find a parking space and spent a fortune in parking fees which were charged by the hour.

They were grim, dark days that even the perfect Australian spring weather couldn't dispel.

I neglected Lola because there weren't enough hours in the day. I insisted on taking her for a daily run, but her training went to pot. I was forever grateful to Emma and Thea for looking after her when I was away too long.

While Joe battled for his life in the ICU, Fred was handling the many problems that arose at home.

I happened to be at home the day Fred confronted father and son, Reg and Kurt. They had turned up to work, for a change, and were laying the travertine pavers around the pool. It was a modestly-sized pool, so the job shouldn't have taken long. However, their frequent absences had slowed work to almost a standstill. The omnipresent tinnies were clearly on view.

I was inside, with the window open, and their raised voices could easily be heard. I couldn't resist peeping around the blind.

"Reg, Kurt, can I have a word?" called Fred.

"What about?" asked Reg, already bridling.

"Eh?" said Kurt. He put down his trowel and walked over.

Both tilers towered above Fred, but he was undaunted.

"I think we have a bit of a problem," he started. "This job is taking far too long."

"Wot you on about? We been working hard," protested Reg.

"Yes, mate, when you're actually here."

I have discovered that in Australia, 'mate' can convey a variety of sentiments which I will attempt to demonstrate, with examples.

It can be used in a friendly way, like, "Hello, mate! How are you?"

Or it can be used to address somebody if you can't remember their name, as in, "Haven't seen you for ages, mate!"

It can be used to express disbelief, "Mate! You *didn't*!"

And it can be used very effectively to threaten or warn somebody, as in, "Watch it, mate!"

Fred was most definitely using the last one.

The father and son tiler team looked at each other, clearly surprised.

"Wot d'you mean, when we're here?" asked Reg, staring Fred down.

"Come on now," said Fred. "Did you think we hadn't noticed you two sneaking off whenever you please and not coming back for days?"

Reg gaped at him and Kurt reached for his tinny. He took a swig, then replaced it on the rock. As always, the can was clothed in a cooler, a foam sleeve designed to insulate it and keep the contents cold. I'm positive the coolers were also used to disguise the contents of the cans.

"And that's another thing," said Fred.

"Wot?"

"You're drinking on the job."

"Just a bloody minute, are you saying we can't have a drink when we're working?"

"Drink, yes, Kurt. Alcohol, no," said Fred, folding his arms.

Kurt's face turned beetroot, his eyes narrowed, and his hands turned to fists. He stepped forward.

"Did you just call me Skirt?"

Fred blinked behind his thick-lensed, horn-rimmed glasses and looked puzzled.

"No, I didn't. I said 'Yes, Kurt...'"

"You just did it again!" bawled Kurt, ready to lunge at Fred.

Reg grabbed his son's arm and pulled him back.

"It's okay, son," he said, "leave it!"

I had to admire Fred. Small in stature, he only reached Kurt's shoulder, but he didn't back down.

"Look," said Fred. "I'm giving you fair warning. I expect you to stay on-site and finish this paving. And no more drinking on the job."

Kurt's face was thunderous, but Reg had a firm hold of his son's arm as Fred turned away, his mission accomplished.

I had to rush away to the hospital, but I made time to first thank Fred. I also thanked him silently for making me smile for the first time in days.

Perhaps I sound as though all our tradesmen were problematic, but that wasn't true. One of our favourites was Bob the Brickie. He was semi-retired and only accepted jobs if he felt like it. Luckily for us, he was happy to build our bathroom wall.

Bob was one of life's gentlemen. His handshake was warm, his smile genuine, and his passion for bricklaying was evident. Bob brought along his battered, cement-splattered radio which was tuned in permanently to a country music station. As he mixed cement and laid bricks, he sang along to Dolly Parton or Tammy Wynette.

Bob was shocked to hear that Joe was so sick and arrived next morning clutching a bottle of Blackmore's echinacea liquid.

"Put a few drops in his coffee," he said to me. "It'll protect him from colds and flu. I take it every day, and I haven't had a cold in sixty years."

In the ICU, Joe was conscious but still unable to breathe by himself. He could, however, write notes so at least we could communicate.

I still have those notes; huge, shaky scrawls across many pages. Rereading them to write this chapter brought everything back. Joe's bewilderment, confusion, love, fear, gratitude, all expressed in malformed, smudgy words, laboriously written with a marker pen on scrap paper.

All the time, the machine breathed for him and the dials, graph lines, and countless lights flickered on and off, displaying numbers.

I tried hard to keep the visit lighthearted and told him a watered-down version of the 'Skirt' incident which made him laugh.

no larf - hurts!!!

I apologised, and he changed the subject to a far more serious matter. His hand clutched the marker, and he wrote:

dr wants speak w you tomorrow

"Oh, really? Does he want to update me on your progress?"

no

"Oh! Okay, do you know why he wants to see me?"

yes. you know my thoughts

"What do you m…"

Before I could finish, two nurses bustled up to us.

"I'm sorry, we'll have to interrupt," said one. "It's time to prepare your husband for his MRI."

I left Joe in their capable hands. I didn't get the opportunity to quiz him further and returned home, wondering what the doctor wanted to see me about or was going to say to me.

I collected Lola from Emma, who had kindly taken Lola and Baxter to the oval for a run. Lola gave me her usual exuberant welcome, breaking every rule about jumping up when meeting people.

I inspected the renovation progress. The travertine pavers were looking fabulous, especially on the new patio outside the bedroom door, covering up the ugly pipework leading from the new en suite bathroom to the drain.

Before I went to bed, I called the hospital and was informed that the MRI went well.

"Ah, I have a note here to say that Dr Gordon would like to have a word with you as soon as possible."

"Yes, Joe told me. Do you know what it's about?"

"I'm sorry, I don't."

I spent a restless night worrying about what the doctor would say. It must be very important if it was on Joe's notes, and a nurse couldn't, or wouldn't, simply tell me. Whatever did the senior doctor want to say to me?

As I dozed, I remembered the date. This weekend the *fiesta* would be taking place in our village in Spain, on the other side of the planet. Had I really been in Australia for more than a year?

Of course, there would be dancing in the village square, noise, games, contests and processions. But had Lola Ufarte and Father Samuel patched up their differences, or had Lola decided that Esteban was more to her taste? And what about Geronimo and Valentina? Had Geronimo agreed to leave the comfort zone of the village and accompany his fiancée on a trip overseas?

I hoped my young penpal would keep me up to date.

And I prayed that Dr Gordon had good news for me tomorrow.

"Would you mind waiting in the Relatives' Room and I'll page Gordon," said the young nurse who had come to collect me from the ICU waiting room.

My heart dropped. The Relatives' Room? *No, not again…*

Dr Gordon arrived, smiling kindly. We greeted each other, and after a short pause, he explained why I had been summoned.

"I've already had a good chat with Joe," he said, "and he was keen for me to talk with you, too."

He told me that they still didn't know why Joe's breathing was failing, as the two viruses seemed to have cleared up.

"Unfortunately," he said, his kind eyes watching me, "the infections have caused his lungs to deteriorate even more. But that doesn't explain why he is struggling to breathe unaided."

"But he'll come off the ventilator, won't he?" I asked, appalled.

"Yes, just as soon as we feel he's strong enough. The reason I called you in for a chat was because you and Joe have options."

"Options?"

And then he spelt it out.

"I need to make you aware that this could happen again with no warning. And if it does, you need to decide."

Long pause. I held my breath and waited, reading the compassion in his eyes.

"Decide?" I whispered.

"Yes, if this happens again, you can make the choice not to put Joe through any more. Unfortunately, the use of ventilators to support breathing can cause further lung injury, particularly in older patients or patients whose lungs are already damaged."

Another long pause. I felt the doctor's eyes on me, but he said no more. I tried to absorb his words.

"So you are saying…"

"Yes. I'm saying that if it happens again, and he is in a weakened state on a ventilator, you may both decide that it might be better not to resuscitate."

There. He'd said it.

"We can sedate patients and keep them in induced comas, but they may never regain any quality of life. And we must take into consideration that ventilators can keep people breathing, but there are huge risks. The breathing tube can allow bacteria to enter the lungs, which may cause pneumonia."

My mouth was dry. I looked down and saw my hands were balled into fists in my lap.

"And you had this conversation with Joe?"

"I did."

"What did he say?"

"He listened very calmly and didn't hesitate. I'll let you talk to him then you can both be clear about how you feel."

I was numb as I made my way back into the ward. How could things have come to this point so quickly? I didn't know what to say to Joe.

But I didn't need to broach the subject.

Even though he was still on the ventilator, propped up on cushions, attached by lines to drips and machines, he was able to read my mind. He began writing.

u chat w dr?

I didn't want to talk about it. I didn't even want to think about it. Not now. Not when he was getting better again.

But I knew exactly what Joe's reaction would have been and what he would have said to the doctor.

Joe's eyes bored into mine above the breathing tube. He raised his eyebrows in question and pushed the paper at me again, ordering me to answer.

I sighed and reached for his hand.

"Yes, I talked with Dr Gordon. He's such a nice man. What an awful job he has sometimes."

Joe squeezed my hand and raised his eyebrows, urging me to get to the point.

"I know how you feel about it, Joe. And I would feel the same if it was me. Don't leave me on a ventilator with no quality of life. And I also agree with you, donate any of my organs if they are of any use. And use my body for science."

Joe nodded vehemently. We'd discussed organ donation many times.

"But you're improving. You're conscious, and you'll get better every day."

Joe nodded, but I knew we were both thinking the same thing.

It could happen again.

He could catch another virus. He could end up on a life-support machine.

He picked up the marker once more and scribbled three words.

pull the plug

AUSSIE HAM AND CHEESE PULL-APARTS

Perfect for any festive party, or TV supper. Kids will love it and I guarantee it'll be gone in seconds. Ham can be replaced with cooked turkey or chicken for a change. From newideafood.com.au

Ingredients (serves 8)

Cooking oil spray

2 crusty baguettes, about 34cm long (12 inches)

Olive oil cooking spray

125g (4½oz) brie cheese

⅔ cup cranberry sauce

150g (5oz) sliced ham

1½ cups grated mozzarella (200g)

Parsley, to garnish

Method

Spray a 35 cm (12 inch) round pizza tray with a perforated base with oil.

Trim ends from baguettes. Cut into 2 cm (¾ inch) round slices. Place slices side-by-side on prepared tray. Spray with oil.

Cook in a hot oven 200°C (390°F) for about 5 minutes, or until crisp.

Remove. Stand for 5 minutes.

Meanwhile, cut brie into thin wide slices. (It's easier if the brie is chilled.)

Spread cranberry sauce over toasted bread. Top with brie then ham. Sprinkle with mozzarella.

Cook in a hot oven 200°C (390°F) for about 15 minutes, or until golden and cheese is melted.

Serve garnished with parsley.

28

WORMS

Joe's health improved daily. The breathing tube was successfully removed and he was able to breathe by himself. At last he was considered to be out of danger. He was moved out of the ICU and given a bed in the general ward.

He was on the mend.

Two days later, on the 13th October, he was discharged. But first we had to wait several hours in the hospital Transit Lounge. Joe, never patient at the best of times, voiced his displeasure at having to wait to go home to all who would listen. The administration staff ignored him, and the other patients rolled their eyes and looked away. It was good to hear him grumbling again, a sure sign that he was feeling better.

At long last, all the papers were signed, and we were given a pack containing up-to-date medical notes and CD records of his scans. We were very grateful, and Joe apologised for his impatience.

Coming home was a mixed blessing because he was appallingly weak. He couldn't walk or stand long without support, so I purchased a walking frame and a shower seat. During those early days, he didn't have the strength to put toothpaste on his own toothbrush and even eating left him breathless. Thea arrived with a beautiful German cake, which I ended up eating almost entirely myself because Joe couldn't manage it.

Thank goodness for the team of after-care nurses who came out daily to check on Joe's welfare. They must have been shocked by the state of the house, with no kitchen, and a bathroom fit for nothing but demolition. But, to my relief, the new bedroom and en suite were ready to move into.

I had painted the bedroom walls white. I couldn't have been more delighted by the lime-washed bed, bedside cupboards, and the white plantation shutters. The white marble tiles in the en suite gleamed, and the black tapware looked sensational. Now Joe had a retreat. A clean, dust-free zone.

But there was a significant problem.

Although our plumber had finished his job, he had gone overseas. That shouldn't have concerned us because we could easily find another for the main bathroom and kitchen, when the time arose. But in his haste to jump on a plane, our plumber had cut corners and left us with a difficult situation.

When we began using the en suite, it didn't take long for a most unpleasant problem to rear its ugly head. Something was blocking the toilet. It wouldn't flush away, and the water rose up the bowl alarmingly.

I've noticed that domestic emergencies alway occur on public holidays, weekends, or during the night. True to form, this happened on a Sunday. I had a card for an emergency plumber, sporting the slogan: Pipework is our Pleasure. So I rang the number.

Dean arrived with a bag of tools and examined the toilet. The water had slowly drained away by now, so he flushed it again.

"A good flush beats a full house," he said happily.

Joe and I looked at each other. We'd never met such a perky plumber before.

The water rose in the bowl and stayed there.

"Hmm," he said. "You definitely have a blockage. Leave it with me, and I'll see what I can do. We're Number One in the Number Two business."

Five minutes later, Dean delivered his verdict.

"Nope, I can't see what's causing the blockage. Whatever it is must be further down the pipe."

"We've just had a new patio laid," I said. "Those pavers won't need to be lifted, will they?"

"Nope. I suggest I come back tomorrow with my jet spray and camera. We'll send them down, and we'll be able to see what's causing that blockage."

"Oh, that sounds like a good idea."

"In the meantime, don't use the toilet, and I'll see you tomorrow." With that, he gathered up his tools and left.

Hola tía Vicky y tío Joe,

I hop you are wells. My family is completely wells and I am sad *tío* Joe is not completely wells. I am writing you a letter because my teacher say i must write very good english like my sister. Papa say why i not work very hard like my sister but my sister not love dancing crazy so much like me and Mama. My sister want be a travel shop person. I want to dance flamenco for the television and in weedings and i am not need very good english.

Now we have the *fiesta* and I and Mama and my sister dance flamenco very much then my dancing shoe have hole. My papa make music with the guitar and all the peoples claps hands. When we finish all the peoples shouts and say dance again. Like MacDonalds I am lovin' it.

Also i have now a secret. If you not say to my mama i will say to you in my next letter.

Felicitations, Catalina xx

I finished reading the email to Joe and looked up.

"Well, it's a very nice email," I said. "I wonder what the secret is? But she hasn't given me all the information I was hoping for."

"What information?"

"Don't pretend you're not interested! You know, village stuff."

"You mean gossip, don't you?"

"No! Not really... I mean like, has Valentina persuaded Geronimo to go on a trip overseas with her? And did her aunt, Lola Ufarte, go to the *fiesta?* And poor Father Samuel, where is he? And what about Esteban, has he come back to the village?"

"Gossip," said Joe, shaking his head. "That's definitely gossip. If you're so interested, why don't you ask her?"

"I think I will. Just to help her improve her written English, of course."

"Of course."

⁂

Dean, the plumber, arrived with not only his bag of tools but also a carry-case housing his camera setup. He lifted the inspection hatch on the patio.

"Does your hosepipe reach this spot?" he asked.

I scrambled to get it, and by the time I returned, Dean was on all-fours feeding the probe with the camera fixed to the end down the drain.

"Let's have a look what we've got here," he said. "Would you like to see?"

Of course we would!

"Right, watch the monitor as the camera travels along underground. It's got its own little light so you'll see everything."

One might think that seeing the inside of an underground pipe as it makes its way to the main drain at the bottom of the garden would be dull. It wasn't dull at all. It was fascinating.

Having travelled some distance, the probe came to a halt, blocked by an obstruction.

"What's stopping it?" asked Joe.

The camera swivelled a fraction until we could see it clearly. Sodden cardboard pieces.

"Who on earth would put cardboard down a drain?" I asked, aghast.

"Well, judging by the writing I can make out, I'd say it was your tiler trying to save time clearing up. He's torn a box up into little shreds, but it's all gathered together and caused an obstruction."

We had to agree that was likely, judging by the '6 ceramic tiles' legend stamped on one shred.

"How do we shift it?"

"I'll aim the hose down there first. See if that and the camera probe will dislodge it. If not, I'll use the water jet."

I turned on the tap and sprinted back, not wanting to miss seeing it on the screen. I was in time to see a mini tsunami hit the cardboard wall, and with a little extra nudge from the camera, the obstruction broke up and floated away.

We all cheered.

"Try flushing the toilet now," said Dean, the dam buster.

I ran inside and flushed the toilet. To my dismay, once again, the water filled the bowl.

"It's still blocked," I reported.

"Right," said Dean. "That can only mean one thing."

"What?"

"The blockage must be *before* this inspection hatch. It must be somewhere under the floor of the house. Let's push the camera in and find out."

His enthusiasm was infectious, but I wasn't really sure I wanted to see what was blocking the drain closer to the toilet.

"Right! All cisterns go!" cried Dean, and thrust the camera back down the hole.

Joe chuckled. He loves a good pun and Dean had a stock of them.

The camera nosed its way along until…

"There it is!" Dean sang out, as delighted as though he'd won the lottery. Then his expression changed. "What the…"

He stopped. We all stared at the screen. The camera was showing us a large pile of white, gleaming worms, all intertwined.

"Good grief," said Joe.

"What *is* that?" I squeaked.

"I'm not sure," confessed Dean. "That's just plumb crazy."

"Are they alive?"

"I don't know. I've never seen anything like this before, but I haven't had the camera very long. They look like worms."

He was right. They appeared to be writhing in and out of each other's coils as the camera hovered around the heap.

"Maybe they're tree roots?" volunteered Joe.

We all looked over our shoulders to check, but there were no trees nearby, so that was unlikely.

"Baby snakes?"

"A strange Aussie fungus?"

"Whatever they are, they're causing your toilet to block."

He prodded the squirming mass with the camera. The whole pile seemed stuck together and sprang back when he withdrew the camera.

"I know what it is!" Dean exclaimed. "It's not a pile of worms at all! It's silicone sealant! Your last plumber must have broken the pipe, and instead of replacing it, he tried to mend it with silicone. The silicone's found a hole and squirted through. Mystery solved!"

Joe and I stared at the screen again. Yes, that's precisely what it was.

"It's too solid and rubbery for the camera to dislodge," Dean decided. "I'll blast it with the pressure jet."

And that's exactly what he did. We had the satisfaction of watching the silicone break away and wash harmlessly down the drain.

The toilet flushed beautifully, and all was well.

"Would you like a magnetic business card to put on your fridge?" Dean asked. "Got a leak, I'll take a peek."

We thanked him and took his card, keen to employ him again in the future, although hopefully not in an emergency. Whistling, he marched off with his bag of tools and camera, back to his van.

"And don't forget, you never need to go to bed with a drip!" he called over his shoulder.

That made me laugh, but Joe didn't find it so funny. In fact he sulked for a good hour afterwards.

Joe encouraged me to leave him and take Lola for walks.

"I'll be fine," he said. "I'm getting stronger every day and Lollipop needs a walk. If I have any problems, Fred will be here. Or I'll phone you. Don't worry, go and enjoy yourselves."

Sometimes Lola and I walked by ourselves, or with Thea and Nixi. At other times, we met up with Deb and Molly. As Molly and Lola possessed more than their fair share of energy, we usually chose to walk along the beach where they could romp unrestricted.

It was low tide, and the beach was almost deserted as Deb and I walked over the wet sand, occasionally dodging over-enthusiastic wavelets that threatened to soak our feet. Lola and Molly dashed this way and that, stopping only to sniff a seagull feather, or heap of seaweed, or other fascinating items the waves had carried ashore and dumped on the sand.

When the tide was high, we often passed lone fishermen casting their lines into the waves. But today there was nobody about apart from a single figure. This man had neither fishing rod nor net, and as we drew closer, his behaviour baffled me. This man stood at the water's edge, dragging something quite heavy, tied to a line, across the wet sand. A bucket stood close by, and in his other hand he held a pair of pliers.

"What is he doing?" I asked Deb, who I always regarded as my personal Aussie reference manual.

"I have no idea."

"Isn't that a *sock* he's dragging around?"

"Certainly looks like it."

Curiosity won over shyness, and I approached the man.

"Excuse me," I said, "can I ask what you are doing, please?"

"Catching beach worms," he said. "I chop 'em up and use 'em for bait."

"Oh! Is that a sock you're dragging?"

"Yep. Called a stink-bag. Stuffed it with rotting fish guts and smelly stuff. Worms love it. Up they pop, drooling at the thought of dinner. Then I grab 'em by the nose with me pliers."

"Oh."

"And then I pull 'em out. Slippery little suckers they are. You have to be fast."

"They're just small, right?"

"Nah."

"Oh, how big are they?"

"More 'n a metre, sometimes."

"Do they just slip out?"

"If yer lucky and yer worm's relaxed, yep. Otherwise I have to drop me stink-bag and dig him out, hanging onto his nose like me life depends on it."

"Gosh! How do you know where to drag your, um, stink-bag?"

"See them holes? That's where the blighters hang out."

We were surrounded by dozens of small holes in the wet sand. Occasionally, a bubble popped out. I'd just thought they were air holes; I hadn't realised a monster worm lurked in each.

I sensed I was outstaying my welcome and the man wanted to continue his worm-hunt. I thanked him and walked back to Deb.

"Thinking about it," said Deb, "I seem to remember there was a Youtube clip about fishing for beach worms. It was in all the local papers because it went quite viral."

I couldn't find that clip, but I found another[1] which shows the art of Aussie beach-worming, with stink-bag and pliers, in glorious detail.

Something was bothering Deb that day. I felt that her mind was elsewhere, and she wasn't her usual bubbly self.

"Deb, are you okay? Is something bothering you?"

She took a deep breath and then she told me.

---

1. Youtube clip: Catching beach worms with stink-bag and pliers. https://www.youtube.com/watch?v=rMhDMkQkyj0

CHEATING APPLE DUMP DESSERT

Delicious with cream and tastes like a pie. Why 'cheating'? Because you use a packet cake mix. Why 'dump'? Because you dump it all in together.

Ingredients

5 medium apples (peeled, cored and sliced)

1 cup chopped nuts of your choice (lightly toasted)

4 teaspoons cinnamon (divided)

1 teaspoon freshly ground nutmeg

½ cup sugar

1¼ cups apple cider (or apple juice)

1 box yellow cake mix

¾ cup butter (melted)

Method

Preheat oven to 190°C (375°F). Lightly grease a shallow oven-proof dish or pan.

In the dish, add apples and nuts with 2 teaspoons cinnamon, nutmeg, and sugar. Spread evenly and cover with apple cider or juice.

Sprinkle dry cake mix over apple mixture then sprinkle remaining cinnamon.

Drizzle melted butter over top.

Bake for 45 minutes or until golden brown and bubbly.

29

SUMMER DAYS

"I've come to a very reluctant decision," said Deb sadly. "I'm going to consider letting Molly go."

I stopped in horror, allowing her words to sink in. Molly and Lola raced each other over the sand and back to the water's edge. They were in doggy heaven.

"Let Molly go?" I echoed. "No! You can't!"

"I must think about it for both our sakes. We can't carry on like this, with Molly spending several days a week at Doggy Day Care. It's unsettling for her and worrying for me. I have to visit my sister regularly, and there's nothing else I can do."

It was hard to take in. I knew Deb adored Molly as much as I loved Lola. Giving up her dog would be heartbreaking for her.

"I've even had discussions with the vet about it, and we tried medicating her. Nothing works. She's just a severely over-anxious dog, and I hate seeing her distressed."

I listened in silence, not knowing what to say.

"And I'm going to enrol for a course at TAFE which will help me find a job, hopefully. I'll have to put Molly in daycare for those days, too."

I knew TAFE stood for Technical and Further Education in Australia.

"Surely we can come up with something, or somebody, that could help? I know a few people I could ask." I was thinking of my dog walking pals at the oval.

"I think I've tried just about everything. Daycare is costing me a fortune, and I don't think I can afford to do it much longer. And finding somebody to look after her for odd days is probably not the answer. Molly needs stability. She needs to live with somebody who understands her terrible separation anxiety. Somebody who doesn't go out to work and can be with her all the time. She's not a demanding, difficult dog; she just needs human company."

It was hard to take in, but I understood. Deb was putting Molly's welfare above her own.

Joe was still weak, but we felt he was gradually making progress. The after-care nurses stopped visiting him, and we were coping alone. Every day he could walk a little further, and his appetite was good.

Not everything went so well. It was only a question of time before we parted company with our troublesome tilers. Fred caught Reg and his son drinking on the job again and sacked the pair of them on the spot.

Work was delayed while we searched for replacement tilers but the team we found was far more professional. They finished laying the silvery-blue travertine pavers around the pool, and the completed job looked terrific. They then began tiling the new main bathroom.

With the outside paving finished, I asked Fred to remove some of the rusty railings surrounding the pool. Then I booked a company to replace it with glass fencing. A date was set, and we happened to be out on that particular day. We left Fred in charge.

When we returned, I rushed out to inspect the new glass fence.

"Joe! They haven't done it. They didn't turn up! I'm really disappointed…"

"Vicky, put your specs on. It's done!"

I looked again and gasped. The glass was frameless, and I hadn't even seen it at first glance. The garden had been utterly transformed.

The pool and garden was revealed through sheets of gleaming and, seemingly, invisible glass. Poor Lola learned about it the hard way. Thinking she now had free access to all that wonderful water, she flattened her nose against one of the waist-high vertical sheets. Happily, no harm was done but she didn't try it again.

"Poor Lola!" I said, but she was already wagging her tail, the incident forgotten.

"She almost turned into a bulldog," observed Joe, chuckling.

Work inside the house also progressed well. The new main bathroom was looking spectacular, and I was delighted with it. I had chosen over-sized white tiles, a freestanding bath, black tapware and a semi-frameless shower cubicle with black trim and a black door handle.

"I'd never choose a black-edged shower panel," said one of the men who had come to install the cubicle, unaware that I could hear.

"Nor me," said his mate. "I'd have chrome or gold trim every time."

They finished the job and stood back.

"Actually, that looks bloody lovely," said the first man, scratching his head.

"I agree! Let's take a photo for the website," said his mate.

I checked their website a couple of weeks later and was amused to see a photo of our bathroom in prime position.

Our new tilers broke the news that they would need to use a jackhammer to remove the tiles throughout the living room area and kitchen. Laying a new floor on the top of the old tiles would bring the level too high.

"It's a really messy job," the foreman told us. "It's loud, and the dust is unbelievable. It will get everywhere. I suggest you seal off the rooms you don't want covered in dust and move out for three days."

Joe's lungs could never have withstood such a dusty environment, so we prepared to leave. The smaller pieces of furniture and TV were moved into the bedrooms and sealed off. The bigger items, like the couch, armchairs, sideboard, and dining room table, were carried outside and placed under the pergola.

"We're going to be homeless while they work on the floor," I told Karly.

"Come and stay with us," she suggested.

"Are you sure?"

"Absolutely! We can take advantage of live-in babysitters."

So for three days we stayed with Karly and Cam. It was a pleasure to spend time with them and the girls, and I tried to be useful by helping out with the laundry and cleaning chores.

Indy loved pretending to make phone calls. One day she was sitting in her child-seat in the back of Bruce. She and I were driving to the shops to pick up a few things for her mum. Indy held her toy phone to her ear.

"Ring-ring!" she called. "Ring-ring!"

That was my signal to pick up an imaginary phone and answer. I took one hand off the steering wheel and cupped my ear.

"Hello? Nanny speaking. Who's that calling?"

"It's me, Indy!"

"Oh, hello Indy, how are you today?"

"Good. I want to know what is your favourite animal."

"Hmm… Excellent question. What is *your* favourite animal?"

"Guinea pig."

"Oh, really? And why is that?"

I don't think I ever heard her answer because I suddenly felt extremely uncomfortable. We had stopped at traffic lights and the car alongside us was a police car. Both uniformed occupants had swivelled their heads in my direction and were staring at me with expressionless faces. Our eyes met.

It suddenly dawned on me that they thought I was making a real phone call. The use of a mobile phone while driving is highly illegal in New South Wales. My window was half open, so they had probably heard me talking, and had seen my hand over my ear.

I dropped my hand and opened it, palm out, fingers outstretched to show them I didn't have a phone.

"Silly Nanny!" cried Indy from the back seat. "You dropped your phone."

"No, I didn't! I don't have a phone!" I protested loudly.

The policeman's eyes bored into me.

"Yes, you have, Nanny!" crowed Indy.

The policeman's eyes narrowed.

"Nanny! Pick it up!"

"Indy, show the policeman your phone!" I commanded.

Indy obediently waved her toy phone at them, but I don't think they saw her. The lights had changed and we all drove off but not before I caught the expression in the nearest policeman's eyes. He clearly thought I was behaving very oddly.

After that, I made sure both my hands were on the steering wheel all the way to the shops.

During our stay, Bandsaw made herself scarce. This wasn't unusual. Bandsaw was probably tired of being hauled around like a sack of potatoes by a toddler. Karly was convinced the cat had adopted another family and was dividing her time between two homes.

"She's like a furry barrel on legs," said Karly. "She can't have put on that much weight with the food we give her. She must be being fed somewhere else as well."

LJ wasn't at all impressed with Lola's presence and made it quite clear she wasn't welcome. Karly took both of them for a long walk, on neutral territory, which helped a little, but LJ remained very territorial. It wasn't an ideal situation.

After three days, I phoned the tiler.

"Is it okay for us to come home?" I asked.

"No, we won't finish lifting the old tiles until tomorrow. And then it's going to be another three days to lay the new ones."

Shocked, I relayed the news to Joe. We both agreed we didn't want to outstay our welcome, so I found a local dog-friendly motel and booked us in.

"You don't have to do that, you can stay as long as you like," said Karly and Cam, but our minds were made up.

The motel accommodation was a trifle cosy for the three of us, but we coped. We went for walks, watched the TV, and read, and tried to stop Lola barking at passers-by.

Another three days crawled by. We had time on our hands and plenty of opportunities to discuss important topics.

"You know what to do, don't you?" Joe often said, even a couple of times in front of Karly and Cam. "If I'm taken to the hospital again and put on a life support machine…"

"I know…"

"Pull the plug. I mean it."

"Well, judging by that huge dinner you've just polished off, I doubt that's going to happen any time soon!" I said.

But his words had struck home. They stayed in my head, and I couldn't dispel a sense of foreboding, a fearful apprehension as though something terrible was waiting around the next corner.

"They must have finished the tiling by now!" Joe complained, changing the subject.

"I doubt it. Don't forget we've just had a weekend. I doubt they worked on Saturday or Sunday."

I was right, unfortunately. When I rang again, I was told the job would take a further three days.

In total, we stayed at the motel for a week.

During that time, the weather suddenly changed, and black storm clouds rolled in across the lake. Strong winds bent the trees and driving rain sent everybody scuttling indoors.

In our motel room, the TV news informed us that the rain would continue for days.

"At least we're warm and snug here," I remarked.

"Have you forgotten all our furniture is outside?" asked Joe. "The sofa, dining room table, everything."

I had forgotten, but there wasn't anything we could do about it.

Eventually, the storm moved on. Deb and I met up and took Lola and Molly for a walk beside the lake. I was almost afraid to ask whether she had thought any more about re-homing Molly.

We stopped for a coffee at a very nice cafe with a slightly alternative menu.

"Do you fancy something to eat?" asked Deb. "How about one of those lemon myrtle slices?"

"Lemon myrtle?"

"Oh, it's bush tucker. No calories."

Deb could always make me smile, and actually, the lemon myrtle cake was delicious.

"I've been asking around," said Deb, reading my mind. "I'm not going to come to a decision quickly, but my sister isn't getting any better, and I know I need to find Molly a new home. I just have to be one hundred per cent sure that it's the right one."

I wholeheartedly agreed. But did a perfect home exist for such an anxious little dog?

"I'm a member of a lot of doggy Facebook groups," Deb went on. "I'm just putting out feelers, but I haven't done anything yet. How's Joe?"

"Oh, getting a little better every day, thank you. I know he'll never be cured, but he managed to beat those viruses, I think. We just have to hope he doesn't pick up another one."

That cold feeling of dread came back as I spoke.

At long last, we were told that the tiling was finished and that we could return home. I couldn't pack our cases fast enough. But all the inconvenience and the long wait were worth it. I didn't even care about our dripping wet sofa and dining room table outside. The floor looked stunning.

"Look, Joe! It looks amazing. It's funny how you forget all the pain, isn't it? Like childbirth."

"I wouldn't know. But the floor does look great."

Our soaked furniture gradually dried out and wasn't much damaged. We still didn't have a kitchen, but we were definitely making huge progress. We had three working bedrooms, two beautiful bathrooms, and a garden to die for. Summer had arrived, and we swam in the pool every afternoon.

"Can Molly swim?" I asked Deb once. Molly and Lola often paddled in the sea, but they didn't actually swim, probably nervous of the waves.

"No, she's never tried as far as I know."

"Instead of a walk, why not bring her with you to our house next week. Let's see what she thinks of the pool."

Deb arrived bearing cupcakes for us and treats for Lola. Joe excused himself, saying he needed a nap.

"I'll leave you ladies together," he said, and disappeared into the house.

Lola adored jumping into the pool, and I threw a toy into the water. Lola leapt in and retrieved it, swimming back with it in her mouth. Molly was very interested and watched her carefully. She stood in the shallow end, the water lapping her belly.

Deb threw a toy for Molly, and she was desperate to get it.

"Molly! Go and get it!" we urged.

She paddled the water with one paw, then the other. Suddenly she launched forward, now out of her depth. For a split second, she looked terrified, and then it dawned on her that she was swimming. She *loved* it.

"Yay! Well done, Molly!"

"Hurrah! Molly's swimming!"

From that moment, both Molly and Lola were in and out of the pool like twin furry seals.

They were happy days, drenched in sunshine and laughter.

It was easy to forget how sick Joe was. And how Molly's days with Deb were numbered.

LEMON MYRTLE CAKE

Lemon Myrtle is a beautiful, native Australian shrub. It grows up to three metres high, and clusters of cream fragrant, feathery flowers occur in autumn.

Ingredients

125g (4½oz) butter, chopped

¾ cup caster sugar

1 teaspoon vanilla essence

2 eggs

2 cups self-raising flour, sifted

⅔ cup milk

1 tablespoon Lemon Myrtle powdered spice

Method

Preheat oven to 180°C (350°F).

Lightly grease a deep, 20cm (7 inch) round cake pan. Line base with baking paper.

Beat butter, sugar and vanilla together in a large bowl using an electric mixer, until pale and creamy.

Add eggs one at a time, beating well after each addition, scraping down sides of the bowl.

Lightly fold flour into creamed mixture alternately with milk, beginning and ending with flour.

Add lemon myrtle in with cake mixture.

Spoon mixture into prepared pan.

Bake for 40-45 mins, or until cooked.

To make the vanilla icing:

Sift icing sugar into a bowl.

Add butter, water and vanilla. Add a little lemon myrtle. Beat well with a wooden spoon until a smooth spreadable consistency.

Spread over cooled cake.

From bindibindidreaming.com.au, a website celebrating aboriginal culture. (bindi bindi means 'butterfly')

30

OXYGEN

Some weekends, Karly, Cam and the children came to stay. Being summer, it didn't matter a bit that we had no finished kitchen yet, because we cooked on the barbecue, as all Aussies do.

Lola adored having the family around. She played with Indy, stole the kids' socks and toys, and never complained when baby Winter yanked her eyebrows. Like most dogs, she soon learned that it was a worthwhile exercise to hang around under the dinner table, vacuuming the scraps that regularly hit the floor.

It was a fundamental rule of mine that Lola must keep off the furniture. Whenever she jumped onto the sofa, I had only to look at her and she would immediately jump off, looking guilty. I was pleased that my training had worked. Or, I should say, I thought it had.

One morning, Cam said, "I got up in the night and guess who I saw fast asleep on the sofa?"

"Not Lola. She knows she's not allowed on the sofa," I said, shaking my head.

"Well, she was!"

"I don't believe you."

Later that day, he tricked me. While I was outside, he sat on the sofa.

"Lola was on the sofa again," he said, when I came in.

"Cam, I don't believe you, she wouldn't do that."

"Honestly! She heard you coming and jumped off quickly. If you don't believe me, feel the sofa here," he said, pointing at the area where he had been sitting. "It's still warm where she was."

Only when he started laughing did I realise he was telling fibs. I was certain that well-trained Lola would never dream of sleeping on the sofa. Unfortunately, at a later date, Cam got up in the night again and produced photographic evidence of Lola blatantly flouting the rules.

It reminded me of my Facebook friend, Elle, telling me about her dogs. They were never allowed onto the sofas. But she and her partner were well aware that when they'd gone to bed, and the coast was clear, the dogs would be on the sofa in a trice. It got to the point where the first person to get up in the morning would cough loudly as he, or she, came down the stairs, giving the dogs time to relocate and look innocent.

I don't know how it happened, but Lola gradually managed to bend the rules. It wasn't long before she was not only allowed on the sofa, but on our laps too, despite her size.

A Facebook friend once showed me a tea towel. It was decorated with cartoons and the following captions, which made me laugh. Dog owners will understand.

DOG RULES

- The dog is not allowed in the house.
- Okay, the dog is allowed in the house, but only in certain rooms.
- The dog is allowed in all rooms but must stay off the furniture.
- The dog can get up on the old sofa only.
- Fine! The dog is allowed on all the furniture but is not allowed upstairs.
- Okay, the dog is allowed upstairs but not on the bed with humans.
- Fine! The dog can sleep on the bed but only by invitation.
- Okay, the dog can sleep at the end of the bed but only on a blanket.

- The dog can sleep between us and share the pillows.
- Humans must ask permission to sleep on the bed with the dog.

One evening, as we were sitting watching TV, my phone lit up, showing an incoming message. It was yet another saucy message from Fred, clearly sent to me by mistake.

I need you to keep me warm.

"Joe, another message from Fred," I said, giggling. "I wonder who that one was meant for?"

I showed him the message, but he didn't reply. I'd noticed he seemed overly sleepy that evening, dozing off in front of the television, which wasn't normal for him.

Suddenly, I remembered the doctor's words. If Joe kept 'drifting off' it could be a sign of high levels of carbon dioxide in his blood and not enough oxygen. He could be losing consciousness.

"Joe? How do you feel?"

"Sleepy. I'm okay, honestly." He stared vacantly at the TV.

The TV show kept playing, but I could see that Joe wasn't concentrating. His eyelids were closing again.

"Joe? I'm worried about you."

He opened his eyes halfway. "No, I'll be okay."

I wasn't so sure as I studied his face. He didn't seem to have much colour. In fact, his lips looked a little bluish, as did his fingernails. Next time I looked, he was asleep again, and now I was seriously concerned.

"Joe? Wake up!"

I sensed he was trying to open his eyelids a crack, but the effort was too much. I grabbed his shoulders.

"Joe!" My heart raced. "Joe! Wake up! I'm going to call for help."

"Yes, call..." he whispered, and his voice faded away. I grabbed the phone and dialled triple zero.

"Which service do you require, Police, Fire or Ambulance?"

"Ambulance, I think my husband is slipping into unconsciousness."

"What is the exact address of your emergency?"

I gave them all the information, then turned my attention back to Joe. He was barely conscious.

"Joe, wake up! An ambulance is coming, and they'll sort you out." I chafed his lifeless hands. "Stay with me, just hold on."

Every second felt like a lifetime. I willed him to breathe. I willed the ambulance to hurry. No! It hadn't come to this! Not now!

But all the time, as I waited for the ambulance to arrive, his words replayed in my head.

"You know what to do, don't you? If I'm taken to the hospital again and put on a life support machine..."

"I know..."

"Pull the plug. I mean it."

My heart thumped so loudly, I could hear it. *Pull the plug, pull the plug,* it drummed.

It seemed like hours, but within ten minutes, blue flashing lights pierced the night outside our home. I leapt up.

"Joe! They're here. Just hold on, everything's going to be okay now."

I threw open the front door and ran outside.

"Quick! He's hardly breathing!"

The ambulance staff hurried into the house where Joe was motionless, slumped back on the sofa, his skin grey. The two men were wonderful. They were calm, exuding an air of confidence as they began work immediately, checking and measuring Joe's vital signs.

One nipped back to the ambulance for more equipment and came back with an oxygen tank. They placed a mask over Joe's face and gave him something from a phial and then oxygen. Slowly but surely some colour returned to his face, and his chest moved up and down as he breathed more easily. His eyes opened.

"You're pretty crook," said the driver. "You should've called us earlier, mate."

Joe spent many days in the ICU. Thank goodness his breathing was gradually stabilised without the need of a ventilator, and I never had to say those three terrible words. However, he needed oxygen twenty-four hours a day and slept with the aid of a BiPap machine in case he stopped breathing in the night.

At first, his skin was almost as white as the hospital sheets, but gradually he took on a healthier hue.

He was encouraged to sit up as soon as possible, but he was pitifully weak. Physiotherapists arrived to teach him how to breathe correctly, and help him walk a few steps. When I thought about the games of squash he had played, the marathons he had run, and the heavy work he had carried out renovating our home in Spain, it seemed incomprehensible to me. It was hard to believe that this frail creature, struggling to breathe or take a few steps, was the same person.

But Joe never gave up. With the help of the hospital staff, he grew a tiny bit stronger every day.

I tried my best, but sometimes it was difficult to stay cheerful with the harrowing sounds of the ICU around us. Curtains surrounded each bed, but they didn't shut out the suffering. Sometimes we heard patients crying out in pain, or relatives weeping. So many tragic stories. Such sadness.

Yet, if I looked out of the ICU window, I could see blue sky stretching for ever, and flocks of cockatoos flying over. Sometimes a single eagle hung in the air, or a group of pelicans in V-shaped formation passed, their silhouettes like prehistoric pterodactyls.

Finally, the day came when Joe could walk to the bathroom by himself, with the oxygen tank in tow.

"They're just waiting for a bed to become available in the respiratory ward," he told me. "Then they'll move me down."

We were delighted when that happened because it was a sign that he was improving. However, the respiratory ward was crammed full, and the nurses were rushed off their feet. The side wards were also full. Every bed contained a very sick person fighting to breathe, whether from lung cancer, COPD, or some other terrible breathing affliction.

I often thought how I'd always taken the act of breathing for granted. Not now. Now I often breathe deeply, sucking in the sweet, fresh air, *just because I can.*

I visited Joe every day, leaving Lola with Emma and Baxter, or taking her to Germany. Lola's tummy grew rounder as I walked her less, and she enjoyed the many treats Thea gave her.

In the evenings, I made myself useful by painting walls. Joe couldn't have coped with the paint fumes, so I rushed to get it finished. As Lola snored, I painted walls, doors and skirting boards, until I dropped into bed, exhausted.

Joe grew stronger, and I was able to wheel him onto the balcony for some fresh air. He was still connected to his oxygen cylinder, and all that paraphernalia had to accompany us. It was a challenge getting through the big swing doors that opened onto the balcony, but worth the battle.

Outside was another world far removed from the hospital ward. That balcony became our escape, our refuge, our favourite place.

I tried to entertain Joe with small events, snippets of what was going on at home. Fred had brought in his son to help him, a big strapping, capable young man who towered over his father. Together they knocked down a wall and rebuilt another. The kitchen began to take shape.

I told Joe which countertops I'd chosen for the kitchen, and which blinds for the windows. I told him how the men arrived to fit the plantation shutters and how Lola had 'helped' them by putting her toys in their toolbox. I told him how she had learned, on the first day, to open the shutters with one paw so she that she could keep a lookout for cats.

"Have you seen Deb and Molly?"

"No, she's been really busy visiting her sister and job hunting. She says she has some news, though. I'm sure she will tell me the next time I see her."

"Does Lollipop still love her walks on the oval?"

"Of course, and the cockatoos are keeping her exercised. She catches sight of a flock grazing on one side of the field, and chases them. Meanwhile, another flock lands on the other side of the field, so she gallops after those. Meanwhile, the first flock has landed again and needs chasing, so she swings around and pelts after them."

It was good to make him smile and see his strength slowly return.

And one welcome thing came out of that hospital stay.

Joe has never been keen on ice cream, but I love it. As his appetite came back, he was served ice cream and discovered he did like it after all. In future, I could add ice cream to our menu.

Joe was eventually able to walk short distances and shower by himself. The overcrowded respiratory ward was probably anxious to free a bed, and the doctors decided Joe was ready to go home.

But first, a technician arrived at his bedside.

"We're going to give you a BiPap machine to take home with you," he explained. "I'm going to set it all up for you and show you how to maintain it. It has a computer chip inside which will record all your sleep patterns. When you come back to the hospital for out-patient check-ups, the doctors will be able to download all the information and see how you're doing."

"How long will I need to use the BiPap machine for?"

"Probably for life. The act of breathing is hard work, but the machine will do it for you. You'll love it, and you'll sleep like a baby, I promise you!"

Joe was sceptical, but the man was right. Joe got used to wearing a mask at night and enjoyed restful sleep. We would never need to worry again about his breathing during the dark hours.

"We're also going to lend you a couple of portable oxygen tanks, which you'll need for a while. I'll give you the number of a local company that the hospital recommends. They'll keep you supplied with oxygen. They'll take the empty tanks away and bring new ones."

"Will I always need oxygen?"

"Not necessarily. Some patients do, but many regain their strength and don't need the extra oxygen after a while."

Joe and I looked at each other. I could read his mind. I knew how stubborn he was. And I knew he would be utterly determined to get well enough to dispense with that oxygen tank.

I squeezed his hand and smiled at him.

There was so much that we hadn't yet done. So many places and beaches we hadn't yet explored. So much wildlife we hadn't seen. We needed to settle into our lovely new home and enjoy the changing seasons and watching Indy and baby Winter grow.

"Do you know," said Joe, reading my mind as usual. "We've been so busy; we haven't even made it to Splinterbone Crag yet, to watch the humpback whales swim past."

"You're right! And it's only five minutes away from home. That's definitely something we must do!"

Joe had battled viruses that had nearly stolen his breath for ever. But he had won.

At last, it was time to thank the staff and leave the hospital that had saved Joe's life three times.

I pushed his wheelchair and the oxygen tank across the car park to Bruce. We were free to go home and build the rest of our lives together. Future adventures were beckoning us.

VEGEMITE PASTA

For the final recipe, I had to include something really Aussie, and what could be more Aussie than Vegemite? From notquitenigella.com

Ingredients

375g (14oz) dried spaghetti

50g (2oz) unsalted butter

1 teaspoon Vegemite (or Marmite)

Freshly grated parmesan cheese, halved cherry tomatoes and baby spinach leaves to serve (optional)

Method

Cook the spaghetti in a large pot of salted boiling water according to directions. Drain and rinse under water keeping a cup of the pasta water.

In the same pan, put on the heat and evaporate the water and then melt the butter and add the Vegemite and a tablespoon of the pasta water and mix to dissolve.

Add the cooked pasta and more pasta water to combine if necessary.

Garnish with grated parmesan cheese if you like, and baby spinach leaves and halved cherry tomatoes.

EPILOGUE

Lola was beside herself with delight when Joe came home. Somehow she knew that the oxygen line was not a toy and never touched it, which was remarkable considering she played with everything else.

Thea made a beautiful German cake to welcome Joe home. It didn't last long, it was far too delicious, and Joe was regaining his appetite fast.

We had one final email from our young 'penpall', Catalina, in Spain.

Hola tía Vicky y tío Joe,

I hop you are well. My family is completely wells and I am content *tío* Joe is very better.

I have many news for you. Geronimo and Valentina they went to London for vacation after the *fiesta*. They have very good times and soon there will be a weeding and my sister and me we can dance flamenco. Valentina she say Geronimo has eyes like a fish he stare at all things in London. Geronimo he say he like London but he like El Hoyo very better. He say the colour of London is very grey and if he want grey he can look at his donkey.

Valentina she say to my mother that they has a big surprise in

London. ¡¡¡¡¡They see *tía* Lola!!!!! She is with her friend Esteban and they have vacation in London also. Mama she say we not talk about it and it is not the business of children. Then she say to papa poor father Samuel and Lola has not change her skin.

I am sad *tía* Lola and father Samuel not have a weeding but i can dance flamenco at the weeding of Valentina and Geronimo and perhaps a man from television see me.

I not be your penpall no more because I must dance and i have a boyfriend also. My boyfriend is Manolo the grandson of Marcia at the shop of El Hoyo. Before it is a secret but now it is not a secret because my little brother Pollito he see me and Manolo he tell mama but mama say it is OK. Manolo say me he think father Samuel will go to the country of africa and be a *misionero*. One day perhaps there will be a weeding with *tía* Lola and Esteban and I can dance flamenco. But perhaps then i will be flamenco dancer *famosa* and you will see me on the television.

My sister not have a boyfriend.

Felicitations, Catalina and Manolo xx

"Well!"

"That answers all your questions, doesn't it, Miss Nosy Parker?"

"I guess it does... Do you know what that story of seeing Lola Ufarte and Esteban in London reminds me of?"

"Reykjavík!"

"Yes!"

We both laughed, recalling the memory. It took place in the nineties, when the flashiest plane in the sky was Concorde, long before the tragic crash that grounded Concorde planes forever.

One of our close friends, Al, booked a flight on Concorde, as a surprise for his father, who was celebrating his 80th birthday. It was an expensive, luxurious day trip and the flight would go supersonic, breaking the sound barrier, before landing in Iceland. There, the passengers would disembark and explore the city of Reykjavík before boarding Concorde in the evening and returning to London.

Al and his dad had a wonderful day. They enjoyed an authentic lunch in a restaurant, then strolled through the streets, admiring the Icelandic architecture and exotic sights.

Imagine everybody's utter astonishment when they bumped into a familiar couple from their small home town back in Sussex.

Al and his father knew the couple well, but the chance meeting was not a happy one. Why? Because the couple walking with arms entwined, were married.

But not to each other.

The unfortunate lovers had probably chosen a trip to Iceland because, not in their wildest dreams, could they imagine they'd be seen by anyone who knew them.

But they were. Coincidences do happen.

Likewise, Lola Ufarte and Esteban must have thought that nobody they knew would ever see them in London.

But they were spotted.

Al and his dad were very discreet and never told us who the couple in Reykjavík were. Even now, years later, I still wonder who it was.

Joe's healing would be slow, and it was unlikely he would be able to join Lola and me on long, brisk walks in the near future. I carried on meeting with Deb and Molly and was keen to hear Deb's news.

"I think I've found the perfect home for Molly," she said, and I could see conflicting emotions in her eyes.

"Where?" I asked, trying hard to sound enthusiastic. "Who with?" It was the worst news, and the best news.

"You remember I put feelers out in some of the Facebook groups I belong to?"

"I remember."

"Well, I never actually posted anything about re-homing Molly, but I did chat privately with a few people. One of them suggested a lady she knew who was looking for a dog, not a puppy, for her grown-up daughter."

"Really?"

"Yes, and she put us in touch with each other, me and the lady with the daughter. It turned out that we actually have friends in common from the time when I used to live in Sydney."

"Gosh, what a coincidence!"

"I know! Anyway, we got talking, and I was very honest about Molly's issues. Whoever takes her on must understand that she has problems. I doubt she'll ever be cured of her anxiety and her new owner must be aware of that."

"Did the mother take all that onboard?"

"She absolutely did. The more we talked, the more we both thought Molly might be the ideal companion for her daughter."

"Why, exactly?"

"That's the extraordinary part! Her daughter, Ruth, suffers from severe social anxiety. She lives alone and is capable of looking after herself, but her mother pops in every day. Ruth's anxiety is extreme. She can't work, except for cutting friends' hair in her own home, and she rarely has the confidence to go out alone."

"Oh my goodness!"

"Ruth's mother believes that being responsible for Molly and having her as a companion will help her daughter in so many ways."

My eyes strayed to Molly and Lola who were chasing seagulls across the sand. My heart was heavy. I would miss these sun-drenched days, watching the pair of them race, side by side, while the sea sang its song and washed their paw prints away.

"So, what happens next?"

Deb sighed. "I can hardly bear to think about it," she said, "but it does seem like a match made in heaven. I've arranged to meet them, to see if Ruth and Molly like each other. Then we'll go from there."

Ruth and Molly did like each other. A lot. A play-date was arranged, and Deb left Molly with Ruth for a few hours. It went well.

Next, Deb and Ruth's mother set up a sleepover date.

"It was so hard leaving her there," said Deb. "Ruth was planning to take Molly out for a walk, and they would visit Ruth's mum round the corner. They were going to have dinner there and introduce Molly to the rest of the family."

"How did that go?"

"Really well. Everybody made a fuss of Molly and she loved it. She sat on everybody's laps and had a great time. I didn't ask where Molly slept, but I imagine she shared Ruth's bed, like she does mine."

Debs smiled but her voice sounded hollow. I couldn't even begin to imagine how she was feeling. Had I been forced to give Lola away, it would break my heart.

A month later, Deb bravely gathered up Molly's bed, toys and leads and drove to Ruth's house in Sydney.

"Please take these," she said, handing over Molly's bag of belongings to Ruth's mother while Molly jumped into Ruth's arms and covered her face with kisses.

"Just one thing," Deb said to Ruth and her mother. "If, for whatever reason, it doesn't work out, please tell me, and I'll take her back."

Both Ruth and her mother promised and insisted that Deb could visit whenever she liked. Deb hugged Molly for the last time.

The deed was done, and Deb turned away to lick her wounds and try to fill the void that Molly had left in her life.

Ruth's mother and Deb did keep in touch.

"Ruth walks Molly every day," Deb told me. "Her mother says the pair of them are inseparable, and that Ruth has become so much more confident and self-sufficient. Ruth's mum and dad have even booked an overseas holiday, which they haven't been able to do for years. Before Molly came, Ruth couldn't cope without them."

"That's wonderful!"

"I know! It's so good to know that not only is Molly happy, but she's brought happiness to somebody else and is helping to heal a troubled soul."

It was the best of all possible outcomes.

Sometimes, after a swim, Lola wears the hooded, yellow *Surf Dog Australia* towel that used to belong to Molly. Immediately my mind is cast back to Molly and Lola pounding along the wet sand, barking at seagulls, and digging holes, simply for the sheer joy of it. And all the while, the rhythm of the sea sent frothy waves to lap at their toes and fill in their newly-dug excavations.

Time has passed. At first, Joe couldn't walk far, but now he can manage a good hundred metres before stopping to rest.

Doctors are keeping a close watch on the tumour in his pituitary gland. It's been pronounced benign and non-aggressive. It has been decided not to meddle with it unless it changes.

In addition, his prostate cancer has been successfully kept at bay.

Work on our house was finally finished, and we are delighted with the result. It's not a big house, but it's easy to maintain, light and airy. I doubt the former owners would recognise it.

Fred, the builder, has since completed other odd jobs for us. Sadly, Dinkum passed away, but Hulk is thriving and, thankfully, has stopped growing. Fred no longer sends me saucy texts.

Baby Winter's first word was "Lola", and Indy prepared to start school.

Sometimes I think of our life in Spain and the folk who enriched it. Will Lola Ufarte ever behave? Will Catalina become a famous flamenco dancer, or will she settle down with Manolo and produce lots of beautiful children just as her mother has done? And what about our lovely neighbours, Paco and Carmen? And Geronimo and Valentina? Did Father Samuel really become a missionary in Africa?

Moving to Australia was a tough decision, but absolutely the right one. We adore everything about Australia. We love the open spaces, the unexplored bush, the endless beaches, the colours, and the Australian wildlife. We love the informality, the friendliness and the humour of Australians.

We are so lucky to spend our twilight years here, where we can watch Indy and Winter grow. Australia is the perfect place for children (and puppies) to be raised, a land of opportunity and adventure.

And I'm convinced that Joe would have died, had we still lived in the tiny, remote village of El Hoyo.

Sometimes I suffer from night terrors. I hear soft voices in my ear.

"*Pull the plug,*" they whisper. "*Pull the plug.*"

Joe may not be as strong as he was, but we have plans. Wonderful, exciting plans. We haven't finished having adventures, and I haven't finished writing about them.

We're not ready to pull any plugs.

A REQUEST...

We authors absolutely rely on our readers' reviews. We love them even more than a glass of chilled wine on a summer's night beneath the stars.

Even more than chocolate.

If you enjoyed this book, I'd be so grateful if you left an Amazon review, even if it's simply one sentence.

THANK YOU!

SO WHAT HAPPENED NEXT?

To find out, please join us in the next Old Fools adventure.

If you'd like to keep up with our lives, and be notified when the next book comes out, please join me on Facebook.

And if you are not subscribed already, or have fallen off our mailing list, do subscribe to our newsletter on my website. I send it every few months and it usually contains news, stories, competitions, photos, free books, book recommendations and a recipe.

As for the next book, I already have a full notebook. The chapters are organising themselves in my head. Now all I have to do is write it…

THE OLD FOOLS SERIES

Book #1

Chickens, Mules and Two Old Fools

If Joe and Vicky had known what relocating to a tiny mountain village in Andalucía would REALLY be like, they might have hesitated...

Book #2

Two Old Fools - Olé!

Vicky and Joe have finished fixing up their house and look forward to peaceful days enjoying their retirement. Then the fish van arrives, and instead of delivering fresh fish, disgorges the Ufarte family.

Book #3

Two Old Fools on a Camel

Reluctantly, Vicky and Joe leave Spain to work for a year in the Middle East. Incredibly, the Arab revolution erupted, throwing them into violent events that made world headlines.

New York Times bestseller three times

Book #4

Two Old Fools in Spain Again

Life refuses to stand still in tiny El Hoyo. Lola Ufarte's behaviour surprises nobody, but when a millionaire becomes a neighbour, the village turns into a battleground.

Book #5

Two Old Fools in Turmoil

When dark, sinister clouds loom, Victoria and Joe find themselves facing life-changing decisions. Happily, silver linings also abound. A fresh new face joins the cast of well-known characters but the return of a bad penny may be more than some can handle.

Book #6

Two Old Fools Down Under

When Vicky and Joe wave goodbye to their beloved Spanish village, they face their future in Australia with some trepidation. Now they must build a new life amongst strangers, snakes and spiders the size of saucers. Accompanied by their enthusiastic new puppy, Lola, adventures abound, both heartwarming and terrifying.

One Young Fool in Dorset (Prequel)

This light and charming story is the delightful prequel to Victoria Twead's Old Fools series. Her childhood memories are vividly portrayed, leaving the reader chuckling and enjoying a warm sense of comfortable nostalgia.

One Young Fool in South Africa (Prequel)

Who is Joe Twead? What happened before Joe met Victoria and they moved to a crazy Spanish mountain village? Joe vividly paints his childhood memories despite constant heckling from Victoria at his elbow.

Two Old Fools in the Kitchen, Part 1 (Cookbook)

The *Old Fools' Kitchen* cookbooks were created in response to frequent requests from readers of the *Old Fools series* asking to see all the recipes collected together in one place.

THE SIXPENNY CROSS SERIES
SHORT FICTION, INSPIRED BY LIFE

A is for Abigail

Abigail Martin has everything: beauty, money, a loving husband, and a fabulous house in the village of Sixpenny Cross. But Abigail is denied the one thing she craves... A baby.

B is for Bella

When two babies are born within weeks of each other in the village of Sixpenny Cross, one would expect the pair to become friends as they grow up. But nothing could be further from the truth.

C is for the Captain

Everyone knows ageing bachelors, the Captain and Sixpence, are inseparable. But when new barmaid, Babs, begins work at the Dew Drop Inn, will she enhance their twilight years, or will the consequences be catastrophic?

The Sixpenny Cross Collection: Books 1-3

D is for Dexter - coming soon

MORE BOOKS BY VICTORIA TWEAD...

How to Write a Bestselling Memoir
How does one write, publish and promote a memoir? How does one become a bestselling author?

Morgan and the Martians - A COMEDY PLAY FOR KIDS
Morgan is a bad boy. A VERY bad boy. When a bunch of Martians gives him a Shimmer Suit that makes him invisible, he wastes no time in wearing it to school and creating havoc. Well, wouldn't you?

Two Old Fools in the Kitchen, Part 1 (COOKBOOK)
The *Old Fools' Kitchen* cookbooks were created in response to frequent requests from readers of the *Old Fools series* asking to see all the recipes collected together in one place.

ABOUT THE AUTHOR

Victoria Twead is the New York Times bestselling author of *Chickens, Mules and Two Old Fools* and the subsequent books in the Old Fools series.

After living in a remote mountain village in Spain for eleven years, and owning probably the most dangerous cockerel in Europe, Victoria and Joe retired to Australia.

Another joyous life-chapter has begun.

For photographs and additional unpublished material to accompany this book, download the

Free Photo Book

from

www.victoriatwead.com/free-stuff

CONTACTS AND LINKS
CONNECT WITH VICTORIA

Email: TopHen@VictoriaTwead.com (emails welcome)

Website: www.VictoriaTwead.com

Old Fools' updates Signup: www.VictoriaTwead.com

This includes the latest Old Fools' news, free books, book recommendations, and recipe. Guaranteed spam-free and sent out every few months.

Free Stuff: http://www.victoriatwead.com/Free-Stuff/

Facebook: https://www.facebook.com/VictoriaTwead (friend requests welcome)

Instagram: @victoria.twead

Twitter: @VictoriaTwead

We Love Memoirs

Join me and other memoir authors and readers in the We Love Memoirs Facebook group, the friendliest group on Facebook.

www.facebook.com/groups/welovememoirs/

ACKNOWLEDGEMENTS

Thanks as always to **Nick Saltmer** who painted the fabulous cover picture. I've lost count how many covers you have designed for me, Nick, and I love them all.

Thanks also to **Julie Haigh, Pat Ellis** and **Pauline Armstrong** for your friendship and beta-reading talents. Skills like yours are essential for knocking any book into shape.

Big thanks and hugs to you, **Joe**, for your input and editing skills, and heartfelt thanks to my family for allowing me to write about you. **Joe, Karly, Cam, Indy, Winter**, my books would be so much duller without you.

Thank you Spain and El Hoyo for putting up with us for eleven years. To say you will always be in our hearts is a huge understatement.

Sincere thanks to all the wonderful **Facebook friends** I have made since I wrote my first book. Your loyalty and support often take my breath away. Particular thanks to the members of the We Love Memoirs Facebook group. You are totes stonking amazebobs…

This memoir reflects my recollections of experiences over a period of time. In order to preserve the anonymity of the wonderful people I write about, some names have been changed, including the name of the village. Certain individuals are composites and dialogue and events have been recreated from memory and, in some cases, compressed to facilitate a natural narrative.

ANT PRESS BOOKS

AWESOME AUTHORS ~ AWESOME BOOKS

Ant Press

If you enjoyed this book, you may also enjoy these Ant Press titles:

MEMOIRS

Chickens, Mules and Two Old Fools by Victoria Twead (Wall Street Journal Top 10 bestseller)

Two Old Fools ~ Olé! by Victoria Twead

Two Old Fools on a Camel by Victoria Twead (thrice New York Times bestseller)

Two Old Fools in Spain Again by Victoria Twead

Two Old Fools in Turmoil by Victoria Twead

Two Old Fools Down Under by Victoria Twead (NEW)

One Young Fool in Dorset (The Prequel) by Victoria Twead

One Young Fool in South Africa (The Prequel) by Joe and Victoria Twead

The Two Old Fools Boxset, Books 1-3 by Victoria Twead

Fat Dogs and French Estates ~ Part I by Beth Haslam

Fat Dogs and French Estates ~ Part II by Beth Haslam

Fat Dogs and French Estates ~ Part III by Beth Haslam

Fat Dogs and French Estates ~ Part IV by Beth Haslam

Simon Ships Out: How One Brave, Stray Cat Became a Worldwide Hero by Jacky Donovan

Smoky: How a Tiny Yorkshire Terrier Became a World War II American Army Hero, Therapy Dog and Hollywood Star by Jacky Donovan

Smart as a Whip: A Madcap Journey of Laughter, Love, Disasters and Triumphs by

Jacky Donovan

Heartprints of Africa by Cinda Adams Brooks

How not to be a Soldier: My Antics in the British Army by Lorna McCann

Moment of Surrender: My Journey Through Prescription Drug Addiction to Hope and Renewal by Pj Laube

One of its Legs are Both the Same by Mike Cavanagh

A Pocket Full of Days by Mike Cavanagh

Horizon Fever by A E Filby

Cane Confessions: The Lighter Side to Mobility by Amy L. Bovaird

Completely Cats - Stories with Cattitude by Beth Haslam and Zoe Marr

From Moulin Rouge to Gaudi's City by EJ Bauer

Fresh Eggs and Dog Beds 1: Living the Dream in Rural Ireland by Nick Albert

Fresh Eggs and Dog Beds 2: Still Living the Dream in Rural Ireland by Nick Albert

Fresh Eggs and Dog Beds 3: More Living the Dream in Rural Ireland by Nick Albert

Don't Do It Like This: How NOT to move to Spain by Joe Cawley, Victoria Twead and Alan Parks

Longing for Africa: Journeys Inspired by the Life of Jane Goodall. Part One: Ethiopia by Annie Schrank

Longing for Africa: Journeys Inspired by the Life of Jane Goodall. Part Two: Kenya by Annie Schrank

South of Barcelona: A New Life in Spain by Vernon Lacey

A Kiss Behind the Castanets: My Love Affair with Spain by Jean Roberts

Life Beyond the Castanets: My Love Affair with Spain by Jean Roberts

FICTION

Parched by Andrew C Branham

A is for Abigail by Victoria Twead (Sixpenny Cross 1)

B is for Bella by Victoria Twead (Sixpenny Cross 2)

C is for the Captain by Victoria Twead (Sixpenny Cross 3)

D is for Dexter by Victoria Twead (Sixpenny Cross 4) - coming soon

The Sixpenny Cross Collection: Books 1-3

NON FICTION

How to Write a Bestselling Memoir by Victoria Twead

Two Old Fools in the Kitchen, Part 1 by Victoria Twead

CHILDREN'S BOOKS

Seacat Simon: The Little Cat Who Became a Big Hero by Jacky Donovan

Morgan and the Martians by Victoria Twead

ANT PRESS ONLINE

Why not check out Ant Press's online presence and follow our social media accounts for news of forthcoming books and special offers?

Website: www.antpress.org
Email: admin@antpress.org
Facebook: www.facebook.com/AntPress
Instagram: www.instagram.com/publishwithantpress
Twitter: www.twitter.com/Ant_Press

HAVE YOU WRITTEN A BOOK?

Would you love to see your book published? Ant Press can help! Take a look at www.antpress.org or contact Victoria directly.

Email: TopHen@VictoriaTwead.com

Lightning Source UK Ltd.
Milton Keynes UK
UKHW010926180522
403179UK00001B/19

Johnstown Castle

A HISTORY

Johnstown Castle

A HISTORY

LIAM GAUL

*This book is dedicated to all those who have walked through
the gates of Johnstown Castle demesne and to the ghosts of
past residents there.*

First published 2014

Reprinted 2019

The History Press Ireland
50 City Quay
Dublin 2
Ireland
www.thehistorypress.ie

© Liam Gaul, 2014

The right of Liam Gaul to be identified as the Author
of this work has been asserted in accordance with the
Copyrights, Designs and Patents Act 1988.

British Library Cataloguing in Publication Data.
A catalogue record for this book is available from the British Library.

ISBN 978 1 84588 826 8

Typesetting and origination by The History Press
Printed and bound by TJ International, Padstow, Cornwall

CONTENTS

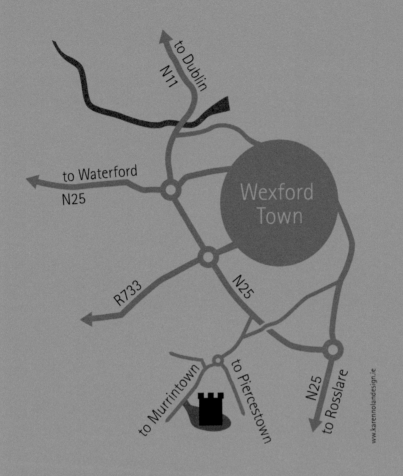

Johnstown Castle is a ten-minute drive from Wexford town centre. Indicated by brown road signs from the N25, it is situated a mile from the village of Murrintown.

GPS coordinates:

Garmin: N52° 17.782, W 006° 30.355
Tom Tom: N 52° 17.761, W 006° 30.335

Map courtesy of Karen Nolan Design

ABOUT THE AUTHOR

A native of Wexford town, Liam Gaul has had a life-long interest in history with a special interest in his local history. He is a member of the Wexford Historical Society and in 2013 he was invited to present the Dr Hadden Memorial Lecture as part of Wexford Opera Festival. To date he has four books published: *Masters of Irish Music, Glory O!, Glory O!: The Life of P.J. McCall, A Window on the Past* and *Wexford – The American Connection.* He is a regular contributor to historical journals, periodicals and newspapers and presents a radio programme during the summer months for the Christian Media Trust on South East Radio.

ACKNOWLEDGEMENTS

My special thanks to: Patrick Browne, Mairéad Esmonde, Aileen Cardiff, Patrick Sills, Edward McDonald and Sarah Lacey at Teagasc, Matt Wheeler and Michael Kelly.

I would also like to thank: D.F. Burchmore; Lily Burns; the Commonwealth War Graves Commission; Niamh Coulter; Alan Cuddihy; Dr Noel Culleton; Gráinne Doran; Laurence Doyle; the EPA in Johnstown; Marie Fane; The Friday Historians – Gloria, Nicky, Ken, Billy, Seamus and Tom; Jarlath Glynn; Ken Hemmingway; Lorcan Kehoe; Gerard Lawlor; Dr Patrick McKiernan; Peter Miller; Canon Arthur Minion; Matthew Murphy; Denise O'Connor-Murphy; the National Gallery of Ireland; the National Library of Ireland; Eoin Ó Donagáin; Gerry O'Leary; Dr Austin M. O'Sullivan; Nicky Rossiter; Georgina Rothwell; the churchwardens of St Mary the Virgin, Winchfield, Hampshire; Jimmy Taylor; Claire Verdun; Dan Walsh; and Michael, Ann, Claire, Susan and staff at Wexford Library.

Finally, I'd like to thank my wife and family for their interest, support and patience.

Photographic credits: Aerial view of Johnstown Castle – Gerry O'Leary; Capt. G.H. FitzGerald's gravestone, France – Commonwealth War Graves Commission; Capt. M.G. Lakin's gravestone, Tunisia – Denise O'Connor-Murphy; Johnstown Castle – EPA; Johnstown Castle – Irish Agricultural Museum Archive; midsummer night at the castle – Paddy Donovan; the National Gallery of Ireland and the National Library of Ireland.

INTRODUCTION

Having worked in the analytical services for thirty years with An Fóras Talúntais and Teagasc, I became very familiar with Johnstown Castle, gardens and grounds. I enjoyed every aspect of this historic estate through the seasonal changes from the new spring growth through lush green lawns and flower-laden shrubbery of summer. I loved the multicoloured fallen leaves of autumn and oft-times the glittering sparkle of winter frost with the occasional dusting of snow which gave the landscape an eerie and serene effect.

The grey architectural pile of the castle dominates the scene like a sleeping giant with so many tales to relate of conquest, eviction and patriot allegiance. There are threads of a lost cause in the 1798 Rebellion and a story to be told from the final stately residents of the Anglo-Irish FitzGeralds, Earls of Kildare in the presence of Lord Maurice and Lady FitzGerald. The long tradition of occupancy from Norman knight and Cromwellian soldier to the demise of Lady Adelaide FitzGerald resulted in the castle and estate being gifted to the Irish State in 1945.

Since that time, Johnstown Castle and its grounds has served as a college for students of agriculture and has been the centre for experimental research and analytical services to the Irish farming community for over fifty successful years. Teagasc still continues with this very valuable service. In the past few years the campus has played host to the Environmental Protection Agency and the Department of Agricultural, Food and the Marine. The Irish Agricultural Museum is housed in farm buildings dating from 1810 and the Famine Museum is also incorporated within this museum of rural life in Ireland.

Over my years at Johnstown Castle my interest was stirred by the fascinating history of this special location just 4 miles from Wexford town and the result is this book which I trust will give enjoyment to its readers and stimulate further and more extensive research into this magical rural demesne. Current expectations indicate a restoration and refurbishment of the interior of the castle to its former glory and opulence.

Liam Gaul, 2014

1

THE NORMANS AND ESMONDES ARRIVE

After the Vikings, the second invasion of the Wexford area was heralded by the arrival of the Normans. The coast of Wexford, separated as it is from Wales by a narrow stretch of sea, was the ideal landing place for the invading Normans and it opened the way forward to the rest of the country. Many historians consider this landing to be one of the most important events in Ireland's history, resulting in change which has lasted to present times.

Following the death of the English king, Edward the Confessor, in January 1066, William, Duke of Normandy claimed the English throne in opposition to Harold II. He invaded and defeated Harold at the Battle of Hastings and was crowned King of England on Christmas Day 1066. William pushed through a more brutal transformation of English society than any other ruler, before or since. He built castles in all the major English towns and confiscated his opponent's estates, transferring them to those he could rely on, nearly all Frenchmen, thus establishing an entirely new French-speaking ruling class.

One family which was granted land by William was the de Clare family who went on to become very influential. Richard de Clare, 2nd Earl of Pembroke from around 1130 to 1176, was a fearless soldier and leader who gained the nickname 'Strongbow'. He inherited his father's title as Earl of Pembroke in 1148 but no land as his father's lands had been confiscated by Henry II when he came to the throne as punishment for supporting King Stephen (c. 1096-1154) during the civil war. Still out of favour at the English court, Strongbow decided to accept Dermot

MacMurrough's offer of marriage to his daughter Aoife and succession to the Kingdom of Leinster in return for military assistance. Dermot MacMurrough, King of Leinster, had been forced to flee his castle at Ferns after being opposed by the Irish chieftains. MacMurrough was said to have been a man of tall stature and strong build, with a warlike spirit, and was described as a despicable character who showed no mercy to his rivals. In 1166, after many years of strife and a litany of treacherous deeds and brutality the Irish chieftains turned on MacMurrough. He set out for Bristol, eventually going on to Normandy and obtained permission from Henry II, King of England, to recruit some of his subjects to help him regain his Kingdom of Leinster. It was Strongbow who agreed to help raise and lead this army.

Dermot returned in secret to Ferns Castle and awaited the arrival of the Norman invaders. When no invaders appeared, Dermot sent Maurice Regan, his secretary, to announce that all who would come over to help Dermot MacMurrough would get lands if they wished to stay and settle in Ireland. For those who wished to return at the finish of the campaign,

Norman knights. (Courtesy of Kevin Lewis)

money or cattle would be given. The offers made by MacMurrough proved too good to refuse. The first Norman knight to land in Ireland was Richard FitzGodbert de Roche in 1167, followed, in 1169, by the first contingent of a party of around thirty chain-mail clad knights landing at Baginbun on the south-west coast of County Wexford. It was on 1 May 1170 that an army of 390 men arrived under the leadership of Robert FitzStephen de Marisco. Meiler FitzHenry, Miles FitzGerald, son of the Bishop of St David's, Maurice de Prendergast and Hervey de Montmorency were also part of the invasion force.

Henry II was keeping a watchful eye on those freelance adventurers and the possibility of them setting up a Norman state in Ireland which might oppose him and undermine his power. In Ireland, the Normans would be out of reach of the king. Henry II therefore resolved his differences with Strongbow and the king sent his own army, under the leadership of Strongbow, to Ireland.

Strongbow embarked from Milford Haven with 1,200 men and landed near Waterford on 23 August 1170. The following day Strongbow was joined by Raymond le Gros and his men with the combined forces marched on the city of Waterford. Although it was bravely defended, it was soon taken by the Normans. Having established his authority in the city, Strongbow and Aoife, daughter of Dermot MacMurrough, were married as agreed beforehand. The Normans soon moved up through Ferns, taking the coast road to Dublin where the principal city was taken by assault and great slaughter. Further expeditions were taken by MacMurrough into Meath and other areas. A few months later MacMurrough died at his castle in Ferns on 1 May 1171 and was succeeded to the throne of Leinster by Strongbow.[1]

Esmondes

Esmonde is a derivation of the ancient family name of d'Osmond. The name d'Osmond reached England for the first time with the ancestors of this family as they migrated following the Norman Conquest of 1066. A branch afterwards returned to Normandy but the main family settled in Norfolk with another branch settling at Huntingdon in Lincolnshire. The name is a reference to Osmandville, on the River Bire in Bessin, Normandy, the principal place of residence of the family prior to the Norman Conquest. The family had been granted lands by Duke William of Normandy, their liege Lord, for their distinguished assistance at the Battle of Hastings.[2] Geoffrey de Estmont, according to tradition, was one of the thirty knights who accompanied Robert FitzStephen to Ireland in 1169 and landed at Bannow, County Wexford. The Esmonde's settled on the lands known as Johnstown and Rathlannon and commenced building tower-houses at those sites from around 1480. The original tower-house at Johnstown was built by Geoffrey de Estmont and his son, Maurice, built a tower-house on the same site at Rathlannon. Maurice died around 1225 and his son, John, built a castle on a new site, the current Johnstown Castle. John died in 1261 and on his death was succeeded by his son, Sir William Esmonde. Sir William had several sons including John who became Bishop of Ferns. Another son, Walter, became a Canon of the Diocese of Ferns and settled at Ballynastragh, near Gorey County Wexford.

These basic tower-houses were developed over the centuries by the different residents right up to Cromwellian times when the estate was confiscated and granted to Lt-Col John Overstreet. Up to that time the Esmonde family had established itself there and had risen to become high-ranking officials in both State and Church. Family members married into local families and built up considerable land holdings across County Wexford. The modern Esmonde family began with James Esmonde, around 1520, who married Isabel daughter of Thomas Rossiter of Rathmacknee castle.[5] Their eldest son, Lawrence, married Eleanor Walsh, daughter of Walter Walsh of The Mountain, and their son William Esmonde succeeded his father to the estates. In turn, William married Margaret Furlong of Horetown, Foulksmill, County Wexford and they had seven sons and four daughters. Robert Esmonde was the eldest son and was described as one of the wealthiest gentlemen of the barony and was owner of considerable family property in north and south Wexford, including the castles of Johnstown, Ballytrent and Rathlannon with adjoining lands.[6] Lawrence, the second son, renounced the Roman Catholic faith of his ancestors and adopted the new religion during the reign of Elizabeth I. He was duly appointed Major General of all the Crown forces in Ireland and was rewarded with a knighthood. It was Lawrence who built a castle and church at Lymbrick, Ballynastragh near Gorey in north County Wexford. He named the castle after the original Norman motte and bailey established by the Esmondes in the Barony of Forth. Lawrence was appointed Governor of Duncannon Fort in 1606, a position he held until his death in 1646. Lawrence had married a daughter of Grace O'Malley (1530-1603) and they had one son, Thomas. He was reared by his mother in Connaught as she feared he might be brought up as a Protestant. Sir Lawrence, although not having divorced his wife, married a second time, to Elizabeth Butler. They had no issue. On the death of his father, the estates passed to Sir Thomas. Following the confiscations of the Cromwellian period, parts of the estates were granted to Lawrence Esmonde, third son of Sir William of Johnstown, and it was Sir Lawrence who built Huntingdon Castle in Clonegal in 1625, on the Wexford–Carlow border. By this time Lawrence had been created Baron of Lymbrick. After his death in 1646, Sir Lawrence was interred in the vault of his church at Lymbrick.[7]

During the Cromwellian Confiscations, the Johnstown Esmondes, who were Catholic, were evicted and their estate granted to Colonel John Overstreet and later came into the possession of the Grogan family. The Ballynastragh lands were also confiscated together with their lands at Ballytramont, near Castlebridge, outside the town of Wexford and were granted to the Duke of Ablemarle (General Richard Monck). It took the Esmonde family sixty years and a huge amount of money to get back parts of their estates in north Wexford.

Sir Thomas Esmonde married Ellice FitzGerald, daughter of Sir John FitzGerald, and they had three sons, Lawrence, James and Patrick. The eldest son, Lawrence, inherited the title and as Sir Lawrence once again reoccupied Huntingdon Castle in 1682. The line of the Esmondes came down through the descendants of Sir Thomas as the 3rd, 4th, 5th and 6th baronets residing at Huntingdon Castle. Following the death of the 7th baronet, Sir James, in 1750 the title devolved to Thomas Esmonde of Ballynastragh who then became Sir Thomas.

Thomas had a brother James, a Franciscan Friar, killed as he was hearing confessions in the friary in Wexford during the 1798 insurrection.[8] Another brother, John, a medical doctor, was hanged on Carlisle Bridge, Dublin, for his part in the rebellion. The property at Ballynastragh was confiscated because of the family's involvement in the rebellion. As Thomas had no family the title passed on to Dr John's eldest son, also named Thomas. He eventually regained the property and lands at Ballynastragh in 1816. The new baronet married twice, firstly to Mary Payne in 1852 and secondly to Sophia Maria Knox Grogan Morgan of Johnstown Castle. Having been confiscated by the Cromwellians the Johnstown Castle estate had once again returned into the possession of the Esmonde family, albeit for a short time. Sir Thomas Esmonde, 9th Baronet died in 1868 aged 82 years.[9] As there was no issue, the Esmonde link with Johnstown was broken.

2

THE CROMWELLIANS

A wet and stormy day at the beginning of October 1649 heralded the arrival of one of the most notorious visitors to Wexford town. The fifty-years-old Oliver Cromwell, together with 7,000 foot soldiers and 2,000 horsemen, camped on the north-west side of the town. His ships had sailed down the coast with his supplies and siege guns and soon block-aded the entrance to Wexford Harbour. He had already taken Enniscorthy Castle on his way to Wexford when the garrison surrendered without a blow. Cromwell had hoped to take Wexford town in a similar manner as the town, with its exceptionally strong 22ft high walls, would provide pro-tection and winter quarters for his army. He had immediately taken the Fort of Rosslare when his cavalry rode across the isthmus as on seeing the approaching soldiers the defenders had evacuated the fort. The gun emplacements at the fort were trained seawards and were of little use against a land attack.

The Wexford town garrison, under the command of David Sinnott, refused to surrender unless certain conditions were met. These Cromwell refused and, following a short siege, Cromwell's forces succeeded in breaching the town walls on 11 October and sacked the town.

Following his Irish campaign, Cromwell returned to England in 1650 and continued to rise through the ranks, eventually being declared Lord Protector for life. He was formally installed at Westminster Hall on 16 December 1653. By 1656 he was rewarding his loyal followers with knighthoods and to those soldiers and officers who remained in Ireland, parcels of land and property which were confiscated from their Catholic owners. The Esmonde family at Johnstown were Roman Catholics and so their land was liable for confiscation and they would have been on the list of Transplantable Catholics in 1653.[10] It was about this date that the abstract of the title to the estates of Johnstown, Whitestown, Little Hayestown and Scoughmolin all formerly the estate of William Esmonde, who was involved in the Rebellion of 1641,[11] were set out to Lt Col John Overstreet in lieu of payment for services rendered to Cromwell.[12]

Following the surrender of Colonel Wogan on the 17 August 1650, Duncannon Fort[13] came into the hands of the Parliamentarians, with John Overstreet appointed as temporary governor. This same Colonel Overstreet was granted the Johnstown Castle estate in 1652, shortly after its confiscation from the Esmonde family. Upon which an order from Waterford, dated 22 July 1652, was sent to the Commissioners of Revenue at Wexford to:

> Take an account upon oath of such money as was formerly ordered for repairing of ye said garrison, and to certify upon a Survey taken how much more money will be necessary to finish ye repairs of ye said Castle, and build competent lodgings for ye soldiers theirin, and likewise to cause a Survey to be made of ye probability of ye sinking of a well within ye said Castle and to reporte their opinions of the charge that may arise thereby, that further order may be taken thereupon.[14]

In May 1655, Commissary Withers of Wexford, on the recommendation of Major Symner, was appointed to 'repaire to Duncannon Fort, and having well viewed and considered the present condition thereof, is to report what repaires will bee necessary together with an estimate of the charge thereof and what else he shall think fitt'.[15]

Major Overstreet was still governor of Wexford town in 1653 when, on application to the council, the former occupant of Johnstown Castle and estate, Sir Thomas Esmonde, was granted protection until 1 August 1653. Sir Thomas was allowed to 'stay in the house he now lives in neer to Wexford'. This order was signed by four of the council members – Charles Fleetwood, Edward Luttrell, Miles Corbet and John Jones – at Dublin on 23 April 1653.[16] Wexford Precinct had its own commissioners appointed for examining the delinquency of the Irish and other proprietors according to the Act for the Settlement of Ireland.[17] On his promotion to lieutenant colonel, Overstreet served as part of a Committee for County Wexford with

Col Sadlier; Col Puckle and Capt. Camby for the apprehension and transplantation of Irish Papists: those who are to be 'kept in restraint' and those who are to be released.

Lt Col Overstreet and his wife Bennett became sole occupants of Johnstown Castle and estate following its confiscation from the Esmonde family. The Overstreets had no issue and after the death of her husband, Bennett married Edward Withers, a marriage also without issue. Research has shown that this is the same Edward Withers who had served with Overstreet on the various committees in Wexford. A former Master Gunner with the Cromwellian train of artillery, Edward Withers was in command of the gunners of the Wexford Garrison and the adjacent one, as shown in his request to be supplied with ammunition dated 5 July 1652.[18] In an order dated 8 September 1654, Withers salary as Woodreve and Commissioner of Survey was to be increased from £80 to £100 a year.[19] On 26 May 1656, an order prohibiting the exportation of timber and for the preservation of wood in and about Wexford was received by Edward Withers and John Moore. The order also instructed both men that timber owned by the State and that belonging to private persons was not to be mixed together in the wood-yard at Wexford.[20]

Edward Withers was obviously becoming quite well-off and in 1657 he leased 44 acres of land at Maudlintown, in the Liberties of Wexford, at £8 a year. In the same year he rented 'one waste plott of ground with ye walls of an old house thereto adjoining. 1 slate house in St. Patrick's Parish. 1 thatcht cabin in Selskars' Parish all for the fee of £1 10s.'[21] Further property was acquired by Withers in St Iberius' parish. In 1661 Withers was one of twenty-one burgesses of the Corporation of Wexford.[22] On his marriage to Bennett Overstreet he entered into a recognisance of £300 and took the lease of Johnstown Castle and estate in 1660.[23]

A niece of Colonel John Overstreet, Elizabeth Lacy, had married a John Reynolds from Wexford town and Reynolds is listed as a property holder in the town. Col. John Reynolds, the officer rank cited by historian P.H. Hore[24] was one of 'The Forty-Nine', a name given to those officers and soldiers who had seen service in Ireland before 5 June 1649, some four years before the arrival of Cromwell. They were ordered the payment of their arrears by Cromwell in 1654-55, and certain lands and houses were reserved for them, but they were overtaken by the Restoration and the officers were only satisfied.[25]

In 1668, Edward and Bennett Withers sold the castle and estate to Col John Reynolds and his wife for £500. John and Elizabeth Reynolds had three daughters, Mary, Jane and Susan, who were heirs to the estate in equal shares.

At the time John Reynolds acquired the castle, Cornelius Grogan, a yeoman, also bought property within the town. It is likely both men would have known each other. Grogan was a merchant, born *c.* 1635, the son of John Grogan, a carpenter, from Enniscorthy. Cornelius Grogan married Mary McDonnell, from Antrim, and their only son, John, was born in 1653. It was this John Grogan who married Mary Reynolds and thus began the Grogan family association with Johnstown Castle. Soon after, John Grogan, purchased his sister-in-laws' shares in the estate. On the death of his wife in 1690 and the death one year later of Edward Withers, John Grogan becomes the sole owner of Johnstown Castle Estate. This was the beginning of the Grogan dynasty.

3

THE GROGAN DYNASTY

The prefix 'O' to the surname Grogan as O'Grogan, or Ó Gruagáin in Irish, was omitted in the seventeenth century and does not seem to have been resumed since. According to Edward MacLysaght, the name Grogan is listed as one of the principal Irish surnames in the barony of Farbill in County Westmeath and in Ballyboy, County Offaly. In the seventeenth century the pedigree of the principal landed family of that name, Grogan of Johnstown Castle, County Wexford, was registered at the Office of Arms in Dublin Castle. In 1878 the Grogan estates totalled upwards of 13,000 acres in counties Wexford, Wicklow, Westmeath and Offaly.[26]

John Grogan

John Grogan and his wife hailed from County Antrim and settled in County Wexford, having been granted houses and lands in Wexford town by King Charles II in the twentieth year of the King's reign (1667).

The Grogans had the following issue: Cornelius, John's heir; John, who lived in Enniscorthy; Edward; and Anne. She married Sir Moses Hall in 1630.

Cornelius Grogan

On the death of his father, Cornelius succeeded to the estate and married Mary Raby. They had a son, John, and two daughters. Following Mary's death in May 1685, Cornelius married Margaret Codd on 26 July that same year at Wexford. There was no issue from this marriage.

John Grogan

Cornelius was succeeded by his only son, John Grogan, born in 1653 who married Mary Reynolds, daughter and co-heiress of John Reynolds of Wexford. John Grogan and Mary Reynolds had the following children:

Elizabeth, born 2 December 1684. She married Richard Waddy of Cloghest Castle, County Wexford. They had a son and a daughter. Elizabeth died on 19 June 1709, aged just 25 years.

John, born 14 January 1686 at Wexford. He died in infancy and was buried in Wexford on 4 June 1686.

Cornelius, born 23 March 1687, who was heir to the estate.

John, born 27 July 1689 at Wexford. He died aged 14 years and was buried at Wexford on 14 October 1703.

William, born 6 October 1690. He died aged 13 years and buried in Wexford on 2 November 1703.

John Grogan's wife, Mary, by whom the Johnstown Castle estate came into the family, died 28 October 1690 and is buried in the chancel of St Patrick's church in Wexford. John Grogan then married Anne Smith Linington (widow), one of three daughters of Captain Charles Smith, on 18 January 1691.[27] They had four sons and two daughters:

Nicholas, born 18 June 1692, died 26 November 1758 aged 66 years. He lived at Ardcandrisk, County Wexford.

George, born 17 November 1693. He worked in the East India Company's Service. He died in India on 11 June 1754 aged 61 years. He had one daughter, Anne.

Edward, born 1 April 1695. He married Anne Lucas from County Carlow. and had three sons, John, Edward and Lawrence.

Lawrence, born 11 March 1701. He sold his paternal property and went to Barbados where he died unmarried. He was the piper, musician and composer.

Mary, born 16 April 1696. She married Andrew Knox, Rathmacknee Castle, County Wexford. They had one child, Catherine Knox, born 17 August 1720. She married her first cousin John Grogan on 8 September 1745. Mary Knox married secondly William Hore of Harperstown, County Wexford, and married thirdly Charles Tottenham of Ballycorkeran. She died in February 1777 aged 81 years.

Sarah, born on 26 September 1699. She married William Morgan, Senior Alderman of the city of Waterford. He died 22 February 1785. They had two sons and two daughters.[28]

John Grogan married for a third time, to Anne Milivard, widow of Clement Milivard of Dublin. She died on 11 May 1743 without issue. John Grogan died on 10 January 1720 and was buried at Rathaspeck.

Cornelius Grogan

John was succeeded by his second son, Cornelius, from his first marriage, born 23 March 1687. He was married on 9 July to Elizabeth White, born 2 February 1684 and died 21 November 1754, aged 70 years. Elizabeth was the daughter of John White, Ballyellis, County Wexford. They had three sons and two daughters:

John, born 18 July 1716. He succeeded his father.

Overstreet, who later lived in Dublin. He died unmarried in October 1761 and bequeathed £60,000 and his house in College Green, Dublin, to his brother John.

George, died unmarried.

Catherine, who married Robert Carson on 7 May 1751. They had three sons and one daughter. Robert Carson, a native of County Down, was an attorney-at-law and died in 1765.

Anna Maria, who married Dubliner Stuchey Simon and had one son, James, and one daughter, Margaret.

John Grogan

Cornelius Grogan, died intestate in October 1724 and was succeeded by his eldest son, John. He married Catherine Knox, his first cousin. Catherine was the only child and heiress of Major Andrew Knox of Rathmacknee Castle. They had ten sons and four daughters:

John, born 23 July 1736, died 10 July 1756. He was a Fellow Commoner in Trinity College aged 19 years. He never married.

Andrew Knox, born 1737 and died unmarried in 1756.

Cornelius, who succeeded to the estate.

Overstreet, born 15 January 1739 and died, unmarried, 4 May 1757 aged 18 years.

George Knox, born 21 April 1744 and on coming of age in 1765 was the second son and, as such, had to take the name of Knox. He became a Justice of the Peace for County Wexford on 9 October 1777 and on 30 November that same year was elected Mayor of Galway. He was a Freeman of the City of Waterford in 1768. He died 11 January 1784, unmarried, aged 40 years.

William, born 24 June 1745. He served as an ensign in the 16th Regiment of Foot and lieutenant and quartermaster in Florida. He died on 2 February 1785, aged 40 years. He was married with two daughters, Catherine and Mary-Anne. Both of them died young.

Overstreet was born around 1750 and died in infancy.

Thomas Knox, born 1758 and on the death of his brother William took the name of Knox as he was now the second son. He later lived at Castletown, County Wexford, and served as cornet and lieutenant in the 2nd Horse and was appointed a Justice of the Peace for the counties of Wexford and Wicklow. He married Hannah Daunt in Dublin in 1785. They had one child, Georgina. She died at Bath in January 1788. Thomas was killed in action aged 43 on 9 June 1798 at the Battle of Arklow at the head of a Yeomanry Corps in a charge against the rebels.

John Knox, who succeeded his brother Cornelius at Johnstown, was born in 1760.

Overstreet, born 1762 married Elizabeth Morrall. He was called to the Irish Bar in 1793. He died 25 June 1814 at his home on Merrion Square, Dublin, aged 52 years.

Catherine, born 11 May 1740. She married Sir Vesey Colclough of Tintern Abbey, County Wexford. They had three sons, Caesar, John and Vesey. Their second son John was killed in a duel on 30 May 1807.

Mary, who married Sir George Ribton, Bart in 1779. He was High Sheriff of County Dublin in 1772. Mary died on 1 February 1781. She is buried at Rathaspeck. They had three daughters, Catherine, Mary-Anne and Alice, who married Francis King of Silverspring, County Wexford.

Elizabeth, married Ebenezer Radford Rowe of Ballyharty, County Wexford. He was High Sheriff of the county in 1772. They had one son, Ebenezer Radford Rowe who married Elizabeth, daughter of Col Irvine of Castle Irvine, County Fermanagh and they had: Ebenezer, died young; John Rowe of Ballycross, County Wexford, married Margaret, daughter of Gabriel Redmond of Wexford; Elizabeth, who married Henry Irvine, her first cousin; Sophia-Maria, who married Hamilton Knox Grogan-Morgan, her first cousin; Letitia, who died young; and Anna Harriott who married John Nunn of Silverspring, County Wexford.

Anne, born October 1746. She married James White, Middleton, County Wexford on 15 February 1784. They had one daughter, Catherine. She married Thomas de Renzy of Clebemon Hall, County Wexford, on 9 March 1805. Anne's husband died in 1808.

John Grogan died 26 December 1783, aged 66 years. During his lifetime he had served as High Sheriff and Justice of the Peace for County Wexford. He was elected Member of Parliament for the Borough of Enniscorthy in May 1761. He was succeeded by his third son, Cornelius.[29] Following the restoration of the Johnstown Estate in 1810, John Knox Grogan became the new heir.

John Knox Grogan

John Knox Grogan was born in 1760. He married Anne Coote, born 28 June 1762, and they had a daughter, born 24 October 1785. She became heiress of Chidley Coote, Ash Hill, County Limerick. Anne died on 25 October 1785, the day after giving birth to her daughter, Anne.

John then married Elizabeth-Geraldine FitzGerald, only daughter of Stephen FitzGerald, Ballythomas, Queen's County, in January 1803. They had three sons:

John Knox, born 1803 and died in Leeson Street, Dublin, on 6 August 1810 aged seven years.

Hamilton Knox Grogan, his heir.

George Gilbert Grogan, born 10 March 1809. He lived at Ardcandrisk and in 1828 assumed by royal permission the name and coat of arms of Morgan in addition to Grogan. He married without having issue.

Hamilton Knox Grogan

Hamilton Knox Grogan was born in 1808 and died in 1854, aged 46 years. He married his first cousin Sophia Maria Rowe, daughter of Elizabeth Rowe of Ballyharty, County Wexford. They had three daughters: Sophia Knox Grogan who died young, Elizabeth Geraldine Grogan[30] and Jane Colclough Grogan.[31] After the death of her husband, Hamilton Knox Grogan Morgan, Sophia Maria married Sir Thomas Esmonde, Bart, of Ballynastragh. There was no issue.

Jane Colclough Grogan

The Earl and Countess of Granard (Lady Jane Colclough Grogan) had two daughters, Lady Adelaide Jane Frances Forbes, born 1860, and Lady Sophia Mary Elizabeth Forbes, born 1861. Lady Adelaide married Lord Maurice FitzGerald and they had one son and three daughters, the youngest, Marjorie, lived from 1896 to 1899. Their only son and heir, Gerald Hugh FitzGerald, was born in 1883 and was killed in action in the First World War in 1914.[32] Geraldine Mary FitzGerald was born in 1881 and died in 1954. Their second daughter, Kathleen, was born in 1892 and married Michael Lawrence Lakin. Kathleen died as a result of a horse-riding accident in 1930. They had two sons, Gerald Michael Lakin, born 1916 and he was killed in action in the Second World War in Tunisia in 1943. Their second son, Maurice Victor Lakin, was born in 1919. He fought in the Second World War, was wounded but survived the war. It was Victor who presented Johnstown to the nation in 1945. He went on to live in France where his descendents are living and in recent years they have visited Johnstown.

4

A GENTLEMAN PIPER

By your leave, Larry Grogan, Enough has been spoken; 'Tis time to give over your sonnet, my boy![33]

(Pierce Creagh, *c*. 1735)

Lawrence Grogan was born on 11 March 1701. His father, John Grogan, had married Mary Reynolds in 1682 and became sole owner of the Johnstown Castle estate having bought out his sisters-in-law, Jane and Susan Reynolds.

John Grogan died in 1720 and in his will Lawrence and his brother, Edward, were to be maintained and educated out of the estate during their minority and to receive £140 out of the estate on reaching their majority at 21 years of age. It is said that Lawrence Grogan moved to Dublin and studied law, eventually qualifying as a lawyer but there is no positive evidence that he practised in this profession.[34] He was known to frequent many places in the city where there were musical evenings and soirées where he entertained with his excellent playing on the bagpipes. Both Lawrence Grogan and another gentleman musician, Jackie Lattin, a renowned fiddle-player from Morristown, Naas, County Kildare, were regular musical contributors at a small public house, The Conniving House, under the ownership of Jack Macklean, just beyond Ringsend.[35]

Lawrence Grogan was a musician of high standing, possessed of that rare talent of fluency in musical composition. Lawrence was an uilleann piper of note and, like the Brownrigg's of Norrismount[36] and Dudley Colclough of Tintern,[37] would have been regarded as a 'gentleman piper' because of his status in the community. The *píob mór*, or war pipes, had enjoyed great popularity in Ireland and Scotland from very early times but their loud volume was not conducive to their use indoors. In the beginning of the eighteenth century the *píob mór*[38] were replaced for indoor use by the more compact and versatile uilleann or union pipes.[39] The use of this instrument gained great popularity in providing the main music at weddings, christenings and of course for dancing. Lawrence Grogan was one of the first performers in the second decade of the eighteenth century on this newly improved instrument for which there is any historical record.[40] It was from about the year 1715 that the uilleann pipes were improved which led to their popular use amongst musicians in preference to the Irish harp.

Many tunes were composed by Lawrence Grogan, including the 'Larry Grogan' jig. Many composers of traditional dance tunes have their own compositions named after them, not by themselves, but by other musicians who would have learned the tune and used the composer's name as a source of authorship. This jig appeared in print in 1737 and was published in the second volume of Walsh's *Caledonian Country Dances*.[41]

Grogan's most famous composition gave rise to great controversy. Known by the title 'Alley Croker', it was written and composed by him in 1725. It is based on an account of the vagaries of a disappointed suitor of a lady named Alicia Croker of Raleighstown, County Limerick. Miss Croker was the daughter of Col Croker of Ballingard and sister of Edward Croker, High

Larry Grogan - Jig

'Larry Grogan' jig. (Music transcription by Liam Gaul)

Ally Croker

Composed c.1725

Laurence Grogan

L.G. 2014

'Ally Crocker' reel. (Music transcription by Liam Gaul)

Sheriff of County Limerick. The charming heroine of the ballad eventually married Charles Langley, of Lisnamrock, County Kilkenny, and she lived to a great age, dying in 1770.[42] Some believe that the disappointed suitor in the ballad is actually Lawrence Grogan himself. Due to the popularity of this melody it was taken up and used in the play *Love in a Riddle* where it appeared as 'No more, fair virgins, boast your power', in 1729.[43]

The successful comedy *The Englishman in Paris*, written by British actor-manager and playwright Samuel Foote, was performed at the Haymarket Theatre, London, in 1747.[44] Within the play, the melody composed by Lawrence Grogan is used without any credit given to its composer. It was from the singing of Maria Macklin, to her own guitar accompaniment, that the Irish actress-vocalist brought the air to a greater audience.[45] In the opera *Midas*, by Irish ballad opera composer Kane O'Hara, there is an adaptation of Grogan's melody used in 1753. The melody appeared in many printed collections, including Thompson's *Collection of 200 Favourite Country Dances, Vol. 1* (published *c.* 1780). In 1803, George Colman set the lyrics of his song entitled 'The Unfortunate Miss Bailey' to this air.[46] Thomas Moore has preserved this melody for our enjoyment to this day when he wedded his immortal lyric, 'Oh the Shamrock' to the tune and published it in the fourth number of his *Irish Melodies* in 1811.[47] However, the English music publisher William Chappell claimed that this melody was of English origin and on this account Sir Charles Villiers Stanford excluded it from his edition of *Moore's Irish Melodies* published in 1895. This opposition to the origins of authorship was strongly defended in Lawrence Grogan's favour by a relative of Alicia Croker, the writer and folklore collector, Thomas Crofton Croker. Lawrence Grogan and Pierce Creagh, a well-known character of his day from Dangan, were great friends as evidenced in the announcement in *Faulkner's Journal*, 'On Wednesday, August 31, 1743, the £10 prize at Loughrea Races was won by Pierce Creagh's horse, Larry Grogan'.[48]

The following is the opening verse of the lyric of 'Ally Croker':

There liv'd a Man in Ballinocracy,
Who wanted a wife to make him uneasy;
Long had he sigh'd for dear Ally Croker,
And thus the gentle youth bespoke her,
Will you marry me, dear Ally Croker?
Will you marry me, dear Ally Croker?

It is thought that Lawrence Grogan may have travelled to Barbados in the West Indies where he died at a young age. He had drawn up a will on 6 May 1728 which was proved on 30 March 1729 leaving one moiety of his goods to his sister Sara Grogan (1699-1785) and the other moiety to Catherine Knox, daughter of Major Andrew Knox of Rathmacnee. It appears that Lawrence Grogan lived for just ten years following his father's death in 1720.[49]

The jig 'Larry Grogan' has survived in the repertoire of many present-day traditional musicians and the musical notation may be viewed in the collected works of Captain Francis O'Neill, Chicago; Francis Roche, Limerick as 'Larry Grogan' and in Brendán Breathnach's *Ceol Rince na hÉireann, Vol. 1* as 'Coppers and Brass' with an added third part and in Pat Mitchell's collection of *The Dance Music of Willie Clancy* also as 'Coppers and Brass' giving two parts with an excellent variation on the repeat of the tune. The ghost of Lawrence Grogan still returns to make an appearance in musical publications such as Mel Bay's *The Complete Fiddling Book*, published in Montreal, Canada, in 1990, which contains a variant of the tune 'Ally Croker' given as a reel under the title 'Allie Crocker'. It all started over 300 years ago in 1701 at Johnstown Castle.

The Johnstown Castle Grounds
by Willie Asple[50]

In the early spring when the birds do sing,
And the ploughman's on his rounds,
The gull and crow they come and go,
To the Johnstown Castle grounds.

The rabbits and hares all run in pairs,
And badgers too are found,
As they frisk and play in their own wild way,
In the Johnstown Castle grounds.

Wild flowers too are grand to view,
As a stroll you take around,
And in early June they are in full bloom,
In the Johnstown Castle grounds.

In the winter time be it wet or fine,
It's grand to view the hounds,
Chase Reynard through a field or two,
In the Johnstown Castle grounds.

In years to come when we're dead and dumb,
And laid beneath the mound,
A stranger's hand will take command,
Of the Johnstown Castle grounds.

Lady Maurice Fitzgerald owned the estate,
And no finer can be found,
But I'm sorry to say she has passed away,
From the Johnstown Castle grounds.

But whoever roams this fine estate,
I hope they will not fail,
Not let it be sold for a ten-bob note,
Like Beaties of Borodale.

The Beauties of Johnstown: 'A Morning Scene in Autumn'
by Francis Whelan[51]

One golden harvest morn, when the yellow waving corn,
The fragrant fields adorn, with the meadows newly mown,
In Johnstown vale reclining, with jessamines entwining,
And odours all combining, I found myself alone.
The fragrant flowers were blooming, the groves around perfuming,
And honey-bees all humming, around me where I lay.
In joyful concert rhyming, each other sweetly timing,
Whilst the solemn tower clock chiming, proclaimed the rising day.

Through glistening arbours glancing, the morning sun was dancing,
The scenery enhancing, by the glory of its beams.
Above the arbours splendid, from waving branches blended,
Sweet honey drops descended, through fragrant ever-greens.

On verdant moss bank sloping, with silver foliage drooping,
In countless numbers grouping, shone Flora's choicest gems.
In beaming beauty waking, their golden blossoms shaking,
With laden dew-balls breaking, their tender trembling stems.

The blue-brow'd cineraria, the bronze calceolaria,
And silver saponaria, with pinks and picotees.
Mid bow'rs of bright lavender, arrayed in gorgeous splendour,
Waving their blossoms tender, before the morning breeze.

And fragrant roses blushing, by amber fountains gushing,
And silvery cascades rushing, mid the golden blaze of bloom.
With sunray'd dews descending, through myrtle arbours bending,
And green magnolias blending, exhaled a rich perfume.

On spangled branches swinging, the wild birds all were singing,
In jovial concert ringing, round the leafy mantled dale.
Through green shades radiated, with music animated,
Their notes reverberated, through the glory-lighted vale.

By streamlets sweetly flowing, wild lusmore-bells were blowing,
And drooping hare-bells showing, in every scented shade.
The purple-eyed azalea, the crimson robed camellia,
And glossy blue lobelia, the verdant vale array'd.

Drooping ash and willow weeping, a wary watch were keeping,
Over water lilies steeping, in the azure bosom lake.
And no breath disturbs the sleeping, of the silent water creeping,
Save when the wild trout leaping, its tranquil slumbers break.

A noble palace splendid, by clustering towers befriended,
On the grassy lawn extended, its giant shadowy mould.
In the morning glory glancing, a radiant sight entrancing,
Its granite crystals dancing, like burning beams of gold.

And sombre pinewoods towering, with woodbine shades embowering,
And bright laburnums flowering, in sunny vistas green.
Looked on the valley seeming, with fairy grandeur teeming,
In silent beauty beaming, in the morning's golden sheen.

The lake at Johnstown Castle, line-drawing by A. Nicholl.

5

HERO OR VICTIM
OF THE 1798 REBELLION?

The Rebellion of 1798 in County Wexford began on Saturday 26 May with a skirmish at the Harrow when Fr John Murphy, Roman Catholic priest at Boolavogue, and a small number of his people confronted Lt Thomas Bookey and the Camolin yeomanry. The yeomen had torched the house of the Boyne family. Lt Bookey and his deputy officer, John Donovan, became separated from the rest of the yeomen group and both men were killed.[52] Fr Murphy had earlier requested his flock to surrender their pikes and firearms so that an uprising might be avoided. He now found himself leading his people against the oppressor, who were better armed and greater in number. Through the long summer months battles raged, lives were lost on both sides and a list of horrific tortures were perpetrated on innocent people by those loyal to the Crown. Following the disaster of Vinegar Hill, Enniscorthy, the rebels scattered in a bid to escape the wrath of the large British force surrounding the hill. The final battle in County Wexford was fought on Wednesday 4 July at Ballygullen.

Many of the landed gentry in County Wexford became involved in the rebellion as did five prominent Protestants, liberal supporters of Catholic political emancipation. Two wealthy farmers – Anthony Perry from Inch, near Gorey, and George Sparks of Blackwater – were joined by Matthew Keogh, a former captain in the British Army and at that time a merchant in Wexford town as well as two other farmers, William Boxwell of Sarshill, Kilmore, and William Hughes of Ballytrent. Beauchamp Bagenal Harvey of Bargy Castle, William Hatton of Clonard and Cornelius Grogan of Johnstown Castle were prominent in the civilian wing of the United Irishmen movement.[53]

Cornelius Grogan, born in 1738, was the third son of John Grogan and Catherine Knox and heir to the Johnstown estate. He was acclaimed to be extremely wealthy, with an income of between £8,000 to £10,000 per annum. He owned many properties and land and was a major shareholder in Wexford Bridge. Many historians disagree as to his age, some claiming he was in his seventies during the rebellion. Yet according to the year of his birth on the family chart he would have been sixty years of age when he was hanged for his involvement in the Rebellion in 1798. He suffered from severe gout which made walking a painful and slow process. When he moved about the countryside or to visit the town it was mainly on horseback or in his carriage. He lived in the family seat at Johnstown with three female servants, a coachman named Madden, a James Furlong, and his butler and servant of many years, John Devereux. He was officially unmarried yet some claimed he was married to his housekeeper, Rebecca Frost, a claim perhaps supported by the fact that he appointed her as one of the executors to his last will and testament.[54] Grogan was a thick-set man, short in stature and wore his white hair at shoulder length. A very popular landlord, renowned for his hospitality, and served on many committees and organisations in the county. He was High Sheriff of County Wexford and Member of Parliament for Enniscorthy from 1769 to 1773. Cornelius Grogan was much respected and an excellent magistrate with a personality to command the affection and respect of a wide neighbourhood. His large fortune and property in the country was so immense that it was unlikely that he would have committed himself to disloyalty to the Crown by any act of treason which would have compromised his wealth, position and his general safety.

Grogan reputedly permitted men to meet in his house to discuss subjects that were totally unfriendly to the cause of law and order but it is quite unlikely that Grogan was involved in any such discussions. On hearing of the rebels approach to the vicinity of Johnstown, he went with many others to take refuge in Duncannon Fort. Very soon he realised his error in leaving his castle and returned quickly as he feared his premises would be looted of the large quantity of money and silver plate he had left behind. He secured his valuables and hoped to join the fleeing loyalists the next day. However, his loyal friends convinced him to remain at Johnstown where they believed he would be safer. When the insurgents entered Wexford town and liberated the prisoners, they appointed a military governor. A party was sent out to Johnstown for Cornelius Grogan. He came to town on horseback surrounded by a cheering crowd, his hat adorned by a green ribbon leaving all in no doubt that Grogan was a sympathiser to the rebels cause. A Civil Committee was established in Wexford for the protection of people and property and Grogan was appointed as Commissary to take charge of all food stocks and other necessities for the use of the people and the insurgent army. In this task Grogan was assisted by Robert Mayler of Gurteenminogue. Cornelius Grogan placed a guard on every house in his neighbourhood to prevent pillage and plunder.

Capt. Patrick O'Brien of the Murrintown corps was ordered by Bagenal Harvey to bring Grogan to the rebel camp at Carrigbyrne. The presence of a wealthy and well-known Protestant gentleman, it was thought, would add prestige to the rebel army. Afterwards, at the trial of Cornelius Grogan, a deposition was made by a paid informer, Richard Grandy, that he saw Mr Grogan and Mr Harvey coming from the Battle of Ross and that he had heard that Mr Grogan was in charge of the barony of Forth corps. This deposition was made before George Ogle; Isaac Cornock; John Lyster and John Kennedy. When the Bill of Attainder was opposed before the parliamentary committee it was very clear that the people who brought Cornelius Grogan to Carrigbyrne from Johnstown got no closer than 5 miles to Ross. As Mr Grogan was ill he was taken to Foulksmills in his carriage and from there back to his home at Johnstown.

Cornelius Grogan, according to his own evidence, was only interested in one thing and that was reform and that he knew nothing of the United Irish Society. During the insurrection he had spent most of his time at his home, attended by his devoted personal servant John Devereux. In the early days of the rebellion, Capt. O'Brien demanded that Mr Grogan take the oath of the society. Mr Grogan sought the advice of the parish priest, a Father O'Connor, who read through the wording of the oath. The priest thought there was nothing contained in the oath that was unacceptable to Christianity or the Constitution. Cornelius Grogan took the oath and became a kindly, charitable, humane and militarily ineffective member of the United Irish Society. [55]

He visited Wexford town occasionally by order of the committee attending meetings in the Assembly Rooms. [56] He visited neighbours and acquaintances in the jail and at times was successful in having some of them released. After the defeat of the insurgent army at Vinegar Hill, General Lake issued a proclamation on 23 June and very soon arrests, trials and executions began.

When the British troops arrived at Johnstown Castle to arrest Cornelius Grogan, he made no efforts to escape or hide from the soldiers as he had not expected to be placed under arrest.

On 25 June Cornelius Grogan was brought from Johnstown Castle to the jail at Wexford. His trial began on the 26th but was adjourned to enable him to bring forth witnesses in his defence. His first witness was shot dead on his way to Wexford to give testimony. Cornelius Grogan, perhaps realising that his fate was already decided, made no attempted to call further witnesses. He defended himself throughout his trial, which lasted much longer than most rebel leaders[57] brought before the court martial. The court martial comprised of Major General Cradock; Lord Bective, Colonel of Meath Militia; Lord Clements; Lord Doneraile, Colonel of South Cork Militia; Lt-Col St Leger, Lieutenant of South Cork Militia; and Lord Frederick Montague, 29th Regiment. The court martials were not sworn, nor was there any judge advocate, as appears in the House of Commons.[58] Cornelius Grogan's trial took place in a building in Wexford's Bull Ring.[59] The trial ended on the 27 June with the death sentence passed and he was marched along the Main Street of Wexford to the jail on that evening.[60] Two days before, on 25 June, Cornelius Grogan had drawn up his last will and testament, appointing his executors and witnessed by Loftus Richards. Written in a steady, if somewhat cramped, handwriting it read as follows:

In the name of God, I Cornelius Grogan do give my personal property of any kind whatsoever to Rebecca Frost as a reward for her love care and attention for many years toward me on all occasions,
Cor. Grogan

Witness present
A. Jacob

I Cornelius Grogan do leave all my other property of any kind whatsoever or wheresoever to my surviving brothers,
Cor. Grogan

Witness present
A. Jacob

I Cornelius Grogan do now appoint to my last Will and testament my Brother Overstreet Grogan and Rebecca Frost and John Grogan my Executors as I fear I have not already done so and I leave to my Brother George Knox's son the sum of five hundred pounds for his future advancement in life to be paid out of my Fortune. 27 June 1798
Cor. Grogan

Witness Present
Loftus Richards

On 28 June Cornelius Grogan was accompanied to Wexford Bridge, the place of his execution, by Revd J. Elgee, rector of Wexford Parish, and a long-time friend of Mr Grogan. Due to his gout, it was observed that he walked very slowly and in obvious signs of pain. He prayed as he hobbled along

CORNELIUS GROGAN'S WILL

Facsimile of the codicil to Cornelius Grogan's last will and testament.

supported by his crutches and he met his fate with bravery and perfect calmness. At 9 p.m. Cornelius Grogan closed his Bible and, looking at the sky, indicated he was ready to die.[61] He faced Sergeant Dunn of the King's County Militia, the official hangman, described locally as a brutal, coarse and savage man, a veritable monster. The victim was stripped, the noose placed around his neck and he was raised up on the hanging frame: a long and torturous method of execution. Dunn collected Grogan's personal possessions and tied them up in a bag ready for sale at another time. On the death of his victim, the executioner mutilated the body, beheaded it and threw the headless corpse into the mud of the river. He took the head with him for to be spiked and displayed to the public outside the courthouse in the Bull Ring where it remained for three or four weeks. Grogan's head was placed together with the heads of Keugh, Harvey and Colclough, previously executed, who were already on the spikes.[62] John Devereux, the faithful servant of Cornelius Grogan for over fourteen years together with some of his neighbours retrieved the body and brought it to the graveyard at Rathaspeck

Commemorative Stone to Cornelius Grogan at Rathaspeck church. (Courtesy of Patrick Sills)

church where it was buried. Some weeks later, Devereux recovered the head from the spikes outside the courthouse and interred it with the body.[63]

Sir Frederick Flood, Bart, a witness to the execution recalled:

Mr. Grogan, just previous to his execution, took out of his sleeves a pair of buttons of Irish gold, and gave them to a gentleman to deliver to Sir Frederic, as otherwise the hangman would have them. Sir Frederic received them, but did not disclose the name of the person who handed them to him. He further stated, that he, on Mr. John Knox Grogan's entering upon the estates of his brother, delivered them to him, considering himself only as a trustee in the business.[64]

Cornelius Grogan, heir to Johnstown Castle, inadvertently became involved in a rebellion which cost him his life and the confiscation of the entire estate and his wealth.

Are you still a footnote,
Long blurred and unread:
Another enigmatic conscript
Of Ireland's glorious dead.

Words from the final verse of the poem, 'Cornelius Grogan of Johnstown Castle' by Wexford poet Anthony N. O'Sullivan, which are inscribed on a memorial to Cornelius Grogan, unveiled in Rathaspeck churchyard by Piercestown-Murrintown Comoradh '98 Committee, 7 June 1998.

6

A DIARY BY
THOMAS LACY

Many eminent visitors over the years to Johnstown Castle demesne have written various descriptions of the castle, gardens and grounds to great and interesting effect. The definitive description of Johnstown Castle, both interior and exterior, must be credited to the writings of Thomas Lacy in his diary dated 1852 entitled *Home Sketches on Both Sides of the Channel*[65] and in a further description in his 1863 publication *Sights and Scenes in Our Fatherland.*[66] Lacy's work would very easily be a 'blueprint' for the proposed restoration of the castle. The following transcriptions of Thomas Lacy's accounts cannot be surpassed. I think the reader will agree, Mr Lacy never missed any detail during his visits.

When I paid my last visit to the Crystal Palace I had the great pleasure of seeing the excellent model of Johnstown Castle, which was situated in the Fine Arts sculpture department.[67] Feelings of pride and gratification took possession of my mind, as I beheld, one after another, numbers of distinguished visitors, both English and foreign, stop to admire, and to bestow their praise upon, this perfect representation of native munificence and taste. Cards in German, French and English, explanatory of the particulars in connection with the castle, were appended to that faithful image of this magnificent pile, and were read with avidity and apparent interest by many of those who, from time to time, entered the department.

I remained for a considerable time viewing this and other objects of a similar description, and can say, with perfect truth, that there was no single object of the kind in the whole department more worthy of notice and attention.

When I thought of the blessings which the noble-hearted proprietor has, for years, been conferring on the artisans and labourers who have been employed in carrying out his grand improvements, I looked upon the model then before me with feelings approaching to veneration.

Not having been at Johnstown for the last five years, and being struck with the extensive additions and improvements which a close inspection of the model rendered manifest, I determined on my arrival in Wexford, to avail myself of an early opportunity to visit this fine seat. In pursuance of this determination I paid my contemplated visit in the month of July, and was astonished at the extent of the improvements which had been made, as well as with those which are at present in progress. I found that a splendid porch had been erected before the grand entrance, which is in the north front of the porch. The carriage-way immediately in front of this porch, is formed by beautiful Gothic arches, with neat light groinings, surmounted by a handsome tower that harmonises with the rest of the building. The door of the porch is in the Gothic style, finely

The north front of the castle. (IAMA Johnstown)

ornamented above with oak carving; there is a niche on each side of it in which a lamp will be suspended, while underneath, statues or fancy figures may be placed. In the daytime this door folds backwards and discloses to the view another, which is composed of one entire sheet of the finest plate glass. The outer door, which is invisible when folded, is again made available at night, and affords the requisite security. On the northern side of the laboratory, and connected with it, a handsome building is now being erected, a portion of which shall be appropriated to a billiard-room. This is considered a desideratum, as, from its detached situation, the noise of the balls, when parties are at play, will not be heard within the castle.

This new building and the laboratory stand east of the castle, from which a communication with them takes place by means of a spacious gallery running over an elliptic Gothic arch, of considerable dimensions, that spans the intermediate distance, and which also affords a carriage-way to the east, or private entrance. Between this arch and the castle, another arch, of smaller dimensions but of a similar character, affords access to the domestics and ordinary visitors while passing from the porch to this entrance. This addition is composed of a fine bluish stone, which is quarried on a part of the demesne; the quoins and ornamental parts are of cut granite. It shows a very handsome front to the north, and is flanked on each extremity by a neat square tower, finished to correspond with that which stands above the porch. A light, lofty, and beautiful octagon tower graces the western front at the point where the new addition is united to the laboratory, on the north side of the elliptic arch. In the main entrance to this building there are three doors, one leading to the laboratory, one to a conservatory, and a third to the new billiard-room, the approach to which is by spiral stairs of cut stone. The billiard-room is of ample proportions, and will be lighted by a dome.

The north front of the castle presents an appearance very different from the others. That part which appears above and at each side of the porch is new, and characteristically ornamented. On each side of this appear what may be called parts of the ancient castle, showing the grey colouring which time gives to edifices of this description; the windows are small, and the walls are partially covered with ivy. A handsome octagon tower, rising above the castle, stands on the north-west angle, and is surmounted by a flag-staff; there are fifteen windows in this front.

The east front of the castle. (IAMA Johnstown)

The east front is, perhaps, the least ornamental of any of the sides of this noble edifice; it has, however, a fine appearance. The south-east angle displays a magnificent round tower, at once characteristic of strength and beauty; while the laboratory, and the newly-erected building in connection with it, which will contain the billiard-room, interferes with its uniformity, and gives it an aspect of a different character, but still very grand. The private entrance to the castle is in this front. On this side there is a very beautiful terrace garden, filled, as a matter of course, with all that is calculated to gratify and delight the beholder, including a very beautiful *jet d'eau*; and on this side also, extending to offices remote from the castle, there is a subterranean passage, lighted from the surface of the lawn, and leading from the underneath apartments of the building.

The west front faces the high road, from which it appears to great advantage, the intermediate space presenting no obstruction to the view; travellers frequently stop to enjoy the pleasure of beholding this rich and magnificent structure. The light and handsome octagon tower, on which stands the flag-staff, presents the same appearance from this side which it shows from the north, it being on the north-west angle. On the southern extremity of this front, a beautiful round tower, of similar character to that mentioned in the east front, displays itself; while in the centre of the front, a flat projection appears with three windows, one in each storey, and above the upper window there is a splendid clock. There are two windows in each storey in the space which lies between the central projection and the south-west tower, and three windows in each storey in the space between the said projection and the north-west tower. In the centre of the rich lawn in front of this side of the castle, there is a fine basin, or large reservoir, in the midst of which a powerful *jet d'eau* throws the water to a great height, producing the usual agreeable and cooling sensations in its fall. Labourers were employed in levelling and forming terraces on this part of the lawn.

The south front is by far the most grand and imposing, combining within it solidity and strength, united with elegance and beauty. It is flanked on the east and west by the beautiful round towers already mentioned, in each of which there are four characteristic windows, while

The west front of the castle. (IAMA Johnstown)

in the centre a semi-hexagon projection displays itself; in this there are three highly-wrought and richly ornamented windows, one in each story, composed of fine plate glass; indeed, all the windows of the castle are of this material. The intermediate space between the central or hexagonal projection and the western tower has also three windows, one in each storey, while the space between the centre and the eastern tower there are likewise three windows, one in each storey, but there is a striking difference in the character and appearance of the latter. Two of these windows are much more highly ornamented than the corresponding windows on the opposite side, and even the rooms which are lighted by them project to a greater extent than do those on that side; and, so far, the uniformity of the front is interfered with, but this I suppose became necessary in order to enlarge the rooms.

The laboratory displays its front to this side, while the connecting part, over which the gallery runs, shows the same appearance as it does from the north front, being that of a strong and lofty elliptic Gothic arch, together with the smaller one already mentioned. Thus I have vainly endeavoured to give a description of this magnificent building. I am fully conscious of my inadequacy to do anything like justice to an object which combines within it such variety in its architectural construction. I might, to be sure, have supplied my want of acquaintance with the rules of architecture by applying to professional friends for assistance, but as I have had to rely upon my own feeble resources in other instances, I made up my mind to trust to chance in this also. Besides, what would have been gained in one way might have been forfeited in other, and while seeking for technicalities perhaps I should have lost enthusiasm. In front of the castle, on the south side, is the beautiful lake, with its numerous aquatic birds. I saw as many as fourteen fine swans and cygnets floating upon its tranquil bosom. In this front also, between the castle and the lake, there is another fine *jet d'eau*. Islands have been formed near the centre and along the sides of the lake, and are closely covered with plantations. On these islands the swans breed and shelter their young, while small wooden houses are placed in various parts of the lake for the accommodation of the several specimens of the feathered tribe – many of them domesticated wild fowl – that feed and dwell upon this element. A handsome flight of fine cut stone leads from the beautiful and extensive space which surrounds the castle, to the commodious and nicely prepared walk that

The south front of the castle. (IAMA Johnstown)

sweeps around the margin of the lake. Between this walk and the edge of the lake, a neat and closely-shaven bank slopes downwards, whereon occasionally may be seen the numerous birds basking in the mid-day sun, and enjoying that pleasure to which all animals seem more or less partial. Abundance of fish, as well as fowl, inhabit and embellish this fine sheet of water.

On the opposite side, and on a gentle acclivity, which rises from the edge of the lake, stands an old castle richly mantled with ivy, and in a state of fine preservation; it is surrounded by a velvet lawn, ornamented with clusters of beautiful trees and flowering shrubs, that form the most pleasing and agreeable objects, and upon which the eye delights to dwell. New and handsome turrets have been built on each side, near the margin of the lake, and present a very fine appearance as viewed from the grounds in front of the castle. At the close of my visit, and when I was about to leave the grounds, I had the good fortune to meet the benevolent Mr. Morgan, the owner of this fine place, who, with his usual kindness, said I would at all times be welcome to view the pleasure-grounds and gardens, and, in addition, was pleased to say that I would be at liberty to view the internal decorations and furniture of the castle. Availing myself of this kind indulgence, I paid another visit to the castle early in the month of September. On this occasion, I entered

Rathaspeck Church of Ireland church. (Courtesy of Patrick Sills)

the demesne by the north-western gate of the deer park, near the foot of the Mountain of Forth, by which it may be said to be bounded on that point. There is a porter's lodge at this entrance; the person in charge of it is attentive and polite to the visitors who use this drive. We saw, as we rode through this part of the park, several herds of fine deer, which were followed by a number of beautiful fawns. Many acres of large furze and fern may be seen in this park, which afford shelter to the deer in winter, and to the fawns in summer. It also abounds in some fine timber. A river flows through the park, which stands upon a richly-planted elevation in the centre of the deer-park, the whole of this extensive and very beautiful demesne falls within the view. Woods, rendered hoary with time, the timber of which must be of great value, with rich and ornamental plantations, are to be seen in every direction; while, through the vistas, appear corn-fields and meadows, teeming with abundance, and of the greatest beauty. The whole demesne contains 936 statute acres, including the deer-park, which contains 222 acres. There are four entrances to the demesne, and a like number to the deer-park. The grand entrance is contiguous to the church of Rathaspeck, which is on the Johnstown estate, and to which the family report for divine worship. The church of Rathmacnee is also on Mr. Morgan's estate, and stands about a mile and a half from the castle.

The entrance-gate is very capacious, with a handsome Gothic porter's lodge on each side: these, together with the arch above the gateway, are entirely covered with luxuriant ivy. The visitor must be greatly struck with the rich and peculiar appearance of this entrance, which leads into a lawn of great extent and beauty. The castle is approached by a very fine new avenue, which is of great width and covered with nice white gravel. Trees of great age and magnitude, and of healthy and vigorous appearance, stand on each side of the avenue as it sweeps in an amole curve towards the castle. The private entrance is about a quarter of a mile from the grand one, and is used by the tradesmen and labourers who are employed at the castle and upon the grounds, or by such as have ordinary business to transact; a porter is in attendance at this gate, who, while he allows the horses and cars to enter, must be careful that no improper person intrude themselves. Within this entrance, on the right hand, there is situated about a mile from the castle, and near to the chapel of Piercestown: cars and carriages occasionally enter by this avenue. The stables, the coach-houses, the dog-kennel, and farm-yard, lie between this entrance and the castle. Here, also, there is a neat porter's lodge of a turreted character, finished in what may be called the appropriate Johnstown style of architecture. An elegant, unique, and commodious cottage has been built under the immediate direction of Mrs. Morgan, and by her appropriated to a school-house for the education of the children of the tenants and workmen, and those who may be considered as dependents on her bounty. Teachers who possess the necessary qualifications are provided to carry out her benevolent intentions, as I have reason to know that the greatest care and attention are bestowed on the pupils who attend the school. This school-house is situated immediately adjoining the handsome church of Rathaspeck, which stands in the centre of the burial-ground, where, within a commodious vault, the ancestral relics of the house of Johnstown lie entombed.

On a slight elevation, on the west bank of the river that flows through the deer-park, the old churchyard of Kildavin appears, with its ancient and small chapel, a complete and ivy-clad ruin. At present this churchyard is not much used as a burial-ground; however, a few of the old neighbouring families continue still to use it, and find 'that sleep that knows not breaking' beside the remains of their virtuous ancestors.

Passing out of the deer-park by the gamekeeper's lodge near the chapel of Murntown, we had to ride about half a mile before we arrived at the new entrance to the demesne. The porter's lodge at this entrance is a neat building of a castellated character, corresponding in style and finish with the new buildings that are to be seen in the immediate vicinity of the castle. On the south of this lodge, you enter the demesne by a gateway beneath an elliptic Gothic arch, which corresponds with the style of the arch that connects the laboratory with the castle. On the other side of the road, and directly opposite to this entrance, a neat turret and similar archway form a handsome entrance to the deer-park. These buildings are composed of the fine bluish stone which is raised from the quarries on the demesne, and like the other buildings, the cornices and ornamental parts are of cut stone. The ordinary high road forms the boundary between the demesne and the deer-park, the former lying on the east and the latter on the west of this road. At a short distance from this entrance are situated the new gardens, which were laid out within the last seven years. These gardens are entered by a door that leads through the centre of the grand conservatory; this conservatory is of circular form, and lofty proportions, composed entirely of glass.

Grogan family tomb. (Liam Gaul Collection)

Ranges of considerable length extend one on each side of the grand
conservatory, and form graperies, which furnish abundant supplies of delicious fruit. Plants and beauteous flowers, both native and exotic, of the
richest and rarest descriptions, are to be seen in the conservatory and
flower-garden. The walks are neat and commodious, branching off, at
right angles, in front of the centre of the grand conservatory. This garden,
which contains over two statute acres, is surrounded by a high brick wall,
along the south-western front of which runs a handsome terrace, and also
a fine sloping bank, the latter entirely under strawberry beds. Through
the centre of this bank, and by an ample flight of fine cut stone steps,
you ascend to the terrace, and thence to the fruit and vegetable garden;
this garden is also surrounded by a high wall of handsome brick, and is
of the same size as the flower-garden. A very neat lodge stands on the
north-west side of this garden, and is occupied by the head gardener, who
is a very intelligent person. He has eighteen men and six women under
his direction, who are exclusively employed upon the pleasure grounds
and gardens. On the south of the fruit-garden lie the melon garden and

pinery, which comprise nearly a statute acre, including within it a recently planted dwarf orchard; here green-houses and hothouses are got up and constructed on the newest and most approved principles; pines, melons, and other rich and delicate fruits are produced here, while specimens of highly prized plants and flowers, both foreign and domestic, fill the green-houses. The mechanism, by which a full supply of air can, at all times, be admitted to the conservatories and greenhouses, is of admirable contrivance, and was executed by that very ingenious and clever mechanic, Mr. James Pierce.

Leaving the gardens, you approach the castle by rich walks, amid trees of a youthful and peculiarly vigorous description. These walks, like the gardens, have been recently planned and laid out, and the perfection they have attained, in so short a time, as well as their general freshness and beauty, is equally a matter of surprise to those who, like myself, had not seen them for the last five or six years. Approaching the castle in this

The conservatory. (IAMA Johnstown)

direction, the south front strikes upon the view, and challenges the unqualified admiration of the visitor. When I reached the terrace upon which the castle stands, I took a seat upon the neat garden chair that is placed above the flight of cut stone by which the descent to the lake takes place. The day was calm and sultry, and the refreshing and cooling sensation, produced by my proximity to the lake, as well as to the beautiful *jet d'eau*, which was playing by my side, created feeling of the purest gratification, such as the rich sense of tranquil beauty then before me was so well calculated to engender. While seated thus, with the castle upon one hand and the lake upon the other, I thought of the beautiful lines which Bulwer[68] puts into the mouth of 'Claude Melnotte', when he describes to the lovely, confiding, but haughty 'Pauline' his 'princely palace by the Lake of Como'. Having rested, for some time, in this delightful situation, I walked around the castle, where all was peaceful tranquillity, which was broken only by the pleasing hum of the tradesmen and labourers who were at work upon the new building and on the lawn.

The entrance gate and the porter's lodge. (IAMA Johnstown)

The entrance
hall to the castle.
(IAMA Johnstown)

I then proceeded to the castle, and was kindly received by the excellent
Mr. Morgan, who not forgetful of his previous invitation, did me the honour
to accompany me through the interior of the castle. The approach from the
porte cochè to the entrance-hall is by a handsome corridor, with beautiful
groined arches, which spring from bosses of the richest character and are
beautiful in execution and design. The edges of the groinings are of oak,
enriched, in some parts, with fine gilding. Curtains of Utrecht velvet of the
finest crimson, deeply trimmed and fringed with gold, ornament the splendid Gothic windows on each side of this corridor. The floor of this approach
is covered and ornamented with the newest and rarest material which can
be applied to such a purpose. The entrance-hall has a fine appearance;
the oak panelling and carving are of the most costly description; amongst

The grand
staircase.
(IAMA Johnstown)

The library.
(IAMA Johnstown)

other beautiful specimens of carving, both by the hand and by machinery,
are the Apostles and the family coat of arms. Nothing can be more truthful
and natural than the apostolic figures; the folds of the drapery will enable
the most incompetent person to form a judgment of their merit. The skin
of a magnificent Bengal tiger, the head finely developed, is spread out as a
hearthrug before the fireplace in the hall.

The grand hall presents a massive and truly characteristic appearance;
so much so, that if an intelligent person was brought thither in his sleep,
he would, upon waking, be at once convinced that he was within the hall

of some grand castle or stately palace. It is lighted by a dome of ornamental stained glass, which subdues the fierce glare of the summer's sun, and throws a mellowed and pleasing light upon the surrounding objects. This hall is surrounded by two magnificent galleries, one on each story, formed of oak, and of the finest workmanship; they are at once strong and beautiful, and perfectly in keeping with the character of the Castle. The floor is of asphaltum, tessellated in black and white. Passing from this hall, you enter the staircase-hall, and become struck with the grandeur of the noble staircase, which was designed by Hopper,[69] an English architect of no mean pretensions.

Having viewed the halls, we next entered the library, a very grand and solemn-looking room, with magnificent carvings and panelling in oak, some of them by poor Mooney, who may be said to have lived and died in the employment of the munificent proprietor. He has been succeeded by another native genius, Mr. Sinnott, who, although but a young man, has transcended even the finest efforts of the deceased carver. I saw beautiful specimens of this young artist's, than which nothing could be more clear or nearer to perfection. The furniture of this grand apartment is in keeping with its character; the chairs, sofas, tables, and book-cases are all of the choicest and best descriptions; this is such a room as Bacon, Newton, Locke, or Walter Scott, would like to call his own. We next proceeded to the dining-parlour, a fine room, of an oblong form: here, also oak panelling and carving can be seen; the darkness of the oak is finely relieved by the rich gilding of the ceiling and the other parts of the chamber. This room has a really gorgeous appearance, and reminds one of the House of Lords, which, in some measure, it resembles both in figure and decoration. Like the lordly chamber, it requires lighting up, to be seen to full advantage. The several articles of furniture are of the richest quality and newest patterns; to recapitulate them would be an impossibility. The tables, sofas, chairs, mirrors, vases, and the mantelpiece, with its unique ornaments, leave an impression on the mind which even time can scarcely erase. I noticed here beautiful candelabra, which are formed by richly-gilt allegorical figures, the glowing light issuing from the hand of each graceful figure; one of these was a carving by Mooney, and was finely executed.

Having viewed these magnificent rooms, we ascended the great staircase, which is lighted by a window of large dimensions, the curtains of which are of Utrecht velvet. In our farther ascent we noticed a splendid

picture, by Parris, of Mr. and Mrs. Morgan, and their elder daughter,
the Honourable Mrs. Deane, then a most interesting child, who is represented as caressing a fine dog, of the Newfoundland breed. This is a
very fine painting; Mrs. Morgan's likeness is as truthful as it is exquisitely
finished, and, although painted many years ago, is a perfect likeness up
to the present hour. Mr. Morgan's was, I am sure, an excellent likeness
when painted, but his figure being more robust now than it was at that
time, renders the identity less striking; the features, however, cannot be
mistaken, they are well defined and correctly truthful. There are in some
of the rooms splendid paintings by the same artist.

On the left of the grand staircase, you enter a large and very fine bed-
chamber; the decorations, although not complete, were in a forward
state, the papering is remarkably beautiful, and of French manufacture,
the pattern chaste, the colouring clear and perfect, and the figures finely
developed. In this room stands a bed of light, lofty, and elegant appearance, richly ornamented with gilding; this room, when finished, will be a
really beautiful one. On the right of the staircase, and opposite to the last
mentioned chamber, a fine room, of smaller dimensions, will form a dressing room to the bedchamber. At present, a small bed occupies the centre
of this room, the curtains of which are of Utrecht velvet. They are hung
in a tent-like shape, the centre ending in a cone, surmounted by a golden
ornament resembling a coronet.

We now arrived at the grand gallery, from which we entered the splendid suite of apartments which comprise the drawing-room and boudoirs.
It cannot be expected that I dare attempt a minute description of these
elegantly-furnished rooms; the ceilings, the rich and gorgeous papering,
the magnificent curtains and the drapery in general; the mantelpiece,
and the articles of vertú that ornament them; the splendid mirrors,
the vases, the candelabra, the tables, chairs, sofas, ottomans, and the other
indescribable articles – so grand, so gorgeous, so chastely beautiful, and so
new – render it impossible that one like myself, so unskilled in the science of elegant luxury, and so limited in point of time, could do anything
but fail in an effort to accomplish what even a very clever person would
be unequal to. Here, indeed, the graphic and glowing pen of Alexandre
Dumas might be employed with effect.

The first drawing-room is a fine oblong room, of elegant proportions;
the decorations and furniture are truly magnificent and judiciously selected,
while everything is so artistically arranged as to call forth the highest

commendation. The window, which is large, admits a full stream of light that falls on the various articles of *vertú*, so as to set them off to the finest possible advantage. The appearance of the lake and the lawns, with the fine old ivy-clad castle, is really beautiful, as seen from this window. The window-curtains are of Irish tabinet – the coverings of the sofas, ottomans, etc. are of the same material – the colour, a mixture of azure and amber. The papering is of green and gold, and of an exceedingly neat pattern. Large and magnificent mirrors, the frames of which are of the carving in oak, grace this fine apartment. One of these frames was carved by native workmen,[70] employed at the castle. Here also gilt figures, elegantly wrought, serve as chandeliers. In this room there is a fine painting, by one of the best masters, representing St. Agnes,[71] her right arm thrown over a lamb, the emblem of innocence and purity; the colouring is true and life-like, and the expression of the saint that of unmistakable piety and sanctity. It would seem that this picture was smuggled into this country from Italy; when it arrived, the saint was represented as leaning, in a pensive posture, upon an urn. Some of the connoisseurs, perceiving that the picture had a stained and dirty appearance, recommended that it should undergo the process of cleaning, and accordingly it was submitted to a skilful renovator, who, while exercising his skill upon it, was surprised to find that the urn entirely disappeared, and along with it the veil which had hitherto obscured its perfections. Thus its rare qualities again displayed themselves, and the ingenious device which was resorted to, in order to lessen the high duty consequent on its importation, became accounted for. Another picture of great merit can be seen in this room, which represents three children, members of the ancient family of Knox, the ancestors of Mr. Morgan, whose name he bears. These children are portrayed as being eminently beautiful – the eldest about ten years old, the second eight, and the youngest six. From this room there is a communication with another part of the castle, by an ingeniously-contrived door, the front of which is a large mirror. A stranger would never imagine that an entrance existed in this quarter. The second drawing-room in size and appearance accords with the first; the ceiling and papering are equally rich, but varying in their style of beauty; the furniture, too, forms to a certain extent, a contrast to that which occupies the first room. The papering of this room is of a claret, brown, and gold, here are to be seen elegantly-wrought figures, highly gilt, representing Atlas supporting the earth, the globes forming splendid candelabra. The window-curtains, and the covering of the furniture, are of Lyons brocade, of a peculiarly elegant appearance.

The first drawing room. (IAMA Johnstown)

A magnificent table, of the rarest material, occupies the recess of the window in this drawing-room. From this window also can be had an excellent view of the lake and the lawns. These splendid rooms are so open to each other, that they may be virtually considered as one and the same.

That which more particularly arrested my attention, as I passed through the state apartments, was the beautiful boudoir, which is entered from the last-mentioned drawing-room. This may arise from its being so limited in extent as to be capable of being taken into view by a comparatively hurried examination; even a momentary glance cannot fail to excite the interest of the visitor. When I approached the door, I paused, and felt almost afraid to enter, nay, I could scarcely think myself at liberty to breathe, lest I should disarrange its light and elegant trappings. This beautiful room, this temple of all that is chaste and delicate in furniture and decoration, is the fitting abode of the pure and refined genius, to whose exquisite taste and rich imagination it owes its existence in its present shape. It is situated in the south-eastern tower, and is, therefore, called the tower boudoir. It is, as a matter of course, of circular form; a neat and beautiful round table occupies the centre of the room; the chairs are of a peculiar shape, and of a light and delicate appearance; the recess, formed by the window, is filled by an elegantly upholstered seat, which is covered with a material of the finest texture; the colour, a rich cerulean. The window-curtains and drapery are of Lyons silk, of a peculiarly delicate and chaste character.

The walls are decorated with tapestry of the richest and rarest description; groups, representing innocent and happy rural life, appear on various parts of it; the figures are chastely and truthfully developed. The artistic execution of these characters is considered as difficult in the performance as they are beautiful in appearance. The lawns and the lake can be seen to full advantage from the window. The style and embellishments of this boudoir are of a truly poetic character, and, to use the same language, it may justly be designated a seraphic dwelling. I have recently seen some rich and elegant apartments, but there is not one amongst the whole number I would so gladly look upon a second time as on this finely conceived and exquisitely executed tiny gem.

Another beautiful boudoir is entered from the second drawing-room also; it is situated on the left hand, and is larger and somewhat different in its style of decoration. The tout ensemble of the tower boudoir is essentially light and delicate, while the character and appearance of this one is more full and gorgeous. The furniture is of the most splendid description: the window-curtains and drapery are of Lyons brocade. The walls are decorated with fine paintings by Parris, consisting of distinct and separate views of the castle, with fancy figures of the richest colouring and finish, representing "chiefs and ladies bright" in equestrian groups on different parts of the surrounding sunny lawns; while other parties are seen, some of them sailing in a fine gondola upon the beautiful lake, and others indulging in pedestrian exercise upon its borders. It would require a genius and an aptitude of no common order to do justice to these unrivalled apartments. All that Moore has said in his 'Epicurean',[72] or in his 'Light of the Harem'; or that Byron[73] so graphically described in 'Lambro's Cottage' in the Grecian Isle, are fully realised in the magnificence and variety of these splendid rooms. It would be a treat for the connoisseur to see this noble suite of apartments lighted up on a gala night: the hundred lights which are available for such a grand occasion, when throwing their lustre on the gorgeous ceilings, the papering, tapestry, and furniture of these rooms, as well as the saloons on the lower story, must have an effect which should be seen to be properly understood.

The music-room is a fine apartment; the furniture and decoration of this room are in keeping with the other grand apartments of the castle. I saw some specimens of the works which have been executed at the castle, consisting of elegant and highly-polished chimney-pieces of white marble. One of these magnificent monuments of native manufacture is composed, in part, of a piece of white marble which, in the lifetime of Mr. Morgan's grandfather, stood as an ornament over the garden gate. The chiselling of the devices on this piece were considered such rare specimens of artistic skill, that the present proprietor was induced to appropriate it to the upper part of a grand chimney-piece; additional parts were prepared by the workmen who were employed at the castle, and, after great labour and skill, they were enabled to produce corresponding portions worthy of the rare and antique original. As a whole, it is now considered very beautiful. In one of the rooms I noticed a rich and beautiful chimney-piece composed of slate; the polish is of the finest character, the colour a jet black; it is intersected with veins of gold: this, of itself, is a great curiosity.

Ascending from this elegant suite of rooms, we entered the second grand gallery. Here, I have no doubt, a skilful architect would pause to admire the grandeur and beauty of the design and workmanship which this part of the castle displays. Around this gallery are to be seen pictures of merit by the best masters; one of them a fine 'Samuel' – a perfect representation of this sanctified character. The 'Ruins of Jerusalem' is a splendid effort, and faithfully represents the desolation of this holy and celebrated city. There is also a fine full-length portrait of George the Third, in his regal robes. In the gallery other rare specimens of painting attract the notice of the visitor.

We now entered the grand bed-chamber, which is immediately above the grand drawing-room. I was equally surprised and delighted with the bed, and the several articles of furniture which are contained in this room. The curtains of the bed and of the window are of the richest description of Lyons brocade. Some very fine pictures are to be seen in this room, but it took so much time to view these magnificent saloons and the several articles of elegance and bijouterie which they contain, that I could not take a note of every object that presented itself; therefore I am not in a position to give a description of these paintings; they appeared, however, to be excellent efforts of art. The view from the window is very extensive and eminently beautiful, embracing within it not only the lawns, the lake, the fine old castle, and the castle of Rathmacnee, but even enables the eye to range over the whole space of the barony of Forth, which lies between Johnstown and the sea, and even a considerable portion of the sea itself becomes open to the view from this commanding eminence. From this window Mr. Morgan pointed out the valley which he purposes to annex to the lake, whereby it will be considerably enlarged.

We entered and viewed several finely furnished bed-rooms on this storey, and then proceeded to that part where the baths and machinery for supplying the castle with water are to be seen: everything which can minister to the safety, the comfort, and even to the luxury of the inmates, has been secured and provided. We now descended by a flight of stone steps, until we again fell in with the grand staircase, and thence descended to the hall, where, in such terms of gratitude as I could command, I endeavoured to express my acknowledgements to the excellent Mr. Morgan, and retired, deeply impressed with his great kindness and condescension. Visitors, specially favoured as I was, must leave Johnstown Castle filled with admiration of its beauty and grandeur, and, if strangers to the neighbourhood, must be forcibly struck with the wealth and liberality of its proprietor; but should they confine their views to the objects to be seen on the demesne, important as they unquestionably are, they will have but a comparatively imperfect notion of the true character of Mr. Morgan. In order to form a just appreciation of this pure philanthropist, it would be necessary that they should make a circuit of the surrounding country for several miles; they would then be enabled to read, in a truly practical volume, the real character of this excellent landlord. The comfortable and substantially-built and slated farm-house, with its neat garden or orchard, and its tasteful parterre, will speak, in language not to be misunderstood, his best eulogium. Many of the tenant farmers on his estate, are frequently to be seen as well mounted as some of the surrounding gentry, following the hounds, in the hunting season; while his day-labourers dwell in neatly-scented cottages, where the creeping woodbine, or mayhap the sweetly-scented rose, declares, in silent but convincing terms, that comfort and comparative refinement are not strangers to those who live within the range of his influence and his bounty. With such generous and bountiful dispositions, and a fortune of £20,000, a year, which is all spent in his own neighbourhood, it may be very naturally supposed that blessings are daily offered up, for the health and welfare of himself, and equally humane and benevolent Mrs. Morgan.

On Thomas Lacy's third visit to Johnstown Castle in 1863,[74] he once again gives a very descriptive insight into the further work carried out by the late Hamilton Knox Grogan Morgan (1808-1854) in his publication, *Sights and Scenes in Our Fatherland*. The following is an extract transcribed from Lacy's writing:

Vast sums of money were expended by the late Hamilton Knox Grogan Morgan, Esq., and by his father John Grogan, Esq., in extensive alterations and improvements, on Johnstown Castle, which Lady Esmonde, who in a few years after the decease of her late lamented husband, Mr. Morgan, married the Right Hon. Sir Thomas Esmonde, Bart., who is now the owner of the castle and adjoining estate, which by articles of agreement devolved upon his lady. As a matter of course, Lady Esmonde has but a life interest in the property, which, on her demise, will pass to her youngest daughter, recently married to the Right Hon. the Earl of Granard, K.S.P., and Lord-Lieutenant of the county of Leitrim.

Among the latest ornamental decorations of the interior of the castle are a series of splendid Parisian mirrors, three in number, which have been placed near the extremity of the grand drawing-room.[75] They are set in magnificently carved frames, manufactured by machinery in London, and richly gilt by Barnascone,[76] an Italian artist, for some years resident in Wexford and are probably the largest to be seen in this country. The appearance of this elegant saloon, which is grand in the extreme, is considerably enhanced by its being reflected in the magnificent mirrors, which rise from the floor to the gorgeous ceiling of the splendid chamber. The pictures, the furniture, and the various articles of *vertú* and *bijouterie*, as they strike upon the view, produce an almost magical effect on the mind of the unsuspecting visitor, who entertains a feeling somewhat approaching to regret when he discovers that, to some extent, he was labouring under a brilliant delusion; although, indeed the beautiful reality might well suffice to satisfy the most ambitious and fastidious craving. Among the fine pictures in this drawing-room is a modern painting by the celebrated Mulrenin, who came down to the castle, at the request of Sir Thomas Esmonde, for its execution. It is of large size and represents the Right Honourable Baronet in his Deputy-Lieutenant's uniform and Lady Esmonde who stands at a short distance on his right-hand side. This is an uncommonly fine painting, which, both as regards the truthfulness of the portraits and their masterly execution, reflects the highest credit on the taste and genius of the artist. That of her ladyship is full of character, being alike replete with elegance, dignity and grace. When I paid this, my last visit to the castle, in July, 1860, workmen were engaged upon the ball-room, which, with the adjoining apartment, called the band-room, occupies the lower storey of the new building erected by the late Mr. Morgan for a laboratory, he being an adept in chemical science. The splendid panelled ceiling was then in a forward state, and required only the finishing hand of the gilder for its completion. The floor was being laid with rich wood panels, prepared in London, with decorations similar to those which appear on the finest description of encaustic tiles.[77] These, when set and polished, present a beautiful carpet-like appearance. Some highly valued specimens of painting on marble are to be seen on the chimney-pieces of the ball-room and music-room, the delicately beautiful floral ornaments of which excite the astonishment of those who have not been previously acquainted with the interesting process by which such decoration is effected. The rich sheen of the verdant leaves, and the warm glow of the ripening fruit, form a delightful contrast with the highly-polished surface of the Bangor slate, upon which they have been so ingeniously and so artistically depicted. Elegant elliptic Gothic arches, each divided by two mullions, with finely ornamented traceried heads, stand on each side of the arcade leading from the castle to the ball-room. These several compartments will be entirely filled up with plate glass; while each side of the great arch which forms the carriage-way that intervenes between the castle and the ball-room will be furnished with folding doors, which, on the occasions of balls and other assemblies, will be closed, and will thereby afford protection and shelter to the company in their progress from the castle to the temple of gaiety and pleasure, from the inconvenience arising from unpleasant air-draughts. The upper part of this fine adjunct to the castle is appropriated to a billiard-room, and is approached from the drawing-room storey by an open corridor, lined on each side with elegant statuary. This noble castle, after many years of continuous improvement, carried out at an immense expense, is now in such a state of perfection as to elicit from those who are capable of appreciating its rare attributes, the most unqualified admiration.

With these few observations I shall conclude my notice of Johnstown Castle, being fully conscious of my inability to convey an accurate notion of its superlative claims to the attention and admiration of the visitor. The man who has the welfare of his fellow countrymen at heart, when he visits this part of the county, will derive much gratification on observing the style and character of the houses on the Johnstown estate, where

The sitting room. (IAMA Johnstown)

not only the habitation of the farmer but even that of the ordinary day-labourer is constructed of stone and roofed with slate; while the areas in front of them, being nicely planted with evergreens and flowering shrubs, impress him with the conviction that in the character of the proprietor, who had been thus sedulously blended the resident landlord and the enlightened philanthropist.

7

ART, ARTISTS
AND ARTISANS

To judge from the number of paintings in oils, water colours and drawings listed in the auction catalogue of the contents of the castle in 1944, Johnstown Castle possessed quite an art collection, amassed over the decades.[78] All of the art works listed were sold, leaving the large family portrait by Edmund Thomas Parris of the Hamilton Knox-Grogan Morgan's as the sole survivor. During the three-day auction a total of eighty-five paintings were sold and included

'North view of castle', sepia wash drawing by E.T. Parris, November 1833.

'South view of castle', sepia wash drawing by E.T. Parris, November 1833.

works by Francia, William Gilliard, H.E. Toner, T.S. Mann and many other unsigned paintings. A portrait of a 'Gentleman in Armour' by Sir Godfrey Kneller[79] and a 'Coaching Scene' by Philip James de Loutherbourg[80] were also on the list of paintings for sale. A painting of the 'Houses of Parliament', London, by architect and surveyor Thomas Hopper hung in the library at the castle.[81] In his *Sights and Scenes in Our Fatherland*,[82] Lacy refers to a large painting hanging in the drawing room of Sir Thomas Esmonde in his Deputy-Lieutenant's uniform with Lady Esmonde standing nearby. The painting is the work of Bernard Mulrenin, the celebrated painter who came down to the castle at the request of Sir Thomas.[83]

Edmund Thomas Parris[84] made a series of oil paintings which decorated the tower-boudoir and consisted of distinct and separate views of the castle. They were described by Lacy as having, 'fancy figures of the richest colouring and finish, representing "chiefs and ladies bright" in equestrian groups on different parts of the surrounding sunny lawns; while other parties are seen, some of them sailing in a fine gondola upon the beautiful lake, and others indulging in pedestrian exercise upon its borders'.[85] This set of oil paintings were listed in the sale catalogue of 1944 as Lot No. 291 and had been displayed in the Cloisters Corridor of the castle.[86] Parris painted the family portrait of Hamilton Knox Grogan-Morgan, his wife Sophie and their daughter Elizabeth-Geraldine during the time he visited Johnstown Castle in 1833. He also made a series of four

'East view of castle', sepia wash drawing by E.T. Parris, November 1833.

'West view of castle', sepia wash drawing by E.T. Parris, November 1833.

sepia-washed drawings of the castle from north, south, east and west positions in November 1833, one of which is shown on a table in the family portrait. Mr and Mrs S.C. Hall visited Johnstown Castle around 1842 and gave an interesting account of the restoration work in progress at that time. The Johnstown section was illustrated by six drawings showing Johnstown Castle; Rathmacknee Castle; Bargy Castle; Cottage at Redmondstown; School-house, Johnstown and The Lake at Johnstown. The six original drawings were by Andrew Nicholl.[87]

It is seldom that the names of the many tradesmen and craft workers involved in a new building or the refurbishment of an older one are recorded for posterity. Thomas Lacy, in his very detailed description of the many magnificent changes, alterations and additions to Johnstown Castle, its gardens and extensive grounds, has left some names of the most prominent and artistic craftsmen involved in this work.

John Mooney

Much of the wonderful and ornate oak carving of furniture and fittings was carried out by County Wexford wood carvers including a John Mooney from the outskirts of Enniscorthy. The family had a long tradition as coopers. Mooney spent several years at Johnstown and some of his work, especially the library with its magnificent carvings and oak panelling, is still to be seen in the castle today. Following Mooney's death, he was succeeded by another young wood carver by the name of Sinnott. This young man's work transcended even the finest work of his predecessor.

James Pierce

Several greenhouses and hothouses to the south of the fruit-garden produced many prized plants and flowers, both foreign and domestic. They required a full supply of air to the conservatories and greenhouses at all times and a mechanism to accomplish this was developed by a very ingenious mechanic, James Pierce.[88] A blacksmith and inventor, Pierce, from Kilmore village in the south of the county, went on to manufacture fire fans in a small premises in Allen Street in Wexford town, eventually setting up Pierce's of Wexford, specialising in making and supplying agriculture machinery and implements nationwide.[89]

Thomas Fagan

Thomas Fagan, Murntown, carried out the principal stonework of Johnstown Castle, as stated in his list of work carried out by him at Castleboro and Wilton Castle and several public buildings in Waterford.[90]

Patrick O'Connor

Patrick O'Connor, a builder from Wexford town, was also involved in work carried out in Johnstown in the 1840s and may have been responsible for the ornate ceiling work at the castle. There is a marked similarity between the work at Johnstown and the ceiling work carried out by O'Connor at the Franciscan friary in Wexford.[91]

Thomas Barnascone

A series of three Parisian mirrors set in magnificently carved frames were gilded by Thomas Barnascone, an Italian craftsman living in Wexford for a

Detail of ceiling in castle. (Liam Gaul Collection)

A pair of carved oak chairs, possibly by Mooney. (Liam Gaul Collection)

number of years and working as a gilder on the cornices and ceiling orna-
mentation at the castle. Barnascone is listed as a 'Carver and Gilder' at
25 Lower Exchange Street, Dublin.[92] Some of the larger pieces of furniture
have survived and with the expected restoration of the castle to its former
glory, they may once again take pride of place.

8

LORD AND LADY MAURICE FITZGERALD

Lord Maurice and Lady Adelaide FitzGerald were the last residents at Johnstown Castle.

The Right Hon. Lord Maurice FitzGerald, his Majesty's Lord Lieutenant and Custos Rotulorum of the County of Wexford,[93] was second son of Charles William, 4th Duke of Ireland and Marquis of Kildare and premier Duke of Ireland, and of Caroline Sutherland Leveson-Rower, third daughter of the Duke of Sutherland.[94] He was born at Carton House, Maynooth, County Kildare, on 16 December 1852. On 13 April 1880 he married Lady Adelaide Jane Frances Forbes, eldest daughter of the Earl of Granard, KP, and Jane Colclough Grogan-Morgan, at Longford.[95] Having finished his education, Lord Maurice spent eight years in the navy, and went round the world with the flying squadron, commanded by Sir Edward Hornby. He returned to his home at the beginning of the Franco-Prussian War, and remained at Carton House for seven years, until his marriage. During this period he was made captain of the Kildare Militia, which he resigned when he left the county. Lord Maurice, previous to his marriage, was a keen sportsman and hunted regularly with the Kildare, Ward and Meath Hounds. He was accounted the hardest rider in the countryside and an all-round lover of sports, including shooting. Lord Maurice was well known to be a crack shot. He settled down at his charming residence at Johnstown Castle, and pursued the life of an ideal Irish nobleman, in every sense. He resided permanently upon his estate, seldom going out of Ireland except for a few weeks every year, and devoting himself to the service of his country and its people.

Soon after his arrival in Wexford he was offered the Hon. Colonelcy of the Wexford Militia, but he declined the office, as he thought others were more deserving of it. In 1883 he was appointed high sheriff but he resigned after the Spring Assizes, as there was some question of the legality of his holding that position with the lord lieutenancy. He acted as foreman of the Grand Jury for one year only, but was on several other occasions was requested to do so but declined as he wished that Col. Alcock or Mr Doyne[96] should act in that capacity. Lord Maurice was a singularly liberal and broad-minded member of his class. He was entirely free from bigotry or intolerance, and above all things he was fearless and courageous in giving expression to and maintaining his opinion on all questions that might arise, always recognising the right of others to differ from him.

For a long time he took an active interest in the proceedings of the Wexford Poor Law Board and District Council, and with Lady Maurice helped to make the lot of the sick and aged poor in the Wexford Workhouse much more comfortable than they had previously been. The comforts of the aged and afflicted in the hospital that the guardians did not see their way to provide, Lord and Lady Maurice provided themselves at their own expense. The Catholics of the county owe Lord Maurice a great debt of gratitude for the fearless manner in which he championed their rights at the County Infirmary Board. More than 90 per cent of the patients in the County Infirmary have always been Catholics, yet not an official of the establishment belonged to the Catholic religion. Catholic patients felt they were deprived of the means to have the last rites administered to them in their dying moments as the majority of the nursing and administrative staff were of a different religious persuasion. Lord Maurice at once took up the matter, to see that justice was done to the thousands of poor Catholics who were seeking relief in the County Infirmary. This he succeeded in doing after a prolonged and severe struggle and his brave and broad-minded action should never be forgotten.

When local government was established in Ireland, Lord Maurice was unanimously co-opted a member of the county council. As a landlord he was considerate and fair and during the great land agitation the tenants on the Johnstown properties enjoyed peace and comfort while others were treated with hardship and turmoil. The charity shown in a material manner by himself and Lady Maurice was well known, but it was always done in a quiet unobtrusive manner.

Lord Maurice served on many committees in County Wexford, including The Society for Prevention of Cruelty to Animals in the role of president.[97]

He was a Governor of the Lunatic Asylum at Enniscorthy[98] and a member of the Her Majesties Prison, Wexford's Visiting Committee[99] and an ex-officio guardian of the Board of Guardians, Wexford Union.[100]

In the early afternoon on Wednesday 24 April 1901 the citizens of Wexford were profoundly shocked by the sad news of the death of Lord Maurice FitzGerald, who passed away after a very brief illness. He was just 48 years of age. The previous Saturday he had taken an active part in the proceedings of the Wexford District Council and afterwards, when in the town, he had appeared to be in his usual excellent health, except that he was a little pale, which was attributed to his recent attack of influenza. On his arrival at Johnstown, late in the evening, he complained of earache, and lay down, and on Sunday became very ill, and on Monday and Tuesday grew rapidly worse, suffering what was described as an affection of the brain. The family physician, Dr Hadden, called Dr Dowse and Dr Drapes in consultation, and so serious did they consider his Lordship's condition that Sir Thornley Stoker, the eminent Dublin surgeon, was wired for, with a view to, if necessary, performing an operation. Sir Thornley Stoker arrived on Wednesday morning, and pronounced his Lordship's condition hopeless, adding that he had but a few hours to live. Lord Maurice passed away at 2.30 p.m. in the afternoon, having lost consciousness several hours previously. It was only late on the previous evening that it became known in Wexford that Lord Maurice was so seriously ill.

The funeral was strictly private, in accordance with his own wishes and those of Lady Maurice. This fact was very disappointing to the public, who were anxious to pay Lord Maurice a last sad tribute of their respect. The interment took place in the family private cemetery in the demesne. The chief mourners were Lady Maurice FitzGerald, Gerald Hugh FitzGerald (son), Geraldine and Kathleen (daughters), Lord Walter FitzGerald and Lord Henry FitzGerald (brothers), Lady Eva, Lady Mabel and Lady Nesta FitzGerald (sisters), Col. FitzGerald, C.B. (brother-in-law), Mr and Mrs Colles (cousins), Mr Wm. B. Nunn and Mr Crozier, family solicitor. The coffin, supplied by Messrs. Sinnott & Sons, was of plain polished oak, lined with satin, and contained the following inscription: 'Lord Maurice Fitzgerald, – Born, 16/12/1852, – Died, 24/4/1901'.[101]

The contents of Lord Maurice FitzGerald's last will and testament were as follows:

The sole executrix of the will dated 3 June 1892, with a codicil of the 17 February, 1897, of Right Hon. Maurice FitzGerald, commonly called Lord Maurice FitzGerald, of Johnstown Castle, Wexford, Lord Lieutenant of the County of Wexford, who died on the 24th April last, aged 48 years, son of the fourth Duke of Leinster, is his widow, Lady Adelaide Jane Frances FitzGerald, daughter of the seventh Earl of Granard, and the testator appointed her and his brother, Lord Walter FitzGerald, as guardians of his children. He bequeathed £1,000 in trust for the benefit of the children of his brother, Lord Charles FitzGerald, and he bequeathed the proceeds of life insurance policies with the Scottish Widows and Royal Exchange Offices for £15,000 in trust to apply so much thereof as may be necessary in discharge of a charge of the Kingstown estate created by settlement as to £10,000 if he should leave three younger children, and any balance from the proceeds of the said policies is to be applied in redemption of a charge on the same estate for £7,900 to Alderman Morgan's trustees, and the testator stated that any sums paid by him in redemption of charges on the estate are to be taken as for the benefit of the inheritance. He left all the residue of his property to his wife, Lady Adelaide FitzGerald, and his personal estate has been valued at £27,081 2s 9d gross, including £3,512 7s 10d in England.

Lady Maurice FitzGerald

Lady Maurice FitzGerald survived her husband by forty-one years during which she kept the huge Johnstown Castle estate operational with the managerial skills of her first cousin, Capt. Ronald Forbes. Through the tragedy of the loss of her only son and one of her daughters and witnessing the First World War and the onset of the Second World War, Lady Maurice immersed herself in a myriad of church, charitable and social activities with an energy that belied her advancing years.

She was the daughter of the 7th Earl of Granard and sister of Lady Sophia Grattan Bellew, widow of Sir Henry Grattan Bellew of Castle Forbes, Longford, and a half-sister of the Earl of Granard. Lady Maurice was a niece of the Hon. Mrs Deane-Morgan of Ardcandrisk. For many years she took a very active part in public life in the county and carried on the good work and traditions of her late husband. She was chairman of the Board of Guardians, of the Wexford Branch of the National Society for the Prevention of Cruelty to Children and of the County Wexford Horticultural Society. She took a prominent part in the Women's National Health Association. There was virtually no organisation across the county for the relief of the often terrible conditions affecting the general public and especially the poor to which she did not give her support and allegiance. During the First World War she acted as chairman of the Wexford Branch of the Queen Mary Guild and in 1914 she opened the Wexford Cinema Palace at a concert and moving picture show in aid of the Belgian refugees. She was always ready and willing to offer her support to every appeal or to make a donation in a quiet and private manner. She gave a great deal of employment at her estate and kept a large staff at Johnstown. Her active interest in the Rathaspeck Nursing Association provided a district nurse in the Rathaspeck area. As a trustee of the Lady Esmonde and Cullimore charities she succeeded in obtaining from the high court an order which helped the Sisters of St John of God in nursing the poor of the town of Wexford. She always expressed an interest in the town and its progress.

Lady Maurice's half-brother, the Earl of Granard, was Deputy Speaker of the House of Lords in 1915 and was also a member of the first Irish Senate. He had served as Post-master General in England from 1906 to 1910.

Lord Maurice FitzGerald and Lady Adelaide FitzGerald. (IAMA Johnstown)

In her final year Lady Maurice FitzGerald was confined to bed for months prior to her death aged 82 years, which occurred at her residence, Johnstown Castle on 18 November 1942. Her funeral took place to the family private burial ground within the grounds of the Johnstown Castle estate in the presence of her daughter Mrs More-O'Farrell, her cousin Capt. Ronald Forbes, her son-in-law Major Michael Lakin, and other family members. Funeral arrangements were carried out by Messrs John Sinnott and Sons, Funeral Undertakers, South Main Street, Wexford directed by Mr Frank Gaul, proprietor.[102]

9

SOCIAL ACTIVITIES AT THE CASTLE

The wonderful castle building and grounds at Johnstown lent themselves as the ideal locations for the many social events and activities held there over the decades right up to present times.

Debutante Ball

In 1910 a Wexford newspaper carried a report on the Debutante Ball held at Johnstown Castle. The occasion was to celebrate the coming out of Miss Kathleen FitzGerald, daughter of Lady Maurice FitzGerald. The splendid apartments of the palatial residence were artistically adorned. The many invited guests were received at the head of the grand staircase by Lady Maurice FitzGerald and her son, Lt Gerald Hugh FitzGerald of the 4th Battalion Royal Irish Dragoon Guards. For this occasion the staircase was lined at each side with many fairy lamps dressed with shades of gold.

The dining room was the ballroom for the night and presented a resplendent scene with exquisite floral decorations contrasting in perfect harmony with the illuminations. The drawing room and library were utilised as 'sitting out' rooms but were no less magnificent in their decor and afforded a pleasant area for relaxation for the many dancers throughout the evening. The central or main hall in which the house party dined was also lighted to great effect and presented as an exotic scene. The supper-room was filled with the fragrance of choice blooms as were the adjoining rooms which served as tea-rooms. The flowers and ornamental plants were arranged with charm and splendour and were from the castle greenhouses and gardens.

Dancing commenced at 10 p.m. and continued until 5 a.m. The music was supplied by the very popular and much sought-after May's Band from Dublin. Miss FitzGerald, the fair debutante, looked charming in a beautiful dress of white satin trimmed with ninon[103] and silver and wore a diamond pendant and a diamond and sapphire brooch. Lady Maurice FitzGerald's dress was black satin with black sequins, and her ladyship's ornaments were a diamond tiara, a diamond necklace and pendant.

Over ninety guests were in attendance on the night, including Lord Frederick FitzGerald, Lord Walter FitzGerald, Lord Desmond FitzGerald, Viscount and Viscountess Stopford, Lord and Lady Carew, Baroness Gray, Sir Henry and Lady Sophia Grattan Bellew, Captain the Hon. Bertram Forbes, the Hon. Mrs Deane-Morgan, Mr and the Hon. Mrs Irvine, Mr and Mrs Gerald Moore O'Farrell, Lord and Lady Templemore, Captain Harvey, Captain Alcock, Major Forest, Mr and Mrs Elgee, Miss Cynthia Paget, Major and Mrs Townsend and many, more prominent members of Irish society.

A varied selection of music was performed for the delight of the packed ballroom floor from May's Band and included such well-known waltzes as: 'Vision D'Amour', 'Dollar Princess', 'The Gold and Silver', 'Songe d'Antomne', 'Eternity', 'The Druid's Prayer', 'Barcarolle', 'The Merry Widow', 'Ciribiribin'. There was also a two-step, 'Moonstruck' and 'Mandolinata' with various lancers, galops, polkas together with special requests and dedications throughout the hours of dancing.

Skating on the Frozen Lake

During the very cold weather of February of 1895,[104] very large crowds of people from Wexford enjoyed the skating on the frozen lake at Johnstown Castle. They were joined by Lord Maurice and Lady FitzGerald who treated the visitors with every attention. Workmen on the estate were engaged in keeping the ice swept and at nightfall torches and flaring oil lamps were hung from the trees around the edges of the lake.[105]

The FitzGerald's skating on the lake at Johnstown, February 1895.

Judges Entertained at Johnstown Castle

A notice appeared on p.3 in the *Wexford Independent* on 21 July 1855 as follows:

> On Saturday last Mrs. Grogan Morgan entertained at Johnstown Castle the Judges of Assize to a sumptuous 'dejeuner dinatoire'.[106] Sir Thomas Esmonde, Bart., Mr. Talbot, High Sheriff; Mr. Walker, D.L., and a large number of the gentry were invited to meet their Lordships.

Fashionable Engagements[107]

Two notices appeared in the *Free Press* on Saturday 31 January 1914 as follows:

> The engagement is announced of Captain Michael Lakin, Master of the Wexford Hounds and late of the 11th Hussars, youngest son of Sir Michael Lakin, and Miss Kathleen FitzGerald youngest daughter of the

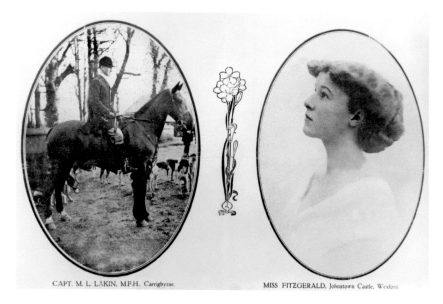

CAPT. M. L. LAKIN, M.F.H. Carrigbyrne.   MISS FITZGERALD, Johnstown Castle, Wexford

Maj. Lakin and Kathleen FitzGerald. (IAMA Johnstown)

late Lord Maurice FitzGerald and of Lady Maurice FitzGerald of Johnstown Castle Wexford. Miss FitzGerald is a cousin of the Duke of Leinster and she is also a niece of Lord Granard, her mother, who was before marriage Lady Adelaide Forbes, being Lord Granard's half-sister.

The engagement is also announced of Miss FitzGerald's only brother, Captain Gerald FitzGerald, 4th Dragoon Guards, his fiancée being Miss Dorothea Spencer-Charrington, youngest daughter of Mr. Spencer-Charrington, of Winchfield Lodge, Hants, England.

Presentation to Miss Kathleen FitzGerald

Following the announcement of Miss FitzGerald's engagement, a meeting was called by some prominent members of the Killinick Harriers Club and it was agreed that a suitable memento be presented to Miss FitzGerald upon the occasion of her marriage to Capt. Lakin. After some discussion, it was decided that a Chippendale pattern tray bearing a suitable inscription and weighing some 85 ounces be presented by Major Irvine, Chairman of the

Killinick Harriers Club, accompanied by Messrs John Codd, Master of the Hounds, Francis Walsh, Secretary and Dr Jeremiah Hadden.

The Cricket Club at Johnstown[108]

Capt. Ronald Forbes was an avid follower and participant in the game of cricket and at one time formed a team at Johnstown Castle. Many matches were played on their home cricket ground on the estate. The team often competed in away games and in return matches

In August 1913 their rivals were a team from Carne. The Johnstown team won both games. The 'home' team were captained by Capt. Ronald Forbes and other team members were: J. Staples, R. Malone, R. Swaby, G.H. FitzGerald, Edward Slavin, T. Esmonde, J. Bowers, the Shea brothers and White.

The club crest carried the motto: 'Crom a Boo'. The crest was a combination of features taken from the crests of the FitzGerald and Forbes families. The club was familiarly known as the Crom a Boo which was the motto and original battle cry of the FitzGeralds, Dukes of Leinster.[109]

At the outbreak of the First World War the cricket club went out of existence.

The crest of Johnstown Cricket Club. (Courtesy of Dr A.M O'Sullivan)

A Strange Visitor

Many important visitors from the ranks of gentry, politicians, clergy and the judiciary came to Johnstown Castle during the residency of Lord and Lady Maurice FitzGerald but the most unusual invitation to lunch was extended to Sequah[110] by Lord Maurice around 1890. It was on the final day of Sequah's visit to Wexford town where this travelling 'doctor' of American Indian origin carried out his healing practise and the extraction of painful teeth, all to the sounds of a buck-skin-clad brass band. In a short report in the *Free Press*, it was stated that the visit by Sequah to Johnstown was in gratitude for the successful treatment of an ankle injury to Lady Maurice some days earlier.

10

JOY AND SORROW

On Saturday 18 July 1914, at 1.30 p.m., the marriage took place at St Brigid's church, Rathaspeck of Major Michael Lakin, MHF, Carrickbyrne House, youngest son of Sir Michael Lakin, Bart, and Lady Lakin, of Warwickshire, and Kathleen FitzGerald, daughter of Lady and the late Lord Maurice FitzGerald. For many months past the wedding of the young couple had been looked forward to in social circles throughout the county, in which they were great favourites. It was little wonder that when the happy day arrived for their wedding the usually placid surroundings of Rathaspeck were invaded by a happy and fashionable throng of well-wishers. Even the weather on the morning of the wedding was smiling as the sun burst forth in all its splendour, dispelling the gloomy clouds of the previous day.

For a time before the ceremony large crowds had gathered along the road at St Brigid's church. The curate of the parish, Revd Harris, arrived early and with the assistance of Col. Ffrench and Mr Nunn of Castlebridge made the necessary arrangements for the reception of the many invited guests. By one o'clock every seat in the church was filled with the exception of those allocated for the bride, bridegroom and their party. Archdeacon Latham entered the church with the bridegroom accompanied by his father Sir Michael Lakin and the bestman, Mr Bell-Irvine. On the entrance of the bride the choir sang the hymn, 'O Father, all Creating'. The bride was accompanied by her mother, her brother, Capt Gerald FitzGerald and the bridesmaid Miss Cynthia Paget. The bride's beautiful wedding gown with its court-train was carried by her pageboy, Master Andrew Horsburgh Porter, dressed in hunting costume. The bride wore a beautiful veil of old lace and carried a magnificent bouquet, as did her bridesmaid. The bride was given away by her mother.

The wedding ceremony was performed by Archdeacon Latham, assisted by Revd C.A. Harris. At the conclusion of the ceremony the choir sang Psalm 67, after which the prayers were recited by Revd Harris. The choir sang 'O Perfect Love' as the happy couple and their witnesses signed the register. With his newly wedded wife on his arm and both smiling the couple walked slowly down the centre of the church to the strains of Mendelssohn's 'Wedding March' to the waiting motor outside where they received numerous hearty congratulations. The choir for the ceremony was comprised of sopranos, altos, tenors and bass voices with musical accompaniment on the harmonium by Mrs Tuach. The entire party of guests returned to the castle where the wedding 'dejeuner' was held and a reception given by Lady Maurice FitzGerald.

Mr and Mrs Michael Lakin.
(IAMA Johnstown)

THE FASHIONABLE WEDDING AT JOHNSTOWN CASTLE.

Standing (left to right)—Capt. M. L. Lakin, M.F.H. (Bridegroom), Lady Henry Fitzgerald, Lady Maurice FitzGerald, Capt. Gerald Fitzgerald. Sir Michael Lakin, Mr. Bell Irvine (Best Man), Miss C. Paget (Bridesmaid), Miss D. Charrington.
Sitting—The Bride. Page—Master Andrew Horsburgh Porter. Sitting—Lady Lakin.

Bride and groom and wedding party at Johnstown. (IAMA Johnstown)

The dresses worn for this fashionable wedding were very much admired. Miss FitzGerald's wedding gown was of ivory charmeuse, with slightly draped skirt, over which fell a full tunic of old Limerick lace. It was a gift from her aunts, Ladies Eva and Mabel FitzGerald. The train was of white ninon embroidered in gold. One side of it was draped with Limerick net, caught with trails of orange blossom, white heather and shamrock. Her veil was of lace held in place with sprays of orange blossom. The going-away gown was of dark mole crepethais with a draped skirt coming very high to the waist, the bodice being composed of fine cream lace over flesh-coloured chiffon outlined with mole chiffon. Over this was one of the new capes in the same material as the gown, lined with the palest pink satin. Her hat was of brown lace straw, with a mount of pink roses.

The bride's mother, Lady Maurice, wore a gown of soft grey moiré. The skirt, which hung in graceful folds, had a small train. The bodice draped with grey chiffon and cream lace, had sleeves of chiffon over lace, and showed an inner vest of pale mauve. The cape worn with this gown was of the same moiré, lined with pale mauve satin, with a rolled velvet collar, and was made in the long straight shape, well open in front. Lady Maurice wore a hat of mauve straw, with handsome grey ostrich plumes.

The wedding presents to the happy couple numbered in excess of 200 items, including jewellery, silver service, silver cutlery, cut-glass, furniture, gold wrist watches, a writing desk and the Mayor of Wexford, James Sinnott, gave a silver afternoon tea service. The bride's uncles and aunts, Lord Frederick, Lord Walter, Lord George, Lord Desmond, Lord and Lady Henry, Lady Eva, Lady Mabel, Lady Alice, Lady Nesta FitzGerald and other relatives all gave presents of a costly nature. During the week prior to the wedding, by kind permission of Lady FitzGerald, the presents were on view at Johnstown Castle and many of the townspeople availed of the privilege to view the gifts. The photographs of the wedding group were taken by the well-known Wexford photographer, Mr. C.E. Vize.

The Lakin's set up home at Carrickbyrne for a time following their marriage and later took up their new residence at Horetown House near Foulksmills, County Wexford.[111] Michael Lakin was educated at Marlborough College in Wiltshire. He joined the British Army and fought in the Boer War in 1900. He gained the rank of major while serving with the 11th Hussars. He also fought in the First World War, holding the rank of Acting Major in the service of the Machine Gun Corps. In 1915 he was decorated with the award of the Companion, Distinguished Service Order (DSO) and was major and second in charge of the South Irish Horse. At the end of the First World War he was decorated with the Military Cross (MC) in 1918. He had a lifelong interest and love of horses and was an excellent horseman and was popular

Staff on duty for the wedding. (IAMA Johnstown)

Kathleen Lakin on her horse, 'Active'. (IAMA Johnstown)

at the various 'meets' around the county. His wife, Kathleen, was also a keen horsewoman and both husband and wife hunted with the Wexford Hounds where they were popular with all who came in contact with them. Major Lakin was Master of Wexford Hunt for many years.

The Lakins had two sons from their marriage: Gerald Michael, born 17 January 1916, and Maurice Victor, born 30 October 1919. In 1930, however, the great joy and happiness experienced by the Lakin family of Horetown House was to turn to sorrow and bereavement resulting from a tragic hunting accident and untimely death by which a husband lost his wife and two young boys lost their mother. Thirty-eight-year-old Kathleen Lakin rode out with the Wexford Hounds on Friday 21 February and while hunting near the village of Gusserane her mare stumbled in the act of clearing a 4ft ditch and dislodged Mrs Lakin, sending her crashing onto her back on the hard surface of the roadway. She struck her head and never moved after that. Due to illness, her husband, Major Lakin had stayed home on that particular day.

Medical assistance was immediately summoned and very soon the injured woman was attended by Doctors McCabe, Walsh and Travers whose joint opinion was a basal fracture. The resident surgeon of Wexford County Hospital, Dr M.K. O'Brien, came to the scene at about two o'clock that afternoon to find Mrs Lakin unconscious and her symptoms pointed clearly to a fracture of the base of the skull. She was in a serious condition and was removed at once to the County Hospital. Sir William de Courcy Wheeler, the distinguished surgeon, travelled from Dublin and everything possible was done for the unfortunate Mrs Lakin but to no avail. She died without ever regaining consciousness about three o'clock on Sunday afternoon. Evidence to the accident was given on the following Monday at an inquest held at the County Hospital by Mr F.M. O'Connor, deputy coroner for South Wexford. Expressions of sympathy were extended to her husband, sons and mother on the great loss they had suffered.

On Monday evening the remains were brought from the hospital to Johnstown Castle accompanied by a large cortege of people, demonstrating the feelings of regret and sympathy of all classes. Her private funeral took place the following Tuesday and she was buried in the family cemetery in the grounds of Johnstown. The remains were borne by members of the Horetown House and Johnstown Castle employees. The funeral service was conducted by Revd Harold Gibb, rector of Sherborne, Warwick; Revd W.L. Shade, rector of Bannow; and Rev. T. Talbot, rector of Horetown.

The family and the many friends and admirers of the late Kathleen Lakin wished to perpetuate her memory for the future and the idea of a much-needed maternity wing to the County Hospital in Wexford town brought an immediate response. A committee was established by the Wexford Hunt which brought extremely generous monetary subscriptions. Two years after her death, the Kathleen Lakin Memorial wing at the County Hospital, Wexford, was formally opened on Monday 23 May 1932. The ceremony was carried out by Lady Maurice FitzGerald attended by a large gathering of representatives of the Wexford Hunt Committee, the County Health Board officials, staff of the hospital and relatives and friends of the late Mrs Lakin. The five-ward new wing was to accommodate maternity patients with a section of the wing to treat poor patients for free. The furnishings of the bright and spacious wards were contributed by Major Lakin. A marble tablet within the building is inscribed as follows:

The Kathleen Lakin Memorial Ward.
In memory of Kathleen Lakin, died 23 day of February 1930,
from injuries received in the hunting field.

Lakin memorial plaque at Wexford Hospital. (Courtesy of Ms Lily Burns)

Mr M.J. Jordan accepted the gift of the new building on behalf of the Health Board from Mr T.A. Colfer, Solicitor and Hon. Sec. of the Wexford Hunt Committee. Mr Jordan thanked all concerned with the project and thanked especially the generous subscribers who made the new wing a reality. He then called on Lady Maurice FitzGerald to formally open the new wing of the hospital. Prior to the ceremony Lady Maurice thanked all those who made this possible and said that she hoped the new wing would be a source of comfort and help to all those who entered it. Lady Maurice unlocked the entrance door to the wing and declared the Kathleen Lakin Memorial Wing open. Afterwards, on behalf of the Board of Health, Miss N. O'Ryan, a near neighbour of the Lakin family, presented Lady Maurice FitzGerald with a solid silver key, embossed in Celtic design surmounted by a Celtic cross inscribed as follows:

Presented to Lady Maurice FitzGerald of Johnstown Castle, Wexford, on the occasion of her opening the Kathleen Lakin Memorial Wing of the County Wexford Hospital, 23 May 1932.

Concluding the ceremony Lady Maurice thanked the Health Board for this special gift and promised it would be treasured and retained within her family for future generations. The Kathleen Lakin Memorial Wing served the people of County Wexford up to recent years.

11

JOHNSTOWN AT WAR

Military historians have written many volumes on the numerous wars since earliest times from the Punic Wars, the Peloponnesian War, The Thirty Years War, Napoleonic Wars, the Boer War to wars of independence and civil wars in America, England, Spain and Ireland. It was the assassination of Archduke Franz Ferdinand, heir to the throne of Austria-Hungary and his wife, Sophie, on 28 June 1914 by Yugoslav Nationalist, Gavrilo Princip, in Sarajevo that brought about one of the deadliest conflicts in history, the First World War of 1914-1918. The war began on 28 July 1914 and lasted until 11 November 1918. The main opponents in this war were the Allied countries of Great Britain, France and the Russian Empire in conflict with the central powers of Germany and Austria-Hungary. Fought mainly in trenches, this war involved an estimated 70 million military personnel resulting in 10 million fighting men killed and 20 million wounded. Millions of civilians were also killed on all sides. This war was supposedly the war to end all wars with a prediction that the fighting would be all over by Christmas. That was not to be as it proved to be the bloodiest war in history.

In country houses in Ireland and Britain the war changed the way of life that had been going on for decades. Even before the war began, the shape of Irish society had altered with the landed gentry having lost most of their lands, being left with just a small acreage and a large house in almost complete isolation. At that time, only 150-170 estates belonged to the Irish aristocracy. So it was on 4 August 1914 that a meeting was convened by

George Kingston[112] at Mitchelstown, County Cork, to review the current situation regarding their lands and properties and how the war might affect them. The meeting was attended by the aristocracy and gentry from all the surrounding counties. Irish aristocratic families had a long tradition of military service, with the younger sons who would have gone on to military academies for training. Following their initial training these young men went on to pursue a military career and joined the British army. The oldest son would have been the heir to the house, lands and any other properties belonging to the family estate and following a good education would have returned home, yet, many of the heirs did complete military service prior to taking over the running of the family estate.

Regarding themselves as still part of the aristocratic class the response to 'call-up' was an opportunity to put themselves to the forefront, especially in the roles of officership and command. Prior to the First World War many of those men had already served as officers in the British Army and seen action in the Second Boer War (1889-1902). Many of the officers and men would have left their regiments but re-enlisted to serve once again. The older retirees organised recruitment drives around the country in an effort to get young men to join the fight. Their wives would have also been involved in fundraising activities to provide parcels to be sent to soldiers at the front. Lady Maurice FitzGerald was a great supporter and served as a member on several committees. The aristocracy stayed faithful to the war effort right to the end of the conflict.

Gerald Hugh FitzGerald, born on 11 April 1886, was the only son of Lady Adelaide FitzGerald and Lord Maurice FitzGerald. Following his early education he went on to study at Eton and joined the Royal North Devon Hussars (Yeomanry). In December 1907 he was gazetted to the Royal Irish Dragoon Guards and was promoted to lieutenant on 17 November 1908.[113] On 25 November 1913 he was promoted to the rank of captain. The young officer and Miss Dorothy Violet Charrington, youngest daughter of Spencer Calmeyer Charrington of Winchfield Lodge, Winchfield,[114] were engaged to be married but brought their wedding forward and were married at South Tidworth on 5 August 1914, the day after war was declared.[115] He left that evening with the Expeditionary Force to France.

The British Army was advancing north from Marne on 13 September 1914 in the hope of crossing the Aisne near the village of Bourg-et-Comin, about 17 miles east of Soissons. Part of the Oise-Aisne canal crossed over the Aisne river here on an aqueduct. The 4th Dragoon Guards were positioned in front

An aerial photograph of Johnstown Castle. (Courtesy of Gerry O'Leary)

Johnstown Castle around 1900,
watercolour by Michael Kelly, Wexford.

A connecting corridor in the castle. (Liam Gaul Collection)

The Apostles Hall. (Liam Gaul Collection)

The entrance hall. (Liam Gaul Collection)

The Mirror Room. (Liam Gaul Collection)

The Italianate Walk.
(Liam Gaul Collection)

Porte Coache.
(Liam Gaul Collection)

The Fishing Tower. (Liam Gaul Collection)

Morning sunrise at the Fishing Tower. (Liam Gaul Collection)

The wheelwright's workshop in the museum. (Liam Gaul Collection)

The blacksmith's forge in the museum. (Liam Gaul Collection)

The castle in the snow. (Liam Gaul Collection)

An autumnal scene. (Liam Gaul Collection)

A midsummer night at Johnstown.
(Courtesy of Paddy Donovan)

Coat of arms.

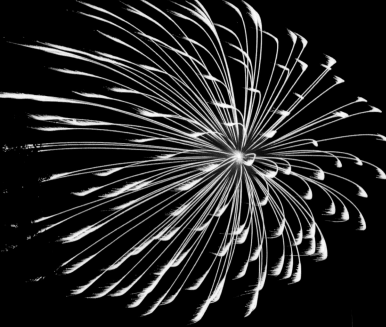

of the village where there were three bridges that crossed the two canals and the river. Earlier, patrols had discovered that the two canal bridges were intact but the road bridge over the Aisne river had been destroyed. The plan was to take the two bridges and make an entry into the village of Bourg which was held by German infantry supported by machine guns at strategic spots on the bridges. The British infantry charged the outposts that guarded the first bridge and took the Aisne canal bridge quickly. During this time the 4th Dragoon Guards were under heavy fire from machine guns on the other side of the Aisne-Oise canal and from the aqueduct. At this point Capt. FitzGerald, the Dragoon's machine-gun officer, rode up and with his machine guns soon silenced the German fire. The way was now clear for the infantry to move up, cross the bridges and use the aqueduct to cross the river and enter the village of Bourg.

Capt. FitzGerald was known to all in the army as 'Pat' FitzGerald and the following account was given by Capt. A. Osborn, RAMC Medical Officer, 4th Dragoon Guards:

> It was at this point in the battle a shot rang out from the church tower in Bourg. Pat got a bullet between the eyes. I was only a few yards from him, trying to do something for Sergeant Langdon when someone shouted to me. FitzGerald was unconscious when I got to him. His wound was no bigger than a blue pencil mark in the centre of his forehead. Then in a moment he was gone.[116]

Capt. Gerald Hugh FitzGerald was just 28 years of age and his loss to his regiment was immense. He was extremely popular and loved by his brother officers and men. He was a keen sportsman, a fine horseman, polo player and cricketer. A brass plaque on a pillar inside the Beauclerk/Charrington family pews reads, 'In memory of Capt. G.H. Fitzgerald, 4th Dragoon Guards. Killed in action, 13 Sept. 1914. Quis separbit.'[117]

The news of Capt. FitzGerald's death was received in a telegram from the war office to the castle on Friday evening. Lady Maurice and the captain's widow, who was staying at Johnstown, were profoundly shocked on receiving the sad tidings. In a letter from Capt. H.S. Sewell, details of Capt. FitzGerald's death were outlined: 'his personal belongings were collected to be sent to Mrs FitzGerald. His remains were buried in the village cemetery. I know you will bear this bravely, and we all mourn with you the loss of so noble and gallant a comrade. Yours Sincerely, H.S. Sewell.'[118]

Capt. G.H. FitzGerald in dress uniform. (IAMA Johnstown)

Lady Maurice FitzGerald was 54 years of age and bereft of both her husband and her only son and heir.

Lt Desmond Otho Paget, another member of the extended FitzGerald family, was killed in action on 21 March 1918 aged 19 years. On Sunday 19 June 1920, two years after the war ended, a memorial window was unveiled and dedicated by Rt Revd Dr J.A.F. Gregg, Bishop of Ossory at St Brigid's church, Rathaspeck, to the memory of Capt. Gerald Hugh FitzGerald, 4th Dragoon Guards and his cousin, Lt Desmond Otho Paget,[119] King's Royal Rifle Corps. The stained-glass window is a fine work of art, depicting Our Lord's Resurrection on the left pane and an angel opening the vault whilst two soldiers armed with a sword and javelin are on duty on the right pane. At the bottom of each pane is an inscription to the memory of the deceased officers with the badges of their respective regiments. On the exterior of the wall in which the window was erected is a marble tablet with the following inscription:

This window is erected by friends in memory of the late Captain G.H. Fitzgerald, 4th Dragoon Guards, who fell in France during the Battle of The Aisne, 13/9/1914, and Lieutenant D.O. Paget, King's Royal Rifle Corps, who fell in France, near St. Quentin, 21/3/1918.[120]

The memorial was commissioned and designed by Messrs Earley and Co., Dublin, and the cost borne from subscriptions by family and friends of the two officers. Following a meeting of the subscribers, prior to the unveiling ceremony, Lady Maurice FitzGerald expressed thanks on behalf of her son's widow Mrs Dorothy FitzGerald, Lieutenant Paget's sister Miss Cynthia Paget, and herself. In Wexford town, at St Iberius' church, another fitting memorial in the form of a pulpit was dedicated to the war dead including names of those who died in the Second World War. The pulpit has the following inscription:

The gravestone of Capt. FitzGerald, France. (Courtesy of The War Graves Project)

This pulpit is erected to the glory of God and to the sacred and honoured memory of the Officers, non-commissioned Officers, and men whose names are heron inscribed who gave their lives for their God, their King and Country in the Great War 1914-1918 'Faithful unto Death'.

In the list of sixteen men who died in the First World War are the names of Capt. G.H. FitzGerald and Lt D.O. Paget and in the listing for the Second World War is the name of Capt. G.M. Lakin.[121]

All male members of the extended FitzGerald and Forbes families answered the 'call to arms' and offered their services and previous military experience and expertise.

Following the death of Lord Maurice FitzGerald in 1901, the Johnstown Estate was managed by Lady Maurice's cousin, Ronald Forbes, who resided at the castle. A year into the war, Ronald Forbes volunteered for active service and was accepted by the War Office. He was granted a commission as a lieutenant in the Royal Wiltshire Yeomanry.

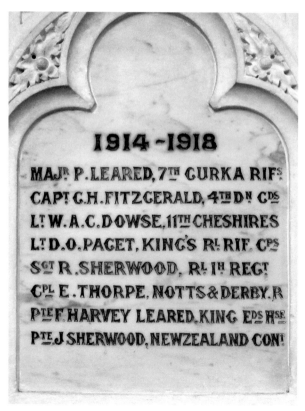

Pulpit inscription at St Iberius' Church, Wexford. (Courtesy of Canon Arthur Minion, rector)

Capt. Ronald Forbes in uniform.
(IAMA Johnstown)

On 30 October 1915, the following notice appeared on p.5 of the *Free Press*:

> Lieutenant Forbes comes of a distinguished military stock, his elder brother was the late Colonel Forbes who was killed in action at St. Eloi while in command of the 1st Battalion Royal Irish Regiment on the 17 March, 1915. Lieutenant Forbes has had previous experience in the South African War where he was taken prisoner but released on the cessation of hostilities. He was awarded two medals for engagements in the Transvaal, Orange Free State and Cape Colony and the King's Medal. Resident in County Wexford for the past number of years he is well known in social and sporting circles. A fine sportsman, Lieutenant Forbes is a keen follower of the Killinick Harriers and is also an excellent cricketer. [122]

Many Wexford men joined the army, answering the call issued by John E. Redmond to join the fight. One of those who went to war was Jem Brien, a stone mason from the maintenance staff at Johnstown as did Sydney Carey-Giltrap, Governess to the 8th Duke of Leinster, who became a secretary at the Civil Engineers Department of the British Admiralty at Buncrana, County Donegal, during the war.

The south-east corner of Ireland was a strategic location for the observation of enemy U-Boats which were causing havoc with shipping in the English Channel. During the war years several stations were set up along the Wexford coast with Tuskar Rock lighthouse playing a significant role.

The Allies needed help with the huge demands and loss of life the war was causing and this finally came on 6 April 1917, when the United States officially declared war on Germany. As part of this action the house and lands at Ely, Ferrybank, just outside Wexford town, were taken over under the Defence of the Realm Act[123] by the British Admiralty and used by the United States Navy as a sea-plane base. At the end of the war the property was vacated and returned once again to its owner, Major-General John Doran. In a similar manner Lady Maurice FitzGerald allowed a wooded section of her estate in Johnstown to be cleared for use as a mooring station for airships.

Airship moored at Johnstown Castle. (IAMA Johnstown)

Airship over Wexford town. (M.J. O'Connor Collection)

During the rapid expansion of the airship service during the First World War it was decided to have as many mooring sites for the servicing and supply of the scout ships as possible and this resulted in two such stations on the east coast of Ireland, namely Johnstown Castle and Malahide Castle in County Dublin. Neither of these two Irish stations had hangars for the ships and relied mainly on the mooring rings set in concrete to hold the airships at ground level.

Considering the prohibitions listed in the Defence of the Realm Act, it is easy to see why the amount of printed information available on the airship base at Johnstown Castle is so sparse. However, some small snippets of information may be gleaned from various national and local newspapers and publications by military historians in recent years. Johnstown Castle was an ideal location for an airship base due to its proximity to Rosslare Harbour as was the seaplane base at Ferrybank[124] for both stations had a clear view of the area over which they flew their reconnaissance and bombing missions. The sight of an airship flying over Wexford town heading in a northerly direction on a mission in the Arklow area or flying southerly at evening time on its return journey to its base at Johnstown was a common sight. Several photographs are extant of these massive air ships.[125] Wexford solicitor Michael J. O'Connor took the above photograph from his home at Westlands in the town.

In comparison to the United States base at Ferrybank, which was a veritable small town with accommodation for 20 officers and 404 men,[126] the base at Johnstown Castle was small, comprising approximately fifty men and officers.[127] The military personnel were billeted in small tents near the actual mooring site of the airship with nearby sheds and outhouses on the estate used as storage areas for spare parts and engine repairs. The closest airship base to Johnstown was across in Pembroke in Wales which was a Class C Airship Station and Johnstown Castle acted as a sub-station for moorings, servicing and repairs. The Johnstown station served the US Navy in 1918.[128]

Equipped with small bombs, these ships proved to be not only observers but also active participants to the fleet's battles. Once a U-boat was spotted the airship would signal the location of the submarine to the fleet and at the same time was preparing to drop its bomb before the U-boat could take a shot at the airship.[129] The larger airships usually carried a crew of three and were 143.5ft in length with a diameter of 30ft and powered by one Rolls-Royce Hawk 75hp engine. They could reach a maximum speed of 53 miles per hour and were equipped with a Lewis Gun and two 50kg or one 110kg bomb.[130]

To moor an airship took between twenty and thirty men hauling them down and tethering the craft to the mooring ring while four other groups of men secured the airship with ropes on either side, front and back. The undercarriage, which carried the crew, had also to be supported to enable the crew members to alight. It would have been a very precarious operation mooring such a large balloon in rough weather with the constant risk of it becoming entangled in the surrounding trees.[131]

The commanding officer at the Johnstown base was H.L. Fuller. He later lived in Crossabeg, and in 1917 he became liaison officer between the Royal Naval Air Service Station and the American Naval Airforce at Ferrybank.[132] In the Wexford notes of the *Free Press*, dated Saturday 3 August 1918, the following account is given:

Two officers attached to the Flying Station at Johnstown Castle have just returned there from London, where they were decorated by the King. Captain John Edward Barres received the Distinguished Flying Cross for his 'heroic and successful action with a submarine last December'. The operator who accompanied him was Mr. A.M. Tattershall who was in charge of the gun and the wireless at the time. He received the Distinguished Service Medal. Congratulations to both men on the honours received.[133]

Captain Barres was stationed at Pembroke from May 1916 and qualified as a coastal pilot in 1917. It was noted that on 1 October 1917 he had carried out four attacks on enemy submarines.[134]

Johnstown Castle played a vital role in anti-U-boat activities at this time and yet life carried on within the castle and the estate under the watchful eye of Lady Maurice FitzGerald.

During the Second World War the FitzGerald family suffered another tragedy, in 1943, with the death of Capt. Gerald Michael Lakin, grandson of the late Lady Maurice FitzGerald. Lady Maurice had died the previous year in 1942 and was spared the awful grief which enveloped the family. Gerald Michael Lakin, born in 1916, was the elder of the two sons born to Major Michael and Kathleen Lakin. Following his college education the young Gerald Lakin joined the British Army and became an officer in the Royal Armoured Corps. He fought in the war in North Africa which ended in Tunisia with the defeat of the Axis power by a combined Allied force. The campaign began on 8 November 1942, when Commonwealth and American troops made a series of landings in Algeria and Morocco. The Germans responded immediately by sending a force from Sicily to northern Tunisia in a bid to halt the Allied advance east in early December. In the south the Axis forces defeated at El Alamein were retreating into Tunisia along the coast through Libya and were pursued by the Allied Eight Army. By mid-April 1943, the combined Axis force was hemmed into a small corner of north-eastern Tunisia and the Allies were grouped for their final offensive. The Eight Army attack on the position at Enfidaville on 19 April captured the village but strong resistance meant no further progress was made. Attacks further north met with greater success and Tunis fell on 7 May and Bizerta on 8 May. By 11 May, the village at Enfidaville was surrounded and all resistance ceased the following day.

Capt. G.M. Lakin in dress uniform.
(IAMA Johnstown)

Gravestone of Capt. Lakin at Enfidaville.
(Courtesy of Denise O'Connor-Murphy)

Capt. Gerald Michael Lakin was killed in action on 20 February 1943 and is buried at Enfidaville War Cemetery.[135] The name of Capt. Gerald Michael Lakin, Royal Army Ordnance Corps, is inscribed on the Second World War Memorial at St Canice's Cathedral, Kilkenny, on the left panel on the west wall of the porch with those servicemen killed in action from the Diocese of Ferns. His name also appears on the pulpit at St Iberius' church, Main Street, Wexford. Thus ended the involvement of the families of the FitzGeralds at Johnstown Castle in the two world wars.

12

CASTLES, GARDENS AND GROUNDS

Johnstown Castle is situated 4 miles from Wexford town and half a mile from the village of Murrintown. By 1863, the demesne was over 1,000 acres, divided by a road from Wexford to Murrintown. On the north side of the road was the deer park and on the south side the castle, gardens and farm. Considerable development had taken place to the castle and the grounds and by the 1900s this remodelling and landscaping had been completed, leaving the castle as we find today. This was a type of major country house erected by many of the landed Irish families in the early nineteenth century. The gardens and grounds are still a major attraction to all those interested in horticulture and landscape. From 1945, Johnstown Castle and estate has been used as an agricultural college and is still vibrant today as a Teagasc research centre. The castle building had, for a time, been used for research purposes, administration and residential use but is now vacant and is awaiting a new purpose. This will be subject to the covenants contained in the Johnstown Castle Act 1945 which already has three amendments applied. Any further refurbishment or remodelling will require a further government amendment.

Johnstown Castle and Rathlannon Castle, situated within the Johnstown estate, were originally built by the Esmondes as tower-houses in the reign of Henry VII (1485-1509). The Esmondes are shown to have lived there from that period.[136] In a list of thirty-eight gentlemen of the barony of Forth for 1608, Robert Esmonde of Johnstown and John Esmonde of Rathlonane (Rathlannon) are shown as residing in those locations.[137] Following the death of John Esmonde on 6 October 1616, the castle passed to his twenty-four-year-old son, Mark Esmonde. There is an understanding that this building was at one time occupied by two sisters of the Esmonde family. The erection of Rathlannon Keep has been attributed to Sir Geoffrey de Estmont of Huntingdon, Lincolnshire, shortly after the Norman invasion of 1169.[138]

In the preface to William H. Jeffrey's *Castles of Co. Wexford*, Dr Edward Culleton writes that soon after the Norman invasion until possibly the sixteenth century the Normans or their descendants constructed strong stone castles throughout most of the country. In County Wexford there is evidence, either in stone or in documents, for the existence of 235 castles, including Rathlannon and Johnstown. The tower of Rathlannon is somewhat unusual, consisting of three storeys and showing evidence of a considerable amount of alteration or rebuilding.[139] Unlike the excellent written descriptions by Thomas Lacy, Mrs S.C. Hall and J.B. Cullen of Johnstown Castle in its present format, very little is documented on Rathlannon Castle that has survived in print. However, in a survey of sites in the baronies of Forth and Bargy, County Wexford, Niamh Coulter gives

Rathlannon Castle, watercolour by Michael Kelly, Wexford.

Johnstown castle in the sixteenth-century, watercolour by Michael Kelly, Wexford.

a very in-depth study of Rathlannon Castle from an archaeological view-point, with measurements of the building both interior and exterior posing many questions still left unanswered.[140] The watercolour of Rathlannon shows the rectangular four-floor tower-house which is turned outwards at the base.

The floors of this tower-house are reached by a mural staircase going straight upwards with a square stone chute or garderobe[141] at the top of the first flight of steps. A machicoulis high above the entrance door was a means of deterring intruders by pouring boiling liquids or stones on their heads. Inside was another means of defence, a 'murdering hole', through which the defenders could shoot arrows or other missiles down an opening on any attackers who had succeeded in gaining entrance to the castle.[142]

The external measurements of Rathlannon Castle are 33ft by 24ft with walls approximately 3ft thick. There are no windows, just one or two narrow slits and no chimneys or fireplaces.[143]

Described as one of Ireland's finest castellated residences in the Gothic revival style, the building at Johnstown was developed to its present

Johnstown Castle around 1700, watercolour by Michael Kelly, Wexford.

structure mainly by Hamilton Knox Grogan-Morgan in the mid-nine-teenth century from a very basic tower-house. The development work commenced around 1810 by John Knox Grogan when the family regained the estate.

Part of the original ivy-clad tower-house was incorporated into the new development of Johnstown but was dismantled due to it being deemed unsafe following the handover of the estate to the nation in 1945. However, some old photographs show this original building, featuring three windows, possibly indicating three floors. Like Rathlannon, it would have had a mural staircase giving access to the floors. It had a high battlemented parapet, as shown in the old photographs and in the early sixteenth-century watercolour giving the artist's impression of Johnstown.

Historian H.F. Hore,[144] when discussing how the name of the castle came about, writes as follows:

I cannot trace the origin of the name, a corruption apparently of Jonickstown, under which I find it in the chief rents in the county, in the early years of Queen Elizabeth I. There still remains the question – who was Jonick? It is not a surname and a very unusual Christian name.[145]

The original structure built by the Esmondes was enlarged around 1700 when a second tower-house was built of similar dimensions and architectural design. Both towers were linked by a narrower building of three storeys in height. This particular structure, as far as can be ascertained, remained unchanged until 1810.[146]

Johnstown evolved from tower-house to 'big house' over three generations of the Grogan family beginning around 1810.[147] It is possible that the English architect, James Pain, who worked mainly in Munster, drew up a new design for the entrance view of the castle resulting in a remodelling and castellated facade. John Knox Grogan's plans also gave a new southern front with a very large circular tower on either side. In 1814, the completion of the proposed remodelling was put in abeyance due to the death of John Knox Grogan, as the heir to Johnstown, Hamilton Knox Grogan, was still a minor.

The new heir married his first cousin, Sophia Maria Rowe, on reaching his majority in 1829. He recommenced the remodelling and extension of

H.K. Grogan-Morgan
and family.
(IAMA Johnstown)

the castle that same year. By 1833 the addition of a striking clock graced the west-end, and the main central block of the castle was of three storeys and a basement.[148]

The main architect employed was Daniel Robertson with later additions to the castle by Martin Day, a native of Gollough, Kilmore, County Wexford. Hamilton Knox Grogan-Morgan (he had added the name Morgan to his surname at this stage) planned a more elaborate remodelling than his father and had Robertson draw-up a new set of plans around 1836 or even earlier as evidenced from the painting of Hamilton Knox Grogan-Morgan, his wife and eldest daughter by Edmund Thomas Parris, dated 1833 – a drawing for the proposed west front of the castle, actually constructed later, was clearly shown in this painting. As Mr Grogan-Morgan had an interest in architecture and science, plans for houses often appeared in family portraits.

Robertson's designs were to transform this castellated house to one that would have the splendour of other 'new' castles of the period, incorporating his own designs into the interior of the building. There is no written and detailed account of the work carried out by Mr Grogan's father, John Knox Grogan. However, Lacy in his *Home Sketches* mentions the addition of the east wing, originally as a science laboratory for Hamilton Knox Grogan-Morgan, and later had further additions of a ballroom and billiard room and an octagonal tower.[149] Between 1846 and 1851 the splendid porch (porte-cochère)[150] was built and is described by Lacy. The additions to the

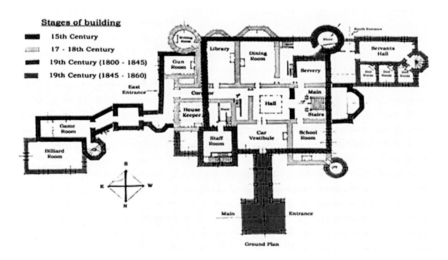

Ground floor plan of the castle. (IAMA Johnstown)

castle were faced with rubble shale stone, reputedly quarried on the estate, finished with fine dressings and quoins of Carlow granite. The western elevation differs in this respect in that it consists of limestone ashlar stonework as a substitute for the rubble stonework. New crenellation was added to all of the walls with a mix of oriel and mullioned windows.

Following the death of Hamilton Knox Grogan-Morgan in 1845, the laboratory, no longer required, was converted and used as a band room (music room). His widow married Sir Thomas Esmonde in 1856 and she continued the work started by her late husband by having the arches between the ballroom and the castle glazed and the sides of the central arch forming the carriageway were provided with folding doors. The doors were closed on the night of a ball. Lady Esmonde also had the ballroom fitted with a panelled ceiling and inlaid timber floor in 1860. The coats of arms of her daughter, Lady Jane and her husband, the Earl and Countess of Granard[151] are carved in the stone work over the carriage arch and on the mantle to the dining room. The earl and countess had come to live at Johnstown Castle and it is likely the nursery wing was added to the western side of the castle at that time. Martin Day was still employed at the castle carrying out various works on the estate so it is most likely he designed the nursery addition, which has similar architectural detail as found on the main building.

The internal decoration and fittings of the castle, in the Gothic revival style, all seem to be the work of Daniel Robertson. Much use was made of carved oak timber panelling throughout the rooms, both for the walls and ceilings. Some very intricate plasterwork to the cornices was used in most of the main rooms with finely detailed marble chimney-pieces in many of the rooms.

During Lady Maurice FitzGerald's years in residence, little further alterations were made to the house, a house that was so carefully created by her grandfather. In Lord and Lady Maurice FitzGerald's years, the offices were in the basement and the dining-room, library, estate office, gun room, school room, entrance hall, grand central staircase and the ballroom were on the ground floor. Located on the first floor were the two drawing rooms, principal bedrooms, nursery and billiard room with the rest of the bedrooms on the second floor.[152]

Over ten years from 1945 to 1955, the original sixteenth-century towerhouse known as Cromwell's Tower was removed. A bathroom was built over the nursery and the lead roof of the entire building replaced by an asphalt roof. The main staircase was removed due to dry rot and replaced by two new reinforced concrete stairways in different locations. The pipe-organ was also removed at this time but the 'Apostles Hall' and highly ornamented ceilings have survived.[153]

The Gardens and Grounds

The grounds are dominated by three man-made lakes created during the nineteenth century. The castle lake covers about 4.9 acres and originally had a number of small islands. The lower lake is around 11.9 acres and is recognised as the largest freshwater lake in the neighbouring counties. This lake originally had two islands. The third lake is the garden lake which covers an area of roughly 2.15 acres.

The middle or main gate is the everyday entrance into the grounds. There may have been a gate lodge at one time as indicated by a blocked-up opening. The large gates are of cast-iron and would have been manufactured in the nineteenth century. The finials are shaped like pike heads and are in

Pike-head finials on the main gate. (Liam Gaul Collection)

Garden gate. (Liam Gaul Collection)

commemoration of Cornelius Grogan. An identical gate across the main Murrintown-Wexford road gave access to the former deer park.

The design of the garden gate is attributed to Martin Day and was erected with its Lodge around 1848. The three-storey lodge is built of rubble shale stone ornamented with granite dressings and a crenellated parapet. It has an oriel window on the first floor overlooking the main road. On the opposite side of the road there is a similar arched entrance which gave access to the deer park but did not have a lodge.

The stables may have been built by John Knox Grogan before his death in 1814. A quadrangle of two-storey buildings, they originally provided stabling for the family horses and work horses that were used to pull carts and carriages and for work on the land. These buildings also housed coaches and carts and had accommodation for the coachman, the chauffeur and their families. The buildings in this entire area are now the home of the Irish Agricultural Museum and Famine Exhibition.

The meat store is the small two-storey tower located near the east entrance to the castle. This building was used for hanging and curing meats and for storing game birds shot on the estate. The servants' tunnel opens out to the ground floor level of the meat store. It leads from the castle basement to the store and is lit from overhead glass skylights set into the paths and lawns overhead.

The Fishing Tower is one of two folly towers on the west and south side of the castle lake. It's a round tower set on the bank of the lake and is part of bastion terraces running along the west side of the lake. On the southern side of the lake is a square tower set near a series of bastion terraces. Daniel Robertson created a prominent feature of the gardens with bastions and terraces used to create variety in the landscape surrounding the castle and castle lake which was originally very flat. In other sections the bastions are used to create raised terraces, lawns and walkways, giving excellent views across the lakes and gardens.

The Italianate Terrace is a very important feature on the south side of the Castle Lake, displaying a row of classical deities and a group of three putti at play with a water jug. There is an excellent view of the castle across the lake from this terrace.

Meat store.
(Liam Gaul Collection)

Putti on the Italianate
Terrace. (Liam Gaul
Collection)

A fountain adorns the south and north lawns at the castle and is still operational, creating a sparkling cascade of cooling water, especially on a fine sunny day.

The walled garden is comprised of two enclosed gardens surrounded by 3m-high brick walls. The former fruit and vegetable garden is elevated and is reached by a flight of granite steps from the lower garden level which was originally used as an ornamental flower garden. This lower garden has an entrance gate with a hideous gargoyle carved in granite over the archway and is known to all as 'The Devil's Gate'.

The head gardener's house was most likely designed by Daniel Robertson and is located in the second or upper garden within the walled garden area. It stands one and a half storeys high and is constructed of random shale stone with granite dressings.

The grounds have fine colourful displays of camellias, azaleas, rhododendrons, heathers, vanilla bush, Australian bottle-brush, pampas grass, fire

Dolphin fountain.
(Liam Gaul Collection)

View from the upper garden. (Liam Gaul Collection)

The Devil's Gate entrance to garden. (Liam Gaul Collection)

bush, fuchsia and magnolia. Many varieties of trees abound throughout the estate including fir, oak, maple, sycamore, birch, chestnut, cypress, beech, laburnum, spruce, redwood (sequoia), rowan, yew, cedar and elm – just some of the trees to be seen in a pleasant ramble around the walkways.

The changing seasons bring many species of wild birds to the estate including blackbirds, bullfinch, goldcrest, kingfisher, linnet, robin, starling, mistle thrush, lapwing, curlew, tree creeper and water birds such as Bewick swan, mallard, coot and moorhen.

The red squirrel is to be seen as it flits at lightning speed along the grass verges or climbing with great agility to the top of the tallest tree. Over

Gargoyle over the
Devil's Gate. (Liam
Gaul Collection)

Head Gardener's House. (Liam Gaul Collection)

the past few years the grey squirrel has invaded the territory of the red squirrel, possibly leading to the annihilation of the favoured red squirrel. Nature will decide.

The gardens and grounds have been open to the public since 1969 and have proven to be a popular venue for many visitors and locals alike for its spacious areas for walking and is a favourite location for the amateur photographer or for wedding couples and families to capture those special moments through the lens of the camera.

Land Measuresments and Architectural Terms

Ashlar	finely dressed masonry, either an individual stone that has been worked until squared or the masonry built of such stone. It is the finest stone masonry unit, generally cuboid or less frequently trapezoidal. Precisely cut 'on all faces adjacent to those of other stones', ashlar is capable of very thin joints between blocks, and the visible face of the stone may be as quarry-faced or feature a variety of treatments: tooled, smoothly polished or rendered with another material for decorative effect.
Bovate	15 acres (approx.).
Carucate	120 acres (approx.).
Cornice	ornamental moulding around the corner of a room just below the ceiling.
Finials	spire or projection on gables.
Gothic	church style of architecture from the twelfth to sixteenth centuries.
Mullioned Window	a window divided into lights by vertical bars of stone or timber, and found in Gothic and Tudor architecture.
Oriel	an oriel window is a form of bay window which projects from the main wall of a building but does not reach to the ground. Supported by corbels, brackets or similar, an oriel window is most commonly found projecting from an upper floor but is also sometimes

	used on the ground floor.
Plough	60 acres (approx.).
Porte-cochère	a large porch with enough space for a wheeled vehicle to pass through.
Quoins	are masonry blocks at the corner of a wall. They exist in some cases to provide actual strength for a wall made with inferior stone or rubble and in other cases to make a feature of a corner, creating an impression of permanence and strength, and reinforcing the onlooker's sense of a structure's presence.
Rubble stone	is rough, unhewn building stone set in mortar, but not laid in regular courses.

13

ARCHITECTS AND LANDSCAPERS – ROBERTSON AND DAY

The designs of many of the great Irish houses were influenced by gardens in other European countries, in particular Italy and France, even to the importation of the many ornaments and statues which adorn those gardens. Johnstown Castle has an array of such statues on the Italianate Walk. Although cast in concrete, they give a striking look across the lake.

Following the Act of Union in 1800, many of the landowners departed from Ireland, leaving their country houses and vast tracts of land. However, some of the absentee landowners returned and once again took up gardening pursuits, bringing in landscape gardeners and designers to rejuvenate tired gardens, lawns and shrubberies. New varieties of trees, plants and water features were introduced and many demesnes had new boundary walls, entrance ways and large ornate cast-iron gates installed, all giving an air of ownership and a sign of permanent residence of the honourable gentleman.

When Ireland was overshadowed with the catastrophic Great Famine of 1845-49 by the failure of the potato crop, thousands of Irish people died of starvation along the roadsides. Many others took the famine ships to America in the hope of a new beginning, yet back in Ireland landscaping activity was on the increase throughout the Irish countryside. Many large landscaping projects were initiated by landlords as famine relief schemes. Although County Wexford was not affected by the famine to the huge extent of other counties, the excavation and creation of the lakes at Johnstown Castle were part of such a relief scheme undertaken by Hamilton Knox Grogan-Morgan.[154] To execute such a gargantuan projects

Hamilton Knox Grogan-Morgan employed the architect Daniel Robertson, who was also a landscape gardener, to draw up the plans.

Robertson may have been born in Charleston, South Carolina, in the United States, according to research carried out by Stephen Massil. He maintains that Daniel was the youngest son of Andrew Robertson (1733-1791) and his wife Helen (*née* Crawford). She died in 1778 and it is probable she died on the birth of Daniel. Robertson's death is 1849, giving him a life-span of 73 years. The Robertson family returned from America to Scotland, their country of origin. Details of Daniel's architectural training are not known but there were relatives, the Adam family, who were architects. In 1800 Daniel and his brother, Alexander, arrived in London as protégés and partners of William Adam, a builder and developer. This partnership proved disastrous.[155]

Robertson had a distinguished practice in Oxford from 1825 to 1829. He left England and came over to Ireland where he won several commissions for country houses and gardens in Wicklow and Wexford. Word of his excellent garden design and building work soon spread and his reputation grew. He had taken on a pupil, Martin Day, and the two of them combined to create Wells House, near Gorey, County Wexford, which is still extant and once again welcomes the public to visit. Robertson's two other Wexford creations, at Castleboro and Wilton Castle, are both ruined shells. His designs for the upper terraces at Powerscourt, County Wicklow, and work at Kilruddery are two of Ireland's most important gardens. Unfortunately, Daniel Robertson seemed to be always in debt and was crippled with gout and in an advanced state of alcoholism. At one stage he lived at Powerscourt and on another occasion at Lisnavagh, County Carlow, while work was in progress. While overseeing the completion of Lisnavagh, he fell seriously ill in the spring of 1849. His long-suffering wife came over to Ireland and took a house in Howth, County Dublin, where Robertson stayed up to his death in 1849. His assets were worth just £20.[156]

Daniel Robertson should not be confused with William Robertson (1770-1850), also a landscape gardener from Kilkenny.

Martin Day

Martin Day was born in Gollough, Kilmore, County Wexford, and flourished from around 1822 until 1849. He was assistant to Daniel Robertson on work at Ballinkeele, Johnstown Castle, Bloomfield and Castleboro, all in County Wexford. He also took his own commissions to design country houses. Martin Day was one of three members of the Day family, along with William and John, who were architects and builders. Martin was the best known of the Day family and he gained notoriety for designing several Church of Ireland churches, for the Board of First Fruits and the Irish Ecclesiastical Commissioners around 1822 and 1849. Day drew up plans for the west-north front and battlemented gateway in Johnstown Castle demesne. However, his best work was the design for the Indian Hindu Gothic gateway in 1849 for Henry Villiers Stuart. This gateway still survives and has been refurbished on two occasions, first by the Irish Georgian Society in the 1960s and then by Waterford County Council in 1990.

Both Daniel Robertson and Martin Day have left a very fine legacy of architecture and landscaping at Johnstown Castle, making it one of Ireland's most beautiful and interesting demesnes.

14

FOND MEMORY
BRINGS THE LIGHT

Part of a line from Thomas Moore's song[157] 'Oft in the Stilly Night' is an appropriate introduction to memories of days gone by at Johnstown Castle. In September 1983, Eoin Sinnott and Laurence Doyle, both members of staff at Teagasc, invited various people to reminisce on their years spent at Johnstown Castle, whether as a resident or an employee. Amongst the people involved were the 8th Duke of Leinster, His Grace Gerald FitzGerald; Mrs Sydney Giltrap, Governess to the Duke; Peter Kehoe; James (Jim) Power and Michael (Mick) Furlong.

On his arrival at Johnstown Castle in September Gerald FitzGerald was greeted by his boyhood friend and playmate, Peter Kehoe, son of the coachman at that time on the castle staff. Both Gerald and Peter had much to talk about and stories to recount from their youth. Following a pleasant lunch in the castle dining room the two friends adjourned to what was once a sitting room where they spoke with Eoin Sinnott. Their conversations were recorded and preserved for posterity on video tape by Laurence Doyle.

Gerald FitzGerald was born in London on 27 May 1914 and was the only child of Edward FitzGerald, 7th Duke of Leinster and his first wife, May Juanita Etheridge. The marriage was not a happy one and following his parents' separation in 1922 and their divorce in 1930 the young Gerald and future Duke spent most of his childhood at Johnstown Castle. He grew up here and was reared by his grand-aunt, Lady Adelaide FitzGerald, widow of Lord Maurice FitzGerald and her cousin, Captain Ronald Forbes.

Lady Maurice stepped in and took responsibility for my upbringing. Both herself and Capt. Forbes travelled to London and collected me and took me back by boat to Johnstown Castle which was to become my home. It was just at the end of the Great War in 1918. As far as I was concerned they were my parents and I was treated as a member of the family. I lived here at Johnstown Castle until I got married in 1936 but I always regarded it as my home.

Capt. Forbes ran the place following the death of my granduncle Lord Maurice FitzGerald. I became friends with Peter Kehoe. His father James, was the coachman, although there was no coaches then but that title was inherited from the olden days. Peter was the youngest of the three Kehoe brothers and he had a sister, Nancy. As I was an only child and the only child here at Johnstown, Peter and I naturally came together as playmates. We spent many happy hours and grew up together and often became involved in many schoolboy pranks as time went on.

People I remember on the estate were John Doyle, the carpenter and Paddy Mahon, the painter on the maintenance staff. When I got married, Paddy came up and painted my house at Ballyragget. I was his painter's mate – he and I painted the whole house together. I also remember Mr Slavin (Slevin).[158] He was the head gardener and lived at the gardener's house in the grounds. There was Dick Brien, he drove the first tractor that was acquired for the farm.

Peter Kehoe briefly interjected at this point saying: 'It was a Fordson tractor and had iron wheels.' Gerald continued, 'John Bowers was the gamekeeper on the estate. He lived in the lodge in the deer park, near Murrintown. Mr Bowers took me out shooting and hunting. He taught me how to stalk rabbits'.

In response to a question from Eoin Sinnott regarding a description of the deer park at that time the duke went on to say:

The deer park was completely covered in bracken except the Burnt Wood and the Rock Wood. The Redshire area was also covered in bracken but it was a great place to pick up a wood-cock. The pond at the little rocks which is still there, I saw it this morning on my walk in the grounds, was where John Bowers used to gut the rabbits and throw the guts in the water to attract the ducks. There was also a stone building nearby, also still there, known as the foal's house which had a little bit of reclaimed land. This area was wired off and it was called the new farm. It is wonderful to see the reclamation that's been done. It was a very fine area for a boy of my age for shooting and hunting. At that time there were about one or two organised wood-cock shoots if a frost came. The wood-cock would come in here of a frosty time. Capt. Forbes used to organise those events. He would invite such people as Capt. Cazalet; Capt. P.J. Roche from Woodville, New Ross, Capt. Barrett, the two Bradish brothers, Mr Manners and Major Lakin, of course.

When asked about his formal education, Gerald replied:

I went to school in England aged seven and a half years. I should have gone earlier but I got measles. I went a term later and it was to Summerfield[159] that I went to school. I used to come back home for the holidays. Capt. Forbes always took me over and he would come and meet me in London for the return journey home at school holiday time. I went from Summerfield to Eton and was there for a number of years before moving to join the army at the Royal Military Academy Sandhurst.[160]

Asked if he enjoyed his childhood in Johnstown, the duke had no hesitation in replying that it was a most marvellous time of his life. He never felt privileged, although at the time he was entitled to be addressed by the courtesy title of Marquess of Kildare. He said:

I was usually called Master Gerald and was never restricted by my aunt from mixing with the many people who worked on the estate and I enjoyed walking all around the area and as I got older I would venture further afield in my walks. Later on I got a bicycle and would cycle to Wexford town to collect the post and go into the local shops where most of the shopkeepers would give me chocolates and sweets. I felt I was completely free and acknowledged the fact that my aunt was very strict yet she kept me on the 'right road'. She thought it was a good idea for me to meet with the people on the estate with whom I got on very well. I loved being on the farm. I thought very highly of my aunt and deemed her to be a wonderful person to be brought up by.

In reply to Eoin's question as to the relationship between him and his aunt, the duke agreed that there was absolutely no problems in having a conversation with her. As he said:

I wasn't banished like one was in those days. I had to put on a special little suit to come down to tea in the evenings in my early years. I would spend an hour or so in the company of Lady Maurice and Capt. Forbes in the sitting room for tea and on occassions we would be joined by Major Lakin. There was always somebody to look after me and then when I went to school I became a member of the household and I came and went as I wanted.

Referring to his friend Peter, the duke went on to say, 'I had spent a short time in Wexford living at Wellingtonbridge and enjoyed my first hunting season there before moving up to Ballyragget. It was there I became Master of the North Kilkenny Hounds. Peter came up and spent two or more years with my wife and I'.

Peter added to the conversation, saying, 'When I first went there I did second horse and later the duke put me into the red coat. I enjoyed my time in Ballyragget.'

The duke and Peter went on to talk about hunting and the state of the 'pack'. Some new hounds were brought over from England, ensuring a first-class pack of hounds which brought great success to the North Kilkenny's.

With the outbreak of the Second World War in 1939, the duke was called to serve while his wife stayed on in Kilkenny. During his service he returned home to Ballyragget on leave but soon returned to his regiment, the Enniskillen Dragoons. He was badly wounded in the head in Normandy and was sent back to convalesce in the North of England. His marriage had unfortunately gone wrong and Gerald FitzGerald had no home of his own. During this period he met his second wife, a farm-worker in the area during the war. They got married in 1946. As a result of his injuries the duke suffered a breakdown and the couple decided to return to Ireland to aid his recovery to full health. Their first son was born in Ireland. A year of hunting, shooting and fishing while living at Carnagh, Ballinaboola, gave the duke time to make plans for the family's future.

The duke continued:

In 1947 we moved to Kilkea Castle in County Kildare to start farming. The Land Commission served a compulsory notice if the FitzGerald's didn't farm and my father sold his interest in the land. At that time they wanted to sell Carton House in Kildare and I agreed provided they gave me Kilkea Castle and that's how I went there to start farming. A neighbour, Johnny Green and his family, had the land before me and were an immense help as I knew little about farming. I walked around looking over the hedges at what they were doing and I learned that way. The Land Commission came along in about nine months to see if I was farming and luckily found me on a tractor cutting grass. I started farming from then on. I had the first combine harvester in Ireland. I had 280 acres which I extended, buying extra fields from Johnny Green and later bought his farm and reclaimed the land, taking out the birch trees which brought in another 60 acres. Following a successful farming career from which I made money, I sold up the farm and began a new career in aviation.

I was always interested in flying, much against the wishes of my aunt. Being a ward in Chancery as a young child and the last of the direct line of the FitzGeralds I was almost wrapped up in cotton wool. I wasn't allowed to ride a bike for a long time and wasn't allowed to use public transport. Later I expressed an interest in flying which was almost unthinkable but I eventually took lessons and got my licence. I turned up here in Johnstown one day with a friend. A rough sort of day with strong winds and it was my first cross-country flight. My aunt and Capt. Forbes were out to meet me and I took about four attempts to land. Anyway, I got to land in the end. I had never landed off an air-field before. My aunt and the captain took me to one side. They always called me 'Kildare' and said: 'Kildare you mustn't fly with that chap again'. The only thing for me to do was to come clean so I said: 'I'm sorry, he's flying with me.' They had a fit.

Eoin asked Peter about flying and he retorted:

I flew a couple of times with His Grace and one Sunday morning he came down to Johnstown and said, 'We'll go up to Carton for a few hours'. We took off from Johnstown and landed safely at Carton House where we spent a couple of pleasant hours there. Later we went to take off. Everything was going well until I saw this big house coming for us pretty fast and I was scared. The next thing I saw the joystick going back and the plane went up and we got over the house anyway. His Grace looked over at me saying: 'By Gee, that was a near one.'

Taking the conversation to a close Gerald expressed his sadness that such a historic place had to leave the FitzGerald family. He always regarded Johnstown as his first home and when he heard about the handover of the castle and estate to the Irish Government he thought:

That's a pity as I thought of Victor Lakin going on and maintaining the family tradition here. As time went on and on my return visit here I cannot but be proud to have been associated with the place in such a small way and the fact that I lived here to see what it's doing for local people and Ireland and in particular Irish agriculture. It's something marvellous and when I tell people in England who have been to Johnstown I am always terribly enthusiastic about it.

The Duke of Leinster took his leave and expressed his delight in having met Peter Kehoe once again and having the opportunity to renew their friendship and walk down memory lane.

As part of his visit to Johnstown Castle the Duke of Leinster paid a visit to his former governess, Mrs Sydney Giltrap, at her home in Sallystown which is close to Murrintown. On the following day Eoin Sinnott and Laurence Doyle met with Mrs Giltrap and recorded her memories of life at the castle and her association with the young Marquess of Kildare. Mrs Giltrap went on to relate that she was born and reared in Dublin and came from a strong Methodist family. She was possessed of a rich contralto voice and as a young woman sang with the church choir at Abbey Street Methodist church. On his transfer to Belfast, the former minister at the Abbey Street church invited Sydney Carey (her maiden name) to sing at a concert in his new parish. During her sojourn in Belfast she heard that a naval base was about to be opened in Buncrana, County Donegal. She interviewed for a position at the base and was successful. She was now employed at

The Duke of Leinster and Peter Kehoe. (Courtesy of Laurence Doyle, Tagoat)

28s a week as a secretary at the Civil Engineers Department of the British Admiralty during the First World War. She stayed until the base closed at the end of the war. On her return home to Dublin she answered an advertisement in *The Irish Times* for a governess at Johnstown Castle. She made her application and soon afterwards received a reply from Miss Hunt, secretary to Lady Maurice FitzGerald, enquiring if Sydney Carey was any relation to a Mrs Carey at Sallystown. Mrs Carey was Sydney's grandmother. She had come to live with her sister Mrs Stewart at Sallystown following her father's death. On confirming her relationship to Lady Maurice's secretary, Sydney Alexandra Carey was offered the position of governess at Johnstown Castle.

Sydney Giltrap took up her story as follows:

I travelled down by train to Wexford and was met at the station by James Kehoe, Peter Kehoe's father, and travelled to Johnstown with him in the market cart. I was thrilled when I first saw the castle, such a grand place for me to live, I thought. I was met by Miss Hunt and introduced to the little boy I was to care for. He was a lovely little fellow with dark wavy hair and I had been given full charge of him. He was about four years of age and we got on very well from the start. He had a tutor who came out to the castle from Wexford town for lessons. In the evenings I would dress him in his little suit, white socks and shoes for his evening visit to see auntie and Capt. Forbes. He thought very highly of Lady Maurice and he often said she was the soul of kindness.

My job was to mind the boy seven days a week and in the evenings I would spend my time sewing or embroidering. I used to go to an occasional dance in the YMCA in Wexford. I was a good dancer and I really enjoyed those dances in town. Minnie, the housemaid, had a bicycle and I'd give her half a crown to hire it to go to town for the dance. I was invited to sing at Temperance Meetings in Wexford on several occasions. I enjoyed singing and at one time I won the gold medal at the Dublin Feis Ceoil. One of my favourite songs was the 'Famine Song'. I often walked over to Sallystown to visit my relatives on a Sunday afternoon.

On Sunday mornings Master Gerald and I walked through the grounds along the lime tree walk to attend Sunday service at the Church of St Brigid, Rathaspeck. Lady Maurice and family went on their own. When we entered the church Master Gerald would join the family in the front pews and I went to the choir seats. After the service we walked back to the castle. In the mornings Master Gerald and I would go for a walk and be back in time for lunch at one o'clock. Sometimes we would go up to the garden and talk with Mr Slavin or take the donkey-trap and go for a drive. The groom used to bring down the donkey every other day and we'd set off up through the deer park and up by Frayne's public house. They used to sell sugar-sticks in Frayne's and the boy and myself used to enjoy this special treat. I never went into the public house myself but I would give the money to someone to buy the sugar-sticks for us. However, the story of the sugar-sticks came back to Lady Maurice. It just shows you how news travels. Cherry was the name of the donkey and sometimes he wouldn't budge, no matter what you did.

This life, although most enjoyable, eventually got lonely especially as Master Gerald was about to go away to England to school. I decided to finish my time at Johnstown Castle and return home to Dublin where I married. My husband had studied at Trinity College and became a solicitor and finally set up his own legal office with his business partner as Giltrap and Lambert. Following my husband's death I came back to Wexford and Sallystown where I had spent such happy youthful days. You know I was only in my early twenties and my pay was £40 a year. Not a fortune, but sure I had nothing to spend it on.

Sydney Alexandra Giltrap died on 23 February 1987 at Lourdes Hospital, Kilcreene, County Kilkenny, aged 89 years.

Michael (Mick) Furlong chatted to Eoin Sinnott in his home at Redmondstown, Rathaspeck. The range of houses in past times were referred to locally as the Red Houses. Eoin began their conversation by asking Mick how and when he came to work in Johnstown Castle:

I came as a chap to work as a passage boy during Lady Maurice FitzGerald's time. My duties involved carrying buckets of coal and armfulls of blocks to the upper rooms to keep the fires burning. At that time there was nine of a staff including a butler, William Carroll. He was from Dublin. Sonny Burrell was the footman and Paddy Power, a brother of Jim Power, later worked on the farm. With the exception of Willie Carroll, the rest of the staff were mainly local people or some from Wexford town. I remember when I came to Johnstown Castle only one man had a bicycle. After some time I left this job but came back here to work in 1932.

I was living in one of the estate houses from [when] I was eight/nine years of age and my father worked on the Johnstown farm. I applied for a job and was taken on with a job on the farm. At that time Lady Maurice always paid more wages than anyone around. Several men were getting 18s a week and other farm workers in the area only getting 16s a week from the gentlemen farmers. Lady Maurice called a meeting telling her men she was going to cut their wages. The local farmers were not happy she was paying so much. There was a man by the name of Paddy Neill and when Lady Maurice was going to cut the wages he said to her, 'Well, Lady Maurice, my wife goes to town every week and she buys one rasher. She puts that on the pan every night and we get the smell of that rasher and if you cut our wages we won't even get the smell of that'. Lady Maurice laughed heartily and she said she wouldn't cut the wages and said, 'When I'm bet we'll all go to the Home together'.[161] She didn't cut the wages. There was always higher wages here than any other place around. As well as my wages I also had three quarts-a-milk a day; four tons of coal a year. Lady Maurice treated her staff well. She was a great lady.

I was two years working on the farm when my father got sick. He was a 'yardman', [looking] after the cows. When my father went out I was put into his job, that was about 1935. The yardman had 29s a week but he was on call at all times. He had to be there when cows were calving. There was no over-time for that. There was 'living' in a house in the yard. I was born in the house down in the farmyard. It was the house on the right-hand side as you went into the yard, formerly the house occupied by Billy Breslin.[162]

When it came to Christmas time we'd all go home on Christmas Eve at dinner time and get ready to go down to Johnstown and she would give us our Christmas box.[163] There would be a roast of beef and a pound of sugar to everybody in the house, a pound of tea and a pair of blankets or a pair of sheets, whichever you liked. That was every year and if there were twenty people in your house you would get 20 pounds of roast beef and so on.

I always worked in the cow-house and there was an old man, Dick Brien, working there. When he finished, Peter Dempsey came in to work there. There was also a dairy maid, Maggie May. She later became Mrs Smithers. The first Superintendant from the Department of Agriculture was John Corkery. After Maggie May left to get married, John Corkery asked me if I would go to the dairy. I did and Mr Corkery showed me how to make butter. I spent four years in the dairy and made the butter.

Sunday morning I would start at 5 a.m. and work to 9 a.m. Come home, have something to eat and attend 10.30 a.m. Mass. I would have my dinner and go back to work at 1 p.m. to 6 p.m. and all for 6 pence. This was in addition to the 29s a week. A lot of work.

I joined the Confraternity Brass and Reed Band in Wexford town and played music with them for fifteen years. I used to cycle to town with my brother and seven or eight other lads from Piercestown who were also on the band. On Christmas morning I would go into town and play with the band at twelve o'clock Mass and afterwards go back to the band room where we would have a few drinks. Back home, no dinner and go straight to Johnstown and work to six o'clock and come home and have my Christmas dinner. In my younger days when I finished work on Sundays I would cycle to Rosslare to meet my girlfriend, later to become my wife, Dorrie.

For light in the cow house and the castle we had a gas system generated from calcium carbide to which a supply of water was added creating acet-ylene.[164] That was the only light in the castle. No electricity then. Then a Captain Cazalet, a friend of Major Lakin, arrived and he installed electric lighting down in the cow house. There was a big old 10hp turbine which was powered by water from the castle and the captain would just turn on the turbine and the lights would come on. The turbine served many pur-poses from churning, grinding corn, grating turnips, driving the sawmill and they even threshed with the power from it. After I finished working in the dairy I went back out to work on the farm.

Eoin enquired as to the various staff working on the estate and the families living in the estate houses at Redmondstown. Mick Furlong's recall was very informative as he went on to relate:

Mr Slavin was the land steward and lived with his family in the stew-ard's house in the upper garden. Mr Slavin was preceded in this position by Francis Whelan and a Mr Johnston from Belfast came as steward and acted in that position until the Department of Agriculture took over the estate. Jimmy Murphy was the head gardener. He had worked in the garden as a young man and eventually left for other work and returned as head gardener. Miley Brien and my own brother John Furlong and Jack Restrick and a young chap by the name of Brien (he was a son of Jem Brien, the mason) all worked in the garden. Tom Sane also worked there. Tommy Kelly came to the garden soon after.

One of the gate lodges was occupied by a man named Doyle, his father Denny Doyle was coachman in Johnstown. The Touhy family lived in the opposite lodge. At one time a Nurse Kehoe came to live in one of the houses on the estate in the late 1930s. She was the district nurse. As Lady Maurice was on the Board of Health, Nurse Kehoe got the house because of her association with Lady Maurice FitzGerald.

I remember Tom Sane, Jem Brien, the mason, all lived on the Piercestown Road. Jem Brien saw active service in the First World War. Mrs Walsh lived in the bee house. She was the lady's maid and when Lady Maurice got married Mrs Walsh looked after the poultry which supplied the castle with eggs and chickens and turkeys at Christmas. My own father used to butcher a sheep every fortnight to supply meat to the castle. The meat was stored at the meat house – it's near the castle.

When the Department of Agriculture took over the Johnstown Estate the first man to arrive in 1944 was John Verling and he was here for about two years. He was a very fair man and good to work under. No 'coddology' about him. He stayed at Bill Devereux' house in Murrintown until his wife and family joined him and they all lived in the steward's house in the garden. Next to arrive was John Corkery, the first superintendent. He was an expert with cows and had a great formula for the food mixture for the animals which gave very high milk yields.

The fourteen houses at Redmondstown were all occupied by people who worked in Johnstown. Starting at the top was Asple's, then Miley Brien lived where I live now. My father and mother lived in the third house followed by Paddy Neill in the fourth and Larry Kearns in the fifth house. The sawyer, Jem Smith, came next and Peter Brien, Lar Leary, Jack Restrick and then the Dempsey family and Ned Reddy, Donnelly's and Johnny Rossiter. I can't remember the last house. They were great times and good neighbours lived in our range of houses. In all, I worked fifty years at Johnstown Castle as boy and man and have lovely memories of those days.

To conclude the visit Mick took down his single-row Hohner button accordion and played a selection of tunes including a pleasant waltz and the reel 'Miss McLeod' to the delight of the listeners. Eoin and Laurence bid Mick Furlong and his wife Dorrie a farewell and moved on to continue their conversation with James (Jim) Power at his house.

Eoin Sinnott opened the conversation saying that prior to the Department of Agriculture taking over the Johnstown Estate there were twenty people on the payroll with only six of them still alive (this was in 1983). Eoin asked, 'When did you start work in Johnstown Jim?':

Willie Rossiter had gone out of the job and I approached Mr Slavin about the position. He told me to come over to Johnstown one Monday morning and that was the start. I began work there just two weeks before Christmas 1939 and worked there until I was pensioned off. I worked for four years for Lady Maurice before the Department of Agriculture took over and I had £2 a week. Before coming to Johnstown Castle I had worked on the South Slob until the Second World War broke out. Without regular work, I used to make headstones and kerbing for graves as a means of survival. I was on the labour [exchange] for weeks with just 5s for myself and 5s for my wife and an additional 1s for my child giving a total of 11s a week. It was very difficult to survive on that money.

On coming to work in Johnstown my first job was to milk a cow belonging to Mr Slavin morning and evening. I brought in the cow in the morning and one of the garden men would have brought her in for evening milking. On the general staff at that time were Michael Furlong, Nicholas Asple, Willie Murphy, my own brother, Peter Power, Laurence O'Leary, Peter Dempsey, Jimmy Murphy, Jack Restrick, Miley Brien, Thomas Kemp, Johnny Doyle, Paddy Mahon, Jim McDonald, Johnny McGuire, John Bowers, James Kehoe, Billy Breslin, James O'Brien, he was the mason and Paddy Murphy, he was the trapper on the estate. Tigh Murphy was a casual worker, coming and going every now and again.

When Lady Maurice died we were sent home on the day of her funeral to wash and shave and get ready to carry her coffin over to the little cemetery for burial. Mr Saville was in charge.[165] The undertaker was Frank Gaul.[166] My job at the funeral was to cover the coffin with a bundle of straw just before the grave was filled in. After two or three days Capt. Forbes told Mr Slavin that Major Lakin's son was keeping the estate going. The major's son was shot out in North Africa and as his brother did not want the place it was to be handed over to the Irish Government. After the handover the estate was to be run by the Department of Agriculture.

A Mr Dempsey, an inspector from the department, came to Johnstown and interviewed us. We were asked to stay on in our jobs and we were only too happy to agree. Mr Verling was in charge and I got on very well with him. At that time I was following a horse, working on the land. The horse always went by the Oylgate Horse as he was bought up there in the area of Oylgate village. With the horse I drew dung, leaves from around the walks. There was plenty of work for the horse in those times. At the finish I worked with Nick Asple and Willie Murphy ploughing. I did a lot of ploughing with a pair of horses and my brother, Peter, did a lot of harrowing with the tractor. He worked here in Lady Maurice's time. When Mr Johnston came from Belfast to manage the estate, Capt. Forbes was getting old, Mr Johnston asked me to work the tractor as my brother was sick and I had to tell him, 'I hadn't a clue'. After that the only one allowed to work the tractor was Billy Breslin as he knew how to drive.

I enjoyed working here and was quite happy with my lot, well I had no other choice. I was involved with the Rural Workers Federation whose aim was to improve the working conditions of rural workers. I was the first shop steward and I worked on behalf of the men in the hope of improving things and conditions on the estate. I was always a union and Labour man as I liked to see fair play. In the last of my working years I worked with Paddy Moloney and Tom Gately. I enjoyed working on the experiments, counting corn weights and labelling samples. This work demanded great care and patience. People associated with the experiments were Dan Fox, Joe Prendergast, Pat Comerford, Pat Carroll was a great man to work for as was Joe Phelan. Johnstown Castle was a great place to work and I have many happy memories.

Alas, with the exception of Laurence Doyle the video photographer, all involved in this film have passed on but they have left a wonderful glimpse into the life and times at Johnstown. The author has continued this exploration of past times at Johnstown in a conversation with Matthew Murphy, son of the head gardener. James and Johanna Murphy lived in the garden gate lodge with their children, Marcella and Matt. From growing up on the estate, Matt's association with Johnstown almost spans an entire lifetime, as he explained when he recounted memories of those times:

My parents, James and Johanna Murphy, were from Tykillen, Kyle, Crossabeg, Co. Wexford. I am named after my grandfather, Matthew Murphy and my sister, Marcella, is named after an aunt of my father. Like a lot of families, names pass down through the generations. My father was head gardener at Johnstown and a house on the estate was part of this position. He had an interesting career as a gardener, which began in March 1916 when he worked as a helper in the garden of Col. C.T. Walker of The Deeps, Tykillen, on the outskirts of Wexford town. This was the second year of the Great War, and budgetary constraints brought a reduction in Col. Walker's staff resulting in my father being let go. A glowing reference from Col. Walker brought work at Johnstown gardens where he was employed for fourteen months as journey-man inside and outside.[167] Edward Slevin was gardener to Lady Maurice FitzGerald at that time and in a letter of reference he stated that Jim Murphy's work was of the highest standard and he was a smart hard-working young man who was leaving at his own request with a view to further improving himself.[168]

Matt goes on to relate how his father moved to Lough Cutra Castle, Gort, Co. Galway, and there he worked for eighteen months in the gardens of the property of Robert, Hon. Viscount Gough.

In 1919, he returned to Wexford and worked as a journey-man gardener under Edward Slevin at Johnstown until 1925. He was offered the position as Foreman by Robert Duthie at the gardens of the Vice-Regal Lodge, Dublin, but opted for the position of journeyman. The pay was £2 a week including a bothy, fuel, light and clean linen.[169] My father allowed he wasn't ready for the more onerous task of foreman until he had gained further experience. He moved to Castlecomer, County Kilkenny, to work at Castlecomer House gardens and remained there until 1934 as general foreman under a Mr Grimsey, head gardener to Captain Prior-Wandesforde. Here he gained vast practical experience in growing grapes, peaches, melons, tomatoes, chrysanthemums and greenhouse plants and all vegetables and hardy fruits for kitchen garden. He was responsible for the construction and upkeep of sand and grass courts, bowling-green and croquet lawns, herbaceous borders, rose garden and bedding-out plants.

Then he moved on to the gardens at Kilkenny Castle as general foreman to Arthur Horton, head gardener to the Earl of Ossory. Eventually, due to the closure of Kilkenny Castle and gardens, my father was aware of a position at Johnstown Castle. Following a letter from William Power, Company Nurserymen and Seed Merchants, Waterford, to Lady Maurice FitzGerald recommending James Murphy as a most suitable man for the position. It brought a response from Capt. Ronald Forbes outlining the duties involved. My father immediately made application for the position which was duly accepted. He returned to Johnstown Castle and took up the position as head gardener to Lady Maurice FitzGerald in 1935. In all his prior employments my father was held in high esteem for his punctuality, honesty, hard work, civility and being strictly sober as evidenced for his reference letters in my possession.

His day began at 7.15 a.m. by opening the garden houses for the commencement of work by the men at 8 a.m. He had twelve men under his direction and when the Department of Agriculture took over the estate in 1945 there was usually eight students for training as well as his own full-time staff. I remember Miley Byrne worked in the glass-houses and Tommy Kelly looked after the spraying.[170] The lawns and general grass cutting was done by Watt Kennedy with Mike Sills doing general gardening work. Trees and shrubs were refurbished on a regular basis and fruit and vegetables were grown and sold to individuals and local people. Strawberries, blackcurrants and raspberries were plentiful with a good supply of pears grown in the walled-garden.

My father was also responsible for recording the weather data at the meteorological station situated in the Sandhill Field. He recorded temperature, rainfall and hours of sunshine on a daily basis all of which were logged at Johnstown Castle. My father worked as head gardener to Lady Maurice for ten years and continued from the transfer from the FitzGeralds to the Department of Agriculture, supposedly, at no less terms and conditions in 1945. However, the new employers reduced the pay and conditions of some of the former Johnstown staff much to their annoyance, my father being affected in this respect. He brought his grievance to the attention of Victor Lakin, former owner, who took up the matter with the Department of Agriculture. A series of letters to my father from Victor Lakin highlight the extremes to which Mr Lakin involved himself with the department, resulting in a satisfactory resolution to the problem. My father happily continued in his work until his retirement.

Looking back through the years I can visualise Mick Furlong seated on the Ferguson tractor while Matty Kielthy drove the American manufactured Allis-Chalmers and Paddy Maher had the Ford-Dexta. There was hay-making in the castle field. A bell rang out at 6 p.m., signalling the end of a day's work and releasing a mass of men on bicycles heading for the main gate (there was very few cars at the time).

As a young lad growing up on the estate I enjoyed the freedom to roam the fields and woodlands in what seemed to me to be never-ending summer sunshine during the school holidays. I fished in the castle lake for perch, roach and eels and the Kildavin river had a stock of brown trout until they were completely wiped out by mink which had escaped from a mink farm and took up residence in the grounds. Hunting rabbits was another pastime. Many men came out from Wexford town to hunt the estate and I remember men going home with the handlebars of their bicycles festooned with rabbits. The gates of Johnstown were never closed in those times and many people from Murrintown crossed the grounds as a short-cut to Piercestown. I picked fruit with two of my best friends, the late Dermot Power and Micker Murray. We got the princely sum of 1½d (one and a half pence) for each pound of fruit picked. Heavy going at times but one year I earned enough money to buy a bicycle. Autumn and winter days also brought their own boyhood memories as the dark evenings seemed to create mysterious shadows around the sombre castle, conjuring up all kinds of spooky effects. Passing the ha-ha wall on the edge of the estate was also scary. The big snow of 1947 is still etched on my memory when the entire countryside was blanketed in five feet of snow. It lasted for weeks causing hardship for the farming community but

Matty Murphy. (Courtesy of Denis O'Connor Photographic Archive)

joy for young lads, especially as there was no school. I still stroll through the grounds and recently spied a herd of young deer grazing in one of the fields. I thought the deer were long gone just like the many happy days spent as boy and man at Johnstown.

Matt Murphy worked in the analytical services at Johnstown for forty years.

Several other families of employees on the estate lived in houses within the walls such as John Kehoe, the coachman and Billy Breslin, the chauffeur. The houses are now part of the Irish Agricultural Museum. John Kehoe's son, Peter and his wife Mary and their children lived there also. Michael (Mick) Coffey, his wife and family and Nicholas (Nicky) Boggan, his wife and family also lived in those houses. Over the years the two gate lodge houses were occupied by Nurse Kehoe; Mr and Mrs Dermot Whelan, grandson of the poet, Francis Whelan; Mr and Mrs James (Jimmy) Ryan and Mr and Mrs James (Jimmy) Ennis and their families.

15

A JOHNSTOWN
MISCELLANY

This miscellany covers many short items of information relating to Johnstown and its environs beginning with an insight into the nearest village of Murrintown as it was recorded around 1885.

Murrintown

The name of this village is sometimes spelled as Murntown. The Irish language name is given as *Baile Mhúráin* (Múrán's town) and it is situated in the civil parish of Kildavin in the barony of Forth and the union of Wexford.

George Henry Bassett, in *County Guide and Directory* (1885), recorded:

This village, which has a population estimated at 70, is four miles from Wexford. It is on rising ground, well sheltered, and is bordered by the plantations of Johnstown demesne. The land surrounding is chiefly adapted for tillage. Lord Maurice FitzGerald and Mr. Ebenezer H. Rowe are the landlords. The Kildavin and Fardiestown streams flow in the vicinity, and contain small trout. There is a fowl market on Mondays and Thursdays. The appearance of the village is neat and thrifty, the houses being in good repair, and slated. Johnstown Castle, the residence of Lord Maurice FitzGerald, and Forthside House, the residence of Mr. Bryan O'Brien, are near. In the same vicinity are Rathlannan Castle, a quarter mile; Rathmacknee Castle, two miles; and Kildavin Church, twelve perches from the village; all situated upon the Johnstown estate. About 12 years since, Kildavin Church was repaired.

Within this location you will find: Catholic Church, Rev. Martin Ryan, C.C.; Protestant Church (I.C.) Rathaspeck, Rev. J.K. Latham, Wexford; Postmistress, M. Browne; Dispensary Doctor, Patrick Donnellan; Relieving Officer, Patrick Keating; Royal Irish Constabulary, Sergeant Canning; Protestant School, Rathaspeck, Miss Irvine, mistress; Fife and Drum Band, J. Kerins, Master, W. Clancy, Secretary and Treasurer; Bootmakers, M. Redmond, W. Whitty; Carpenters, Robert Sylls, James Walsh; Milliner and Dress Maker, Julia Byrne; Grocer, Flour Dealers, (Those marked thus* are licensed to sell Spirits), Browne, M.; *Frayne, James.; *O'Keeffe, John; Millers, James Duggan, Laurence Fortune, Kellystown; Sawmill Owner, William Moody, Smiths, P. and T. Sylls; Tailors, M. Doyle, M. Synnott.

Notice

An advertisement on p.1 of the *Wexford Independent*, 27 February 1878, read, 'John Hayes begs to inform his friends and customers that his Stalls in the Lower Shambles will be supplied for the present Season with PRIME VENISON, taken from the well-known Park at Johnstown. All orders attended to with dispatch. Lower Shambles, Wexford, 28 December 1877'.

Transmission and Interment of the Remains of Mr Morgan

The following report appeared in *The People*, 24 June 1854:

The remains of Mr. Morgan reached Wexford, per the Emerald steamer on Thursday at 3 o'clock. A vast concourse of people, many from a great distance, awaited the arrival with the intention of accompanying the body to Johnstown Castle where it was to remain for the night, but on the body being deposited in the hearse the horses were immediately driven a different course from that expected and cars and horses, as well as foot people were left behind disappointed. The funeral took place on Friday morning. The cortège moved slowly and orderly along the grand avenue, and proceeded to the Church at the entrance. The remains were encased in three

coffins, the outer one covered with black cloth and magnificently ornamented. The hearse was drawn by six horses bearing plumes, and was
preceded by the London undertaker. It was followed by a line of carriages
and other vehicles to the number of nearly two hundred. About the same
number of gentlemen wore scarfs and hatbands of black silk, and hardly
less than a thousand appeared in scarfs and hatbands of linen. On arriving in the Churchyard the coffin was placed in the vault, and the 'service'
performed by the Protestant Ministers in attendance.

Eighty-Five Cocks of Hay by Auction

The following advertisement appeared on p.1 of *The People*, Saturday
17 August 1858: 'To be sold by auction on Friday the 13th. Instant, at
Johnstown Castle, 85 cocks of very superior upland hay, saved green and
without rain. Terms – cash. Sale to commence at 12 o'clock. WALSH & SON,
AUCTIONEERS, Wexford 6th August, 1858. The above Hay will be sold in
Lots to suit the Public'.

Lost

The following notice appeared on p.4 of the *Wexford Herald*, Thursday 23
May 1811: 'IN THE WALKS OF JOHNSTOWN, On Sunday the 19th. Inst.
A SILVER SNUFF-BOX, with the Letters S.A. on the Cover. Any person who
brings it to Mr. Allen's, Lattimerstown, shall be handsomely rewarded'.

Murder – and £726 17s 6d Reward

The following notice appeared on p.1 of the *Wexford Herald*, Monday 28
January 1811. A list of sixty-six names of the most influential people in
County Wexford and their subscriptions amounting to the sum of £726 17*s*
6*d*, was also printed with this news item.

On Sunday night last, the 16th Instant, about the Hour of 10 o'clock,
a most inhuman and shocking MURDER was committed, by some person
or Persons at present unknown, on the Body of JOHN LOZELL, Park-keeper

for John Knox Grogan, of Johnstown Castle, in this County, Esq. Now we, the undersigned, holding in Abhorrence so barbarous and cruel an Action, and wishing to bring the Perpetrators thereof to condign punishment, do hereby offer the several Sums annexed to our respective Names, to any Person or persons who will, within the space six Calendar Months from the Date hereof, give such Information as may lead to a Discovery and Conviction of the Person or Persons concerned in so nefarious an Outrage. And we hereby pledge ourselves to make Application to Government to obtain his Majesty's Pardon for any of those concerned in so horrid and sanguinary a transaction (save and except the Person who actually committed the Murder) upon his or their prosecuting him, the said Murderer to Conviction. Dated at Wexford, 17th December, 1810.

Barney Roche

A description of Barney Roche, the established 'natural' of Johnstown Castle, by Mrs S.C. Hall. Mr and Mrs Hall visited Johnstown Castle on their Irish tour.

> Many of the old families encourage the presence of one of these half-demented creatures, who attach themselves to their patrons with a sort of animal instinct but an incorruptible fidelity. They are usually valuable assistants to the huntsman, know the fox earths, and pick up the birds in the shooting season; watch over the 'young heir' with the deepest anxiety, and cater for the sports of the younger children; eat up the leavings of the servant's table, and sleep in the hay-loft; indeed, all of the class dislike the restraint of a bed, to which they attach an idea of confinement, and prefer nestling in hay or straw to anything else. Some of the resident gentry tolerate rather than encourage them; while others sanction their attendance as a matter of course – an appendage to their dwelling that could not be dispensed with. Barney was a mixture of absurdity and shrewdness, although devotedly attached to the family, whose fortune and influence act as perpetual blessings to their neighbourhood, Barney is no way chary of his opinion, and does not hesitate to 'blow up the masther whin he vexes him widout rhyme or rason'. In his youth he achieved a considerable degree of notoriety, in Wexford, as a devourer of candles and soap, a practise, we believe, he has discontinued since his adoption as 'Castle fool'. Barney's great infirmity,

however (an infirmity that certainly is apt to 'bother' his countrymen), is falling in love. Whenever the pretty face of a pretty girl is stamped upon his imagination, Barney scales the castle walls to get a peep at his enchantress, and sometimes pays dearly for his peeping. One evening we espied him shouting and jumping, and rolling down the terrace banks head over heels, and at last he came towards us. 'Barney, will you be a good boy?'

'Oh then, sure I can't be much better than I am.'

'Yet I have not seen you at work these five or six days.'

'They wouldn't give me a spade.'

'That is not true, Barney.'

'Pon my honour it is! Well, what will you give me if I go to work?'

'Sixpence!'

'Well, give it to me first; people say, "Barney, I'll give ye sixpence," and they get a bad memory after. Come, give it ti me now, and I'll be off yer conscience.'

'Here it is. What will you buy with it?'

'Coffee!' said Barney, making a solemn face. We gave him the sixpence; the instant he got it within his fingers, he broke into wild laughter.

'Hurroo!' he exclaimed, 'Thank ye, and God bless ye; but I've changed my mind. I'll buy whiskey – whiskey – ah! ah!'

And so he did, and instead of going quietly to his favourite bed in the stables, he attempted to climb to a window, some forty or fifty feet from the ground to catch a glimpse of a pretty servant, and in the morning

Barney Roche, a line drawing by E.T. Parris, November 1833.

poor Barney was found almost a shapeless mass under the castle walls. We never expected to see him again, but at this present time of writing Barney is alive, and as ready to fall in love as ever'.

(Transcribed from *Ireland: Scenery, Character, etc.* by Mr and Mrs S.C. Hall, Vol. II, 1842, pp. 26-28)

Thomas Lacy – Writer

Thomas Lacy, Wexford-born writer of renown, visited Johnstown Castle in 1852 and again in 1863 during the restoration work being carried out by Hamilton Knox Grogan-Morgan in the mid-1800s. Lacy's description of the castle, both interior and exterior, must rank as the most accurate and informative writings of that period. He gave a first-hand account of everything, even to the material used in the various window curtains and drapes, mirrors, furniture, landscaping, ornate gardens and in particular the names of some of the various craftsmen involved in the restorative works. With the proposal of building a railway line connecting Wexford with Dublin, a Mr George Little was appointed one of the solicitors for this great project and Thomas Lacy was engaged by him as one of his assistants. Lacy's work entailed taking references along the line and also in serving notices on the owners, lessees, and occupiers of property whose holdings might be interfered with by the intended railway. This task eventually took Lacy to Dublin and London to give evidence before the committees of both Houses of Parliament. During his journeys both in Ireland and England Lacy took notes on the many places he visited which were eventually published in his two volumes: *Home Sketches on Both Sides of the Channel, A Diary by Thomas Lacy* (1852) and *Sights and Scenes in Our Fatherland by Thomas Lacy Wexford* (1863). He was often referred to as 'the dacent Lacy'. He was appointed treasurer for Wexford Corporation with the responsibility of overseeing and receiving rentals from the corporation lands. His account books are preserved in the Wexford County Archive as *Account Book of Thomas Lacy 1846-1872*, and *Wexford Corporation – Rental of Corporation Lands 1846-1891*. The books are written in copperplate writing in pen and ink.

Mrs S.C. Hall.
(© National
Gallery of Ireland)

Mrs S.C. Hall

Anna-Maria Fielding was born in Anne Street, Dublin, in 1800. Her mother's family were of Huguenot descent with family at Graigue House, Bannow, County Wexford, where Anna resided until 1815. Eventually her family moved to England and settled in London where Anna met and married Samuel Carter Hall in 1824. Samuel Hall was born at Geneva Barracks, Waterford, in 1800. His father was a soldier garrisoned there at the time. A literary man, Samuel Hall was founder and editor of the *Art Journal* while his wife, Anna, also followed a literary career. Her published work appeared under the name Mrs S.C. Hall and in collaboration with her

husband on over fifty books. In her book, *Sketches of Irish Life*, she describes
life in the village of Bannow where she spent many happy years yet seemingly never returned there again. The couple visited Johnstown Castle of
which she gives an account in *IRELAND: Scenery, Character etc.* in 1842.
A charitable lady, she supported many causes and was responsible for
having a memorial window installed in Bromham Church, Bedfordshire,
to the Irish poet, Thomas Moore. She died on 30 January 1881 and is
buried in Addlestone Churchyard.

(Bernard Browne, Living by the Pen, pp.63-64)[171]

Rathaspeck Church Restoration and Renovation

A movement is on foot for the restoration and renovation of the Church
of Rathaspeck, which is an out-lying Church in the Union of Wexford,
one of three Churches which are served by the Venerable the Archdeacon
of Ferns and his curates. The project had been warmly taken up, and we
already notice among the subscribers Lady Maurice FitzGerald and the
Hon. Mrs. Deane Morgan, Miss Gonne Bell, Mr. E. Moody, Archdeacon
J.K. Latham, D.D.; Mr. E. Jefferies, Mrs. J.R. Cooper, Colonel Villiers
Hatton, Rev. Canon Blacker, Mr. W.B. Nunn, Mr. J. Percival, Mrs. Huson,
Mr. R.W. Elgee, Messrs. W. and G. Hadden, and Captain A.G. Richards.
There are eleven parishes included in the Union of Wexford, many of
them within the walls of that ancient town, and the ruins of several of
the Churches still exist.

(Church of Ireland Gazette, 4 September 1903, p. 720)

Lady Esmonde, Deceased

NOTICE IS HEREBY GIVEN that all persons who were employed in the
employment of the late Lady Esmonde, (of Johnstown Castle, County
Wexford), at the time of her death in 1867, as servants or workmen,
or the legal representatives of any such party who was so employed, are
required to send to us on or before the 1st. July next, their full names and
addresses, stating the position they occupied in her service, and the wages
they were then receiving.

(Milward Jones & Cameron, Solicitors, May 1888)

Clearance Sale

TO BE SOLD BY AUCTION ON MONDAY, DECEMBER 22, 1919, AT THE RECTORY, RATHASPECK,BY DIRECTIONS OF REV. J. LEWIS (WHO IS GOING AWAY)

Superior Cow, due to calve March 1st. Rick of hay, about 3 tons. Hay Knife, Heap of Manure, Wheelbarrow and Garden Tools, Bees and Hives, Llewellyn Barrel Churn, end-over-end, 16 gal. capacity; Dairy Utensils, Steel and Brass Fenders, Brussels and other Carpets, Kitchen Utensils, Lady's Bicycle, with B.S.A. 3-speed gear (Almost new), etc. Books, comprising "The Horse, its Treatment" etc. by Professor Worthley.

Terms – Cash. Sale at Twelve o'clock. G.W. Taylor, Auctioneer.

(*Free Press*, 13 December 1919)

Christmas Tree at Rathaspeck National School

The annual entertainment known as the 'Christmas tree' in connection with the above school was held on Friday evening of last week. The school-room was most tastefully decorated for the occasion, the centre of attraction being, naturally, the 'Tree' on which was hung, amidst glittering ornaments lighted by fairy candles, the many various and useful presents, so soon to gladden the hearts of the bright-eyed youngsters seated expectantly around. Punctually at 4 o'clock Lady Maurice FitzGerald arrived, and was received by Rev. C.J.A. Harris, Curate in charge of Rathaspeck, and the schoolmistress, Mrs. Tuach. No time was lost, but instantly the work of stripping the 'Tree' commenced, and the presents and prizes distributed. While the debris was being removed from the school-room, tea was served to all present in the teacher's residence adjoining, and was thoroughly enjoyed. On returning to the school-room a programme of entertainment ensued.

(*Free Press*, 25 January 1913)

Interrment of John Knox Grogan

On Monday last the 27th. March the remains of the late John Knox Grogan, Esq., of Johnstown Castle, were consigned to the tomb. The multitude, of all ranks, which attended the funeral, was immense, far exceeding what we ever witnessed on a similar occasion. The regularity of all the arrangements reflected the highest credit on the undertaker, and the whole proceeded from the Castle in the following order, which we briefly sketch – The Undertaker, Mutes, Children of the Wexford Lancastrian School, Female Servants, attending Clergy, Physicians, Firing Party of the Johnstown Yeomanry; Pall-bearers, with Coffin in the midst, Horse of the deceased, led by his Groom, mourning carriages; 100 Poor men, to whom great coats had been given; Carriages of the Gentry; Gentry on foot, wearing scarves and hatbands, in number five hundred; and the procession closed by his numerous tenantry, to all of whom hatbands had been distributed. The whole formed a coup d'oeil equally solemn, impressive and affecting.

(Wexford Herald, 3 April 1815)

Death of Lord Walter FitzGerald

The death of Lord Walter FitzGerald occurred in Kilkea Castle, Co. Kildare. He was 4th. son of the Duke of Leinster, and was brother of Lord Maurice FitzGerald, Johnstown Castle, Wexford. Born in 1858, he had served in the British Army in India and was a member of the Society of Antiquaries in Co. Kildare, and the Archaeological Society, and had written many historical articles for publication.

(Free Press, August 1923)

Staff at Johnstown in 1945 at the Handover to the State

Farm Hands: Michael Furlong, Nicholas Aspel, William Murphy, Peter Power, James Power, Laurence Leary, Peter Dempsey.
Garden Employees: James Murphy, John Restrick, Myles O'Brien, Thomas Kelly.
Gamekeeper: John Bowers.
Coachman: James Kehoe.
Chauffeur: William Breslin.
Indoor Staff: Margaret Dunphy; Cook, Margaret Doyle; Kitchen Maid, Mary Forde; Housemaid, Kathleen Kane; Laundry and Dairy Maid, Margaret May; Butler, William Carroll and Footman John Fitzhenry.

Rejoicings

The birth of an heir to the Johnstown Estates on Sunday last, 11 April, caused general rejoicing in the various parts of the county, but in no place so marked as on the banks of the Slaney, from Ferrycarrig to Carrigmannon. Tar barrels and bonfires blazed on the hill tops; and at Ardcandrisk and around the demesne a beautiful pyrotechnic display took place. Cheers were given for Lady Maurice FitzGerald and the Hon. Mrs. Deane Morgan. Music, dancing, and other enjoyments followed; and at the festive board, long life, health and happiness, to the young heir was the ardent wish and prayer of all. The health of the Hon. Mrs. Deane Morgan was given and responded to most warmly and affectionately, as well as that of Miss Gonne Bell, her absence being much regretted. The whole was admirably carried out although the time allowed was so short.

(The Watchman, 17 April 1886)

Field Names as Listed on Field Maps

As is the practice and sometimes tradition on many farms and estates, various fields are given names or are associated with people or events as a means of identification and ease of direction, particularly on farms. Field names are also an excellent means of showing their positions on maps of a property, large or small. Such names have also been used in mapping the Johnstown Castle Estate and go back to former usage of the land such as the wheat field or the meadow and so on. The following is a list of the field names shown on a map of the Johnstown Demesne in the time of John Knox Grogan. The map was copied by A.R. Neville, City Surveyor, 1811:

1. Long Meadow; 2. Church Field; 3. Cow Pasture; 4. Pond Field; 5. Calf Park; 6. Garden; 7. Lawn; 8. Haggard; 9. Big Field; 10. Ox Pasture; 11. Orchard; 12. Castle Park; 13. Green Meadow; 14. Castle Meadow; 15. Turnip Field; 16. Wheat Field; 17. Oat Field; 18. Clover Field; 19. Willow Meadow; 20. Little Meadow; 21. Sally Park; 22. Shrubbery's Park; 23. Part of Kildavin – part of river at edge; 24. Piercestown.

An area of land measuring 57 acres and 6 perches but known as the Twenty Acres was at one time the 'old' village of Murntown with thirty-four

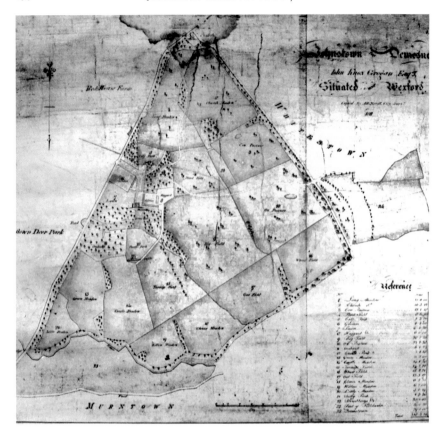

A.R. Neville, map of Johnstown Estate. (IAMA Johnstown)

people in residence in ten houses. The houses were occupied by workers on the Johnstown Estate. After 1851 the houses were gone and the land reclaimed as part of the Johnstown Estate. The 'new' village of Murntown emerged on the opposite side of the road and has developed over the years in its present location.

On a map prepared by the Cartographic Section, National Soil Survey, Johnstown Castle, the field names have gone through a name change due to some smaller fields being taken in to make larger field areas and are shown on the map created for An Foras Talúntais as follows:

Burrel's Field; The Warren; Redshire Field; Hoarstone Field; Field above Burnt Wood; Burnt Wood Field; Foal's House Field; Sandhill Field – Kildavin Church (in ruins) and a Reservoir also marked on the map.

An Fóras Talúntais field map, Johnstown Estate.

Back of Bowers; Bower's Field; Twenty acres; Castle Field; Willow Meadow. Cricket Field; Tower Field; Middle Field; Moate Field. These fields are on the left hand side of the road going from Murntown to Wexford.

The Lawn; Burrow Field; Whitegate North; Whitegate South; Knocklands; Hospital Field. Johnstown Castle and Rathlannon Castle are indicated on this section of the map. Upper Drill Field; Lower Drill Field; Bocher's End.

The Johnstown motor car. (Photograph by Chas. E. Vize)

The Johnstown Castle Motor Car

This well-known photograph of the Johnstown motor car has appeared in many motoring magazines over the years. The car is a 14/20 4-cyl. poppet valve 80 × 130, 2614 cc Siddley-Deasy dated around 1908. The cost would have been around £375. The Johnstown model was supplied by Thompson Brothers, Custom House Quay, Wexford. Capt. Ronald Forbes is pictured in the driving seat with Lady Maurice FitzGerald seated in the front passenger seat. Miss Kathleen FitzGerald and the estate chauffeur Billy Breslin are seated in the rear of the vehicle. This particular photograph may have been taken by Charles E. Vize, photographer, Wexford.

The school house, a line drawing by A. Nicholl.

School House

A school, for the education of the children of her tenants and dependents, was, several years since, erected by the good Lady Esmonde, in which, as I have reason to believe, teachers, who possess the necessary qualifications, are provided to carry into effect the benevolent intention of this kind and generous lady. This school-house, which is in the Elizabethan style of architecture, is situated in the immediate vicinity of the handsome church of Rathaspeck, which, with the surrounding cemetery, is on the estate of the late Thomas Willimsdorf Richards, Esq., whose fine old mansion, a quadrangular building, of ample proportions, approached by a spacious avenue lined with handsome trees, is about a furlong from the church.

(Transcribed from the writings of Thomas Lacy)

Death and Funeral of Mrs Deane-Morgan

The death occurred at her home, Ardcandrisk, Wexford, of Elizabeth Geraldine Deane-Morgan, widow of the late Hon. Robert FitzMaurice Tilson Deane, and eldest daughter of the late Hamilton Knox Grogan Morgan of Johnstown Castle, on 13 May 1920. Her funeral took place to the family vault at Rathaspeck where the Service at the graveside was conducted by Rev. T.E.G. Condell, Kilscoran, Rev. W.L. Shade, Rathaspeck and Rev. Mr. Cooke, Wexford. The chief mourners were her son, Lord Muskerry, Lady Muskerry, daughter-in-law, Mr. Cecil Deane-Morgan, grandson, Lady Maurice FitzGerald, niece and Mrs. Massey, wife of the late Hon. Hamilton Deane-Morgan.

For many years Hon. Mrs. Deane-Morgan was in failing health, which confined her to her residence. She was owner of extensive estates in Co. Wexford and many southern counties and was one of the few landowners to maintain permanent residence in the country. A very benevolent lady and a generous contributor towards all projects for charitable purposes. A life governor in the management of the County Infirmary she took a deep interest and frequently sent donations to assist in the alleviation of their material welfare. Having attained the wonderful age of 91 years she passed away peacefully following a short illness. He only son is the Earl of Muskerry and resides in Springfield Castle, Drumcolligher.

(*Free Press*, 22 May 1920)

Marriage at Rathaspeck Church

The marriage took place at Rathaspeck Church of the Right Honorable George Arthur Hastings Forbes, Earl of Granard, Castle Forbes, Parish of Clongish, Co. Longford, son of Rt. Hon. Viscount Forbes, Major General in the Army, to Jane Colclough Grogan Morgan, Gentlewoman, Johnstown Castle, Parish of Rathaspeck, daughter of Hamilton Knox Grogan Morgan, Esq., D.L., J.P., Co. Wexford.

(Rathaspeck Marriage Register, 2 June 1850)

Marriage in High Life

At the recent marriage of the Right Hon. the Earl of Granard, K.P., Lord Lieutenant of the County Leitrim to Jane Colclough, youngest daughter of the late H.K. Grogan Morgan and Lady Esmonde of Johnstown Castle, the bride was given away by her step-father, Right Hon. Sir Thomas Esmonde, Bart. The bride was magnificently attired in a rich white satin dress, the flounces of Brussels lace, looped with bouquets of orange and myrtle blossoms; a Brussels lace veil being thrown over the head, au dernier, attached by a wreath of myrtle and orange blossoms, relieved by pearls – the ornaments becoming a youthful bride. She was attended by six bridesmaids handsomely dressed for this auspicious occasion. After the ceremony, the bridal party repaired to Johnstown Castle where at a sumptuous dejeuner, Lord and Lady Granard received the congratulations of their numerous friends, and subsequently left for Ballynastragh, the finely wooded and beautifully situated seat of Sir Thomas Esmonde, in the North of the County.

(Wexford Independent, 5 June 1858)

Johnstown Castle – RSVP

The following invitation was sent to Mr Thomas P. Fane, editor of *The People* newspaper in Wexford town: 'Lady Maurice Fitzgerald requests the pleasure of Mr. Thomas P. Fane's company at the marriage of her cousin, Cynthia Paget to Mr. Nicholas Lambert, at St. Martin's Church, Piercestown on Tuesday 9th. August, 1921 at 3.15 o'clock and afterwards at Johnstown Castle, Wexford. R.S.V.P.'

Grogan Houses and Properties

David Rowe and Eithne Scallan, in their book *Houses of Wexford*, record the following properties that belonged to the Grogan family:

• Belvedere House, Belvedere Road, Wexford, built 1730. This was the property of H.K. Grogan Morgan and later used by Lady Adelaide Jane Frances FitzGerald until its sale in 1922.

- Kildavin Lodge (Kildavin House), Deerpark, Murrintown. This may have been built in the early 1900s by Lady Maurice for her daughter, Kathleen, as a wedding present for her marriage to Major Michael Lawrence Lakin. The Lakins lived there for a short time prior to moving to Horetown House. The house was later occupied by Capt. Ronald Forbes, cousin and agent to Lady Maurice. Following the handover of the Johnstown Estate to the Irish Government in 1945, Kildavin House, plus 9 acres of land, was bought back and used by An Foras Talúntais as a temporary residence for some of its personnel. It is now a private residence.
- Ardcandrisk, Glynn, County Wexford. This house was built around 1833 and was the residence of Mr Morgan. A grand ball was held here in 1833 to celebrate the marriage of Lady Adelaide Forbes to Lord Maurice FitzGerald. The house was inherited by the Hon. Mrs. Deane-Morgan and has since been demolished.
- Castletown House, Castletown, Gorey, County Wexford. This property was bought by the Grogans of Johnstown Castle prior to 1777 and was occupied at one time by Thomas Grogan, brother of Cornelius Grogan, Johnstown Castle. Thomas was killed during the 1798 Rebellion.
- Healthfield Manor, Killurin, County Wexford. A three-storey country house built around 1796 and extended in 1820 by the Beatty family. The house was part of the Carrigmannon Estate and John Grogan had the property in 1798.
- Monaseed House, formerly Marwood Castle, Hollyfort, County Wexford. The Grogans bought this property from the Masterson family county around 1780 and later rented the residence to a family named Byrne.
- Rathjarney Cottage, Killinick, County Wexford. This property was part of the estate of Johnstown Castle.

16

THE ACT OF 1945 – END OF AN ERA

This act was an agreement made on 28 December 1944 between Dorothy Violet Jefferies of Carrigbyrne, Adamstown (The Settler), and Maurice Victor Lakin of Horetown, Foulksmills, County Wexford, and the Minister for Agriculture whereby the lands, tenements hereditaments and premises formerly part of the family estates were given to the nation.

The document is couched in the legal parlance usual in making such an agreement and declared the following conditions between the parties:

(1) The Settler and Maurice Victor Jefferies convey and assign as a Free Gift to The Nation, The Estate to The Minister subject to the provisions listed and otherwise free from encumbrances.

(2) The Estate will be conveyed to The Minister with the exception of the Family Private Burial Ground, with the rights of The Settler and Maurice Victor Lakin and their respective heirs and servants at all reasonable times to the said Family Private Burial Ground.

(3) The Estate shall be henceforth known and described as 'Johnstown Castle Agricultural College' and the name shall not be changed. The Property shall be used by The State exclusively for the purpose of a Lay Agricultural College and for no other purpose whatever.

(4) The District Jubilee Nurse at Rathaspeck for the time being shall have the right to reside in the Gate Lodge at Rathaspeck on the Estate free of rent and taxes and The Estate shall be conveyed charged with the obligation to maintain and preserve the said Gate Lodge as a Residence for the purposes aforesaid and to keep at all times in good order and repair and condition.

(5) The Estate shall be conveyed and assigned to The Minister free from all restrictions as to the user thereof.

The agreement conditions continue between the three parties with The Settler and Maurice Victor Lakin relinquishing all rights and interests in the estate. The Conveyance and Assignment was to be executed in escrow and placed in the hands of Thomas Crozier and Son Solicitors, 14 Ely Place, Dublin to be delivered up to The Minister. A date was fixed for the completion with the minister's entitlement to possession and receipt of the rents and profits starting from 21 April 1944. Also included in the gift were all crops growing on the estate at the date of completion. The minister or other body or person managing or controlling the estate was authorised to retain the services of the servants and employees and to remunerate the pensioners employed and connected with the estate. The sum of £4,170 7s 10d was the proportionate amount of all death duties (estate and succession) paid to the State in respect of the estate on the death of Lady Adelaide Jane Frances FitzGerald and the late Gerald Hugh FitzGerald and on the succession of The Settler. The sum of £627 14s 9d was estimated to have been paid or payable by Maurice Victor Lakin for wages and pensions to the employees and pensioners on 1 January 1944 to 21 April 1944. The sum of £155 19s 6d in miscellaneous expenses and outlay incurred by Maurice Victor Lakin from the 1 January 1944 to the date of completion. The sum of £287 12s was granted to cover the costs of The Settler in carrying out this gift. All Deeds and Instruments entered into and executed by The Settler and Maurice Victor Lakin were exempt from Stamp Duty.

It was also agreed that the ornamental nature of the gardens and pleasure grounds on the estate would not be altered and the ornamental timber would not be felled or cut save in the ordinary course of management.

The document was signed and witnessed by Dorothy Violet Jefferies and Maurice Victor Lakin in the presence of their legal advisors. The seal of the Minister for Agriculture was affixed and authenticated by the signature of

D. Twomey on behalf of the minister, J.J. Crowley, Department of Agriculture. A list of the properties on the estate was included as was a list of employees that were to be retained and those whose services were no longer required, along with wages and compensatory amounts. All documents for the first and second schedule were signed by Dorothy Violet Jefferies, Maurice Victor Lakin and D. Twomey.

17

PEACE
PERFECT PEACE

A small private cemetery in the castle grounds is the final resting place of some members of the FitzGerald, Lakin and Forbes families. Other family members are also commemorated. The cemetery ground was consecrated on 25 March 1896 by the Rt Revd W.P. Walsh DD, Bishop of Ossory and Ferns. The memorial slabs in cruciform are in memory of:

- Lord Maurice FitzGerald, died 24 April 1901 aged 49 years.
- Lady Adelaide FitzGerald, widow of Lord Maurice FitzGerald, died 18 November 1942 aged 82 years.
- Kathleen, wife of Major Michael Laurence Lakin, died 23 February 1930 aged 38 years. She was daughter of Lord and Lady Maurice FitzGerald.
- Marjorie FitzGerald, died 2 January 1899 aged 3 years. She was the daughter of Lord and Lady Maurice FitzGerald.
- Major Michael Laurence Lakin, DSO, MC, died 18 October 1960 aged 79 years.
- Capt. Ronald Forbes, cousin of Lady Maurice FitzGerald, died 1960 aged 81 years.
- Capt. Gerald Michael Lakin, died 20 February 1943 aged 27 years. He died of wounds in the Second World War and was buried at Enfidaville, Tunisia.

The Lakin and Jefferies families retain the right of burial in this cemetery as part of the agreement with the Irish Government in 1945.

Entrance gates to the private family cemetery. (Liam Gaul Collection)

A quiet oasis in the castle grounds, the cemetery has some mature varieties of magnolia, camellia and rhododendron inside the entrance gate to the cemetery. The ornate gates were specially manufactured in Italy and are an excellent example of wrought iron craftsmanship.

18

THE IRISH AGRICULTURAL MUSEUM

The idea for an Irish Agricultural Museum was first mooted in the early 1970s and in 1974 Dr Thomas Walsh, Director of An Fóras Talúntais, now Teagasc, agreed to the establishment of an agricultural museum at Johnstown. It was to be located in old farmyard buildings. The museum

The entrance to the Irish Agricultural Museum. (Liam Gaul Collection)

Displays at the Irish Agricultural Museum. (Liam Gaul Collection)

first displayed its exhibits for public viewing in 1979 when it was officially opened by the President of Ireland, Dr Patrick Hillery. The museum gradually evolved and actively engaged in collecting artefacts for display in the renovated buildings. The support from Teagasc has played a major role in the development and ultimate success of this venture. Dr Austin M. O'Sullivan, a research officer at Teagasc, Johnstown, led the development of the museum and become its part-time curator. Eventually, Dr O'Sullivan was released by Teagasc from his other duties, enabling him to devote more time to progressing the museum. Now retired, Dr O'Sullivan has been succeeded by a full-time curator/manager, Matt Wheeler.

The Irish Agricultural Museum has amassed a collection in excess of 2,000 items during the past thirty years and many are displayed in sections across the two floors of the building. Overall there are eighteen areas to visit, including the Curator's Choice which gives a brief preview of the various categories to be seen in the other displays in the museum. The areas include: Transport, The Tractor, The Garden, Power Driven Barn Machines, Sugar Beet Growing and Processing, A Bicycle Display, Village Crafts, A History of the Castle, The Equestrian Room, A Picture Gallery of Times Past, The Dairy, Poultry Keeping, Land Management, Irish Country Furniture, The Furniture of Wexford Craftsman James O'Keeffe. The Great Famine of 1847 is also shown in a very detailed exhibition within the same building.

The museum shop sells a range of souvenirs, gifts and books and the Peacock Tearoom serves a variety of delicious refreshments. Free Wi-Fi is also available. For more information visit the museum website at www.irishagrimuseum.ie.

FAMILY CHARTS – OVERSTREET TO LAKIN

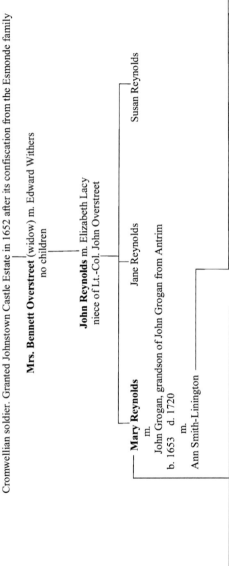

Fig. 1 The Cromwellian period.

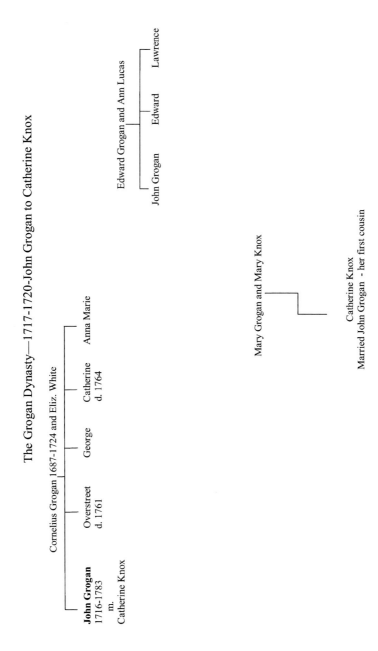

Fig. 2 The Grogan dynasty 1717–1720, John Grogan to Catherine Knox.

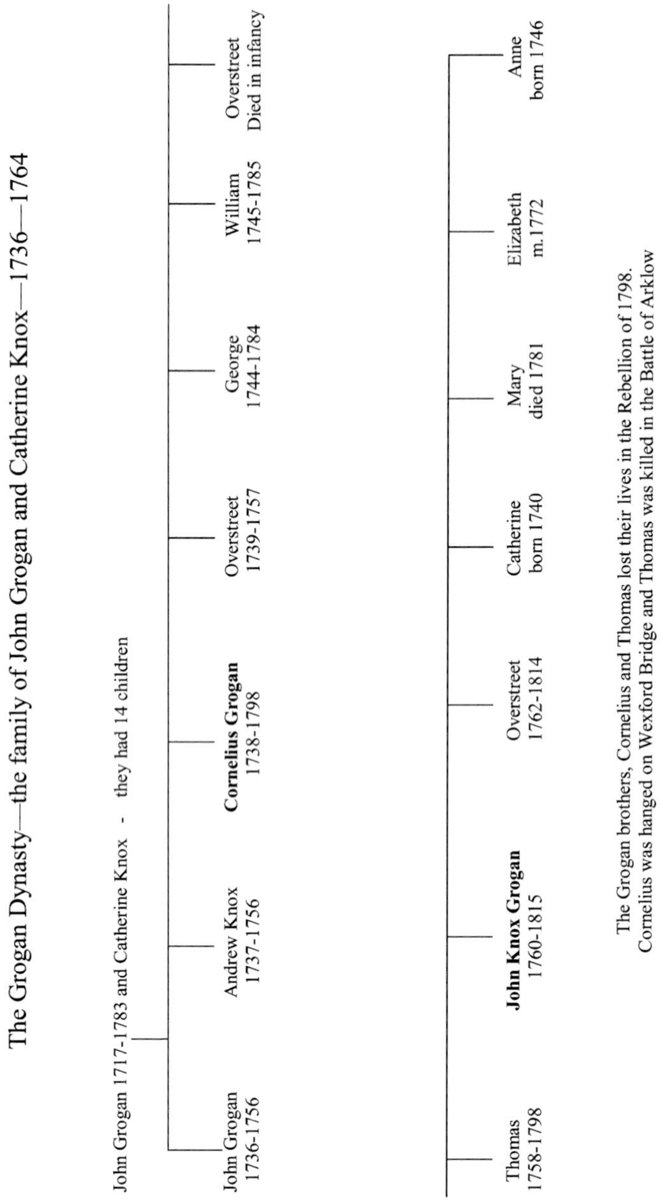

The Grogan Dynasty—the family of John Grogan and Catherine Knox—1736—1764

John Grogan 1717-1783 and Catherine Knox - they had 14 children

John Grogan
1736-1756

Andrew Knox
1737-1756

Cornelius Grogan
1738-1798

Overstreet
1739-1757

George
1744-1784

William
1745-1785

Overstreet
Died in infancy

Thomas
1758-1798

John Knox Grogan
1760-1815

Overstreet
1762-1814

Catherine
born 1740

Mary
died 1781

Elizabeth
m.1772

Anne
born 1746

The Grogan brothers, Cornelius and Thomas lost their lives in the Rebellion of 1798.
Cornelius was hanged on Wexford Bridge and Thomas was killed in the Battle of Arklow.

Fig. 3 The Grogan dynasty – the family of John Grogan and Catherine Knox.

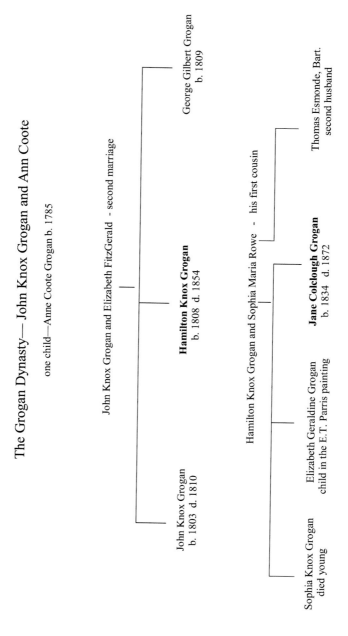

The Grogan Dynasty— John Knox Grogan and Ann Coote

one child—Anne Coote Grogan b. 1785

John Knox Grogan and Elizabeth FitzGerald - second marriage

George Gilbert Grogan
b. 1809

Hamilton Knox Grogan
b. 1808 d. 1854

John Knox Grogan
b. 1803 d. 1810

Hamilton Knox Grogan and Sophia Maria Rowe - his first cousin

Thomas Esmonde, Bart.
second husband

Jane Colclough Grogan
b. 1834 d. 1872

Elizabeth Geraldine Grogan
child in the E.T. Parris painting

Sophia Knox Grogan
died young

Fig. 4 John Grogan and Ann Coote.

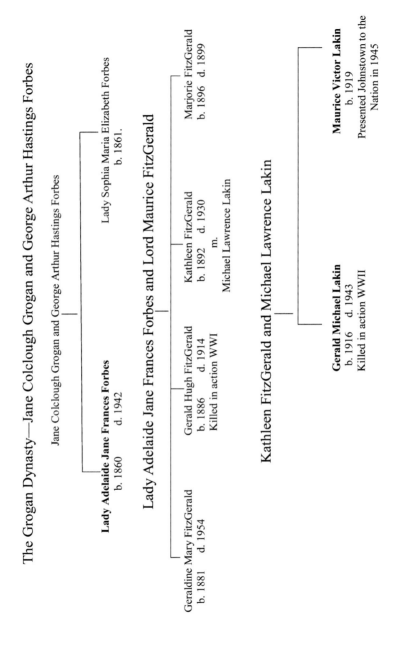

Fig. 5 The Grogan dynasty – Jane Colclough Grogan and George Arthur Hastings Forbes.

NOTES

1   For an in-depth assessment of Dermot MacMurrough, King of Leinster
    and the Norman invasion of Ireland the author suggests the following
    publications: *The Norman Invasion of Ireland*, Richard Roche (Anvil, 1973);
    Diarmait, King of Leinster (Anvil, 1973) by Nicholas Furlong (Revised in
    2000 by Mercier Press, Cork); *Arrogant Trespass*, Dr Billy Colfer (Duffry Press,
    2002).

2   *Genealogical Memoir of the family of Montmorency* by Hervey
    de Montmorency-Morres, p.583 (Paris, 1817).

3   See *The Dialect of Forth and Bargy, Co. Wexford, Ireland*, T.P. Dolan, Diarmaid
    Ó Muirithe, p.7.

4   Gordon, *History of Ireland*, Vol. 1, pp.81-82.

5   Thomas Rossiter's son, Michael, brother of Isabel, was born in 1648 in
    Bargy Castle where the family were living at that time. He was ordained
    in Lisbon in 1672. He was Dean of the Dioceses of Ferns in 1692 when
    he was nominated for the bishopric by King James II. He was consecrated
    bishop in 1698 and in July was named as one of the four Catholic prelates
    then supposed to be in the country. In 1704, he registered as parish priest
    of Killenick, Kilmacree and Rathmacknee. Bishop Rossiter was living in
    Ringaheen where he died in 1709. Tradition says that his remains are
    buried with his ancestors in the churchyard of Rathmacknee. *The Secular
    Priests of the Diocese of Ferns*, Revd John V. Gahan, p.399.

6   *The Castles of County Wexford*, W.H. Jeffrey, p.21.

7   *Genealogical Memoir of the family of Montmorency* by Hervey
    de Montmorency-Morres, p.583/84 (Paris, 1817).

8   James Esmonde's name is shown on a list of friars who were killed during the Cromwellian massacre in the Bull Ring and the 1798 Rebellion.

9   *The Wexford Gentry*, Art Kavanagh and Rory Murphy, pp.97-111.

10 *The Wexford Gentry*, Vol. 1, Art Kavanagh and Rory Murphy, pp.104-105.

11 The Rebellion of 1641 commenced on 23 October and continued for seven months to May 1642. It came about as Charles I attempted to maintain control over Ireland and his own parliament. On the eve of the planned attack on Dublin Castle, at that time the seat of English authority in Ireland, the proposed rising was compromised, its leaders arrested and the attack never came about. This led to the occupation of Ireland after Oliver Cromwell's New Model Army decisively defeated the Irish Catholics and Royalists and re-conquering the country. The almost complete disenfranchisement of the native Irish Catholics and the increasing seizure of land and power from the established English settlers known as the 'Old English'. *Irish History*, Séamus Mac Annaidh, pp.106-107.

12 The name Overstreet is a compound of two elements usually an adjective indicating size or an attractive quality as a prefix attached to a given or locational name. Overstreet is such a combination meaning a person who lived at a Roman road over a river bank. The name was first found in Cheshire where the family held a seat as lords of the manor.

13 'Duncannon Fort is situated on a rocky point on the County of Wexford shore. The principal battery to the sea is about 40ft above high water. It is very well situated to command the channel which becomes very narrow where it is opposite to the fort. The fort to the land has a good scarp wall about 23ft high with a sufficient parapet to resist common shot, a ditch near 30ft wide, a covered way and glacis. The ground in front descends to about 80 yards distance, from thence ascends gradually to a distance of three or four hundred yards, part of it above the level of the parapet. The Barracks being parallel to the Rampart cover the Parade, and a Traverse covers the guns that point to a ship's broadside. The guns are of 24 and 18 pounders, in number 25.' P.H. Hore, *History of the Town and County of Wexford*, Vol. 4, p.253.

14 Ibid., p.224.

15 Ibid., p.225.

16 P.H. Hore, *History of the Town and County of Wexford*, Vol. 5, p.309.

17 Members of the Commissioners in the Wexford Precinct were: Col Thomas Sadlier, Col John Overstreet, William Woodward, Edward Tomlins, Thomas Hart, John Walker, Ambrose Andrews, Barth Hussey, Thomas Dowse, Thomas Dancer, John Moore, Mathew Stoddard and Edward Withers. P.H. Hore, *History of the Town and County of Wexford*, Vol. 5, p.310.

18 Ibid., p.307.

19 Ibid., p.314.

20 Ibid., p.319.

21 Ibid., p. 321,322.

22 Ibid., p.351.

23 Ibid., p.328.

24 Ibid., p.348.

25 Ibid., p.350.

26 *More Irish Names*, Edward MacLysaght, p. 118.

27 Prior to 1795 there was no bridge across the river at Wexford town. The only means of crossing was by ferry, originally operated by the municipal authorities of Wexford. Following the occupation of the town by Cromwell a large tract of land, along with the ferry rights, was conferred on one of his favourites, General Monck and his descendants. These rights continued to the reign of William III. The King also had a favourite, a Captain Charles Smith, known among his acquaintants as 'Spit-fire Charley'. The king ordered the descendants of General Monck to give up part of the right in the ferry and half of the adjoining lands to 'Spit-fire Charley'. In the course of a few years after this, John Grogan, the owner of Johnstown Castle married one of Captain Smith's three daughters and with her received as a dowry her father's right in the Ferry and the adjoining land which up to the advent of a bridge over the river was named as the 'Monck and Grogan property' eventually becoming the property of Grogan. Mr Monck, father of Lord Rathdown, owned three-fourths and Mr Grogan, one-fourth of the ferry. They received £3,200 for their interest in this venture. The ferry of Wexford continued in the hands of the lines of Monck and Grogan for nearly a full century. The owners of the Ferry invested a portion of their interests in the 'new bridge' as shares. *Chronicles of the County Wexford*, George Griffiths, p. 259.

28 John Morgan died in Trinity College, Dublin. He was unmarried. Samuel Morgan was Alderman and twice Mayor of Waterford. On his death in September 1827 his estates and large funded property was shared equally between Hamilton Knox Grogan of Johnstown Castle and his brother George Gilbert Grogan of Ardcandrisk. They were to take the name and coat of arms of Morgan as an addition to their own.

29 See chapter 5.

30 Elizabeth Geraldine Grogan is the child featuring in the family portrait by E.T. Parris. This painting still hangs in the castle. She married the Hon. Robert Deane-Morgan and lived at Ardcandrisk, County Wexford. She was aunt to Lady Maurice FitzGerald. She died in May 1920.

31 Jane Colclough Grogan was born in 1834 and married George Arthur Hastings Forbes, Earl of Granard. She died in 1872.

32 Gerald Hugh FitzGerald had married Dorothy Violet Charrington in 1914.
    She married again, becoming Mrs Dorothy Jefferies, and lived at Carrigbyrne,
    County Wexford. She was one of the signatories for the handing over of the
    estate to the nation in 1945.

33 Lines from 'The County Limerick Buck-Hunt' and sung to the air, 'Nach
    mbaineann sin dó'. Published as Song No. 13, p.16 in *The Irish Songbook*,
    edited by Alfred Perceval Graves (London, 1894), this air was used by
    Thomas Moore for his poem, 'They may rail at this life – This earth is the
    planet', in *A Selection of Irish Melodies Nos. 7 and 8, London, 1818*. A jovial
    melody in 6/8 time, it may be enjoyed from the singing of Aoife O'Sullivan
    with piano accompaniment by Mairéad Hurley in a six-CD set entitled
    My Gentle Harp, the complete collection of Thomas Moore's Irish Melodies (TMF,
    2008). 101-106, Disc 4, Track No. 11. An ideal melody as used by Pierce
    Creagh for his song, 'The Limerick Buck Hunt'.

34 'A Wexford Gentleman Piper: "Famous Larry Grogan" (1701-1728/9)', Sean
    Donnelly, *Journal of the Wexford Historical Society*, No. 16, 1996-97, p.41.

35 'Ecstasy in Eighteenth-Century Kildare?' Sean Donnelly, *Journal of the County
    Kildare Archaeological Society* No. 4 (1998-9), pp.565-588.

36 Robert Brownrigg, Norrismount, County Wexford was a fine performer
    on the uilleann pipes. He was a magistrate in the area of North Wexford.
    Brownrigg was a frequent visitor at weddings and merrymaking or wherever
    good pipers might appear. He died about the middle of the nineteenth
    century at an advanced age. Henry Brownrigg was the eldest son of Robert
    and inherited his father's patrimony and the talent of playing the pipes.
    A barrister by profession, the melody of the bagpipes had more attractions
    for him than the intricacies of the law. He was known for his playing of
    the Highland pipes. Surviving his father by just ten or twelve years he
    died around 1860. *Irish Minstrels and Musicians*, Captain Francis O'Neill,
    pp.186-189 (Chicago, 1913).

37 Dudley Colclough lived in the nineteenth century and was one of the
    landlord class. His estates of 13,000 acres included Tintern Abbey in
    south-west County Wexford. Unlike a lot of landlords the Colcloughs enjoyed
    great popularity among their tenantry. O'Neill, p.186-189.

38 Píob Mór (War Pipes), used mainly in battle to lead troops into the fray. Some
    renowned Wexford war pipers were, Bryan MacGillechrist; Fergus O'Farrell;
    Donal MacFergus O'Farrell and Richard Buí MacJames. O'Neill, p.57.

39 Bellows-blown bagpipe with chanter, three drones and keyed melody
    pipes capable of providing harmony to accompany the melody.
    This instrument evolved from the simple bagpipe in the early 1700s.
    Originally known as the Irish Union bagpipe. In comparison to most other
    bagpipes this instrument is relatively quiet and are essentially indoor

pipes. *The Companion to Irish Traditional Music*, (ed.) Fintan Vallely, Cork University Press,1999, pp.410.

40 *The Story of the Bagpipe*, W.H. Grattan Flood, p.146-147 (London, 1911).

41 See *Sources of Irish Traditional Music c.1600-1855*, (ed.) Aloys Fleischmann, Volume 1, Tune No. 743.

42 Donnelly, *Journal of the Wexford Historical Society*, No. 16 (1996-97), p.54.

43 *Love in a Riddle* was written by Colley Cibber (1671-1757), English actor/ manager, playwright and Poet Laureate. He wrote twenty-five plays for his own acting company at Drury Lane.

44 Samuel Foote (1720-1777), *Dictionary of Theatre* (ed.) (London: David Pickering, 1988), p.182.

45 Maria Macklin, was the daughter of Charles Macklin (McLaughlin) (c.1697-1797). Charles Macklin was a strolling player in his early days. He appeared in leading roles at Drury Lane and excelled in Shakespearian roles as Shylock, Iago and Macbeth. He wrote a number of plays of which *Love á la Mode* (1759) and *The Man of the World* (1781) were frequently revived. Pickering, *Dictionary of Theatre*, p.312.

46 O'Neill, *Irish Minstrels and Musicians*, pp.181.

47 *Irish Melodies*, Thomas Moore, (ed.) J.W. Glover (James Duffy & Co.), p.233.

48 W.H. Grattan Flood, *A History of Irish Music*, p.252-254.

49 Donnelly, *Journal of the Wexford Historical Society*, No. 16 (1996-97), p.55.

50 Willie Asple worked for many years at Johnstown Castle.

51 Patrick Berry, *by Bishop's Rath and Norman Fort* (1994), pp.147-151. Francis Whelan worked as a steward in Johnstown Castle towards the end of the nineteenth century. Born in Castlemartyr, County Cork around 1857, he studied agriculture making him a much sought-after farm manager. In his younger days he held positions on large estates in several counties and at one time was farm manager for the Knight of Glin in County Limerick. He lived for a time at Landscape, Drinagh, during his years as farm steward for Lady Maurice FitzGerald at Johnstown Castle. Moving away from the Johnstown Estate, Francis bought property in Bellfield, Enniscorthy, in 1919 and after ten years moved back to live in the parish of Piercestown with his son, James, a dentist and very fine musician. James's sons Dermot and Seamus Whelan worked in the analytical services under An Fóras Talúntais and Teagasc. Seamus is the holder of an All-Ireland Hurling medal with Wexford's Senior Hurling team and his late brother, Dermot, was a virtuoso button-accordionist and member of the famous Mayglass Céilí Band. The numerous writings and poetry of their grandfather, Francis, are preserved in a bound volume entitled, *Songs of Leisure*, in the Whelan family archive. Francis died in 1930 aged 90 years and is buried in Piercestown Cemetery.

52 Daniel Gahan, *The People's Rising, Wexford 1798*, p.19.

53 Ibid., p.8. For a comprehensive examination of this rebellion the author suggests the following publications: *Reluctant Rebel*, E. Barrett; *Sowing the Whirlwind*, B. Cleary; *The 1798 Rebellion in Wexford*, L.M. Cullen; *The Wexford Rising in 1798*, C. Dickson; *Fr. John Murphy of Boolavogue*, N. Furlong; *The Mighty Wave*, (ed.) D. Kehoe and N. Furlong; *Memories of the Irish Rebellion*, Sir Richard Musgrave; *The Year of Liberty*, T. Packenham; *Here's Their Memory*, R. Roche; *The Tree of Liberty*, Dr K. Whelan; and *County Wexford Trials of 1798*, William Sweetman.

54 *Reluctant Rebel*, E. Barrett, pp. 7 and 8.

55 Article by T.D. Sinnott, *The People*, 1959.

56 The Assembly Rooms are in Cornmarket, Wexford town, and are now used as Wexford Art Centre.

57 Ibid. p.62.

58 *County Wexford Trials of 1798*, William Sweetman, p.368.

59 Barrett, p.62.

60 Ibid., p.67.

61 Ibid., p.68.

62 Ibid., p.68.

63 Ibid., p. 68/69.

64 *County Wexford Trials of 1798*, William Sweetman, p.371.

65 *Home Sketches on Both Sides of the Channel, A Diary by Thomas Lacy*, pp.258–276 (1852).

66 *Sights and Scenes in Our Fatherland 1863*, p. 437-442.

67 A model of Johnstown Castle is listed in the Fine Arts – Class 30 section of the *Guide to the Great Exhibition*. The model was situated on the north side of the British Nave at the Great Exhibition at Crystal Palace, London, from 1 May to 11 October 1851. The model is described in comparison with a miniature 'dolls' house' as follows: 'of equal, though more staid merit, is the model of Johnstown Castle, Wexford, Ireland' on p.97.

68 Edward George Earle Lytton Bulwer-Lytton, 1st Baron Lytton (1803-1873). Born in London, he was a novelist, poet, playwright and politician. Melnotte and Pauline are characters in his play *The Lady of Lyons*. Bulwer coined the phrase, 'the pen is mightier than the sword'.

69 Thomas Hopper (1776-1856), architect and surveyor. Born at Rochester, he was the son of a surveyor in that town. He was commissioned to make alterations at Carton House and among the mansions built or altered by Hopper were Slane Castle and Gosford Castle in Ireland and other castles in Wales and England. *Dictionary of National Biography, 1885-1900*, Volume 27.

70 Possibly John Mooney, a noted woodcarver from the Enniscorthy area of County Wexford. The family were coopers. John Mooney was employed at

Johnstown Castle as a woodcarver and some of the furniture in the castle was attributed to him.

71 St Agnes – see top left of The First Drawing Room, p.62.

72 *Epicurean* was the Irish poet Thomas Moore's only attempt at writing a novel. It was published by Longman's in London in 1827 and proved to be a very successful work. The illustrations of the book were by the English artist William Turner (1775-1851). *Irish Minstrel*, Linda Kelly, pp.198-199 (London, 2006).

73 Lord Byron (1788-1824) published the first two Cantos of his seventeen Canto work The Isles of Greece (Don Juan) in 1818 and was finalised in 1823. Lambro, a pirate features in the third Canto.

74 Prior to his visit to the grand exhibition at the Crystal Palace of 1851 Lacy commented in his diary published in 1852 as follow, 'Not having been at Johnstown for the last five years, and being struck with the extensive additions and improvements which a close inspection of the model rendered manifest, I determined on my arrival in Wexford, to avail myself of an early opportunity to visit this fine seat'.

75 Two of the Parisian mirrors are still in this splendid drawing room. The middle mirror has been removed to be replaced by a wooden door.

76 Thomas Barnascone is listed in *Wilson's Dublin Directory for the year 1832*, working as a carver and gilder from 25 Lower Exchange Street, Dublin. His work at Johnstown Castle would have meant residing in Wexford during this work at the castle. *Wilson's Dublin Directory*, Dublin, p.46.

77 Encaustic tiles – usually ceramic tiles where the pattern is composed of different colours of clay. They were used in nineteenth- and twentieth-century Gothic revival. Encaustic painting, known as wax painting, uses heated beeswax with coloured pigments. Wood and canvas were often used in this medium.

78 The auction of the contents of Johnstown Castle, Wexford, by direction of the executors of the late Lady Maurice FitzGerald commenced on Monday 1 May 1944 and continued until Friday 5 May finishing at 12 noon each day. The auction was conducted by Jackson Stops & McCabe, College Green, Dublin. Catalogue, price 2s 6d.

79 Sir Godfrey Kneller, 1st Baronet (1646-1723) was the leading portrait painter in England during the late seventeenth and early eighteenth centuries and was court painter to British monarchs from Charles II to George I. Kneller (Kniller) was born in the Free City of Lübeck, the son of Zacharias Kniller a portrait painter.

80 Philip James de Loutherbourg was an English painter of French origins. He studied engraving and painting in Paris and moved to London in 1771. His main focus was on landscapes and battle scenes. Loutherbourg was employed as historical painter to the Duke of Gloucester.

81 Thomas Hopper (1776-1856), architect and surveyor was born at Rochester where he trained in his father's office. He carried out many commissions and alterations in England, Wales and Ireland. His Irish work included Slane Castle, Dromoland, County Clare, and at Johnstown Castle, County Wexford. The design of the main staircase is attributed to Hopper. *Dictionary of Architecture; Builder,* xiv, p.481.

82 *Sights and Scenes in Our Fatherland,* Thomas Lacy, p.441.

83 Bernard Mulrenin (1803-1868). Sligo born, Mulrenin was encouraged by the local gentry to pursue a career as a painter. In 1825 he came down to Dublin to exhibit some of his works in the Royal Hibernian Academy. He spent the rest of his life in Dublin and gained a considerable reputation as a miniature painter. He was elected a member of the RHA in 1860. He died at No. 23 Great Brunswick Street, Dublin, where he resided from 1837. *Dictionary of Irish Artists,* 1913.

84 Born in the parish of St Marylebone, London, Edmund Thomas Parris (1793-1873) was history painter to Queen Adelaide, Queen Consort of William IV. He painted the Coronation of Queen Victoria in 1838 and the funeral of the Duke of Wellington in 1852. He was listed as a history, portrait, subject and panorama painter, book illustrator, designer and art restorer. He supervised the painting of the huge panorama in the London Colosseum in Regent's Park and invented 'Parris's medium'. When mixed with oil the medium produced a dull fresco-like surface. Edmund Thomas Parris died at 27 Francis Street, Bedford Square, London, on 27 November 1873.

85 *Home Sketches on Both Sides of the Channel, A Diary by Thomas Lacy,* 1852, p.273.

86 See p.14 of the Catalogue of the Sale of Contents of Johnstown Castle May 1944.

87 Andrew Nicholl (1804-1886) was born in Church Lane, Belfast. Apprenticed to H.D. Finlay, a printer and owner of the *Northern Whig,* Nicholl worked for several years as a compositor on that paper. He always had an interest in painting and moved to London to study. He settled for some time in Dublin and was elected an Associate of the Royal Hibernian Academy in 1832 becoming a full member in 1860. He made over 100 illustrations for Mrs S.C. Hall's *Ireland, its Scenery and Character.* His Wexford illustrations feature on pp.163, 165, 167-170 of Mrs Hall's book.

88 *Home Sketches on Both Sides of the Channel, A Diary by Thomas Lacy,* 1852, p.267.

89 *Wexford Then and Now,* Jarlath Glynn, p.40.

90 'Irish and Italian Marble and Stone Works. Thomas Fagan, Murntown, near Wexford, respectfully informs the Nobility, Clergy, and Gentry of the Town and County of Wexford, that he has on hands and is prepared to execute Statuary, Stone Monuments, Altar Fonts from the plainest

to the most enriched in Carving and Sculpture. He has also on hands, and prepares upon the shortest notice, Head and Tomb Stones, Chimney Pieces, the material for which he is enabled to purchase cheaper than any other in the county. T. Fagan also desires to state his prices for every article are most moderate. All work done by him, sent carriage free to any part of Ireland.

References: The principal Stone Work of Johnstown Castle, Castleboro and Wilton Castle, was executed by him also that of several Public Buildings in Waterford and recently in this neighbourhood, the monuments over the late William Whitty, Esq., in Wexford and Rev. Nicholas Codd, Mayglass Chapel.

N.B. A Branch of the Business in connection is kept with James Doran, John's Bridge, Waterford to which place or in Murntown, Wexford all communications addressed will be promptly attended to. Murntown, October 26th. 1855.' An advertisement which appeared in the *Wexford Independent*, 27 October 1855, p.3.

91 The interior of the friary has a fine ornate barrel ceiling with beautiful panels. This work was completed by the Wexford builder Patrick O'Connor in 1861-62. *Wexford Then and Now*, Jarlath Glynn, p.65.

92 *Wilson's Dublin Directory for the Year 1832*, p.46.

93 Custos Rotulorum – Keeper of the records. A principal justice of a county who keeps the rolls or records of the sessions of the Justices' Court.

94 Charles FitzGerald, 4th Duke of Leinster (1819-1887) was an Irish peer and politician. He was born in Dublin and was son of Augustus FitzGerald, 3rd Duke of Leinster and Lady Charlotte Augusta Stanhope. The Duke was High Sheriff of Kildare for 1843 and Member of Parliament for Kildare from 1847 to 1852. He married Lady Caroline Sutherland-Leveson-Gower, third daughter of the 2nd Duke of Sutherland and Lady Harriet Elizabeth Georgiana Howard in 1847 at Trentham, Staffordshire. They had fifteen children: Lady Geraldine FitzGerald (*c.* 1848-1867); Lady Mabel FitzGerald (*c.* 1849-1850); Gerald FitzGerald, 5th Duke of Leinster (1851-1893); Lord Maurice FitzGerald (Carton, 16 December 1852 – Johnstown Castle, 24 April 1901); Lady Alice FitzGerald (Carton, 1853-1941), married at Carton House 2 May 1882 to Sir Charles John Oswald FitzGerald (1840-1912); Lady Eva FitzGerald (Kilkea Castle, 1855 – February 1931) unmarried, no issue; Lady Mabel FitzGerald (Kilkea Castle, 1855-1931) unmarried, no issue; Major Lord Frederick FitzGerald (1857-1924), Captain 60th Rifles, unmarried and without issue; Lord Walter FitzGerald (1825-1923); Lord Charles FitzGerald (Kilkea Castle, 1859-1928), married in Calcutta, November 1887 Alice Sidonia Claudius (died July 1909); Lord George FitzGerald (1862-1924); Lord Henry FitzGerald (Kilkea Castle, 1863-1955), married in Taplow, 21 January 1891, Inez Charlotte Grace

Boteler; Lady Nesta FitzGerald (Kilkea Castle, 1865-1944), unmarried, no
issue; Lady Margaret FitzGerald (c. 1866-1867); Lord Robert FitzGerald
(23 December 1868 – 23 December 1868).

95   George Arthur Hastings Forbes, KP, 7th Earl and a baronet. Born
5 August 1833, he succeeded his grandfather in 1837. He married Jane
Colclough Grogan, youngest daughter of Hamilton Knox Grogan Morgan,
Esq. of Johnstown Castle and had two children: Adelaide Jane Frances born
1860 and Sophia Maria Elizabeth born 1862. Creations: Viscount Granard
and Baron of Clanhugh, 1673; Earl of Granard 1684, all in the peerage of
Ireland; and Baron Granard of Castle Donington, Leicester in the peerage
of the United Kingdom 1806. He was made a baronet in 1628. The family
seat is: Castle-Forbes, Longford. Their motto translates as: 'The incitement to
glory is the firebrand of the mind'. *Debrett's Illustrated Peerage of the United
Kingdom of Great Britain and Ireland 1865*, p. 169

96   Col. Harry Alcock, Wilton Castle, Enniscorthy and Charles M. Doyne,
Wells, Gorey were both serving Deputy Lieutenants of County Wexford.
Bassett's Wexford County Guide and Directory, George Henry Bassett, p.31
(Dublin, 1885).

97   The County Wexford Society for Prevention of Cruelty to Animals had
offices at 14 High Street, Wexford. Bassett, p.41.

98   Ibid., p.41.

99   Ibid., p.41.

100 Ibid., p.45.

101 *Enniscorthy Guardian*, 20 April 1901, p.5.

102 From the obituary of Lady Maurice FitzGerald, *The People*, 21 November 1942.

103 Ninon – a light-weight silk dress fabric (né-nawn).

104 'The scene on Windermere Lake on Saturday, when 15,000 to 20,000
people went on the ice, was one never to be forgotten by those who
witnesses it. The Lake was frozen from end to end, 12 or 13 miles, with a
single break at the ferry, kept open by the ferry steamer, which couples the
Kendal and Hawkshead highway. The ice was as smooth as glass, and 1 ft.
to 18 inches thick. The Furness Railway Company's steam yachts have been
frozen up for some weeks. From the summit of Biscay Howe, above Bowness,
a vantage point which commands a view of the Lake almost for its entire
length, the scene on Saturday was ever to be remembered. A perfect sheet
of ice was seen north and south, dotted over either end with skaters or with
sleighs drawn by the otherwise "unemployed" men.' The Great Frost as
reported in the *Kendal and County News and Lakes Courier*, February 1895.

105 *Wexford Free Press*, February 1895.

106 A lunch that lasts so long and is so copious it becomes dinner.

107 Both notices appeared in the *Free Press*, Saturday 31 January 1914, p.5.

108   *Free Press*, Saturday 23 August 1913, p.10.

109   *Guide to Johnstown Castle and Nature Trails*, Dr Austin O'Sullivan, Inside cover, 1969.

110   Sequah was the name used by a travelling 'doctor' who claimed to have cures for rheumatism, arthritis, and disorders of the stomach and liver by an alleged combination of botanic and mineral substances. His potions were sold as Prairie Flower and Indian Oil. His real name was William Henry Hartley, a Yorkshireman who became so successful as this bogus 'doctor' he had to recruit some more 'Sequahs' to cover different areas of the country. There were twenty-three of them by the late 1890, practising throughout Britain and Ireland. *The Graphic*, 11 July 1891.

111   Horetown House is a Georgian square block country house standing three storeys above a basement situated a mile or so from the village of Foulksmills. It has 220 acres and the present appearance of the house is based on the plans of Wexford architect, Martin Day. Horetown was the family seat of the Goffs for many generations since 1693. The house was purchased by Major Lakin and proved to be the ideal area for hunting and other field events. *100 Wexford Country Houses*, Dan Walsh, pp.57-58.

112   George Kingston was a member of the Kingston family of Mitchelstown, County Cork. The castle, the former home of the Earls of Kingston was eventually demolished in the 1920s.

113   *The Bond of Sacrifice, A Biographical Record of all British Officers who fell in The Great War*, Vol. 1, p.135 (eds) Col. L.A. Clutterbuck and Col. W.T. Dooner with Commander the Honorable C.A. Denison, (Naval Editor), London.

114   Spencer Calmeyer Charrington (1854-1930) was a landowner and member of the Charrington brewing family. Charrington Brewery was based in the East End of London and was a major employer. He moved to Winchfield, Hampshire. He was a deputy lieutenant for the county and held a commission in the Hampshire Carabineers Yeomanry.

115   Marriage Notice on p.1 of the *Enniscorthy Guardian*, 8 August 1914; 'Fitzerald and Charrington, 5/8/1914 at Tidworth Church, Hants, England by special license, by Rev. H. Delme Radcliffe, assisted by Rev. J.H. Gibb, B.A. –.'

116   *An Unwilling Passenger, One Man's Story of the Great War*, Arthur Carr Osborn (London: Faber and Faber, 1932).

117   This memorial plaque is in St Mary's church, Winchfield. A short biography of Captain FitzGerald was written by Andrew Renshaw. Permission to quote from this work was granted by the churchwardens of St Mary's church, Winchfield.

118   *Enniscorthy Guardian*, 26 September 1914, p.4.

119   Desmond Otho Paget was grandson of Lord Otho Augustus FitzGerald (1827-1882). Lord Otho was brother of Charles FitzGerald, 4th Duke of

Leinster (1819-1887) and uncle of Lord Maurice FitzGerald of Johnstown Castle. Lord Otho FitzGerald had two children, Major Gerald Otho FitzGerald and Ina Blanche Georgie FitzGerald. Ina married Major Arthur Leopold Paget in August 1856 and they had three children: Cynthia Geraldine Ursula Paget (b. 29 October 1888); Desmond Otho Paget (b. 8 May 1898, killed in action, 21 March 1918); and his twin brother, Brevet Major Oswald Leopold Paget (b. 8 May 1898, d. 22 February 1955). The Pagets were cousins of Gerald, Kathleen and Marjorie FitzGerald of Johnstown Castle. www.thepeerage.com, p.724.

120 *Free Press*, 26 June 1920, p.2.

121 *Unending Worship, A History of Saint Iberius' Church, Wexford*, Ruddock and Kloss, pp.38-39.

122 *Free Press*, 30 October 1915, p.5.

123 The Defence of the Realm Act (DORA) of 1914 governed all lives in Britain during the First World War. The act was added to as the war progressed and it listed everything that people were not allowed to do in time of war. The first version of this act was introduced on 8 August 1914. The act included the censorship on all newspapers giving details of military activities and gave the government power to over any land it wanted to use for military purposes. Other things prohibited included any talk about naval or military matters in public places or spreading rumours about military matters, the purchase of binoculars, trespassing on railway lines or bridges, the ringing of church bells, even the feeding of bread to horses or chickens. www.historylearningsite.co.uk.

124 Liam Gaul, *Wexford – the American Connection*, pp.10-26.

125 Nicholas Furlong and John Hayes, *Co. Wexford in the Rare Oul' Times*, Vol. IV, pp.80-84.

126 See *Wexford – the American Connection*, p.10.

127 Siobhán Hayes, unpublished essay, *Perspectives on Local History*, MA in Local History, 2013, p.8.

128 Information supplied by The Airship Heritage Trust through its archivist, Mr Den Burchmore.

129 The Airship Heritage Trust archive.

130 Ibid.

131 Siobhán Hayes, unpublished essay, *Perspectives on Local History*, MA in Local History, 2013, pp.11-12.

132 Nicholas Furlong and John Hayes, *Co. Wexford in the Rare Oul' Times*, Vol. IV, p.82.

133 *Free Press*, Saturday 3 August 1918, on micro-film at Wexford library.

134 Siobhán Hayes, unpublished essay, *Perspectives on Local History*, MA in Local History, 2013, p.14.

135 Commonwealth War Graves Commission at www.cwgc.org.

136 *The Castles of County Wexford*, W.H. Jeffrey, p.20.

137 'The Barony Forth', Part 1, P.H. Hore, *The Past*, p.97.

138 Ibid., p.99.

139 Jeffrey, p.31.

140 *An Archaeological Study of Sites in the Baronies of Forth and Bargy*, County Wexford, pp.34-37. Unpublished to date.

141 Garderobe – French word for wardrobe but is used to describe a medieval latrine or toilet.

142 *Guide to Johnstown Castle and Nature Trails*, Dr Austin M. O'Sullivan, p.14.

143 Jeffrey, pp.31-32.

144 Herbert Francis Hore, b. 1817, near Clonattin, Gorey. His copious notes on family pedigrees, Co. Wexford history and land tenure were later published by his son Philip Hore.

145 Jeffrey, pp.20-21.

146 O'Sullivan, pp.5-6.

147 *Wexford Castles*, Dr Billy Colfer, pp.222-23.

148 O'Sullivan, p.6.

149 *Home Sketches*, Thomas Lacy, p.260.

150 Ibid. p.259.

151 Lady Jane was mother of Lady Adelaide FitzGerald, wife of Lord Maurice FitzGerald. Lady Jane was sister of the Hon. Mrs. Deane-Morgan of Ardcandrisk.

152 O'Sullivan, p.7.

153 Ibid., p.7.

154 *Irish Gardens and Demesnes from 1830*, Edward Malins and Patrick Bowe, p.17.

155 *Dictionary of Irish Architects* at www.dia.ie/architectsview/4570/Robertson+Daniel.

156 Ibid.

157 Thomas Moore (1779-1852). His mother, Anastasia Codd was born in Cornmarket, Wexford. Moore's melodies were published in ten volumes between 1808 and 1834 and comprised of a total of 124 songs.

158 Mr Slevin's son, Eddie, became an electrician and carried out a very successful electrical contracting business and retail shop from his premises at Stonebridge in Wexford town.

159 Summerfield also known as Summer Fields is a boys' independent day and boarding preparatory school based in the North Oxford suburb of Summertown. Founded in 1864 by Archibald MacLaren.

160 Sandhurst is the British Army Officers initial training centre and is located near the village of Sandhurst, Berkshire, which is 35 miles south-west of London.

161 The Home was a reference to the County Home – the Poor House.

162 William (Billy) Breslin was the chauffeur to Lady Maurice FitzGerald.

163 Christmas Box – the tradition of giving gifts to those who have provided services all through the year.

164 Sills, *By Bishop's Rath and Norman Fort*, p.118.

165 Henry Walton Saville was General Manager of the Wexford Gas Company for thirty-three years and lived at 'Dubross' – the house opposite the gasworks. A native of Yorkshire he was a prominent member of the Church of Ireland and served as organist in St Iberius' church for a long period. Mr Saville was a member of the Institute of Gas Engineers. *Free Press*, Friday 15 February 1957, p.5.

166 Frank Gaul was proprietor of the business and premises formerly owned by John Sinnott and Sons, Main Street, Wexford. It was a general hardware store and funeral undertakers. Later this premises was occupied by F.W. Woolworth and today trades as Penney's.

167 Journeyman was a name originally applied to a worker who was hired by the day. Later it was used to describe any competent worker, especially a craftsman or artisan. The word comes from the French word *journée*. *Dictionary of Phrase and Fable*, Brewer, p.720.

168 Matt has a copious collection of reference letters, documents and notebooks and other memorabilia of his father's gardening career over a lifetime.

169 A bothy is a hut or cottage in which workers especially farm or garden workers are housed. *Oxford Dictionary* p.87.

170 Tommy Kelly worked in the gardens at Johnstown Castle for fifty years and on his retirement was awarded the long-service medal by the Royal Horticultural Society.

171 *Living by the Pen*, Bernard Browne, pp.63-64.

BIBLIOGRAPHY

Books

Aird, James, *A Selection of Scottish, English, Irish and Foreign Airs*, Vols I-VI (Glasgow, 1790-1797).

Barrett, Eamonn, *A Reluctant Rebel* (Wexford, 1998).

Bassett, G.H., *Wexford – Borough and County Guide and Directory* (Dublin, 1885).

Bay, Mel, *Complete Fiddling Book* (USA, 1990).

Browne, Bernard, *Living by the Pen* (Wexford, 1997).

Browne, Elizabeth and Wickham, Tom, *Lewis's Wexford* (Enniscorthy, 1983).

Bunbury, T. and Kavanagh, A., *The Landed Gentry and Aristocracy of County Kildare* (Dublin, 2004).

Clutterbuck, Col. L.A., Dooner, Col. W.T., (eds) *The Bond of Sacrifice*, Vol. 1 (London, 1914).

Colfer, Dr Billy, *Wexford Castles* (Cork: Cork University Press, 2013).

Colfer, Dr Billy, *Wexford, a Town and Its Landscape* (Cork: Cork University Press, 2008).

Coulter, Niamh A., *An Archaeological Study of Sites in the Baronies of Forth and Bargy Co. Wexford*, (Cork, 1996).

Coulter, Niamh A., *Johnstown Castle, Its History, People and Heritage*, Dissertation (UCC, 1998).

Culleton, Dr Ed, Furlong, Nicholas and Sills, Patrick, (eds) *By Bishop's Rath and Norman Fort* (Wexford, 1994).

deBreffny, Brian, *Castles of Ireland* (London, 1977).

Dolan, T.P., Ó Muirithe, D., *The Dialect of Forth and Bargy Co. Wexford, Ireland* (Dublin, 1996).

Donnelly, Seán, *A Wexford Gentleman Piper: Famous Larry Grogan (1701-1728/29)*, Journal of Wexford Historical Society No. 16 (Wexford, 1996-97).

Fleischmann, Aloys, (ed.) *Sources of Irish Traditional Music c. 1600-1855* (New York and London, 1998).

Gahan, Daniel, *The Peoples Rising* (Dublin: Gill and Macmillan Ltd, 1995).

Gahan, John V., *The Secular Priests of the Diocese of Ferns* (Editions du Signe, France)

Gaul, Liam, *Laurence Grogan, Gentleman Piper, by Bishop's Rath and Norman Fort,* (Wexford, 1994).

Glynn, Jarlath, *Wexford Then and Now* (Dublin: The History Press Ireland, 2013).

Grattan-Flood, William Henry, *History of Irish Music* (Dublin, 1905).

Graves, A.P. (ed.), *The Irish Song Book* (London, 1894).

Griffiths, George, *Chronicles of the County Wexford* (Enniscorthy, 1890).

Hall, Mr & Mrs Hall's, *Ireland: Its Scenery, Character etc.* Vol. II (London, 1842).

Hore, P.H., *History of the Town and County of Wexford,* Vols. 4 and 5 Reprint (Oxford, 1979).

Hore, P.H., 'Some Commonwealth Orders and References on Petitions Relating to Waterford' *Journal of the Waterford and South-East of Ireland Archaeological Society,* Vol XIV (1911).

Hore, P.H., *The Barony of Forth,* Part IV, Uí Ceinnsealaigh Historical Society No. 5 (Enniscorthy, 1949).

Hore, P.H., *The Barony of Forth,* The Past Nos. 1-3 (Enniscorthy, 1920-1923).

Jackson Stops and McCabe, *Catalogue of the Contents of Johnstown Castle* (Dublin, 1944).

Jeffrey, W.H., *The Castles of Co. Wexford,* Old Wexford Society (Wexford, 1979).

Johnson, John, *A Choice Coll. of 200 Favourite Country Dances,* Vol. VII (London, c. 1760).

Kavanagh, Art, Murphy, Rory, *The Wexford Gentry,* Vol. 1 (Wexford, 1994).

Lacy, Thomas, *Home Sketches on Both Sides of the Channel, A Diary by Thomas Lacy 1852* (London, 1852).

Lacy, Thomas, *Sights and Scenes in Our Fatherland, Wexford 1863* (London, 1863).

Le Clerc, M.H., *The Trees and Shrubs of the Amenity Lands of Johnstown Castle* (A.F.T., 1980).

MacLysaght, Edward, *More Irish Names* (Dublin: Irish Academic Press, 1982).

Madden, Richard R. *The United Irishmen, Their Lives and Times* (London, 1860).

Malins, Ed and Bowe, Patrick, *Irish Gardens and Demesnes from 1830* (London, 1980).

Moody, T.W. and Martin, F.X., (ed.) *The Course of Irish History* (Cork, 1967).

Moore, Thomas, *A Selection of Irish Melodies,* Nos 5 and 6 (London 1813-1815).

Moores-Montmorency, Hervey de, *Genealogical Memoir of the family of Montmorency* (Paris, 1817).

Murphy, Hilary, *Families of Co. Wexford* (Wexford, 1986).

Ó Cléirigh, Brian, *Wexford in 1798: A Republic Before its Time* (Cardiff, 1998).

O'Brien, Jacqueline, Guinness, Desmond, *Great Irish Houses and Castles* (London, 1992).

O'Dwyer, Frederick, *Modelled Muscularity, Daniel Robertson's Tudor Manors,* Irish Arts Review

O'Hara, Kane, *Midas, a Comic Opera* (London, 1764).

O'Neill, Francis, *The Dance Music of Ireland 1001 Gems* (Chicago, 1940).

Osborn, A.C., *An Unwilling Passenger* (London, 1932).

O'Sullivan, Anthony N., *Cornelius Grogan of Johnstown Castle* (Private Publication, 1998).

O'Sullivan, Dr Austin M., *Johnstown Castle Estate and Research Centre* (A.F.T., 1969).

Pickering, David (ed.), *Dictionary of Theatre* (London, 1988).

Reck, Padge, *Wexford – A Municipal History* (Wexford, 1987).

Roche, Francis, *The Roche Coll. of Traditional Irish Music* (Cork, 1982).

Roche, Richard, *The Norman Invasion of Ireland* (Dublin, 1970).

Rossiter, Nicky, *The Little Book of Wexford* (Dublin: The History Press Ireland, 2013).

Routledge, George, *Guide Through the Great Exhibition at the Crystal Palace* (London, 1851).

Rowe, David, Scallan, Eithne, *Houses of Wexford* (Clare, 2004).

Ruddock, Canon Norman, Kloss, Naomi, *Unending Worship, A History of St. Iberius' Church* (Wexford, 1997).

Sadler, John, *Apollo's' Cabinet or the Muses Delight*, Vol. 1 (Liverpool, 1756).

Smith, Alexander, *The Musical Miscellany* (Perth, 1786).

Sweeney, Frank, *The Founding of the Tenant League and the Elections of 1852 in Wexford*, Uí Ceinnsealaigh Historical Society No. 30 (Enniscorthy, 2009-2010).

Sweetman, William, *County Wexford – Trials of 1798* (Wexford, 2013).

Thompson, J., A. and P., *The Hibernian Muse* (London, 1790).

Walsh, Dan, *100 Wexford Country Houses* (Enniscorthy, 1996).

Warner, Guy, *Airships Over the North Channel*, April Sky Design (Newtownards, 2005).

Newspapers

Church of Ireland Gazette
Enniscorthy Guardian
Kendal and County News
Lakes Courier
The Free Press
The Graphic
The Irish Times
The People
The Watchman
Wexford Guardian
Wexford Herald
Wexford Independent

Journals

County Kildare Archaeological Society
The Past
Waterford and South-East of Ireland Archaeological Society
Wexford Historical Society
Wilson's Dublin Directory 1832

Also from The History Press

Irish Revolutionaries

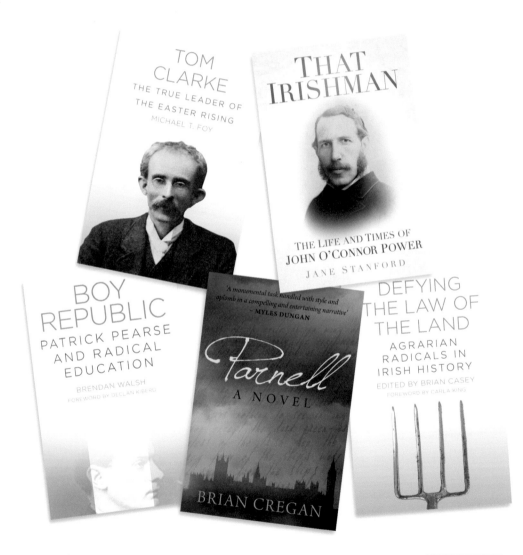

TOM CLARKE
THE TRUE LEADER OF THE EASTER RISING
MICHAEL T. FOY

THAT IRISHMAN
THE LIFE AND TIMES OF JOHN O'CONNOR POWER
JANE STANFORD

BOY REPUBLIC
PATRICK PEARSE AND RADICAL EDUCATION
BRENDAN WALSH
FOREWORD BY DECLAN KIBERD

'A monumental task handled with style and aplomb in a compelling and entertaining narrative'
— MYLES DUNGAN

Parnell
A NOVEL
BRIAN CREGAN

DEFYING THE LAW OF THE LAND
AGRARIAN RADICALS IN IRISH HISTORY
EDITED BY BRIAN CASEY
FOREWORD BY CARLA KING

Find these titles and more at
www.thehistorypress.ie

The History Press Ireland